THE CONSTITUTIONAL HISTORY
OF
THE UNITED STATES

1776–1826

THE MACMILLAN COMPANY
NEW YORK · BOSTON · CHICAGO · DALLAS
ATLANTA · SAN FRANCISCO

MACMILLAN AND CO., Limited
LONDON · BOMBAY · CALCUTTA · MADRAS
MELBOURNE

THE MACMILLAN COMPANY
OF CANADA, Limited
TORONTO

THE CONSTITUTIONAL HISTORY OF THE UNITED STATES

1776–1826

The Blessings of Liberty

by HOMER CAREY HOCKETT

Professor of History in The Ohio State University

NEW YORK

THE MACMILLAN COMPANY

36142

12 Aug. 46

JK 31
.H6
v. 1

Vxori Consilio et Modestia Eximiae

We the People of the United States, in Order to form a more perfect Union, establish Justice, insure domestic Tranquility, provide for the common defence, promote the general Welfare, and secure *the Blessings of Liberty* to ourselves and our Posterity, do ordain and establish this Constitution for the United States of America.
—*Preamble of the Constitution.*

PREFACE

ONE hundred and fifty years ago today was the date set for the first meeting of Congress under the Constitution. Even as I write these lines, President Franklin D. Roosevelt, the justices of the Supreme Court, and the two houses of Congress are assembled at the nation's capitol to celebrate this event and to discuss the principles of our government. These principles were in large part the product of a reaction against monarchy. But they did not spring into being suddenly with the meeting of the Constitutional Convention, nor did the Declaration of Independence evoke them out of the void. The continuity of our institutional development has too often been overlooked by those who have stressed the significance of our secession from the British empire. Independence, indeed, permitted our development to take a course which was in many ways new, but the roots of our constitutionalism must be sought in the contest between England's middle class and the royal authority.

The ideology of the Fathers of the Constitution was essentially that of this English middle class. It was liberal because it shifted the source of authority in government from monarch to those who had been subjects. But it was not democratic, since the privilege of participating in government was narrowly restricted to those who were regarded as fitted therefor by training or by the owning of property.

On such an ideology our government was originally based. It is correctly described as representative, or republican, rather than democratic. Yet in contrast with the monarchies of contemporary Europe it was remarkably liberal. Enthusiastic Americans confidently expected the United States, like a beacon in the night, to guide other nations to political liberty and light. And during the nineteenth century the example of the great republic of the West was a powerful influence in shaping governmental development throughout the world.

But the framers of the Constitution could not foresee the future. They did not even foresee the coming of political democracy—

of universal suffrage—much less the reversion to autocracy in new forms which was to come in our own day. In the course of the evolution of ideas it was reserved for our generation to face the competition with the American way of life which has been brought about by the rise of communism and fascism.

This volume is the first of a series each of which will deal with fifty years of our constitutional history. This work is undertaken because the times demand an intelligent understanding and appraisal of the origin and growth of the principles of our system of government, if this system is to survive on its merits or to be wisely modified and adapted to twentieth-century conditions and needs. Many of our citizens hold mythological ideas concerning the origin and nature of the Constitution, and errors of this kind can be combatted only by presenting the true history. These volumes represent an attempt to present that history. It has been the aim of the author to treat the subject realistically, avoiding the uncritical laudation which has marred so much of the work of constitutional historians in the past, and avoiding as well the cynicism so current nowadays. The subject-matter is intrinsically difficult, but an untechnical treatment has been aimed at, in the hope of rendering the work readily intelligible to any thoughtful reader. The story is not confined to the narrative of events; the desire of the author has been to interpret events in such fashion as to indicate trends and tendencies, and to show how circumstances and experience have led to changes for better or for worse.

The materials for constitutional history are almost without limit in quantity. It is quite beyond the competence of any one to digest them all, and scholars will doubtless miss references in these volumes to works which they would regard as of prime importance. Nevertheless it is believed that the works cited afford a reasonably representative selection from the vast literature of the subject, supplying a basis for the statements of fact and the judgments set forth in the text and a guide for students who wish to go further.

It is futile for a writer to protest that he is objective and impartial. Of these qualities readers are the judges. The present author admits that there is a moral to his tale. It is that the freedom which independence brought to Americans was only an opportunity, at best, amid conflicting counsels and clashing interests, to work out their own salvation under the obligation to regard the general welfare, and that THE BLESSINGS OF LIBERTY are to be gained and preserved only through incessant pains and vigilance.

HOMER CAREY HOCKETT

TUCSON, ARIZ.
March 4, 1939

CONTENTS

CHAPTER XIV. THE NATURE OF THE CONSTITU-
TION AND THE UNION (Continued)

CHAPTER XV. JEFFERSON IN POWER

CHAPTER XVI. FEDERAL AUTHORITY VERSUS
STATE'S RIGHTS

CHAPTER XVII. BROAD CONSTRUCTION IN CON-
GRESS

CHAPTER XVIII. THE SUPREME COURT AND THE
CONSTITUTION

accident of birth. In medieval Europe one was born a noble or a serf, and ordinarily nothing ever happened to alter one's social status. Fixity was the rule, a change of lot the exception. When the barriers which had held the "lower" classes in their ancestral status were broken down, the modern era came in.

In England, these more fluid conditions were beginning to prevail during the thirteenth and fourteenth centuries. The new age was marked by the rise of a new group somewhat loosely called the middle class. It consisted of the free townsmen who lived by the production or exchange of commodities or professional services, using money as a medium, and is to be distinguished from the nobility on the one hand and the peasantry and wage-earners on the other. Out of it grew in time the capitalist class; for political purposes it came to include a considerable section of the landed gentry. In seeking the origin of the ideas which eventually took form in the Constitution of the United States, we must begin with certain experiences of this English middle class. The first fact which it is important to notice is that, through organization and wealth, this element of the population became dominant in the social and political as well as the economic life of the towns. The next is that to it was due the spread of English commerce and the inception of the colonial empire. Thirdly, with the rise of Parliament the same class became the real rulers. Again, the two branches of the class, separated by the Atlantic, sought with partial but only temporary success, to work out a plan of government embracing both realm and dominions and capable of caring for the interests of all parts of the empire. Finally it must be emphasized that in the course of these developments legal and political ways of thinking were evolved which, although they failed to establish a satisfactory imperial constitution, supplied at least much of the stuff of which our own Constitution was made. It should be noted also that the word "constitution" has as its primary meaning the accepted way of carrying on government, although, especially in America, it tended increasingly to denote a superior law which prescribed the duties and limited the powers of all governmental agencies.

I

THE RISE OF ENGLISH LIBERALISM

HE explorer who encounters a river in its middle course
will not map it accurately unless he goes up stream as well
as down. Many students of the origin of our constitutional
system have nevertheless been content to begin the study of its
development with the era of independence and the Convention of
1787. The practical men who composed the famous Convention
sought to solve problems encountered in their actual every-day
experience, but they took much for granted and performed their
task within the confines of habits of thought which had taken form
in the course of generations. The sources of the Constitution will
not be discovered unless one traces the origin of the ideas which
possessed the minds of the framers. "The history of what the law
has been is necessary to the knowledge of what the law is." Law
tends to become crystallized in "principles," "codes" and "constitutions," but even these seemingly fixed and permanent forms
are but phases of a continuous growth.

Anglo-American legal history, which includes the principles of
our fundamental law, differs from ordinary narrative history in
that it deals with *ideas* as affected by events and human experience,
ideas which have eventuated in laws designed to promote the interests or welfare of those who made them. Such history is as
much concerned with psychological processes as with economic
activities or religious controversies. It embraces all of these in their
interactions; but it has little to do with purely abstract thinking.
The milieu of legal history is the social order from which law
springs. The roots of American constitutionalism are therefore
to be sought in the experiences of the social order which arose
coincidently with what we call the modern era. This period con-
trasts sharply with the medieval age, particularly in that the individual's lot in life is to a much less extent determined by the

3

PART ONE

THE EVOLUTION OF A BRITISH IMPERIAL CONSTITUTION

FROM GILD TO CHARTERED COMPANY

The growth of trade following the Norman Conquest made the English towns the seed plots of the new modern order. By the thirteenth century at least one third of them possessed gilds of merchants and craftsmen, the members of which had become the most substantial class of citizens. No man could ply his calling unless he belonged to the appropriate gild, and as a gildsman he was subject to the regulations adopted by the organization. As one of the holders of a charter conferring liberties or "franchises" the member was known as a "freeman." Town and gild were legally distinct institutions, under separate charters, but the same individuals often held membership in both, thus creating an identity of interest and control. Social distinction as well as political influence followed economic success, and a new aristocracy of wealth gradually developed alongside the old one of birth. Originally many of the gilds were democratic in character, but as time passed differences in wealth tended to divide the membership, and a small group of the most prosperous often became the governing body. The number of apprentices was limited more and more, and those who completed their training became less and less certain of promotion to the rank of master craftsmen. Many were compelled to remain journeymen working for wages while the successful master craftsmen became an employing class.[1]

A new type of association was called into being by the growth of foreign commerce. The merchants of the older gilds were mostly engaged in retail trade in a small way; those of the new organizations were wholesalers whose operations beyond seas required considerable capital. The gild of mercers in London was

[1] On gilds and chartered companies, among the older works which are still useful is Joshua Toulmin Smith, *English Gilds*. Charles Gross was an American scholar whose book, *The Gild Merchant*, has long been regarded as a standard authority. To these may be added Rev. J. Malet Lambert, *Two Thousand Years of Guild Life*.

In the footnotes throughout this volume the titles of books are printed in *italics*, while the titles of articles and essays in magazines and composite books are placed in quotation marks. To save repetition the place and date of publication of books and the volume and pages of magazines, etc., in which articles and essays are to be found, as well as full titles, are given only in the List of References at the back of the volume. All entries in this list are arranged alphabetically under the names of authors or editors.

the nucleus of the first of the new associations about which there is definite information—the Merchants Adventurers. They monopolized the export trade with the Netherlands in certain manufactured articles, especially cloth. The company's earliest charter was obtained in 1407, but its privileges were increased from time to time until in 1564 it received a final charter from Queen Elizabeth.[2]

This organization was the first example of the so-called "regulated" company, in which each merchant or "freeman" traded "in his own bottom," subject to the ordinances of the association. This system was clearly an extension of the practice of the gilds. The Company of Merchants Adventurers was a private profit-seeking organization. In spite of this character, however, circumstances forced it to perform functions which fell within the field of public law. Since members, in the pursuit of their calling, necessarily sojourned in the Low Countries for considerable periods, the charter of 1564 conferred upon the governor (as the chief officer was called) and his assistants "full jurisdiction power and authority lawfully to rule and governe the same Fellowship of Merchants Adventurers of England and their successors and all and every merchant and member of the same in all their private causes and suits, quarrels and demeanours, offences and complaints amongst them in the . . . countries and towns of Holland [and] Zealand . . . and to reform decide and pacify all manner of questions discords and variance, between themselves and between them or any of them and other merchants in the said countries."

The Elizabethan age was an era of great commercial expansion for England, and numerous other regulated companies sprang up which followed in general the model of the Merchants Adventurers. Each enjoyed a monopoly of the trade with a specified foreign country or region. As the seventeenth century dawned, a superior plan of operation was introduced (1612) by the East India Com-

---

[2] On the chartered companies and their relation to the expansion of trade and beginnings of colonization, see Sir Charles P. Lucas, *The Beginnings of English Overseas Enterprise,* and George Cawston and Augustus H. Keane, *The Early Chartered Companies.* A useful collection of source materials is William E. Lingelbach, *The Merchant Adventurers of England.* On corporations see John P. Davis, *Corporations.*

pany, known as the joint-stock system. Abandoning the former method of trading "in his own bottom" with its attendant heavy individual risk, each member now contributed to the capital fund by purchasing shares of stock, and participated in the profits or losses in proportion to his investment, without liability beyond the amount represented by his shares. The device brought together larger capital sums than the wealthiest individual could command, and at the same time avoided the risk of ruinous losses by any one person. Without such a plan, English commerce could hardly have ventured upon the precarious enterprises which actually resulted in its enormous expansion.

THE CORPORATION

The joint-stock company approximated in form the modern corporation. Destined to play a vital part in American as well as in English economic and constitutional life, the corporation was itself the product of a long process of evolution. In primitive form it existed among the Romans, from whose law the English derived their earliest notions about corporate bodies. Before the Tudor period any group which held a charter of liberties from a competent superior was regarded as a corporation. The chief types were the chartered towns (boroughs) and the gilds. Some of the early charters were granted by abbots and other clerical and lay dignitaries, but Henry VIII's attack upon the monastic orders led to the adoption of the rule that no corporation could exist legally without the royal sanction.

The earliest chartered bodies lacked some of the characteristics of the later corporations. A notable advance was made when the corporation was recognized as an artificial person. As such it had the right to engage in the activities indicated in the charter and to perform the acts incidental thereto, such as the making of contracts and the holding of property. The right to sue and to be sued followed of necessity. The rule in interpreting charters was to construe them strictly, allowing no powers or privileges to pass by implication.[3] Consequently, if a corporation performed an un-

---

[3] The case of Dr. Bonham may be cited as an illustration. The Royal College of Physicians in London was incorporated by Henry VII under a charter, con-

authorized act, the deed was *ultra vires* and might result in the abrogation of the charter.   The trend of legal development was against arbitrary action, however, and the corporation, although the king's creature, was not in theory dissoluble at his pleasure; the concept crept into law that the charter was a contract to which the king was a party, and hence that a judgment as to violation should be given by a disinterested tribunal.   The courts were subservient to the king down to the Revolution of 1688, but the principle that judicial process was necessary to void a charter was one of increasing significance.

These and other features of the law of corporations developed gradually.   The types of internal organization also changed slowly. The Merchants Adventurers' charter of 1564 created "one perpetuall fellowship and comminalty and body Politick and Corporate" which was declared to have full power "to sue and implead to be sued and impleaded."   Its constitution followed the model of the gilds of the later undemocratic type, vesting its powers in the governor and assistants rather than in the membership at large. The "fellowship and comminalty" had the right to elect the officials, but the legislative and judicial functions were exercised by the latter.

By contrast the East India Company was a democracy.   The members in general assembly, provided that either the governor or his deputy was present, were empowered to "make all reasonable laws, constitutions, etc., agreeable to the laws of England, for their good government, by plurality of voices and [to] punish by fines and imprisonment, the offenders against their laws. . . ."

The evolution of the corporation illustrates an English tendency inherited by America, "to expand if it be possible, some old habit or method, already found fruitful, into new growth for the new need." Here the germ was the gild; expanded and modified to meet the requirements of an enlarged sphere of activity, it became the trading

firmed by later statutes, giving it power to license physicians and to fine any who practiced without its permission.   Dr. Bonham, holding a degree from Cambridge University, denied the jurisdiction of the College, and the court upheld his contention, on the ground that the charter did not grant an exclusive power, but was intended only to insure the competence of practitioners, which in Dr. Bonham's case was sufficiently guaranteed by the certificate of Cambridge.—Louis B. Boudin, *Government by Judiciary*, I, 503.

corporation. This in its turn, in the New-World environment, was to expand into the commonwealth and eventually into the state in the American union.

PRIVATE INITIATIVE

The history of gilds and corporations indicates the importance of private initiative (the ancestor of "rugged individualism"), and proves that a large liberty of association was from an early time a significant phase of English freedom. In general the force impelling to organization was not the royal will or other superior authority, but the prospect of advantages to be gained by those who united for group action. Even though from Tudor times the king's sanction was a legal prerequisite of corporate existence, the *will to associate* had to be made known to the ruler before he could act. His permission was intended to prevent harmful organizations; it was only a partial limitation of a fundamental liberty; and so deeply imbedded was the English habit of forming associations to promote common purposes that mutual agreement may well have seemed to be the real creative force even in the case of corporations chartered by the king. So strong indeed was the impulse of individuals to act with others that legal obstacles were likely to be evaded or disregarded.

INFLUENCE OF PROTESTANTISM

The tendency to trace the real source of group organization to the agreement of the persons concerned was greatly enhanced by the Protestant Revolution. The spirit which repudiated the authority of the Roman Church engendered dislike of the Anglican establishment as the heir of its authoritarian attitude; and as a next step those who rejected the state religion were prone to deny the right of the government to enforce religious conformity. Banned by the law of the land, the sectarian leaders, instead of conforming, fell back for the sanction of their associations upon the law of God as they conceived it to be set forth in the Scriptures. This was substantially equivalent to asserting the sufficiency of mutual agreement as the basis of their groups.

The forms which Robert Browne, founder of Independency,

adopted for the use of his "Separatist" followers in their "covenant of believers," were apparently derived from gild statutes.[4] Thus the Separatist Church as well as the trading corporation bears witness to the pervasive influence of the early gild. But conscience and the Bible formed the chief reliance of the Separatists. Browne asserted that a church is founded in the true scriptural way when believers covenant together and with God to form an association for worship. By the covenant, he held, they are gathered together in a self-governing body, so far as religious affairs are concerned. As for the king or other civil authorities, they rightly "doe nothing concerning the Church." Browne then took a third step and extended his theory of contractual origins to the state itself, declaring that "for civil magistrates, there must be an agreement of the people."

It would be a plausible guess that experience with gilds and companies had brought Englishmen to the verge of this last idea, for these societies not only originated in private agreement, but in many of them members were on an equal footing, and the use of elections in choosing officers rested obviously upon the principle that power resided in the membership and was merely delegated to officials to be exercised on behalf of the body. One would expect to find the same idea arising in the political sphere, where the growth of the elective system in choosing the members of Parliament paralleled the advance of the gilds and suggested that the nation itself was a great association, whose officers derived their powers from the people. As a matter of fact this is just what did happen.[5]

[4] Large numbers of social and religious gilds, the outgrowth of the earlier economic gilds, survived the measures of Henry VIII and received royal sanction. Many of these were in Norfolk County, Browne's home. See Andrew C. McLaughlin, *Foundations of American Constitutionalism*; Charles Borgeaud, *The Rise of Modern Democracy*; Joshua Toulmin Smith, *English Gilds*. McLaughlin's book is an excellent examination of the contributions of the gilds, companies, and religious institutions of England to American political philosophy.

[5] For a recent study of the rise of the middle class in England and elsewhere see Franklin Charles Palm, *The Middle Classes*. Chapters in Harold J. Laski, *The Rise of Liberalism*, deal brilliantly with the same theme. R. H. Tawney, *Religion and the Rise of Capitalism*, and Max Weber, *The Protestant Ethic and the Spirit of Capitalism*, deal with the religious changes of the early modern period as a factor in the middle-class movement.

RISE OF THE HOUSE OF COMMONS

The beginnings of Parliament seemed by no means to promise a development of the kind just indicated; some three or four centuries passed before conditions were ripe for the enunciation of the theory that the people were the source of power. Representation itself was not at all the offspring of liberal theory or the result of popular demand; nor was the House of Commons the house of the common people at any time before the nineteenth century.[6] The knights and burgesses of the lower house were not originally sent to Westminster by their constituents to check the tyrannical propensities of royalty. The feudal barons had indeed united on occasion to curb the king when he became too overbearing, as Runnymede and the Great Charter testify. But not before the seventeenth century were the Commons in position to act with equal effect.

Representation, in fact, was an incident of the feudal system. Even serfs had once owed attendance at the local courts, but attendance was a bother, and representation was in origin a privilege only because it allowed all inhabitants except the deputies to absent themselves.[7] In the period which saw the rise of Parliament

[6] Albert F. Pollard, *Evolution of Parliament*, 107–109. The nucleus about which Parliament developed was the royal council, of which the king himself was the essential element. The council attended the king and was *his* council rather than the council of the *land*, or realm, of England. The word *parliamentum* was first applied to any formal parley of the council, and then to the body itself. The presence of the Lords and elected representatives of shires and boroughs was not essential, and in early times they may not have shared in the council's deliberations. The legislative and judicial authority of the king in council was complete without them. Except during the revolutionary period from 1642 to 1660, acts of Parliament have been theoretically the expressions of the king's will. See Robert L. Schuyler, "A Retrospect and a Theory." Also references cited by Schuyler in this article.

Bishop William Stubbs, in *The Constitutional History of England*, made one of the earliest of the modern scholarly studies of institutions in the era of parliamentary beginnings. Notable studies of limited scope are: J. F. Baldwin, *The King's Council in England during the Middle Ages*; Charles H. McIlwain, *The High Court of Parliament and Its Supremacy*; D. Pasquet, *Origin of the House of Commons*; and Pollard's book, just cited. George Burton Adams, *The Council and Courts of Anglo-Norman England*, treats of a somewhat earlier period.

[7] In 1765, James Otis of Massachusetts combatted the view that attendance in Parliament was a "duty arising from a tenure of lands, or the feudal system," asserting, on the contrary, that it sprang "from the nature of man, of society, and of all original, just, social and civil compacts for forming a state."—*A Vindi-*

(the thirteenth and fourteenth centuries), it had become difficult to secure an adequate attendance at the county court. The attendance of the more substantial element consequently came to be all that was insisted upon, and even freeholders were excused if their lands did not yield as much as forty shillings per year. Thus since members of Parliament were chosen in the county court, it resulted that by the time representation became a valued privilege the smaller landowners were definitely excluded from the suffrage. Representation in Parliament, like that in the county court, was in the beginning imposed from above, chiefly, perhaps, in the hope of rendering the acts of the central government more acceptable to the constituencies.

The control of local affairs was the first stage of political power reached by the middle class or burghers. Their influence is attributable to the power of the purse. Under even the most liberal town constitutions it seems clear that the voters were the substantial citizens who formed the *bourgeoisie*, and equally clear that the growth of their influence in Parliament paralleled their advance in local importance.[8] The burghers had been originally no more

cation of the British Colonies, 29 (see *infra*, Chap. V, note 2). Otis's philosophy prevented him from recognizing historical fact.

[8] In the early days the towns were represented in Parliament as parts of the shires in which they were located. The customary procedure was to direct the sheriff, by writ issued from chancery, to hold the county court of elections. It was his duty also to notify the towns by "precept" of the meeting of the court, and qualified burghers attended to vote or to announce the names of candidates already selected by the townsmen. The formal election of both knights to represent the body of the county and of burgesses as deputies of the towns was the work of the court, but the actual choice of burgesses was probably made beforehand in the towns by whatever methods prevailed in the election of town officers.

Information concerning these methods is meager, but they varied greatly. Some towns still followed medieval customs; some adopted the forty shillings rule of the counties; some were relatively democratic, holding meetings of the "inhabitants of the franchise" in the guildhall and choosing "by the most voice"; in others the choice was made by small oligarchies. Towns changed their practice from time to time, and the later changes seem as a rule to have been in the direction of more restricted suffrage. In London, under Edward I, members of Parliament were chosen by the mayor, aldermen, and delegates from the several wards of the city. By 1375 the election had come to be made by persons selected from a larger body named by the trading companies; while under Edward IV the franchise was formally vested in the liverymen of the companies. The practice of London suggests the growing influence of the *bourgeoisie*, but there is no sufficient evidence that the case of London is typical, since the procedure in each town was a matter to be determined by itself. See Stubbs, *Con. Hist.*, II, 216 *et seq.*; III, 414 *et seq.*

eager for representation in Parliament than the county landowners. The burden of supporting "burgesses" was more apparent than any advantages to be derived from the practice; moreover the system committed the constituencies to the measures proposed by the king and his councilors. However, little was to be gained by neglecting to send representatives to Parliament, since its acts were none the less binding.

Representation, nevertheless, implied a theory of government by consent. It became increasingly difficult to levy or collect taxes without Parliament's assent, and the middle class at length perceived that its control of the purse might be made a means of influencing government policy. The representative system, in short, initiated by the royal government as a mechanism for centralizing control, presently began to work quite otherwise than its authors intended. Royal policy was autocratic enough in purpose. During the very years when Parliament was taking form, the aim of king and council, not to mention the Church, was to establish a far-reaching system of control over the lives, beliefs, and conduct of subjects. Under the forceful but diplomatic Tudors considerable progress was made in this direction, but with the accession of James I the current of events took a new direction.

THE SEVENTEENTH-CENTURY REVOLUTION

By the opening of the Stuart era middle-class self-reliance and impatience of restraint had received the reinforcement due to the Protestant Revolution. Men whose wealth was not derived from land,[9] merchants especially, were becoming restive under a régime

[9] The Wars of the Roses had to a great extent destroyed the old feudal nobility and a new class of nobles had arisen based in considerable degree on grants of lands confiscated from the monastic orders by Henry VIII. The landowning class as a whole, including both the gentry and the new nobility, was inclined to support the Anglican system. The nobles were attached to the crown because it had recently conferred their estates upon them, and all Anglicans were natural, even if half-hearted, defenders of the prerogatives of a royalty which was so closely allied with the ecclesiastical system that to attack the one was to attack the other. Wealth acquired in trade, however, had given many of the new nobles the wherewithal to purchase lands from the king; in short, the order had a strong infusion of *bourgeois* blood. This factor helps to explain why, in the course of the seventeenth century, the landed class and the burghers tended to draw together and make common cause against the king. After the Revolution of 1688 the government rested on these allied classes.

which united church and state as joint exponents of authoritarianism in politics and business as well as religion. The *bourgeoisie* in general accepted Puritanism, the spirit of which was congenial to their habit of taking the initiative in bold ventures and of meeting the challenge of new opportunities.[10]

The Stuart stage was set for the conflict which the more tactful Tudors had succeeded in avoiding during the "adolescence" of the middle class. By this time the rising spirit of *bourgeois* Protestantism could no longer be repressed, for it was determined not to submit to any system of regulation in either religious or secular affairs which its own representatives did not formulate. First to gain control of Parliament and then to place Parliament above the king was its inevitable program.

James I found his plans checked through the control of the purse enjoyed by the middle class in the House of Commons. That House, which was the stronghold of Puritanism, refused grants of money unless the king's measures were shaped in conformity with its wishes. The obnoxious projects of his son Charles I were met by similar tactics. His attempt to levy forced loans was checked, for the moment, by his agreement (in the Petition of Right, 1628) that there should be no taxation except by act of Parliament.

Charles's subsequent attempt to rule without the dubious aid of Parliament failed chiefly because the power to tax had passed from his hands. When, needing money, he summoned the two houses once more, the debate over proposed measures became a quarrel between Parliament and king, the quarrel became a civil war, and the civil war became a revolution. The victory of the parliamentary forces was followed by Charles's execution and the setting up of a new government resting upon the political theories of the Puritan leaders. Their domination was threatened in turn by the more radical program of the peasants, apprentices, and wage-earners who had filled their armies and won their battles. To avert this danger, the Puritans effected a compromise with the Anglican

[10] "Calvin did for the bourgeoisie of the sixteenth century what Marx did for the proletariat of the nineteenth."—Palm, *Middle Classes*, 53, quoting Tawney, *Religion and the Rise of Capitalism*. On the influence of religious changes see also Weber, *Protestant Ethic and the Spirit of Capitalism*, and discussion by Laski, in *Rise of Liberalism*, 1–90 *et passim*.

landlords and agreed upon the restoration of the House of Stuart as a limited monarchy. The second Charles accepted the invitation to ascend the throne fully aware that he held it by consent of the nation and only during good behavior, and carefully refrained from policies which might have caused him to "go again upon his travels."

The quieter era which succeeded the turmoil of the middle decades of the seventeenth century was a period of new economic advance on the part of the middle class, and Charles lent himself willingly to schemes of commercial and territorial expansion. In no previous age had the commercial group enjoyed so large an influence in Parliament and with the king. As its position had been gained at the expense of the royal authority, its leaders were not likely to wink at the efforts of any king to regain lost ground. This, however, was just what the injudicious James II seemed bent on doing; his reign was consequently cut short after three years by the Revolution of 1688.

THE COMPACT THEORY

The overthrow of the Stuarts was an illustration of the fact, announced in this epoch by the philosopher Harrington, that political power follows economic power. It represents also the working out in practice of the doctrine set forth by Robert Browne in the previous century, that "for civil magistrates, there must be an agreement of the people." Browne's phrase contained the germ of the compact theory to which the Puritans appealed during their contest with the royal power. John Milton, less renowned as philosopher than as poet, was among those who expounded the theory of the contractual origin of government. He held that men were by nature equal because they were created in the image of God, and that violence and oppression entered the world through Adam's sin. To save themselves from destruction "they agreed by common league to bind each other from mutual injury, and jointly to defend themselves against any that gave disturbances and opposition to such agreement. Hence came cities, towns, and commonwealths." [11]

The Puritan régime from 1642 to 1660 rested upon the truly

[11] *Tenure of Kings and Magistrates*, quoted by McLaughlin, *Foundations*, 65.

revolutionary philosophy that rulers derive their powers from an agreement of the people. Although Parliament could not exist legally apart from the king, since by definition the king, Lords, and Commons constituted the "king in Parliament," yet the Lords and Commons assumed the legislative function after the breach with Charles I, on the false theory that the two houses made the law and that the king was bound to assent to bills unless he could give reasons for dissent which were satisfactory to the houses. When the Lords in 1649 rejected the ordinance for creating a court to try the king, the Commons went a step further and acted alone, declaring that whatever it enacted as law "hath the force of law." The act establishing the Commonwealth declared that the supreme authority of the nation was vested in "the Representatives of the People in Parliament, . . . without any King or House of Lords." [12] The execution of the king was followed by a number of proposals for the erection of a new government by resorting to an agreement of the people. It fell to the lot of John Locke, however, justifying the Revolution of 1688, to give the compact theory the statement which best satisfied the triumphant parliamentary party.[13]

Locke assumed an original state of nature in which mankind was without government although not without rights or law. Each man had a natural right to his life, liberty, and property, and the principles of natural justice bound him to respect the same rights in others. In the state of nature, however, each individual depended upon himself for the defense of his rights. Hence there was no security or order until by compact or agreement with others government was established. By entering into the compact the individual surrendered the right of self-help (a part of his natural liberty) in return for the protection by government of the more precious rights of life, liberty, and security of property. Thus

[12] Schuyler, "Retrospect," 2–8.
[13] The original edition of John Locke's *Two Treatises on Civil Government* appeared in 1690. A standard modern edition is that edited by Henry Morley, and published in London in 1884. The second treatise, entitled *Of Civil Government,* is the one in which Locke presents his version of the compact theory and his ideas concerning the relations between government and people. Copious extracts are conveniently accessible in Francis W. Coker, *Readings in Political Philosophy,* 385–436.

the agreement "puts man out of a State of Nature into that of a Commonwealth." "The great and chief end . . . of men uniting into Commonwealths, and putting themselves under government is the preservation of their property," under which term Locke includes "lives, liberties and estates." "The liberty of man in society is to be under no other legislative power but that established by consent in the commonwealth."

The government thus created is not absolute; it not only owes its origin to the consent of the governed, but is limited by the purposes for which it is created as well as by the principles of natural law. "These are the bounds which the trust that is put in them by the society and the law of God and Nature have set to the legislative power of every commonwealth, in all forms of government. First: They are to govern by promulgated established laws, not to be varied in particular cases, but to have one rule for rich and poor, for the favorite at court, and the countryman at plough. Secondly: These laws also ought to be designed for no other end ultimately but the good of the people. Thirdly: They must not raise taxes on the property of the people without the consent of the people given by themselves or their deputies. . . . Fourthly: Legislative neither must nor can transfer the power of making laws to anybody else, or place it anywhere but where the people have."

If the "legislative" grasps at absolute power, by the "breach of trust they forfeit the power the people had put into their hands and it devolves to the people, who have the right to resume their original liberty, and . . . (as they shall think fit), provide for their . . . safety and security. . . ." "What I have said here concerning the legislative," Locke adds, "in general holds true also concerning the supreme executor [king], who having a double trust [as part of the legislative as well as the executive] acts against both [trusts] when he goes about to set up his own arbitrary will as the law of the society." Such a ruler becomes a tyrant, for "tyranny is the exercise of power beyond right."

NATURAL LAW *v.* COMMON LAW

In the perspective of two centuries and a half it is easy to perceive that Locke's limitations upon the powers of legislatures and kings, instead of springing from the laws of God and nature, were reactions against the very practices of which the Stuarts had been guilty. Of the real origin of rights and of government he and his contemporaries knew little, but he gave the middle class exactly the rationalization it desired. In the dawn of the scientific age, illumined by the great generalizations of Newton and his fellows, men suspected that human relations, like other natural phenomena, must be subject to natural laws, and human society must be capable of rational adjustment if these laws could be discovered. Men in quest of justification of their attempts to curb arbitrary power believed that they had found it written in the book of nature itself.

It has been an achievement of modern scholarship to discover that rights, instead of antedating society, have resulted from a gradual process of social creation. For example, the origin of the principle that one can be taxed only by a body in which he is represented, which came to be regarded as a fundamental right of Englishmen, is to be found in the story of the rise of Parliament. It has been a trait of Englishmen to imagine that they were defending "ancient liberties" when often, in fact, they were demanding new ones. The history of the growth of English freedom is in considerable part the story of the establishment of rights in law through recognition of the binding force of customs of forgotten origin. The appeal to the "law of the land" in Magna Carta as against the arbitrary claims of the king illustrates this process in the establishment of rights. It is akin to the method by which the principles of the common law were shaped, for the common law consists of crystallized custom. In the days when itinerant justices first visited all parts of the realm hearing causes in the king's name, they recognized as law in cases before them, where no statutes applied, such local customs as had been followed since, as the phrase ran, "the memory of man runneth not to the contrary." The sources of the common law thus lay in the very heart of social experience, and the body of principles which composed it was continuously growing. Since the recognition of the justices gave custom definite legal status, their function became a vital factor in the growth of the common law—sometimes a retarding factor, because a judgment might impart to legal principles a fixity which hindered progressive adaptation to changing social conditions.[14]

Common law principles originating in the forgotten past were easily conceived by the philosophers to be rooted in the natural order.[15] English mental habits made it easy to think of any privilege or immunity which had been enjoyed for a long time as an imprescriptible right, not readily, if at all, distinguishable from a natural right. Such fixed natural principles determined the metes and bounds of governmental power, in Locke's thought, much as written constitutions later came to do in the thinking of Americans. Twentieth-century perspective suggests many questions which Locke did not attempt to answer. How were the principles of natural law to be discovered? If not already known *in toto*, but to be apprehended progressively as the result of experience, to what body or governmental agency did it pertain, at any given moment, to give these principles authoritative and binding form? If parliamentary enactments from time to time professedly embodied an increasing understanding of natural right and justice, and these enactments failed to conform to concepts taking shape in the

[14] It was even not impossible for a judge to misinterpret the common law intentionally, and to change it by foisting his own opinion upon it, sometimes corruptly, in order to support some special interest. England's famous justice, Sir Edward Coke, is charged with a perversion of the common law of libel. According to W. S. Holdsworth, truth had been a defense in common law actions for defamation until Coke persuaded the Court of Star Chamber that the correct principle was "the greater the truth the greater the libel." This doctrine Coke misrepresented as correct common law through his report of the case *de Libellis Famosis,* thus procuring its acceptance by the common law courts.—*History of English Law,* V, 205–207.

That the English common law is of fundamental importance in our own constitutional history may be mentioned here. "The interpretation of the Constitution," said Justice Gray in U. S. *v.* Wong Kim Ark (124 U. S. 478), is necessarily influenced by the fact that its provisions are framed in the language of the English common law, and are to be read in the light of its history." This statement gives point to the pronouncement of Oliver Wendell Holmes, Jr., that "the history of what the law has been is necessary to the knowledge of what the law is." His book—*The Common Law*—is a standard treatise and has recently been reprinted. It treats the subject from the legal rather than the historical point of view. More attention is given to origins by Roscoe Pound, in *The Spirit of the Common Law.* Consult also John H. Wigmore, *Panorama of the World's Legal Systems.*

[15] "By a natural transition, the common-law limitations upon royal authority became natural limitations upon all authority; the common-law rights of Englishmen became the natural rights of man."—Pound, *Spirit of the Common Law,* 89–90.

social consciousness, who was to question the validity of such legislation? Two generations before Locke's time, Sir Edward Coke had declared that the common law would adjudge an act of Parliament to be void if contrary to "common right and reason," [16] and his saying has been made the starting point in the argument of those who have maintained that from an early time the *courts* have possessed the power to hold acts of legislation void on the ground of repugnance to natural right or the "constitution." So long, however, as no such theory was acted upon, so long as Parliament was the final interpreter of the law of nature, limitations upon parliamentary authority were practically non-existent. Nor was there any clear-cut distinction between acts of fundamental character and those of ordinary legislation. Although Locke insisted that the legislature cannot delegate its powers, he failed to work out even in theory, as remedies for misgovernment, any system of checks and balances, elections, judicial review, or other control devices short of the ultimate corrective of revolution. The "appeal to Heaven," as he euphoniously calls it, was the remedy for misuse of power. Minor evils must be endured, for only "a long train of abuses, prevarications, and artifices all tending the same way" should be deemed proof of tyrannical purpose. As a last resort, however, the right of revolution is fundamental—a natural right which the people cannot surrender, for God and nature forbid men to abandon their own preservation.

Despite the lack of the devices of a later time for controlling government, the seventeenth century witnessed great advances in governmental practice as well as theory. The Revolution of 1688 attained objectives long sought; its fruits were garnered in the form of a series of statutes of constitutional significance which established habeas corpus, periodical parliaments, a new measure of religious toleration and of freedom of the press, independence of the judiciary, the supremacy of the civil over the military authorities, and control of the national forces and finances by the legislative branch of the government.

[16] In the case of Dr. Bonham. See *ante*, note 3.

TRIUMPH OF THE MIDDLE CLASS

The Revolution of 1688 was not a victory of democracy. The present-day reader of treatises of the type of Locke's essays on government is in danger of being misled by the democratic implications of the constantly recurring references to the "public good," and to "the people" as the source of authority. The writers were apparently unconscious of such implications. For them the term "people" meant those of their own class, and the "public good" was identified with their class interests. Their creed, held by Anglican landlord as well as Puritan man of business, stressed soberness and thrift as a "specific for prosperity"; but they looked contemptuously upon the poor as victims of their own idleness or vice, and hailed the successful man as the incarnation of the social virtues. In spite of Locke's insistence upon "one rule for rich and poor," he thought that the only good citizen was the prosperous one. It is these who in Locke's ideal state are to be regulated only with their own consent; only these, says Harrington, have a true stake in the country and it is they who ought to rule. The rich, says Locke again, should be educated for government in both state and private affairs; the poor should be trained in piety and useful obedience.

II

PROBLEMS OF IMPERIAL GOVERNMENT: SEVENTEENTH CENTURY

FROM CHARTERED COMPANY TO COMMONWEALTH

THE preceding chapter traced the advance of the English middle class in economic and political influence and indicated the chief elements of the ideology developed by it. At the beginning of the modern period the trading corporation, evolved from the gild as its germ, was the mechanism favored by this class in its economic expansion beyond the realm. Its creed embraced faith in private initiative, the habit of association for common purposes, belief in natural law, and the theory of the contractual origin of government with certain corollaries concerning its functions and powers. Employing the mechanism of the trading corporation the middle class reached out to America in the seventeenth century and began the English colonization of the New World with little assistance from the government beyond the grant of charters of incorporation by the king. Colonization was thus a phase of middle-class enterprise and the leaders carried to the New World the ways of their class at home including not only the mechanism of the corporation but their patterns of thought. Moreover, while colonization was motivated largely by economic purposes, the inevitable consequence was the emergence of political communities and the creation of a widespread empire for which an adequate government must be devised. Our next task is to trace the evolution of the political communities in English America.

In 1612, under the provisions of a revised grant, the Virginia Company became a self-governing corporation similar to the East India Company, with the privilege not only of managing its own business affairs but of governing the inhabitants of the plantation. The charter of 1612 authorized the holding of a meeting in London four times each year, known as the "general court," at which a majority of the stockholders present could make "such Laws and

22

Ordinances for the Good and Welfare of the said Plantation" as they thought "requisite and meet," so long as they were not contrary to the laws of England. Once each year in general court the stockholders elected officers, who carried on routine business between sessions of the court.

It is significant that the organization of the Virginia Company was of the democratic type rather than the restricted kind represented by the Merchants Adventurers. The stockholders were entitled to equal privileges, and the powers of the officers were derived from the body of the membership. The primary purpose of the company was to seek profit; it was organized for business purposes; but the terms of the charter did not distinguish between its economic and political functions. In the "treasurer" (as the head officer was called) and his assistants it is easy to recognize the prototype of the president and board of directors of a modern business corporation; but there is in this official group as marked a suggestion of the governor and council of a commonwealth, while the general court and stockholders foreshadow the modern state legislature and body of citizens.

The stockholders of the Virginia Company were of two classes: those who remained in England were the "adventurers," while the actual colonists were known as "planters." The planter might be the owner of shares of stock by purchase, but he was entitled to a share if he only "adventured his person." For several years after the granting of the new charter the adventurers completely controlled the general court, since the planters were too far away to attend its sessions. In the colony, the authority of the court was wielded by a governor and council, chosen by it. To give the planters an active voice in the common enterprise was a measure well calculated to promote its success; moreover it was no more than their right as owners of shares. But to give them such a voice a new mechanism had to be devised. For this purpose the general court instructed Governor Yeardley to invite the planters to send representatives to join with him and the council at Jamestown in passing ordinances for the welfare of the colony. As representative districts the settlements were grouped into eleven "boroughs," in each of which the "free inhabitants" chose deputies who were called "burgesses." The ordinances passed by the assembly so constituted were subject to the approval of the general court in London, while those of the court were equally subject to approval by the assembly before going into effect. Under these instructions the first assembly met in 1619, and two years later the system was confirmed by an ordinance of the general court which has been called the "first written constitution granted to an American colony." [1]

Whether or not the assembly thought of itself as a political body is an interesting question. Members were necessarily concerned with their interests as associates in an economic undertaking, but from the first meeting the transactions had to do largely with crime and its punishment, relations with the Indians, and other matters which we would now regard as political in nature.[2] The close association of economic and political functions reminds one of the blending of the two in the early English borough; indeed since the trading company grew out of the gild, it appears to be a continuation of the old union. The use of the term "borough" to designate the electoral districts is similarly cognate with the English system of parliamentary representation, and possibly there is significance in the facts that members of the first assembly sat with their hats on, like members of the House of Commons, and that bills were read three times, as in parliamentary procedure.[3] It is at least certain that when the charter was revoked in 1624 Virginia was already equipped with the necessary mechanism of a political community.

The democratic charter of the Virginia Company, like those of the gilds of the earlier time, tended to familiarize stockholders with the idea that officials derive their powers from the consent of the members of the corporate body, of which they are not the masters but the responsible agents. When members of the company were

---

[1] W. C. Morey, "Genesis of a Written Constitution."

[2] The official account of the proceedings of the first assembly was kept by Secretary Pory, who seems also to have acted as speaker. It is printed in Henry R. McIlwaine, ed., *Journals of the House of Burgesses*, I, 2–17. *Cf.* W. W. Henry, "The First Legislative Assembly in America."

[3] Elmer I. Miller, *The Legislature of the Province of Virginia*, 21, 24.

transformed by events into residents of a *de facto* political community, the concept of derivative power was readily carried over
from things economic to affairs political. The corporation charter
by restraining action within certain limits foreshadowed, moreover, the written constitutions of a later time in which the powers
of government are enumerated. Where colonizing groups had
not received the king's grant of corporate rights, circumstances
emphasized the significance of the mutual agreement. This was
especially true in the case of religious colonists like the Pilgrims
who, as followers of Browne, accepted his teaching that "for civil
magistrates, there must be an agreement of the people." Already
united as a church "by a covenant of the Lord," they formed, before landing, a second organization by entering into the celebrated
Mayflower Compact.

The immediate occasion for this action was the fact that since
their patent contemplated a settlement in Virginia, and they were
about to land outside of the limits of that colony, certain malcontents began to whisper that there would be "none to command
them." [4] Thereupon, for want of other authority, the Pilgrim
Fathers had recourse to that inherent in their own group, deeming
that this, "(their condition considered) might be as firme as any
patent, and in some respects more sure."

By the words of the agreement the signers "doe . . . solemnly
and mutualy in the presence of God, and of one another, covenant
and combine ourselves togeather into a civill body politick, . . .
and by vertue hearof [agree] to enacte, constitute, and frame
schuch [*sic*] just and equall lawes, ordinances, acts, constitutions,
and offices, from time to time, as shall be thought most meete and
convenient for the generall good of the Colonie, unto which we
promise all due submission and obedience."

The simplest explanation of this proceeding is to regard it as a
resort to the covenant for political purposes in accordance with

[4] An ordinance of the general court of the Virginia Company gave leaders of
"particular plantations" (group settlements within the limits of the company's
grant) the liberty of "Associatinge unto them divers of the gravest and discreetes
[*sic*] of their Companies, to make Orders, Ordinances and Constitucons for the
better orderinge and dyrectinge of their Servants and buisines provided they be
not Repugnant to the Laws of England." Quoted by McLaughlin, *Foundations*, 19.

the Brownist view. Just as no need was felt for civil sanction of their church covenant, they now considered their mutual agreement as sufficient warrant for the exercise of political powers, even to the extreme of inflicting the death penalty.[5]

From the point of view of English law the Pilgrims' agreement was of doubtful validity. It was not unlike the preliminary step in the formation of a corporation, but the step necessary for its legal consummation, namely, the procuring of the king's consent, was never taken. Thus we have a new example of the adaptation of old ideas or practices to meet new needs in a new environment. As in the case of Virginia, experience gave practical force to the notion that governments derive their powers from the consent of the governed. Practically, the king's authority receded for the time being into the background.[6]

Virginia illustrates the emergence of the political community under the auspices of a commercial corporation operating in the wilderness; Plymouth shows the translation into actual practice, in similar conditions, of the theory that government originates in compact. The history of the Massachusetts Bay Colony affords further illustration of both operations.

The plan of colonizing the Massachusetts Bay region owed its origin to the friction between the Puritan party and the Stuart kings. When Charles I dissolved Parliament in 1629, some of

[5] John Billington was executed in 1630 for the murder of John Newcomer. Billington had been "foisted into the 'Mayflower' by some supposed enemy of the Pilgrims," and had been a source of constant trouble. The Plymouth authorities consulted the Massachusetts Bay leaders before carrying out the sentence. See John A. Goodwin, *The Pilgrim Republic*, 352.

[6] It is possible that the compact found a warrant in an old custom of the sea under which passengers sometimes associated themselves for order and self-government during a voyage which would terminate presumably in a country with an organized government. Some such association the Plymouth settlers may have made on the eve of their voyage, and since the voyage brought them into the wilderness, it might be held that the compact was a stretch of the sea-law to provide for their unforeseen situation upon landing. In that case the sea-law could hardly do more than sanction a temporary agreement pending recourse to the crown. The historian encounters at this point a case of fact versus theory: the government of Plymouth for two generations rested actually on the basis of the agreement of those concerned. If the explanation is found in an extension of the sea-law, the result coincided with the procedure called for by the compact philosophy. See discussion of the sea-law in McLaughlin, *Foundations*, 21–25.

the Puritan leaders, including John Winthrop who had actively opposed the king while a member of the House of Commons, turned their hopes to New England as a new Canaan. Disgusted with Charles's pro-Catholic policies and his arbitrary measures in general, they set on foot a plan to found in the New World a "bulwark against the Kingdom of Anti-Christ." Taking advantage of the fact that a charter had recently been granted for a new trading corporation under the name of "The Governor and Company of Massachusetts Bay," it was arranged, by means of an agreement made at Cambridge, that all stockholders who did not wish to migrate to the colony should transfer their rights to such members of the company as would themselves undertake to go. By this course the seat of the corporation was removed to the colony, and the charter was speedily converted in effect, and perhaps by design, into the constitution of a commonwealth.

The Massachusetts colony was born of the same ideology which led to the Civil War and Commonwealth in England. If the minds of these colonizing Puritans may be read in their deeds, they hoped that the corporate form of organization, functioning so far from the king's watchful eye, would enable them to carry out without interference their purpose of setting up a "Bible Commonwealth." In form and provisions their charter was much like that of the Virginia Company. The stockholders, or in technical terms, the "freemen of the Company," were to hold general court four times yearly for passing ordinances and admitting freemen, and at one of these meetings officers were to be chosen—a governor, deputy governor, and eighteen assistants. The presence of the governor or his deputy, and at least seven of the assistants, was necessary to constitute a quorum at the general court meeting. The official group met monthly as a "court of assistants" to transact routine business. The charter permitted the court to choose its place of meeting, thus facilitating the transfer from London to Boston.

The leaders of this Puritan project undoubtedly had their eyes on the possibilities involved in the grant to the general court of authority to make "all manner of wholesome and reasonable orders . . . and ordinances," so long as they conformed to the laws of

England. As in the case of Virginia, mere distance from England dictated this delegation of governmental functions to the corporation, and although they stood in the king's stead, the promoters saw in the words of the grant the possibility of deviating sufficiently from his wishes to accomplish their purposes. With them the commonwealth concept outweighed the commercial corporation from the outset; but, unlike Plymouth, they enjoyed the advantage of a charter which supplied a definite legal basis for the exercise of governmental authority.

It would have been a further advantage to the Massachusetts leaders, bent upon the establishment of a particular type of society, if the provisions of their charter, instead of following the democratic model, had reproduced the features of the Merchants Adventurers' organization with its concentration of powers in the hands of the governor and his assistants. There is no direct evidence that the Massachusetts leaders were acquainted with the terms of the earlier charter, although it is not unlikely that they were, since it was the "grandfather" of all the subsequent grants. Lacking such provisions, they sought to act just as if their charter had been of the restricted type. Of some two thousand persons who came to the Bay Colony in 1630 only a dozen or so were "freemen of the Company" under the Cambridge agreement. These formed for the time being the entire body of stockholders, and, assembled as the general court, possessed all the privileges and powers granted by the charter, including that of governing the large population of non-freemen. The entire number of freemen, at the outset, was insufficient to supply the full complement of eighteen for the court of assistants. Nevertheless, sitting as a general court, they elected themselves to membership in this inferior body.

This step, legitimate in itself, was preparatory to another which violated the charter. Numerous persons, dissatisfied with the rule of the little handful of resident stockholders, were soon clamoring for admission to the corporation as "freemen." If the new members were to be admitted with full rights in the general court the Bible Commonwealth would be endangered, since many of the settlers were not zealous Puritans. Unable to resist the pressure, the oligarchs consented to admit a number of new freemen, but instead of allowing them the full charter rights of freemen, they were permitted only to vote for members of the court of assistants "when such are to be chosen," while the legislative function and the choice of governor were reserved to this latter body. As an additional safeguard the assistants presently "ordered . . . that for time to come noe man shalbe [*sic*] admitted to the freedome of this body polliticke, but such as are members of some of the churches within the lymitts of the same." The substitution of church membership for stock ownership as the requisite qualification of a freeman is significant of the view taken of the nature of the "body polliticke." From this time on the member of the corporation was in fact the citizen of a commonwealth rather than the freeman of a company.[7]

Whether or not the people suspected that these arrangements violated the charter is doubtful, but new causes of discontent soon arose. The court of assistants having levied a tax to provide funds for fortifications, the men of Watertown protested that "it was not safe to pay moneys after that sort, for fear of bringing themselves and posterity into bondage." The incident proves that the idea that taxation and representation go together was already rooted in the colonists' minds. Governor Winthrop's reply, that the court of assistants was "in the nature of a parliament," both admitted the correctness of this view and indicated that he regarded the corporation as having been raised from the domain of private law to that of public law.

Warned by this incident to proceed with circumspection, the court soon afterwards invited each "plantacion" to send two residents to confer with it about the raising of a "publique stocke." The action recalls the first summons to the boroughs in the thirteenth century; it seems not to have been intended to introduce a permanent system of representation in the law-making body, yet it led to it. Apparently it was some of these "committeemen"

---

[7] Herbert L. Osgood points out that at about this time the freemen are beginning to be called "commons" and "people." His treatment of the whole matter of the removal of the Massachusetts Bay Company and the evolution of the commonwealth is illuminating. See *The American Colonies in the Seventeenth Century*, I, 141 *et seq.*

who asked Winthrop in 1634 to show them the charter. He complied, at the same time giving his opinion that the freemen did not have among them men qualified to share in legislation. It seems that he did not have in mind so much the unwieldiness of a large primary assembly, as the lack of capacity of the rank and file and the superior ability of the assistants. But the terms of the charter had been revealed and concession was again necessary. Hence Winthrop intimated that the assistants would not be unwilling to listen to any suggestions which a committee of the freemen might wish to offer. Already, as noted, a few freemen had begun to sit with the assistants, and in May, 1634, a general court containing twenty-four freemen in addition to governor, deputy-governor, and a quorum of the assistants decided that thenceforth the general court should include deputies chosen by the freeman in each of the towns.

This action restored the general court within the sense of the charter; it regained the legislative function which the court of assistants had usurped, deputies replacing the primary gathering of freemen. In choosing magistrates and other officers, however, every freeman was still "to give his owne voyce." As in the case of Virginia, the introduction of the representative system seems not to have been directly due to imitation of British parliamentary practice. The right of representation was implied in the charter of a trading corporation, and likely to come into use whenever the attendance of freemen at the general court was rendered impossible or inconvenient.

From the point of view of English law, Massachusetts and the later colonies based on corporate charters (Connecticut and Rhode Island) were nothing more nor less than corporations subject to the legal principles governing such bodies. But the early Massachusetts leaders possessed slight knowledge of English law; indeed, they held it in light esteem.[8] For them the command of God was

---

[8] Throughout the colonies lawyers were regarded with little favor during the whole of the seventeenth century. The only man in early Massachusetts who had had any legal training was Roger Ludlow, who was invited to the colony in 1630 as assistant to the governor. There seems to have been no barrister in Massachusetts until Thomas Newton came to Boston in 1688. See Joel N. Eno, "First Court Trials in America."

the only true law, and they preferred to go directly to the Scriptures for their rules of action. Yet they recognized that the charter could not be flouted with impunity; and when the people demanded a definite legal code to guide magistrates, the leaders feared that they could not embody their ideas in such a code without conflicting with the provision that no law should be made which was repugnant to those of England. Apprehension that a code based in part on the Old Testament might involve them in difficulty with the king led them for awhile to oppose the popular demand.

It may be seriously questioned whether the Puritans regarded the charter as the chief source of their powers. Like the Separatists of Plymouth, they were deeply imbued with the philosophy of the church covenant and its political corollary, the compact theory of the origin of government. John Cotton, "the father and glory of Boston," and most prominent of the original group of Massachusetts ministers, voiced the common view when he asserted that "all civill Relations are founded in Covenant." It was possible for the Puritans to cite the charter on occasion and to fall back upon the compact theory when charter restrictions proved inconvenient.

The early history of Connecticut and Rhode Island cumulates the evidence concerning the transfer to America of middle-class traits and institutions and of the emergence of the commonwealth concept. Like Plymouth, these new settlements in the wilderness lay outside the organized jurisdiction of the crown or any existing corporation, and, as at Plymouth, each little group of settlers at first provided for the maintenance of law and order by a "plantation covenant" establishing government of a simple kind resting upon the consent of the settlers themselves.[9] In 1639 a union of the Connecticut settlements was effected, under the plan known as the "Fundamental Orders of Connecticut." The Fundamental Orders were more specific than the Mayflower Compact as to the frame of government, and mark another step in the evolution of a written constitution. They fell short of the modern conception in that they were not superior to ordinary acts of legislation.

For the first quarter-century of its existence Connecticut re-

[9] Lois K. Mathews, "The Mayflower Compact and its Descendants."

mained a "squatter" colony with no other sanction for the powers which it exercised than the consent of the people expressed in the Fundamental Orders as a compact. The confusion which prevailed in England during the Civil War and Interregnum tended to prevent an application for recognition, and it is not certain that a population holding the compact philosophy deemed such recognition essential, except as a prudential measure to establish their status in the king's eyes. Connecticut showed the same self-sufficiency in the management of her affairs as Plymouth was displaying, and it was not until the Restoration enabled the crown to look into the colonial situation rather carefully that she sought a charter.

This first chapter of Connecticut history gives excellent evidence of the constructive vitality of the compact philosophy. In the application for the charter, moreover, is shown again the habit of initiative on the part of subjects, while the charter itself bears witness to the continuing importance of the corporate form of organization. The charter which Charles II gave to Connecticut in 1662 created a corporation authorized to enjoy the very liberties and powers which the colony was already in fact exercising. All these facts are evident from the opening words:

"Whereas . . . We have byn informed by the humble Petition of . . . John Winthrop [and others] . . . that the . . . colony . . . was . . . obteyned . . . with much difficulty, and att the onely endeavours, expence and charge of them and their Associates . . . and . . . [has] become a considerable enlargement and addition of our Dominions . . . ,—NOW KNOW YEA, that . . . WEE HAVE thought fitt . . . to Create and Make them a Body Pollitique and Corporate, with the powers and Priviledges herein after mentioned. . . ."[10]

It is to be noted that although the idea of a trading company has now disappeared, and political organization alone is contemplated, the charter of incorporation still follows the pattern worked out in connection with companies formed for commercial purposes.

---

[10] Text in *Connecticut Colonial Records*, II, 3–11; reprinted in William MacDonald, *Select Charters*, 116–119. The John Winthrop mentioned in the charter was the son of Governor Winthrop of Massachusetts.

With the charter conferring powers "herein after mentioned," there comes into operation also the principle of corporation law which confines the exercise of powers within the terms of the grant. Thus what Connecticut gained in definition of status she lost in freedom of action; hence also the charter marks another step along the path leading to the written constitution, for no longer can the general court, as under the Orders, disregard the provisions of what is now the fundamental law. The charter lacked but little of being a true constitution like that of a state at a later time: the difference was that it rested upon the act of the crown instead of one by the people. But the crown's action was perfunctory, and while it gave the legal basis required by English law, it was not more important than the fact back of the act, namely that the plan of government embodied the will of the people and was established in the first place by their agreement. So true was this that Connecticut, after independence was won from England, retained the king's charter as her constitution instead of framing a new one as other states were doing.

The history of the origin and progress of government in Connecticut is repeated almost exactly in Rhode Island. The religious exiles driven thither from Massachusetts first organized each little settlement under a plantation covenant, and later united by framing and adopting a general agreement. Like Connecticut, too, they sought and obtained a charter from Charles II (1663) confirming for their future government the arrangements which they had adopted by mutual consent, and, like Connecticut, they retained this charter as a constitution when the Revolution brought statehood.

Other examples might be cited, notably that of New Haven, to show the prevalence of the Englishmen's habit of providing their own governments whenever they were thrown upon their own resources. Wherever Puritans settled in the wilderness, they established their churches by covenant and formed self-governing groups with an ease born of their politico-religious philosophy. The Puritan practice was only a phase of the even more fundamental and even more ancient habit of forming associations by mutual agreement for any common purpose; and regardless of creed the Anglo-American throughout our history has set up "home-spun" governments wherever occasion has seemed to require it.

In examining the history of the origin of the basic ideas in American constitutionalism it is important to know that New England affords so many examples of governments arising from actual agreements made voluntarily by the people. That such governments derived their powers from the consent of the governed was not a theory but a fact. In the recurrence of such events one can hardly fail to perceive a shift from the old-time view that the subject's rights and privileges emanate from the king as the fountain of law and justice, to the belief that the people themselves are the source of authority—that liberty springs not from the gracious grant of a sovereign but is the natural right of man. It is true that none of the American communities claimed to be independent of England; they admitted subordination, but it was ill-defined, in part because they did not recognize fully the limitations imposed by the law of corporations or any other kind of English law. They conceived of their condition of dependence not so much in legal phraseology as in the terms supplied by the philosophy of natural law and the compact. The influence of the compact theory in seventeenth-century England has already been traced. It was only in America that conditions permitted, indeed almost compelled, actual resort to compact-making; in England the process hardly escaped from the realm of theory.

America provided fertile soil for the development of legal concepts. The origin of law is a problem in itself, and scholars are by no means agreed in their views. But it is a fact and not a theory that in the colonies new concepts were emerging which could not be fitted into the mold of English law. New conditions engendered a new psychology, a new outlook and spirit; existing law had sprung from earlier and different conditions; the new was struggling to break the bonds of the old. A corporate colony was in a legal position very similar to that of an English borough; but a new reality was emerging—something no less real because as yet it only existed, and that vaguely, in the colonial mind, something real because it was to become embodied or "institutionalized" in the autonomous state in a federal union.[11]

GOVERNMENT IN THE COLONIAL COMMONWEALTHS

A court decree of 1624 dissolved the Virginia Company and placed the "plantation" under the administration of the crown. Thus it became a royal colony. The ruler's habit of leaving the initiative in distant enterprise to the subject received a setback when the defunct Virginia Company left the colony like a foundling on the king's doorstep. Not that James I was reluctant to assume the duties thus thrust upon him; in fact he had sought them when he brought action against the corporation, with which he was quite out of humor; and upon the decision of the court he declared his intention of retaining the government of future colonies in his own hands.

Nevertheless, so far as the planters were concerned, the change did not greatly alter the existing governmental machinery. They were allowed to continue to elect representatives to an assembly, but the king replaced the general court of the company in appointing the governor and councilors. The governor became the agent of the crown, acting under the terms of the royal commission and such instructions as were issued from time to time. The assembly lost the right which it had enjoyed under the company of assenting to measures relating to Virginia decided upon by the general court, and its acts became subject to the governor's veto.

Of all the rising colonial commonwealths, Virginia followed most closely the English parliamentary model. Indeed it has been held that she showed "remarkable adherence to English forms and practices." [12] In particular, the rules of procedure and privileges

[11] "At the first designation of these [colonial] assemblies, they were probably not intended for anything more . . . than the municipal corporations within this island. . . . But nothing in progression can rest on its original plan. We may as well think of rocking a grown man in the cradle of an infant. Therefore as the colonies prospered . . . it was natural that they should attribute to [their] assemblies . . . some part of the dignity of the great nations which they represented. No longer tied to by-laws, these assemblies made acts of all sorts and in all cases whatsoever . . . following all the rules and principles of a parliament to which they approached every day more and more nearly."—*The Works of Edmund Burke*, II, 33.

[12] S. M. Pargellis, "The Procedure in the Virginia House of Burgesses," second installment, 156.

of members which gradually came into vogue in the assembly were copied in considerable part from the practices of Parliament.[13] But the colonials were not mere imitators, and showed ingenuity in adapting English practices to their needs, and, where necessary, in inventing new devices. The relative weight of habit, English example, and the American environment as factors influencing colonial development presents many problems for investigation.

Charles I ventured another experiment when he reverted to the feudal fief for the model of his grant (1632) of Maryland to Lord Baltimore. Despite the greater part played by the corporation, one cannot wholly ignore the fief in tracing American institutions to their English germs. In the patent given to Lord Baltimore, the Palatinate of Durham was specifically mentioned as the model which Maryland as an American "county palatine" was to reproduce. Feudal institutions in some degree provide the background for all of the proprietary provinces, of which Maryland was the first successful example.[14]

Notwithstanding this peculiarity in its origin, the government of the proprietary colony, when matured, differed but little from that of a royal province. In the former the proprietor stood in the king's stead, appointing governor and councilors, and issuing commissions and instructions for their guidance. Although, like the corporation, the proprietor held his privileges by royal grant, his type of government was like that in the royal colony. The proprietary and royal colonies were in fact only varieties of the "provincial" type. In both forms there was an assembly composed of two elements, whether sitting as one or two chambers: the councilors represented the authority of king or proprietor, while the deputies, delegates, or burgesses (different terms being employed in the several provinces to designate the representatives)

[13] *Ibid.*, 143–157. Pargellis points out that the aims and problems of the Virginians were similar to those of the House of Commons in combatting the royal prerogative, and that they kept in constant touch with the work of Parliament. The *Virginia Gazette* carried details of its proceedings, and the burgesses sometimes cited parliamentary practices as precedents to be followed. See also Miller, *Legislature of Virginia.*

[14] See G. T. Lapsley, *The County Palatine of Durham;* also Osgood's discussion of Durham as the model for Maryland, *Am. Cols.*, II, 4 *et seq.* Cf. Charles M. Andrews, *Our Earliest Colonial Settlements.*

were the elected agents of the voting class among the people. In the corporate type (Massachusetts under the first charter, Connecticut and Rhode Island) councilors and governor as well as members of the popular branch of the legislature were chosen by the voters. The corporate colonies obviously possessed the fuller degree of self-government, being in fact petty republics.

ENGLISH LAW IN THE COLONIES

A phrase commonly employed in the grant of legislative power in colonial charters was that no law should be made which was repugnant to the "laws and statutes" of England. The one word "laws" might seem sufficiently inclusive unless it was the intention of the crown to impose the common law as well as the statutes of Parliament upon the dependencies. The phraseology therefore raises the question: Did the whole body of English law extend to the colonies *ex proprio vigore?* Such a notion seems absurd. Common sense required that the code of the mother country should be followed only so far as applicable, or that colonial legislation should keep within the general bounds set by English law as a superior system. A degree of discretion had to be lodged somewhere, and in the first instance the body exercising it was naturally the legislature of each colony. But what were the limits of this legislative discretion? They were not well defined by the charters, nor for some time was there an organ of the British government definitely invested with the function of judging of transgressions except in cases so extreme as to warrant the abrogation of the charter. Then the courts were resorted to. Even under the charter of 1691, the powers of the Massachusetts House of Representatives were not enumerated, and that body had no means of determining their scope except as its measures were disputed by the governor or council. Not unnaturally it came to regard itself as the sole or final judge of its powers. The ensuing contest with the governor over the question of a fixed salary for that official was a factor in revealing the need of a superior authority such as the Privy Council increasingly became.[15]

[15] See William Seal Carpenter, "The Separation of Powers in the Eighteenth Century."

Besides this question of colonial legislative power, there was the related one of Parliament's right to make law for the dependencies. These problems were fundamental in colonial relations with England, and in fact almost the identical problems were carried over into our constitutional period, in the field of the relations of Congress with the territories.

The common law was rooted in the experience of the English people, as a set of principles which had grown with its growth. Its spirit called for constant adaptation to changing needs, and the situation of the colonists indicated that by a continuation of the old processes a body of principles would gradually take form in the New World better suited to its needs than any set which could be transplanted *in toto*. Through a long succession of English decisions the common law had lost much of its original elasticity and had become by the seventeenth century a highly technical system, much of which was inapplicable in America, or at least ran counter to the desires of a forward-looking people engaged in laying the foundations of a new society.

Even if the builders of the colonial commonwealths had wished to follow English law closely, they would have been unable to do so for want of acquaintance with it. They were not without notions of justice derived partly from the English legal system and partly from the tenets of their religion, but reduced to primitive conditions of life on what was really a frontier, the utmost approximation to English practice was a rough and ready justice meted out according to the judgment of persons who had no technical training. In the early days of Plymouth the whole body of adult males was called together to pass judgment upon persons charged with misdeeds. Accused persons, at Plymouth and elsewhere, were often left to defend themselves as best they could.[16] Before many years passed provision was made in each colony for courts of

[16] Eno, "First Court Trials." John Billington conducted his own defense against the charge of murder in Plymouth Colony in 1630. See *ante*, note 5. The laws of East Jersey in 1675 allowed any person to plead for himself and forbade any one to take money for pleading for or advising another. Pennsylvania also allowed any one to plead his own cause. In Rhode Island untrained judges were elected from the body of inhabitants; the same was true in East Jersey; in the towns of early Massachusetts judicial officers were appointed.—Paul S. Reinsch, "The English Common Law in the Early American Colonies," *passim*.

several grades, and the use of juries became general. In Massachusetts the court of assistants became a judicial as well as legislative body, and a set of inferior local courts was established, with provision for appeals to the court of assistants. The general court itself became the final tribunal of the judicial system.[17] More or less similar steps were taken in the other colonies. Judicial and legislative functions were habitually vested in the same bodies. Each colony developed quite independently of the others, and came to differ both from its neighbors and from England in its laws and in its judicial organization and procedure. American jurisprudence, although much indebted to England, became a highly original system or systems, deriving many features from the Old Testament and from frontier surroundings.

Rulers, wrote Locke, should "govern by promulgated established laws, not to be varied in particular cases." Owing to lack of knowledge of the "established laws" (and for other reasons to be noted), this precept could not be followed at first in America. Perforce, the discretion of the judges, whether consisting of the whole community or a select group, was relied upon. But the general feeling was in keeping with Locke's doctrine, and popular insistence upon fixed rules to guide the magistrates led to the enactment of simple codes in nearly every colony within a few years after the first settlement.

The story of the development of law in Massachusetts is one of the best illustrations of what, in a general way, took place throughout English America, although it must be remembered that the Puritan colonies were more zealous to follow Biblical rules than were the settlements to the southward.[18] The Puritan oligarchy would gladly have relied permanently upon magisterial discretion: if each cause were judged on its merits, with due regard to circumstances, it seemed that a substantial body of precedents

[17] Charles J. Hilkey, *Legal Development in Colonial Massachusetts, 1630–1686,* 29 *et seq.*

[18] On the controversy over the English common law in Massachusetts see R. B. Morris, "Massachusetts and the Common Law: the Declaration of 1646," and G. L. Kittredge, "Robert Child, the Remonstrant." Pound, *Spirit of the Common Law,* is suggestive of the effect of the American environment on the older English legal principles.

might be built up somewhat after the manner in which the English common law had attained its status.   These leaders did not wish to recognize the principles of the common law as an obligatory subsidiary body of law.   As has been noted already, they preferred the "law of God" as found in the Mosaic code, and wished to make large allowance, as far as the common law was concerned, for the exigencies of their situation.   But in Massachusetts as elsewhere the people were dissatisfied with magisterial discretion: they wished to live under a government of laws not men.   Yielding to popular pressure, the general court resolved in 1636 that a code should be drafted "agreeable to the law of God," although Governor Winthrop feared that such specific legislation could not be enacted without transgressing "the limits of our charter, which provides that we shall make no laws repugnant to the laws of England." Lawmaking by judicial process, such as the leaders desired, they evidently did not regard as subject to the charter limitation upon acts of the general court.

The Body of Liberties resulting from the resolution of 1636 was adopted in 1641.   In conformity with the purpose of follow- ing the "law of God," the sections dealing with capital crimes were based upon the Old Testament.   Penalties for lesser offences were apparently to be prescribed by acts of the general court, but in cases not covered by such acts the magistrates were to apply the word of God at their discretion.   Winthrop, it appears, adhering to the view expressed before the adoption of the code, would have had the legislature refrain from fixing penalties for all non-capital offences in order that magisterial discretion might remain as wide as possible.

Although the superstition of the age is reflected in the inclusion of witchcraft in the list of capital offences (following Exodus XX, 18), the criminal code as a whole, in its departure from English practice, is a tribute to the humanitarianism of its authors.   England inflicted the death penalty for some one hundred and fifty offences; the Body of Liberties reduced the list of capital crimes to a scant dozen, including blasphemy, idolatry, adultery, sodomy, murder, and treason, in addition to witchcraft.   For all of these except treason there was a scriptural basis, and for some of these offences the current penalties in England were less severe. Blasphemy, perjury, and adultery (Leviticus XX, 10), were more lightly dealt with in the less Biblical-minded mother country. On the other hand, offences against property rights were less seriously regarded in Massachusetts than in the older society; theft, for example, was a minor offence instead of a capital crime.

The departures from English practice in civil matters were as marked as in criminal. While they also sometimes show the influence of Scripture, they reveal particularly the effects of local conditions. Under the Massachusetts code, the eldest son, instead of receiving the entire landed estate according to the common-law principle of primogeniture, was given a double portion only. This rule followed the Bible, but its defenders tried to reconcile it with the English law by the plea that both preferred the eldest son above his brethren. In fact, the relative abundance of land in America partially explains this law; land ownership was losing the significance it possessed in Britain. Similar influences are shown in the tendency to minimize or ignore the distinctions made by English law between real and personal property.

In many other details respecting rules of evidence, court procedure, etc., the Liberties departed from English legal practice. Most of the changes could be justified at least superficially by clever reasoning, as was presently attempted. But it would be difficult to reconcile the state of mind which produced them with the presumption of subordination to England. This state of mind is betrayed especially in the provisions relating to treason. Treason to the sovereign, the greatest crime known to the English common law, was not among the capital offences listed in the Body of Liberties. The treason for which it provided the death penalty was treason against the Commonwealth of Massachusetts. To attribute to the Puritan mind which could conceive of this crime the view that Massachusetts was a mere trading corporation would be an absurdity indeed.

As Winthrop had anticipated, it was not long before complaint was made against the Body of Liberties as violative of English law. Dissatisfaction came to a head in 1646, when a remonstrance signed by Robert Child and others was presented to the general court.

The petitioners complained of the disabilities incurred by those who did not conform to the established Congregational Church polity, and protested against the discretionary judgments of the magistrates. They asserted that Massachusetts lacked "a settled form of government according to the laws of England," and, with an implied aspersion upon the local attempt to reform the law, asked for the "establishment of the wholesome laws of England which are the result of long experience and are best agreeable to English tempers."

At about the same time other complaints were sent to England, and in fear of an investigation the general court appointed a committee to prepare a statement designed to show the conformity of the Massachusetts code with English law. The resulting "Declaration" admitted some deviations, but urged that, just as English laws were constantly undergoing modification to meet new conditions, so also colonial laws must be shaped by similar considerations. From this sensible position the declaration departed, however, by attempting to show conformity where it did not exist.

In answer to Child, the general court asserted that there could be no real conflict between the laws of the colony and of England, if the latter like the former were based on the law of God, adding the startling statement that the laws of England are binding only on those who live in that land, for "neither do the Laws of Parliament nor the King's writ go any farther." Edward Randolph, a royal official, reported in 1678 that the laws of England were regarded as not pleadable in the Massachusetts courts unless they had been accepted by the assembly.

Admitting that a reasonable interpretation of the charter permitted some departure from English practice to meet new situations, the course of Massachusetts went beyond all limits. For more than fifty years her behavior was a constant irritation to the English government. In addition to adopting her own criminal code, she established an independent church, passed harsh laws for the suppression of heresy, treated members of the Church of England with intolerance, coined her own money, issued writs in the name of the Commonwealth instead of the king, stoutly resisted all attempts to appeal from colonial to English courts, and evaded as far as possible every effort at interference on the part of the king's government.

A commission appointed by Charles II to investigate the colony declared in indignation: "The King did not grant away his Sovereigntie over you when he made you a corporation. When His Majestie gave you power to make wholesome laws and to administer Justice by them, he parted not with his right of judging whether those laws were wholesome or no." Even this warning that Massachusetts was, after all, a corporation subordinate to the king did not overcome the commonwealth "complex," and a few years later she paid the penalty when the king's advisers informed him that her government was conducted without the slightest regard for the authority of the crown. The charter was annulled under *quo warranto* proceedings, in 1684. Somewhat chastened by this lesson, Massachusetts was glad to obtain a second charter in 1691, under which the governor was appointed by the crown, and the assembly's choice of councilors was made subject to the governor's approval.

Connecticut and New Haven similarly deviated from the English law. In 1642 Connecticut law provided the death penalty for a list of crimes which is practically the same as that of contemporary Massachusetts. Its code was likewise based on the Scriptures. A revised code adopted in the late forties safeguarded life, liberty and property against all damage and interference "unless it bee by the vertue or equity of some express Law of the Country warranting the same established by a Generall Courte, and sufficiently published." But the reader may judge of the actual procedure in the light of the concluding words—"or in case of the defect of a Law in any particular case, by the word of God." New Haven asserted emphatically that divine law was the binding common law in all temporal matters, to be observed as the guiding rule in both civil and criminal jurisdiction.

While legal development throughout the colonies was not uniform, certain tendencies appeared everywhere. Instead of a bodily transfer of the principles of the common law, the colonists desired a restatement of its applicable principles in the form of a code, and in many colonies this was made. Such codes are notable, especially for their inclusion of the principles of freedom in so far as they had been established in the unwritten law of Britain. In this way they rank as important antecedents of the bills of rights which were placed in the early state constitutions. Americans generally tended to work out their own legal systems, establishing rules dictated by the primitive conditions of life in which they found themselves, and judges were expected to be guided by the laws of their respective provinces rather than by the English common law or statutes. Conditions, nevertheless, left a wide discretion for judicial decision as to what law was applicable in given cases.[19]

With the passing of frontier conditions and the increase in the number of trained lawyers, America became somewhat more hospitable towards the English common law. This was partly due to the fact that it was discovered that it contained liberal principles which could be invoked against the arbitrary conduct of officials such as Andros.[20] At the outbreak of the Revolution, in-

[19] The common law entered the several colonies in different degree, and each showed a mixture of its own, composed of common law principles plus features due to local conditions, besides sometimes practices derived from the Bible. Massachusetts retained its peculiar system in marked degree well into the nineteenth century. Chief Justice Attwood observed in 1700 that the methods of the Superior Court at Boston "were abhorrent from the laws of England and all other nations."—Reinsch, "English Common Law," 24.

The old popular law was still administered in considerable measure in derogation of the rules of common law. It was not until 1712 that the first professional lawyer became chief justice. In 1810 Jefferson noted that Massachusetts law remained *sui generis*, making it necessary to appoint a member of the United States Supreme Court who was familiar with it.—*Ibid*.

[20] "The arbitrary government of Andros did more than anything else to introduce a knowledge of the common law into New England. A genuine admiration for the system sprang up when it was realized that its principles contained safeguards against governmental tyranny."—Carpenter, "Separation of Powers," 25. For example, as the English Habeas Corpus Act of 1679 did not extend by its terms, to the colonies, the Americans assumed that it rested on the common law, and began to claim its benefits.—*Ibid*.

Blackstone held that the colonies had "only so much of the English law as is applicable to their own situation and the condition of an infant colony. . . . The common law of England as such has no allowance or authority there, they being no part of the mother country, but distinct though dependent dominions. They are subject, however, to the control of Parliament, though (like Ireland, Man, and the rest), not bound by any acts of parliament unless particularly named."—*Commentaries on the Laws of England*, Introd., sec. 4, p. 107. This was a new attitude due perhaps to the Privy Council's decision in such cases as Clark *v.*

deed, the framers of the Declaration of Rights drawn up by the First Continental Congress were ready to claim the common law as among the rights of Englishmen and consequently as one of their own rights, and in later years many of its principles entered into the constitutional system of the United States.

The refusal to accept the whole body of the common law and the various modifications of it by American assemblies led to several clashes with British authority and called for some device to bring colonial and English law into working relations. How the problem was dealt with will be considered later. A similar problem was involved in the colonial attitude toward acts of Parliament. The tendency was to regard them as having no force in the colonies unless the latter were specifically mentioned.[21] Even then some colonies, notably Massachusetts, were inclined to deny their validity unless expressly re-enacted by the colonial assembly.

Tousey (see *infra*, p. 56). In 1720 the law officers said that "The common law of England is the common law of the plantations."—Carpenter, 25.

The historian Richard Hildreth, writing in the mid-nineteenth century, deplored the introduction of slavery by Virginia as a violation of the common law.—*History of the United States*, I, 119, 518, 521.

[21] See Blackstone's comment in preceding note.

III

PROGRESS TOWARDS AN IMPERIAL CONSTITUTION: EIGHTEENTH CENTURY

THE troublesome question of the extent to which British law was *ex proprio vigore* in force in the colonies was well in evidence before the close of the seventeenth century. It was a symptom of a difficulty which contemporary statesmanship proved unable to meet, and which was to rend the empire asunder —the difficulty of devising a plan of government which would protect and advance the rights and interests of both Englishmen and colonists. The habit of local self-government was ingrained in the English people, and the necessity of untrammeled action in such matters as concerned only the life of the people within each colony was emphasized by the remoteness of the colonial establishments from the home land. Even the kings had recognized this fact to a degree when they deputed governing power to the trading corporations, and the prompt transformation of these into political commonwealths heightened the devotion of Americans to the principle of local autonomy.[1] The need of such autonomy supplied the impulse behind the controversy with the mother country over the binding force of English statutes and common law. After the Revolution of 1688 considerable progress was made towards a working system of divided authority, under which the home government tacitly acquiesced, in the main, in the control by each colony of its own "internal police," while Parliament legislated in matters which concerned the empire as a whole or the interrelations of its parts. To the latter category belonged plans for the extension and regulation of commerce and international relations including war.

In the end, in spite of the gradual establishment of a system

---

[1] In 1623 James I empowered the officers of the East India Company "to punish all capital or other crimes committed on land in India, either by martial or common law, the accused being in all cases entitled to be tried by a jury of twelve." —Cawston and Keane, *Early Chartered Companies*, 95. In 1661, by a new charter, "The Company was . . . constituted a sovereign State, subject only to the supreme authority of the Crown of England."—*Ibid.*, 105–106.

which might, with further modifications, have led to a satisfactory organization of the empire, and did in fact foreshadow in important ways the constitutional system of the United States, the experiment broke down.   British and American ideology diverged more and more, leading the colonists eventually to regard the policies of the home government as subversive of their fundamental rights.   These developments must now be traced.

PARLIAMENT AND COLONIAL POLICY

The Revolution of 1688, as has been seen, is to be interpreted as a triumph of the middle class.   The policy which this class pursued, both before and after the Revolution, was the logical outgrowth of the thought of the *bourgeois* group which since Tudor times had been concerned with the expansion of trade.   Incorporated as trading companies by complacent kings, they had spread England's influence into Asia and America.   They operated at first, as in Virginia, as private companies, although invested with political powers; but after the Restoration their influence over the British government grew steadily and its policies more and more followed their views.   Finally, by the Revolution of 1688 they thrust the king aside, and in alliance with the landed class became the government. After 1660, then, the development and extension of colonial policy and administration are to be credited mainly to this class, and in final analysis the eighteenth-century imperial system represented their views and promoted their interests.

This system was the legitimate descendant of the principles of commercial monopoly which underlay the great trading companies of the sixteenth and seventeenth centuries.   It was not admittedly conceived in the spirit of narrow class interest; the professed intent was to promote the welfare of all classes and all parts of the empire; but the interest of the class rulers was easily confounded with the good of the empire, and there was none to say them nay.   They believed that colonial industries should be regulated under a program of reciprocal or supplementary relations.   Colonies should be made to contribute to the general prosperity not only by stimulating the carrying trade, but by affording a market for English manufactures and confining their own productive efforts to articles which did not compete with the output of the mother country.[2]

Such reasoning led to the extension step by step of the system of regulation. It seemed obvious that England required a powerful navy which could protect both colonies and mother country in time of war. A large and prosperous merchant marine was indispensable as a foundation for such a navy, and to create it the "mercantilists" embarked immediately after the Restoration in 1660 upon the far-reaching program known as the navigation system. The Revolution of 1688 did not alter the trend of policy as related to colonial trade, since it confirmed the power of the very class which had devised it.

This class, which had attacked the soundness of the old system of royal regulation of industry within the English realm, saw no inconsistency in adopting a similar system of regulation on the larger scale of the empire. The year 1696 saw the passage of a navigation act which set up vice-admiralty courts for the trial of infractions of the regulations, and improved the mechanism for the supervision of colonial administration. The name of the new agency—the Board of Commissioners for Trade and Plantations—in itself indicates that the colonies were regarded as mere economic appanages. Colonial enterprise was strait-jacketed with little or no regard for colonial opinion; and while undoubtedly American economic life was benefited in some respects, it would have been strange indeed if selfishness and stupidity had not rendered the measures oppressive and unjust at times.

[2] The standard treatises on British mercantilism are the works of George Louis Beer: *British Colonial Policy, 1754–1765; The Origins of the British Colonial System;* and *The Old Colonial System, 1660–1754.* A very recent study is Conyers Read, "Mercantilism."

The system of domestic regulation which accompanied the mercantile policy in colonial affairs—a natural reflection of the supreme authority of a Parliament controlled by merchants and landlords—is expounded by E. S. Furniss in *The Position of the Laborer in a System of Nationalism: a Study in the Labor Theories of the Later English Mercantilists.*

The third volume of Osgood's *American Colonies in the Seventeenth Century* deals with the beginnings of imperial control. His posthumous work, *The American Colonies in the Eighteenth Century,* becomes of great value for the period covered by this chapter. It tells of the struggles between governors and assemblies in the various colonies, and of the gradual organization of a unified system of British control, as well as of the growth of the spirit of independence. The emphasis throughout is on institutional development.

The acts increased the prices of imported goods, decreased the returns on exports, and drove colonials to violations and evasions. Colonial governors, upon whom the duty of enforcing them was at first imposed, performed the function so laxly that special collectors of customs had to be appointed with salaries paid by the British government. Colonial juries refused to find violators guilty. It was difficulties of this kind which led Parliament to establish the vice-admiralty courts in 1696. These courts were tolerably free from local influence, because they dispensed with juries and left the decision on points both of fact and law to judges appointed by the crown. But evasions and lax enforcement continued. Britishers when appointed to colonial offices were likely to remain at home, enjoying their income while their duties were performed (or neglected) by deputies who were often provincials with slight disposition to enforce unpopular laws.

All of the acts relating to navigation and trade bore the aspect of regulations conceived in the interest of the empire as a whole. If the shoe pinched here and there, it was expected that the suffering part would endure sacrifice for the common good. The colonial objections were for the most part economic. While there was some disposition to deny the legality of trade regulations, the practical necessity of some general superintending power in a composite empire was so obvious that Americans in general yielded a theoretical even if grudging acquiescence in the power of Parliament to legislate on those matters which lay beyond the competence of their individual legislatures. There was undoubted need of some general supervisory authority which could make uniform rules in matters affecting the interests of the colonies collectively, where separate action was ineffective or tended to confusion. To this class of legislation belonged acts creating a general postal service and regulating the currency. The whole matter of the currency was taken up by Parliament as being closely related to imperial commerce, and several measures were enacted fixing the rates at which foreign coins should circulate throughout the dependencies, or prohibiting paper money issues. One of the last extensions of imperial authority took Indian relations out of the hands of the separate colonies and placed them under the supervision of crown officers who watched over trade, acted as judges in disputes between members of the two races, and made all purchases of lands from the natives.

War, of course, was a concern of the empire as a whole. The series of French and Indian wars taught the need of unified action. The necessity of calling upon each province separately for its quota of troops and funds, and the delay caused by awaiting responses which were reluctant in proportion to remoteness from the theatre of war, led to some advocacy in England of levying taxes and calling out men by direct action of Parliament. The centralized control enjoyed by the enemy's government seemed much superior to the English system at such critical times, and many Englishmen favored the reorganization of colonial administration along the lines of the French model. The soberest statesmen agreed that at least some plan should be devised by which the colonies would be brought into permanent cooperation to deal with such a vital common danger as war presented.

Several plans of colonial union were suggested, some by Americans and some by British thinkers. The most notable was the one offered by a congress of delegates from seven colonies which met at Albany in 1754, at the instance of the British ministry, on the eve of the last French and Indian war. The draft was prepared by Benjamin Franklin. It provided for a grand council composed of delegates from each colony chosen by its assembly, to meet under a president-general appointed by the crown. This body was to have power to carry on wars in which the colonies were involved, and to raise troops and collect taxes for this purpose. If put into effect such a plan might have enabled the British, by dealing with one general council instead of so many separate assemblies, to command the combined resources of the dependencies to much greater advantage.

At the same time that the "Albany Plan," as it is called, promised to facilitate the handling of imperial problems by the British government, it gave the Americans an opportunity to emphasize the necessity of local autonomy, by carefully providing that each colony should retain control over its own purely internal affairs. Thus, the plan recognized the possibility of a definite distribution of authority between imperial and provincial governments.   The British ministry was unwilling to sanction this principle of colonial autonomy, and for this and other reasons (the mutually jealous colonies also finding the scheme unacceptable) the project fell through.

However, the idea of an agreed-upon scheme of distributed powers did not die.   It came up again and again in discussions of the respective powers of Parliament and the colonial assemblies, and after independence, it played a prime part in determining the re- lations of the states to the Union under the Constitution.   In the meantime, at least previous to 1763, a rough system of distributed powers was followed in practice, in the British colonial administra- tion.   While Parliament dealt with imperial affairs each colony was allowed to make its own laws regulating such matters as in- heritance, the relations of husband and wife, master and servant, guardian and ward, providing for the health, safety, and education of the people, and fixing and defining the punishment for crimes.

THE CROWN AS A FACTOR IN COLONIAL GOVERNMENT

This legislative autonomy of the colonial assembly did not leave the English government wholly without influence over colonial domestic affairs.   But it was the crown, not Parliament directly, which shared in the internal political life of the American common- wealths.   The links between the king and his American subjects were the royal governors and the Privy Council.

The governor of a royal province was an agent of the crown, a kind of vice-king originally, governing under the terms of the royal commission and of instructions issued from time to time. It was a part of his duty to prevent the legislature from acting con- trary to British policy.   For this purpose he was given the veto. He was expected also to persuade the lawmakers to cooperate in imperial undertakings, for example, by supplying troops and funds for war.   In the post-Restoration period, acts of royal colonies required the assent of the Privy Council, even after approval by the governor.   They might be "disallowed" by the Council on grounds either of inexpediency or lack of authority in the enacting body. In 1660 the Council set up a Committee for Trade and Plantations (the forerunner of the Board of Trade already mentioned) to supervise colonial affairs and exercise this power of disallowance. In 1677 the committee annulled three acts of the Virginia legislature on the ground that it had exceeded its powers.[3]

In the eighteenth century the task of drafting instructions for the governors and other crown officials devolved upon the Board of Trade, and to it came provincial laws for examination and presentation to the Privy Council with recommendation as to the appropriate action.

This negative or veto of the Privy Council was designed to preserve the compatibility between the laws of England and those of the dependencies. It involved considerable potential control over the domestic affairs of the royal and proprietary provinces. But in the case of the corporate colonies there was no charter provision for the submission of legislation for approval. Hence, when demand was made upon Massachusetts in 1677 for the repeal of certain acts which were held to be repugnant to the laws of England, the colonials held that their charter rights were attacked. The acts in question forbade the celebration of Christmas, required Sabbath observance, and made the marriage contract a civil ceremony. All of these fell under the classification of internal police, and would presumably have been disallowed by the Privy Council if they had come before it as the acts of a province.

Thus the power of disallowance made the king, through the Privy Council, in the last analysis, a part of the legislature of the colonies of the provincial type. There was need of some device which could attain comparable results in the corporate colonies. It was neither desirable nor feasible to institute proceedings for abrogation of the charter in every instance of unwarranted action.

[3] Charles M. Andrews, "The Royal Disallowance." Andrews holds that disallowance was "not a veto, but an act of regulation and control" to be classed with instructions to the governor. The leading purpose was "to defend the law and custom of the British constitution," which included the acts of trade; but the internal police might also be affected, since disallowance was intended to prevent "ill-advised legislation" and "oppressive, improper, or technically defective" legislation. Cf. E. B. Russell, *The Review of American Colonial Legislation by the King in Council.*

Among older works, important and useful studies are: Evarts Boutell Greene, *The Provincial Governor,* and Oliver Morton Dickerson, *American Colonial Government, 1696–1765.*

Forfeiture of the charter was an appropriate remedy only in cases of extreme recalcitrancy such as led to the *quo warranto* suit against Massachusetts. Measures taken in good faith by a dependency honestly desirous of keeping within the limits of its authority called for some mechanism of every day utility to remedy minor errors. Such a means of preserving essential harmony between the domestic policies of the corporate colonies on the one hand, and imperial interests and law on the other, was found in the exercise of the judicial power of the Privy Council, acting as a court of appeal from the decisions of colonial tribunals.[4]

The practice of carrying appeals from the dependencies to the Privy Council began in the sixteenth century, with cases arising in the Island of Jersey.[5] Attempts in the next century to apply the system to Massachusetts Bay were combatted by the government of that colony, however, so long as the first charter remained in force. As early as 1637 the general court refused to allow an appeal to be taken by the Reverend John Wheelwright, on the ground that the king by charter had given the court final jurisdiction over all causes arising in the colony.[6] In 1664, when a royal commission was sent to Massachusetts to investigate sundry charges of irregular and unwarrantable conduct, the court stoutly maintained the same position. The commissioners insisted, on the contrary, that the right of appeal was implied by the very nature of a charter,[7] and in 1684 a general order in council was issued, resting upon this assumption (although meantime new charters contained stipulations concerning appeals), and providing regulations governing procedure.[8]

The second Massachusetts charter provided expressly for appeals of "personal actions" to the King in Council, and also extended the royal disallowance to the Bay Colony, which by that charter was partially converted into a royal province. The general court interpreted the new charter to suit itself and passed an act allowing

[4] Studies of the Privy Council as a court of appeals are: Harold D. Hazeltine, "Appeals from the Colonial Courts to the King in Council," and Arthur M. Schlesinger, "Colonial Appeals to the Privy Council."

[5] Hazeltine, 306.

[6] Schlesinger, 446.

[7] Osgood, *Am. Cols. in the Seventeenth Century*, III, 321–323.

[8] Schlesinger, 280.

appeals in personal actions "and no others." This and two subsequent acts of similar nature were disallowed, after which the colony gave up the contest.[9] Not so Connecticut. In 1698 she refused to allow an appeal on the ground that her courts were tribunals of last resort. The issue was brought before the Privy Council by petition, whereupon the Council declared that it was "the inherent right of His Majesty to receive and determine appeals from all his Majesty's colonys [sic] in America." Connecticut's protest against this ruling was finally submitted to the legal advisers of the crown, who upheld the Council in an opinion asserting that in spite of the lack of any provision for appeals in the Connecticut charter, the right to entertain appeals was inherent in the crown.[10]

This ruling placed Rhode Island, Connecticut, Maryland, and Georgia, whose charters contained no clauses concerning appeals, in the same class in this respect with the colonies whose charters dealt expressly with the matter. There were, indeed, provisions in all the charters guaranteeing to the inhabitants the liberties and immunities of British subjects and forbidding the passage of laws repugnant to those of the realm. From these passages the right of appeal might be inferred. But the British doctrine went behind all charters. The chief statement of it was elicited by the case of Christian *v.* Corren, appealed from the Isle of Man in 1716, in which counsel for the appellant successfully urged that even "if there had been . . . express words in the grant to exclude appeals, they had been void; because the subjects had an inherent right, inseparable from them as subjects, to apply to the crown for justice." [11]

The right of appeal was thus sustained by reasoning parallel to that by which the colonists placed inherent or "natural" rights above charters and even acts of Parliament, although in the contentions of Massachusetts and Connecticut against appeals the application was quite different.

Except in Massachusetts and Connecticut there was little or no denial of the correctness of the principle involved in appeals to the King in Council, although there was some tendency to manipulate

[9] *Ibid.*, 443.
[10] *Ibid.*, 295.
[11] *Ibid.*, 288.

procedure according to provincial desires. For example, a court might deny an appeal on the ground that the amount involved was less than the minimum fixed by the regulations of the Privy Council, or for other technical reasons, when the real design was to prevent review of a local regulation. Offsetting this evasion was the privilege a suitor enjoyed of petitioning the Council to hear his cause, which the Council might do regardless of its general rules governing appeals.

It is estimated that between 1680 and 1780 the Privy Council reviewed some 265 cases taken up from provincial courts. Some of these were heard on appeal, others on petition after refusal of the lower court to grant the appeal.[12] The great majority of the suits involved only the interests of the parties and possessed no public or constitutional significance. A few, however, bore upon the problem of preserving the subordination of colonial to British law. The chief cases of this class arose in Massachusetts and Connecticut.

Both of these colonies passed acts late in the seventeenth century departing from the English common law governing the distribution of intestate estates. Under the common law in such cases the eldest son became sole heir, but these colonial statutes gave him only a double portion. In 1717 Wait Winthrop of Connecticut died intestate, leaving a son and daughter. John, the son, became administrator and claimed the whole estate under the common law, holding that it was superior to the Connecticut act, and that the latter was invalid because it conflicted with the common law. The claim of the daughter, wife of Thomas Lechmere, to a share of the estate under the Connecticut law was upheld by the probate court of Connecticut. Winthrop was denied an appeal to the King in Council, but the Council heard his plea on petition. The case presented a direct issue between the English common law and the colonial statute, and potentially involved the whole question of the power of a colony to deviate from the common law in any respect whatsoever. As practically every colony had departed from English customs wherever its situation seemed to require it,

[12] *Ibid.*, 446 *et seq.* Some fifty cases were heard by the Council on petition after colonial courts had refused to grant an appeal. In 76 cases the Council reversed decisions; in 57 cases colonial decisions were affirmed. In other cases no decision is recorded; some were dismissed or discharged without judgment.

the decree of the Council, issued in 1728, declaring the Connecticut law null and void, as "contrary to the laws of England . . . and not warranted by the charter," was well calculated to cause consternation throughout America.[13]

Since the direct effect of the decree would be to invalidate the law under which a large portion of the lands of Connecticut were held, steps were taken at once to obtain a reversal of the decision. Meantime a Massachusetts case had reached the Council. Distribution of the estate of one Henry Phillips having been made among his heirs according to the provisions of the Massachusetts statute, Gillam Phillips, sole brother of the deceased, claimed the entire estate under the common law.[14]

Like the Winthrop case, this suit—Phillips v. Savage—raised the question of the validity of a colonial act which did not follow the English common law. Unlike the Connecticut act, however, the Massachusetts statute had been duly submitted to the Privy Council and had not been annulled within the three years prescribed by the charter for such action. When the Phillips case reached the Privy Council it was therefore too late for that body to void the colonial legislation.

Encouraged by this decision, given in 1738, the Connecticut government assisted a party in a new suit presenting the same issue of colonial statutes *versus* the English common law, to get his private cause before the Council, in the hope of a reversal of the decision in Winthrop v. Lechmere. Samuel Clark was seeking the recovery of certain lands, under the English law, which Connecticut law had given partly to others. Failing in the colonial courts, he petitioned the King in Council, whereupon Thomas Tousey, the appellee, finding himself unable to bear the expense of a trip to England to present his defense, obtained a loan of £500 from the assembly for the purpose. Connecticut's agent in London was in addition instructed to engage legal aid for him.[15] The result was a decision upholding the Connecticut law.

[13] *Ibid.*, 440–441. It is noteworthy that Winthrop explained, after the decision, that the act, being void in its own nature, could not be said to have been annulled by the decree. This was an early recognition of the principle that the nullity of an unconstitutional act is not imparted by the court, but only recognized by it.

[14] *Ibid.*, 442–443.

[15] *Ibid.*, 444–445.

This case shows a recognition on the part of the statesmen of the Council "of the injustice of enforcing the customary law of one country on another country, where [conditions] had brought into existence" a very different customary law. Although the decision may be criticized as a political judgment in which legal principles were disregarded, it shows the British attitude towards the American dependencies at its best, proving that statesmanship could at times rise above purely legal considerations to meet realities. Indeed, the evidence warrants the conclusion "that the king in council was in general an unbiased tribunal of justice . . . well adapted for the adjudication of colonial appeals." [16]

COLONIAL CHECKS ON ENGLISH AUTHORITY

In none of the colonies were the people at the mercy of arbitrary power, and in contests with royal provincial governors they frequently had their way. The chief weapon of the provincial assemblies in such contests was the old one of control of the purse. Without acts for raising and appropriating money the administration was paralyzed; in nearly all of the provinces moreover, the governor depended upon such acts for his salary and was incapable for economic reasons of making a stiff fight for measures called for in his instructions. The British ministry insisted vainly that permanent provision be made for the salaries of officials; and provincials were greatly alarmed whenever steps were taken in England to make independent provision for them. [17]

Provincial acts often had a long effective life before they were

[16] *Ibid.*, 450.

[17] In 1742 the Massachusetts house of representatives rejected a demand made by Governor Shirley for a permanent salary, on the ground that it "would greatly tend to lessen the just weight of the other two branches of the government, which ought ever to be maintained and preserved, especially since the governor has so great authority and check upon them." Taking their idea of the British constitution as their model, they urged that its strength and beauty "chiefly consists in that mutual check which each branch of the legislature has upon the other." A similar system of checks and balances they thought ought to be preserved in Massachusetts. "There ought not to be an independency in either branch of the legislature, forasmuch as to be independent and arbitrary are the same things in civil policy."—Carpenter, "Separation of Powers," 38. The passage is significant as evidence of the dawn of the concept of checks and balances which Americans came to regard as so essential a device to prevent tyrannical government.

disallowed. The charter of Pennsylvania required submission of statutes "within five yeares," and if disallowed such action must be taken within six months after submission. Such requirements made it possible for the assembly to reenact dubious measures just before the expiration of the five-year period, and by repeating the process to keep them in force indefinitely without submission to the Privy Council. The second Massachusetts charter, although more carefully phrased and requiring submission "by the first opportunity after the makeing [*sic*] thereof," allowed statutes to be effective from date of passage, and disallowance was required within three years "next after the same shall have been presented to us." Failure to disallow therefore was equivalent to positive approbation, as the case of Phillips *v.* Savage proved.

In part because the ministry desired to have at hand a source of information relative to American affairs, some of the larger colonies supported representatives in England known as the colonial agents. These men were often skillful lobbyists and were sometimes able to prevent the passage of acts which would have been detrimental to the interests of their constituents. The influence of the Connecticut agent in connection with the case of Clark *v.* Tousey, noted above, illustrates another way in which these agents were able sometimes to serve their commonwealths.

There are in the practices just described a number of significant foreshadowings of the constitutionalism of the later United States. The Privy Council's power of judicial review was in a strict sense only the power to judge of the compliance of corporate bodies with the terms of their charters. Regarding these bodies as commonwealths, however, the concept emerged that their legislation was subject to a paramount law. This superior law was not merely the charter, but a somewhat vague body of what may be called "imperial" law, including the acts of navigation and trade and other general police regulations, orders in council, and within limits some phases of common law. The colonial mind was thus familiarized with the idea that the powers of their own governments were limited. Their charters and English law stood in somewhat the same relation to their legislative powers that the state and federal constitutions of the later period hold to the powers of the state legislatures. Moreover, the existence of a tribunal exercising the right to judge of infractions of the paramount law by the colonial legislatures anticipated the function of the United States Supreme Court in reviewing state legislation. There is a connection also between the vice-admiralty courts and the federal courts of the constitutional period. Admiralty and maritime jurisdiction descended directly to the federal courts as will be seen later. As courts enforcing imperial law (navigation acts relating to the general police) through judges appointed by the crown, vice-admiralty courts functioned in the colonial communities somewhat as the federal courts do in the states. Finally, the colonial agent was the prototype of the territorial delegate of the national era following 1789.

IV

DEFECTS OF THE CONSTITUTIONAL SYSTEM

THE SUPREMACY OF PARLIAMENT

THE Revolution of 1688, for all of Locke's philosophy, was not a triumph of the people, but only a victory of Parliament over royalty. From this moment, England marched straight towards the actual omnipotence of that body—which meant, in fact, as has been so often observed, government by the mercantile and landed classes. William and Mary accepted the throne vacated by James II on terms dictated by Parliament, and soon afterwards the same body prescribed the conditions governing the succession. In the next reign the royal veto of acts of Parliament fell into disuse. The unfamiliarity of the first Hanoverian with the language and ways of the English threw the responsibility for policy-making largely upon ministers who represented the views of the parliamentary majority, creating a system which is said to have caused the second George to exclaim in disgust that in England it was the ministers who ruled. Ministers had in fact become the servants of Parliament instead of the king, since without the support of their policies by the majority, especially in the House of Commons, their functions could not be carried on. The king's power to choose his ministers was thus rendered purely nominal, for upon an adverse vote it was necessary for him to form a new ministry composed of men acceptable to the majority. The only alternative was to dissolve Parliament and call for an election to determine whether the voters would uphold the ministry by returning a majority of members favorable to its program.

In practice this system meant that executive functions as well as the initiative in legislation were shifted from the king's hands to what was actually a committee of the legislative body.[1] Even the

---

[1] The case of Godden v. Hales well illustrates the effect of the Revolution of 1688 upon the royal prerogative, as well as the efforts of James II to maintain a status superior to both the legislative and judicial branches of the government. Parliament had by a Test Act excluded Catholics from certain offices. James

term "crown" took on in consequence a new meaning, denoting the mechanism by which the will of Parliament, rather than that of the king, was given effect.

Nor could a court hold void an act of Parliament. It was assumed that the legislature could not intend to violate the great principles of justice; hence if an enactment seemed to do so it became the duty of the court to construe it, if possible, in such a way as to reconcile the apparent contradiction, but at all events to give effect to the law.[2]

The middle of the eighteenth century found Parliament without effective check from either king or judge. The consequence of the Revolution of 1688 had been to place that body in the position of supremacy which Locke had denied to both king and Parliament. The compact philosophy had been of essential service to the middle class while on its way to power. Especially was this true of that phase of the philosophy which held that all governments are limited in their authority. But the class which had promulgated this dogma while striving to bring the prince under control now inconsistently rejected the doctrine as applied to the agency through which its own will was made law, and substituted for it the doctrine of parliamentary supremacy. In this way the philosophy of the previous century was twisted to suit the interests of the dominant class.

Reacting against the regulations which the royal government had imposed on business, the middle class should, logically, have proceeded on the theory that the public good would be best served

---

claimed the right to dispense with the act in individual cases, and desired to obtain a court decision upholding the dispensing power. By dismissing and appointing judges he obtained a subservient court which gave the decision he desired. But an act passed in the first year of William and Mary expressly abolished the royal power of dispensing with any statute. See account of the case in Macaulay's *History of England*, I, 587, *et seq.*, and discussion in Boudin, *Government by Judiciary*, I, 45–50, *et passim*.

[2] In the eighteenth century Blackstone carefully formulated the rules for such construction on the part of courts as would reconcile statutes with fundamental rights and still preserve the theory of parliamentary supremacy. It is possible that Coke's saying in the Bonham case was not intended to imply any other power in the judiciary than this. The position taken by the Supreme Court of the United States is analogous. Thus in the case of Murray *v.* Schooner Charming Betsy (2 Cranch 64, 118) (1804), it was held that an act of Congress should not be construed as violating the law of nations "if any other construction were possible"

by leaving each man free to pursue his own course.[3] They should have reasoned that this was nature's way; that man as a rational being would follow nature if left alone and thus promote the general prosperity as well as his own; that the government's true rôle was protection rather than restraint or regulation. However, having taken power to themselves, they yielded to the temptation to experiment with a system of regulation of their own devising. The result was eighteenth-century mercantilism, which shaped both English industrial life and colonial policy. For several generations the masters of Parliament identified their class interest with the general welfare, quite unable to understand why the "lower" classes and the colonists regarded their policies as a system of exploitation.

The reform legislation of the nineteenth century made Parliament responsible to the masses of the British people; the democratization of the system created a very effective check in the shape of public opinion which makes itself felt through elections. But in the eighteenth century parliamentary government rested on a base which was far from popular. The Lords Spiritual and Temporal held their seats, as they still do, by virtue of birth or position in the Church, but members of the Commons, although elected, were chosen under a highly restricted franchise little changed since the thirteenth or fourteenth centuries. In the boroughs it was still the rule that only those voted who were "of the franchise"; in the rural communities the possession of the forty-shilling freehold was still required. Unchecked even by a broad electorate expressive of public opinion, Parliament became a corrupt as well as an irresponsible oligarchy. The apportionment of seats in the lower house had not been revised for centuries, and some of the boroughs which originally deserved representation had declined until they were almost or entirely without inhabitants. New centers of population like Manchester and Liverpool had grown up; yet members still sat for the "decayed" boroughs while the new towns were without representation except as parts of the shire in which they were situated. This system was defended on the ground that inhabitants of the new towns were "virtually" represented as part of the great

[3] It was nearly a century after the Revolution that the *laissez faire* philosophy was given its classic statement by Adam Smith, and still longer before it was accepted in practice.

class of commons. The landed aristocracy was quite skillful in marshalling the rural vote. Owners of small holdings were likely, for one reason or another, to support the candidates preferred by the local squires, while in the case of the "rotten" boroughs the choice of members had become in effect a power of appointment. Bribery was a common practice, as well as the buying and selling of seats. So fully had the electorate been regimented that it was charged in 1780 that about one hundred fifty men controlled the choice of the majority of members of the lower house.

The Lords were even less representative of the masses than were the members of the lower chamber. Theoretically they formed a superior social order, but in fact they were not sharply separated from the commons either by blood or economic interests. Under the law of primogeniture the eldest son of a noble inherited his estate and title. Younger sons belonged to the upper middle class, and often sat in the House; often, also, they sought a livelihood in industry or commerce, thus merging their interests with those of the *bourgeoisie*. Any commoner, moreover, might for sufficient reason be elevated to the peerage. The line of separation between middle and upper class was, in short, not sharply drawn, and the nobility was much affected by the economic and political thinking of the class below it—a fact which helps to explain its weak resistance to the political rise of that class. Thus as a whole Parliament, instead of being truly representative of the nation, was composed virtually of the great landlords, merchants, and manufacturers, or their agents.[4]

By 1763 the rulers of England had well-nigh forgotten Locke's teaching concerning limitations on the powers of government;[5]

[4] On the parliamentary system at this epoch see Edward Porritt, *Unreformed House of Commons*. For the cabinet system as it functions today, see W. Ivor Jennings, *Cabinet Government*.

[5] The repudiation of Locke was promoted by the treatment of the Revolution of 1688 in the *History* of the Tory historian, David Hume. See Wilbur C. Abbott, "David Hume: Philosopher—Historian." According to Alexander Hamilton, Hume even pronounced "all that influence on the side of the crown, which went under the name of corruption, an essential part of the weight which maintained the equilibrium of the Constitution."—Max Farrand, *Records of the Federal Convention of 1787*, I, 376. John Dickinson was perplexed as to what could replace this crown influence in independent America.—*Ibid.*, 86. For Hume's influence on American statesmen see Carpenter, "Separation of Powers."

they had forgotten likewise his saying that when the "legislative" grasps at absolute power the people may resume their original liberty. The American Revolution was to give them a rude awakening.

COLONIAL IDEAS OF RIGHTS

Locke's discussion of natural law and the compact theory fell readily into the current of colonial thinking and practice, and in the light of their own actual experience Americans saw in him "an authority on constitutional law" who enunciated "not theories of what *ought* to be, but pronouncements. of what actually was." [6]

The doctrines which had served the English middle class so well in the contest with the prince were those to which Americans appealed when their own privileges were menaced. This was not only true in cases of dispute with the royal authority, but as parliamentary claims of power over the colonies were extended, the same theories of limitations on government were at hand as a defense against that body. Disputes with the English government during the first half of the eighteenth century kept the compact philosophy alive in the colonial mind.

Another means of preserving the philosophy of 1688 as a vital force in American life was its constant reiteration in sermons. It was an age when the pulpit supplied the chief intellectual stimulus and preachers largely determined the patterns of thought. Elections were frequently the occasions for discourses which dwelt upon the powers and duties of public officers. Puritan pastors especially rang the changes on the natural equality of men, the popular source of the powers of government, and the impossibility of preserving liberty under governments wielding unlimited power.[7]

Reinforcing the last idea, the Frenchman Montesquieu expounded the theory of checks and balances in *L'Esprit des Lois* (1748). Although his interpretation of the contemporary English government was erroneous, his theory fitted colonial practice closely and con-

[6] Andrew C. McLaughlin, *Constitutional History of the United States*, 93.
[7] Alice M. Baldwin, *The New England Clergy in the American Revolution.* See also B. F. Wright, Jr., "American Interpretations of Natural Law."

firmed the belief that freedom could not survive unless government was under due restraint.[8]

So long as the charters stood, the rights which they conferred upon the corporate colonies, despite disputed interpretations, seemed fairly secure. Even in most of the proprietary provinces, the right of representative government was protected by the requirement in the patent that legislation must receive the assent of the freemen. By contrast, in the royal provinces the representative assembly rested, in form, on the monarch's permission given in the governor's commission or instructions. Unlike charters and patents, these lacked the character of contracts; the grant was a unilateral act, and the privileges it gave seemed to be revocable at any time without judicial action. Perhaps this was true under existing law. If so, the colonial attitude illustrates anew the power of ideas to break the fetters of outgrown law. In Plymouth which had no charter, in Massachusetts under its charter, and even in Virginia which had lost its charter in 1624, there was always in the background the theory of the natural rights of men and their function of creating government through agreement. In the royal provinces these doctrines were at their maximum worth; the very want of a charter impelled the people to appeal directly to fundamentals. Assuming that there were limits to the king's power, fixed by the rights of the subjects, they contended in the mid-eighteenth century that "the clause in the commission directing the governor to call together a legislature . . . is declarative and not creative . . . he is directed to act conformably to a *right actually already existing in the people*. 'The crown cannot establish any colony upon—or contract it within a *narrower scale* than the subject is entitled to, by the great charter of England.'"[9]

[8] P. de Rapid-Thoyras published a *History of England* in 1732–1733 in which the doctrine of the separation of powers was expounded several years before Montesquieu's more famous book appeared. That Americans were familiar with the earlier work is shown by quotations from it by revolutionary pamphleteers. Such theoretical discussions aided in fixing the conclusions derived from experience. See Carpenter, "Separation of Powers," 38, note.

[9] Thomas Pownall, *Administration of the Colonies*, 39–47. Extract in Allen Johnson, *Readings in American Constitutional History, 1776–1876*, 26–30. Italics in extract in text are mine. Cf. James Otis: "What could follow from [an act of Parliament voiding all charters], that would shake one of the essential, natural, civil or religious rights of the Colonists? Nothing. They would be men, citi-

This claim of an inviolable right of representative government did not explicitly invoke the theory of *natural* rights as taught by Locke; it rested upon what was assumed to be the English constitution—"the great charter of England." The right was "inherent and essential to the community, as a community of Englishmen." Another step would bring colonists to the assertion that the great principles of English liberty were natural rights embodied in the English constitution as a compact defining and limiting the powers of both king and Parliament.

DIVERGENCE OF COLONIAL FROM BRITISH THOUGHT

The control of their internal police by the colonies respectively and the restriction of Parliament to the general police made the British system in its actual workings a government of distributed powers. English authority had never expressly recognized any fixity in the scheme of distribution, and with the growth of the dogma of parliamentary supremacy it became less and less inclined to do so. In English theory the American right of local self-government was no more immune from parliamentary intrusion than that of localities at home; English statesmen continued to regard even the chartered colonies as mere corporations, like boroughs or trading companies.[10] In practice, the abstinence from interference was probably due more to distance, preoccupation, or negligence than to calculated policy, but it allowed the colonial view to crystallize that "home rule" was not only guaranteed by the charters but was part of a fixed order which could not be changed by Britain without violating principles of natural right incorporated in the British constitution.[11] The view was a manifestation of the old English habit of identifying privileges long enjoyed with imprescriptible or natural rights. It seemed to Americans not inconsistent with their relations to the crown, in spite of the

zens and british [*sic*] subjects after all. No act of Parliament can deprive them of the liberties of such."—*The Rights of the British Colonies Asserted and Proved*, 33. (See *infra*, Chap. V, note 2).

[10] James Otis accused the defenders of the English position of judging "of the reciprocal rights that subsist between a supreme and subordinate state or dominion, by no higher rules than are applied to a corporation of button-makers."—*Ibid.*, 63.

[11] See Thomas Hutchinson's interpretation of colonial opinion in 1767, *infra*, 84.

gubernatorial veto and the system of disallowance and judicial review. The significance of the subtle transformation of the king's status in the English system seems to have escaped them in large measure. If they perceived that the king had been superseded by the ministry, they viewed his eclipse as an aberration from correct constitutional principles. From the king the charters and patents had emanated in the first place, and to the king and his instruments of administration the colonists still regarded themselves as subject. By what right Parliament had taken over the powers of royalty was not clear to them; that governors, Board of Trade, and Privy Council, known as agencies of the crown, had come to be in fact a part of the governing mechanism of the parliamentary aristocracy was either not perceived or not admitted.

At any rate, the capture of these agencies by Parliament gave Americans little or no concern so long as the old relations were maintained in appearance and Parliament refrained from claims of unlimited power and from direct legislation affecting colonial internal affairs. Granting its function as a supreme legislature in matters of general police, it was, or came to be by many Americans, regarded in other respects as a body coordinate with the colonial assemblies rather than their superior. The latter were thought of as in a position similar to that of the Scottish parliament before the Act of Union, the bond between the Americans and the English consisting in the possession of a common king.[12]

For another reason the Americans rejected the claim of parliamentary supremacy. A *working* system of checks and balances seemed to be the only practical way of giving effect to the doctrine that the powers of government—of each branch as well as the whole—are limited by natural law and the terms of the social compact, and that limitations are essential to preserve liberty. The

[12] "All of a sudden . . . we have it advanced that acts of parliament . . . have no more relation to us than acts of parliament of Scotland had before the Union." "The King of Great Britain indeed is our Sovereign, but . . . not merely those acts which lay taxes upon us, but no other acts any further than we adopt them, are binding upon us."—Horace Gray, ed., *Quincy Reports on Constitutional Law, with Notes, 1761–1772*, I, 443, quoting Thomas Hutchinson. Far from being new doctrine, this was the theory which the Massachusetts general court had advanced 120 years before, when it asserted that the laws of England were binding only on those who live in England. See *supra*, Chap. II.

control of the purse afforded a check upon the crown's agent, the governor; recognition of the legislative autonomy of the local assemblies seemed necessary as a check upon Parliament. The claim of such autonomy was not a claim of sovereignty or independence (there was little effort as yet to define the meaning of sovereignty for the king was still the "sovereign"); rather, autonomy offered a check which would tend to render unnecessary resort to Locke's doctrine of revolution.

Nevertheless, with all due subordination to the British government, the right to regulate their own affairs rested ultimately, in many minds, as much or more upon the compact theory—the agreement of those concerned—as upon the legalistic view that the royal grant conferred all the rights which they possessed. Americans not only conceived that their natural rights, as well as those of Englishmen, were guaranteed by the British constitution, and that both king and Parliament were limited by the principles of this constitution, but some of them were ripe for the view that it would be the duty of the courts to set aside as void acts of Parliament if in conflict with the principles of the constitution. The idea may have been suggested by the function of the Privy Council in passing on acts of colonial legislation, but there was thought to be ground for believing that it was warranted by British legal precedents.

If the American view of the constitution was correct, some mechanism was required to maintain the proper balance of powers. If the courts could have checked Parliament, the function would have supplied another practical device, which, like legislative home rule, would have tended to obviate the necessity of resorting to revolution.

From this review it becomes apparent that colonial ideas of the rights of Englishmen had ceased by 1763 to coincide with those of contemporary Britons. Along with trial by jury and other personal rights which they shared with their kinsmen across seas, Americans claimed that of being taxed only by representatives of their own choosing, for the meaning of representation was among those concepts which had diverged on the two sides of the Atlantic.[13] In

[13] The charter of Pennsylvania was unique in containing a provision to the effect that taxes were to be laid only with the consent of the assembly "or by Act of Parliament."

England the whole class of commons was held to be represented in the lower house of Parliament. This fiction permitted the existence of such abuses as the rotten borough system, and the actual non-representation of new centers of population. English statesmen applied the theory of "virtual" representation to the colonies and held that they were represented as part of the great class of commons, or as legally parts of certain English shires. In America, on the contrary, representation meant the election of a resident of a particular locality as its delegate.

The eighteenth century added several concepts to the stock of American constitutional ideas. To Locke's theories of natural law and the social compact with which the century opened, experience as parts of the British imperial system added the conviction that the doctrine of limitations on government, to be effective, must be supported by some working scheme of checks and balances. The concept of distributed powers, involving home rule for the colonies in matters of internal police, had taken firm hold. These were major steps in the development of American constitutionalism. There were others of no small importance, such as the meaning of representation.

But the working system of relations between realm and dependencies did not rest on ascertained principles mutually agreed upon. It had developed gradually, little by little as need arose, and from the British point of view was subject to change at the will of Parliament. "It is my opinion," wrote Governor Francis Bernard of Massachusetts, "that all the political evils in America arise from want of ascertaining the relations between Great Britain and the American colonies." [14] "Instead of certain constitutional law, adapted to the nature of governments, established by the sovereign or imperial state and recognized by the dependent and subordinate states, America has hitherto been governed by temporary expedients." [15] The imperial constitution was ill-adapted to withstand severe stresses and strains.

[14] Edward Channing, ed., *Barrington-Bernard Correspondence, 1760–1770*, 96.
[15] Francis Bernard, *Select Letters*, iii. Quoted by Randolph G. Adams, *Political Ideas of the American Revolution*, 19.

CLASS DOMINATION IN THE COLONIES

The growing rift between England and America cannot fairly be attributed to the greater democracy of the latter. It was rather a contest between two branches of the middle class, one of which had abandoned its earlier liberalism. The colonial leaders adhered to the middle-class ideas which they had brought to America, not only concerning business enterprise and the religious and political compact, but also of class dominance. Their control might rest, as in early Massachusetts, upon a religious basis, through the exclusion of non-church-members from the franchise, or, as elsewhere, upon the ownership of land or other property. As late as the beginning of the revolutionary era seven colonies maintained a freehold qualification upon the franchise, while the other six accepted personal property as an alternative qualification. Higher requirements were stipulated for holding office.[16] The nearest approach to equality was found in New England, but even there high property qualifications for seats in the legislature bore heavily upon the inhabitants of new settlements. Virginia reproduced the English laws of primogeniture and entail, and in several colonies the apportionment of representation was comparable in its inequities to the rotten borough system of England.

A supercilious attitude towards the plain people was manifest from the earliest colonial times. When the Massachusetts general court was considering the submission of the Body of Liberties to the towns for approval by the freemen, Nathaniel Ward, the minister who had done the chief work of drafting the code, questioned "whether it be of God to interest the inferior sort in that which should be reserved 'inter optimates.' "[17] Although this narrow-minded view did not prevail, and the code was actually submitted for consideration by the freemen, the action was hardly due to the spirit of democracy. The freemen to whose participation Ward objected were full members of the political and ecclesiastical community. Beneath them still was the majority of the

[16] Albert E. McKinley, *The Suffrage Franchise in the Thirteen English Colonies in America*, 480.
[17] Reinsch, "English Common Law," 13.

inhabitants, and for these the feeling of the leaders was little short of contempt. John Cotton, most prominent and influential of the ministers, could not conceive that God "did ever ordain democracy as a fit government for either church or commonwealth. If the people be governors," he asked, "who shall be governed?" Governor Winthrop, like-minded, held that "the best part is always the least." Democracy has "no warrant in Scripture." "Among nations it has always been accounted the meanest and worst of all forms of government."

The property-owning classes everywhere feared popular government and took pains to keep control in their own hands. In Pennsylvania, when inland communities were tardily organized as counties, the danger of disturbing traditional ways was curtailed by allowing them not more than four representatives each, while the old counties elected eight.[18] Virginia attained similar results by making the new counties so large that their two burgesses represented many more people than the same number of delegates of the old counties.

Nevertheless liberalizing forces were more active in the New World than in England. The requirement of land ownership as a condition of political privilege or social rank did not so effectively handicap the common man, because land was plentiful and easily obtained. The relative scarcity of the human factor in a country of vast resources awaiting development tended to enhance the social as well as the economic value of the wage-earner, and to promote humanitarian and democratic ideals. The amelioration of the penal code is one evidence of this, and the growth of religious toleration another. The great religious revival of the 1730's stressed the value of the individual soul, and joined with these other influences and the natural-law philosophy to enhance the value of the common man and the sacredness of human rights. The democratic leaven in the philosophy of Locke had so far worked its logical effect by 1764 that James Otis questioned: "If upon the abdication [of James II] all were reduced to a state of nature, had not apple women and orange girls as good a right to give their respectable

[18] Charles Henry Lincoln, *The Revolutionary Movement in Pennsylvania, 1760–1776*, 44–51.

[*sic*] suffrages for a new king as the philosopher, courtier, petit maitre and politician?" [19] Even more strikingly Otis declared that "no good reason . . . can be given in any country why every man of a sound mind should not have his vote in the election of a representative. If a man has but little property to protect and defend, yet his life and liberty are things of some importance." [20]

In America an important source of liberalizing influences was the frontier. Natural forces operated to attract to the outer edge of settlement many members of the class which in an old and stable culture would form a proletariat. In some cases the emigrants were exiles driven from their earlier homes, as was true of the early settlers of Rhode Island. Throughout the colonies, those elements of the population who found themselves discriminated against by the dominant minorities tended to migrate, if free to do so. The frontier was a region of freedom and opportunity and actual democracy and equality, notwithstanding the political control which the older settlements·took great pains to maintain.

American conditions, indeed, engendered a liberalism which was definitely in advance of English middle-class ideology. It manifested itself, even before the Revolution, in the demands of the frontier settlements for equal rights under the colonial governments. But the liberal views of Otis were not characteristic of the ruling class. Their reluctance to grant the demands of the "common" people made the domestic phase of the revolutionary movement a contest between the conservative Patriots who wished to perpetuate their rule, and the radicals who demanded the democratization of government. The contest went on during the making of the state and federal constitutions; indeed, this conflict between the heirs of English middle-class ideology and the exponents of American frontier democracy may be regarded as the forerunner of the "class struggle" in·America.

[19] *The Rights of the British Colonies Asserted and Proved*, 51. (See *infra*, Chap. V, note 2).
[20] *Considerations on Behalf of the Colonists in a Letter to a Noble Lord*, 110. (See *infra*, Chap. V, note 2).

V

THE GREAT DEBATE

WRITS OF ASSISTANCE

BY 1763 the British constitution had succeeded in evolving mechanisms for adjusting minor conflicts between the realm and the dependencies. But it failed to provide adequate ultimate means for the peaceful reconciliation of the diverging ideologies of the home and provincial populations. Incompatible theories threatened no serious clash so long as Parliament and the local assemblies confined their legislation within the spheres respectively of general and local police, as they substantially did before 1763. But efforts to act upon the theory of parliamentary supremacy at the actual expense of provincial interests, by incursions into the field of internal police, were certain to evoke irreconcilable arguments; and the actual system offered no recourse if argument failed—no appeal to elections, no scheme of amendment, no resort to the courts, nothing except the ultimate "appeal to Heaven."

As the long struggle with the French and Indians drew to its close in the early 1760's there were ominous signs of impending changes in the British plans of colonial administration. Vexed by the lukewarm cooperation of the American assemblies in military measures, irritated by their disregard of imperial interests, and burdened by the problems of an enlarged empire and a mounting debt, the ministry planned to embark upon a policy of close control based upon the theory of parliamentary supremacy and crossing long-established boundary lines. In the course of the verbal resistance of the provincials to the new British measures, their views were brought into sharp definition.

Particularly annoying to the British government was the violation of the navigation acts by colonial traders. The practice of smuggling was nothing new, and had long been condoned by lax officials; but the continuance of illicit commerce with the island possessions of France and Spain while England was at war with those countries smacked of disloyalty and was hardly to be over-looked. In compliance with instructions from the English govern-ment to enforce the navigation acts strictly, the customs officers in Massachusetts petitioned the superior court in 1760 to issue writs of assistance. Ordinary search warrants authorized entrance only of designated premises on reasonable suspicion that they harbored smuggled goods; but writs of assistance were general warrants which enabled officers to enter and search almost at will, and with-out making a return to the court, places where it was suspected that smuggled goods were hidden. Their sweeping terms made possible unreasonable searches, violating the maxim that a man's house is his castle. The ground on which the request for the writs was based was an infrequent practice of the English court of exchequer authorized by ancient statutes. Although possibly justifiable as a wartime measure, their actual legality in Massachusetts was de-batable.[1]

JAMES OTIS

To oppose the issue of the writs, certain Boston merchants en-gaged Oxenbridge Thacher and James Otis, Jr., and the petition was argued before the court in Boston, at the February term, 1761.[2]

[1] John Adams, "Autobiography," in Charles Francis Adams, ed., *The Works of John Adams*, II, 124, note 1. *Cf.* "Life of John Adams," *ibid.*, I, 57 *et seq.* Boudin, *op. cit.*, I, 69, is evidently in error in saying that no act of Parliament authorized the writs. Adams's biographer says that the writs were authorized by acts of 12 and 14 Charles II and 7 and 8 William III. The provisions of 14 Charles II were extended to the colonies. Hutchinson says that Governor Shirley issued writs of assistance until he (Hutchinson) warned him that his action was illegal, and suggested that application be made to the superior court. No act of the Massachusetts legislature had recognized the authority of the court to issue them. —Adams's "Life," 58.

[2] James Otis, Jr., was the son of Colonel James Otis, of Barnstable, Mass. He was born in 1725, graduated from Harvard in 1743, received the degree of A. M. in 1746, and began to practice law in Boston in 1748. At the time of the argu-ment over the writs of assistance he was regarded by judges, lawyers, and public as "by far the most able, manly and commanding character of his age at the bar." (Adams's *Works*, I, 57 *et seq.*, II, 124). He resigned the position of advocate-general, which made him the official legal adviser of the government, rather than defend the writs of assistance. His mind became clouded in his later years, and the incipient stages of his disease may account for certain inconsistencies in his political writings which have puzzled students. His death was caused in 1783 by a stroke of lightning. William Tudor's *Life of James Otis* is still the main source of information.

Otis contributed five or six pamphlets to the revolutionary discussion; it may

Otis's colleague urged that "the most material question is whether the practice of the Exchequer will warrant this Court in granting" the writs, and Otis agreed with him that the precedents were insufficient.[3] Otis went further, however, and declared that the writs were against natural equity; consequently not even an act of Parliament could make them legal, because an act against the constitution is void. It would be the duty of the courts, he asserted, to pass such an act "into disuse." [4]

Otis was arguing in effect that natural rights are embodied in the common law and form a part of the British constitution,[5] and that the constitution fixes the limits of the legislative power. To support his contention he cited "8 Rep. 118 from Viner," a contemporary authority on British law, wherein is quoted the comment of Lord Coke in the case of Dr. Bonham, to the effect that "it appears in our books that in many cases the common law will control acts of Parliament and sometimes adjudge them to be utterly void." [6] Otis thus sought to bring the weight of English authority to the support of the American view of the limited character of the powers of Parliament.

be that he wrote certain other essays which cannot be positively identified as his. Some of these pamphlets were reprinted during his lifetime, and received much attention in England as well as America. After his death there were no reprints for many years and the early editions have become quite rare. Five of the essays have been published in the University of Missouri *Studies*, under the editorship of Charles F. Mullet, with the title: *Some Political Writings of James Otis*. All citations of Otis's works in this study refer to this edition.

[3] Adams's *Works*, II, 521. There is no official report of Otis's argument. John Adams heard his speech and made some notes which are printed, *ibid*. An elaborated form which Adams may have supplied is given in G. R. Minot, *Continuation of the History of the Province of Massachusetts Bay*. The passage is reprinted in Adams's *Works*, II, 523–525. See discussion of Otis's speech by Justice Horace Gray, in *Quincy Reports*, I, 48.

[4] According to Adams's notes Otis said: "An act against the constitution is void; an act against natural equity is void; and if an act of Parliament should be made, in the very words of this petition it would be void. The executive Courts must pass such acts into disuse." The term "executive courts" is used by Otis to distinguish the judiciary from the legislative branch in Massachusetts, known as the "general court."

[5] Expressions in Otis's writings show his belief that natural rights are embodied in the common law. Thus "life, liberty and property, are, by the law of nature as well as by the common law, secured. . . ."—*Vindication of the British Colonies*, 11. *Cf.* passage in which he cites English statutes as declaring "the great charter . . . to be the common law."—*Rights of the British Colonies Asserted and Proved*, 57.

[6] Charles Viner, *A General Abridgment of Law and Equity*.

Otis's reliance upon Coke calls for the explanation that the latter's utterance was not a valid presentation of the English law as it stood in 1761: indeed, it is very doubtful whether it was a correct statement of the law even in Coke's own time, the early seventeenth century.[7] None of the five cases which he mentions as appearing "in our books," properly understood, involved a court decision holding void an act of Parliament because of conflict with the common law or natural right.[8] Coke himself, in his later years, became a champion of the legislature in its contest with the king, and declared that the power of Parliament to legislate "is so transcendent and absolute, as it cannot be confined either for cases or persons within any bounds." [9]

Not in Coke's time, however, was the supremacy of Parliament established. Indeed, for some years there were tendencies away

[7] Sir Edward Coke was born in 1552 and died in 1634. He served as attorney-general under Elizabeth and during the early reign of James I. From 1606 to 1616 he was Chief Justice of the Court of Common Pleas and of the Court of King's Bench. From 1620 to 1628 he served in Parliament and shared in the framing of the Petition of Right. His fame rests chiefly upon his legal writings, but their soundness has been questioned. The principal biography is by Cuthbert W. Johnson, *Life of Sir Edward Coke*. See the sketches in the *Encyclopedia Britannica*, and Lord F. E. S. Birkenhead, *Fourteen English Judges;* also H. Lyon and H. Block, *Edward Coke, Oracle of the Law*.

[8] Theodore F. T. Plucknett, "Bonham's Case and Judicial Review." *Cf.* Boudin, I, Appendix A, 485–517; also S. E. Thorne, "The Constitution and the Courts."

[9] Boudin, I, 495–496, quoting Coke's *Institutes*, Part IV, 36. This part of the *Institutes* was published after Coke's death. The words are not quite conclusive proof of his acceptance of parliamentary supremacy. A little earlier he had written: "Magna carta is such a fellow that he will have no sovereign." To him the Great Charter incorporated principles of the common law which were inviolable by the "sovereign," by which term he doubtless at the time meant the king. But elsewhere he declares that if "any Statute be made contrary to the great charter . . . that shall be holden for none." (*Third Institute*, 111, quoted by Mullett, *op. cit.*, p. 9, note 12). It may therefore have been his view that both Parliament and king were limited by Magna Carta, although his latest utterances trend towards the doctrine of parliamentary supremacy. This seems to agree with the view expressed by Professor Edward S. Corwin: "Coke took the position that there was no such thing as sovereign power in England, even for Parliament; for, said he: 'Magna carta is such a fellow that he will have no sovereign'." These words, plus his dictum in Dr. Bonham's case, seem to Professor Corwin to "indicate Coke's belief that the principles of 'common right and reason,' being part of the Common Law, were cognizable by the judges while interpreting acts of Parliament. . . . Being the highest court . . . Coke regarded Parliament itself as the *final* interpreter of the law by which both it, the King, and the judges were bound."—"Marbury v. Madison and the Doctrine of Judicial Review," 28–29.

from the omnipotence of that body. During the mid years of the seventeenth century radical thinkers were busy with the problem of discovering devices by which limitations could be imposed upon the legislative power, then in a fair way to supplant the king and establish its own sovereignty.[10] Locke's essays on government afforded the theoretical basis for limiting the legislative as well as the royal authority; but the middle class, triumphant in the Revolution of 1688, cast aside his philosophy, as has been shown. Some traces of the seventeenth-century doctrines were carried over into the eighteenth century by the English legal writers who did their work before 1750.[11] But Blackstone's great treatise promptly superseded these earlier works. His *Commentaries* established the doctrine of parliamentary supremacy beyond all cavil so far as English thinking is concerned; yet even he attempted to reconcile statutes with the demands of natural justice by rules of interpretation which resulted sometimes in "torturing statutes almost out of recognition" as the only alternative to a frank rejection.[12]

Only in America did the seventeenth-century doctrines survive in full vigor. Even there, diligent research has failed to reveal any cases before 1761 in which a colonial court set aside an act of a colonial legislature on the ground of unconstitutionality.[13]

In spite of these qualifications, Otis's argument against the writs of assistance is a landmark in the rise of American constitutionalism.

[10] Charles H. McIlwain, *High Court of Parliament and Its Supremacy*, discusses the English belief in a fundamental law and the efforts to apply its principles as limitations upon the legislative power, especially during the middle years of the seventeenth century.

[11] Following Coke, Lord Hobart declared that an act of Parliament against natural equity, as to make a man judge of his own cause, is void. Lord Holt added: "What my Lord Coke says in Dr. Bonham's case . . . is far from any extravagancy, for it is a very reasonable and true saying, That if an Act of Parliament should ordain that the same person should be party and judge . . . it would be a void act. . . ." Cf. Boudin, I, 506 *et seq.* These comments became the basis of statements in several summaries of English law prepared in the eighteenth century, including—besides Viner's *Abridgment* cited by Otis—Bacon's *Abridgment* (1735) and Comyn's *Digest* (written before 1740 but published 1762 to 1767).

[12] Andrew C. McLaughlin, "Power of a Court to Declare a Law Unconstitutional," 63–69. McLaughlin does not direct this statement at Blackstone in particular.

[13] Brinton Coxe, *Essay on Judicial Power and Unconstitutional Legislation*, 202–203. The various alleged colonial precedents are discussed in Boudin, I, Appendix B, 518–530.

There was, indeed, little if any originality in his contention that the legislative power of Parliament was limited, but his reference to the courts as in duty bound to void unconstitutional acts introduced into American thinking another of those ideas which while not wholly new, was destined to undergo a remarkable development in New-World practice.[14]

Otis's plea against the writs of assistance was unavailing, although Chief Justice Hutchinson continued the case to the next term, "as the practice in England is not known." [15]   It was not long, however, before the policies of the Grenville ministry, involving taxation of the colonies as well as regulation of their trade, led Otis to elaborate his views. He was one of the first to discern the significance of the revenue provisions of the Sugar Act of 1764 and to urge that if Parliament had the right to tax colonial trade, it had an equal right to tax lands and other property. He perceived also that there was no foundation for the distinction between an "internal" and an "external" tax, of which so much was made a few years later.

These views were set forth in a pamphlet which the passage of the Sugar Act induced him to write, under the title *The Rights of the British Colonies Asserted and Proved*. In this essay he applied seventeenth-century liberal philosophy to the problems of his own day and country. Following Locke he assumed that the people are the source of authority, that in establishing government they entrust rulers only with the powers necessary to advance the general peace and prosperity, reserving to themselves essential rights including that of altering the government if it acts contrary to its trust. As a true son of New England Puritanism, he holds that the laws of God, the author of nature, are the basis of inalienable rights. The compact is the formal method of putting divine law into operation among men.

These premises prepare the way for an examination of the powers of Parliament. Here Otis seems to contradict himself. At one moment he apparently accepts parliamentary supremacy to the

[14] The question of the origin and growth of the practice of judicial review in America has given birth to a considerable volume of literature of a controversial nature. More will be said on this topic later.

[15] James K. Hosmer, *Samuel Adams*, 40.

fullest extent, while at the next he deals with the limitations upon legislative authority. "The power of parliament is uncontroulable, but by themselves, and we must obey. They only can repeal their own acts. . . . Reasons may be given, why an act ought to be repeal'd & yet obedience must be yielded to it till that repeal takes place." Yet in various places he makes a distinction between the *actual* powers of Parliament and those which it *rightfully* possesses under natural and divine law. "Matter of fact is one thing, matter of right another." [16] The supremacy of that body does not mean that it may rightfully be arbitrary. God is above all, and an act of Parliament contrary to any of his natural laws would in consequence be void. Parliament itself would so hold, when convinced of its mistake, and repeal the unjust act.

But Otis is not content to depend wholly upon the enlightened judgment of Parliament to insure conformity to natural equity. Sensing the need of an actual mechanism of government to check the legislature if it should err, he asserts as historical fact that "when such mistake is evident and palpable, . . . the judges . . . have declared the act 'of a whole parliament void.' " [17] Thus, instead of accepting the supremacy of Parliament in the current English sense, he contends that the British constitution not only should but actually does embrace a system of checks and balances. That system, to his mind, constitutes its grandeur. "See the wisdom of our ancestors! The supreme *legislative*, and the supreme *executive*, are a perpetual check and balance to each other. If the supreme executive errs, it is informed by the supreme *legislative*, in Parliament: If the supreme legislative errs, it is informed by the . . . King's courts of law." [18]

Applying these principles to parliamentary legislation for the colonies, Otis admits that the British law-makers have the right to pass acts for the general good and by naming the colonies to bind them like subjects within the realm. He adds that to his personal

[16] *A Vindication of the British Colonies*, 142.

[17] *Rights of the British Colonies Asserted and Proved*, 78–79. "If the reasons that can be given against an act, are such as plainly demonstrate that it is against *natural* equity, the executive courts will adjudge such acts void. It may be questioned by some, tho' I make no doubt of it, whether they are not obliged by their oaths to adjudge such acts void."—*Ibid.*, 73–74.

[18] *Ibid.*

knowledge this principle has been accepted in Massachusetts for twenty years. But, he holds, the supreme power cannot take a man's property from him without his consent given in person or by representative. "There is an extreme difference between [the power to lay 'prohibitions' on trade for the good of the whole] and the exercise of unlimited power of taxation over the dominions, without allowing them a representation."

Otis apparently did not intend to advance new ideas. He accepted Locke's positions; but in fact he broke new ground, and went beyond anything contemplated by Locke. His discussion suggests three possible checks upon parliamentary action: one is the power of the courts to hold that acts against natural equity are void. To his mind this was the chief existing check, but as we have seen, relying on Coke's dictum, he went beyond both the theory and practice of the English courts. The second check, on which he does not dwell, is the force of public opinion. The third is colonial representation. He differed from Locke also in seeking a means of preventing arbitrary action on the part of government without resort to revolution. "His intent was to avert, not hasten revolution." Independence he thought would be a calamity: "Were these colonies left to themselves, to-morrow, America would be a meer shambles of blood and confusion." [19]

In various essays Otis dealt with the question of representation. In *A Vindication of the British Colonies*, inspired by the Stamp Act of 1765, he once more admitted the supreme power of Parliament over the dominions, but urged that it was not rightfully exercised unless they were represented. "An equal representation of the whole state is, at least in theory, of the essence of a perfect parliament, or supreme legislative." "Admitted the parliament have the same right to levy internal taxes on the colonies, as to regulate trade; and that the right of levying both, is undoubtedly in the parliament. Yet 'tis humbly conceived and hoped, that before the authority is fully exerted in either case, it will be thought to be reasonable and equitable, that the dominions be in *fact* represented." [20] Representation, he urged, arose "from the nature of

[19] *Vindication*, 140.
[20] *Ibid.*, 143–144.

man, of society, and of all original, just, social and civil compacts forming a state." [21]   He attacked the theory of virtual representation as a cloak which hid from view the viciousness of parliamentary practices: "No good reason . . . can be given in any country why every man of a sound mind should not have his vote in the election of a representative. If a man has but little property to protect and defend, yet his life and liberty are things of some importance. . . . To what purpose is it to ring everlasting changes to the colonists on the cases of Manchester, Birmingham and Sheffield, who return no members? If those now so considerable places are not represented, they ought to be. . . ." If " 'by far the major part of the inhabitants of Great Britain are nonelectors,' the more is the pity." [22]

In various writings Otis reiterates Locke's dictum that government must rule by known and settled laws rather than by extempore arbitrary decrees, and strengthens his position by citing Vattel, the Swiss authority on international law, who held that the constitution of a state should be fixed, and that as the legislature derives its power from the constitution, it cannot change or exceed it without destroying the basis of its own authority. Applying this principle and relying once more upon Coke's dictum, the hope is expressed that "it will not be considered as a new doctrine, that even the authority of the parliament of *Great-Britain* is circumscribed by certain bounds, which if exceeded their acts become those of meer *power* without *right*, and consequently void." [23]

OPPOSITION TO GRENVILLE'S MEASURES

Otis wielded the cudgels of argument while Parliament under George Grenville's lead passed the Sugar Act of 1764, prepared to enforce the navigation acts, and planned to raise a revenue in America. Although the Sugar Act shifted the duties on foreign sugar and molasses to a revenue basis, it was on its face an extension of the system of trade regulation long nominally accepted in

[21] *Ibid.*, 143.
[22] *Considerations on Behalf of the Colonists in a Letter to a Noble Lord*, 110–111.
[23] Appendix to *The Rights of the British Colonies Asserted and Proved*, especially pages 95–96.

America, and most of the arguments against it dealt with its economic unsoundness. The merchants, concerned with its practical effects, hardly noticed the shift; the public was still less aware of the portentous change. But public indifference vanished when the Stamp Act brought home to every American the claim by Parliament of the right to tax unrepresented communities. The Sugar Act was accepted because it seemed to be merely a new trade regulation; [24] the Stamp Act, as a direct tax, was denounced because it encroached upon a right which had long been regarded as reserved exclusively to the colonial legislatures. With great spontaneity the colonies denounced it on the ground that they could not be taxed by a body in which they were unrepresented. Patrick Henry's resolutions in the Virginia assembly asserted that it violated the fundamental rights of Englishmen and the hitherto uninterrupted right of Virginians to be governed by their own assembly "in the articles of their taxes and internal police." He referred to the charters as affirming that the colonists possess all the rights of the people of Great Britain, among which taxation by representatives was one of the foremost, and concluded that the general assembly was the only body which could rightfully lay taxes upon the people of Virginia.[25]

Henry's argument, however, did not rest merely upon the claim of rights granted by charter, for Virginia no longer had a charter. Charters were referred to only as evidence that the rights of colonists were the same as those of Englishmen, and were guaranteed by the very nature of the British constitution. His doctrine was endorsed in effect as that of America by the Stamp Act Congress which met in New York in October, 1765. In its resolutions against the act the delegates acknowledged their allegiance to the crown and claimed all the rights and privileges of subjects within the realm. One of these is that no taxes shall be imposed upon them without their consent, given in person or through their

[24] Edmund Burke said a few years later: "The Act[s] of Navigation attended colonies from their infancy, grew with their growth, and strengthened with their strength. They were confirmed in obedience to it even more by *usage than by law*."—*The Works of . . . Edmund Burke*, quoted by McLaughlin, *Con. Hist.*, 29. The italics in the quotation are mine. Note the evidence of the significance of usage or custom.

[25] Moses Coit Tyler, *Patrick Henry*, 69–71.

representatives. Otis's idea of colonial representation evidently seemed impracticable to the delegates. They held that their situation precluded representation in the House of Commons, from which it followed that no taxes could be constitutionally levied upon them except by their respective assemblies.[26] The resolutions did not clearly reject duties on commerce, but seemed rather to accept them by professing "all due subordination" to Parliament, as "the general superintending power and authority of the whole empire . . . whose authority is freely admitted here, so far as our circumstance is consistent with the enjoyment of our essential rights as freemen and as British subjects." The supremacy of Parliament, the congress seemed to say, might be a sound principle in the constitutional law of the realm, but not of the empire, its authority over the colonies being limited by the principle of local autonomy evoked by their peculiar circumstances.

While the Stamp Act Congress was in session, the governor of Massachusetts, in a speech to the assembly, urged that the act be obeyed. The appeal called forth a reply by the House of Representatives which was probably drafted by Samuel Adams. It asserted that there were boundaries to the power of Parliament. Unlike Henry's resolution, since Massachusetts possessed a charter, the reply stressed the power given to the general assembly of "making laws for its internal government and taxation; . . . this charter has never yet been forfeited." But like Virginia, Massachusetts found an even firmer basis for her rights. "The Parliament has a right to make all laws within the limits of their own constitution. . . . There are certain original inherent rights belonging to the people which the Parliament itself cannot divest them of. . . . Among these is the right of representation in the same body which exercises the power of taxation." [27]

A few days later the house passed resolutions declaring "That there are certain essential rights of the British Constitution of government, which are founded in the law of God and nature, and are the common rights of mankind." After enumerating some of these it is asserted that as the representation of the colonies in

[26] The resolutions are reprinted in MacDonald, *Select Charters*, 313–315.
[27] H. A. Cushing, ed., *The Writings of Samuel Adams*, I, 23 *et seq.*

Parliament is impracticable, "subordinate powers of legislation in America" are the only method by which the constitutional rights of its inhabitants can be secured. As for Massachusetts, such powers are granted in the charter.[28]

Opinion on the Stamp Act outside of the congress and such bodies as the Massachusetts assembly is reflected in the comment of Thomas Hutchinson.[29] Otis's constitutional views were evidently shared by others, for Hutchinson wrote in the fall of 1765 that the prevailing objection to the act was that it "is against Magna Charta, and the natural Rights of Englishmen, and therefore, according to Lord Coke, null and void." [30] John Adams argued before the governor and council of Massachusetts that the act should not be recognized by the courts, on the ground that it was void, being "in Defiance of the first Principles of Justice. . . . There are certain Principles fixed unalterably in Nature;" [31] while in Virginia a court of law is said to have declared that the act was "unconstitutional," and hence that officers might disregard it without incurring penalties.[32]

Two years later Hutchinson reported that the colonies challenged the authority of Parliament to pass any act whatever affecting their

[28] *Ibid.*

[29] Thomas Hutchinson, born in 1711, came of an illustrious and wealthy family. Educated at Harvard, he engaged in mercantile pursuits for a short time, but at twenty-six years of age, as a selectman of Boston, he began a long public career. He was successively representative, speaker, councilor, probate judge, lieutenant-governor, chief justice, and governor. As chief justice he heard the arguments for and against the writs of assistance; he attributed Otis's conduct to chagrin because his (Otis's) father had not been appointed chief justice instead of himself. Samuel Adams was also heir to an enmity between his father and the Hutchinsons. Hutchinson was the author of the notable *History of the Colony . . . of Massachusetts Bay.* During the stamp act riots his house was sacked and a part of the manuscript of the *History* disappeared; it was found in England many years later.

Hutchinson became acting governor upon Bernard's withdrawal in 1769, and governor in 1771. By temperament and from experience a conservative, he became a Tory and withdrew to England in 1774. He died in 1780.

[30] Gray, ed., *Quincy Reports, 1761–1772*, Appendix, note pp. 527–528.

[31] *Ibid.*, 198 *et seq.* Adams argued that the act was void because it violated the natural right of the colonists as men and Englishmen to be represented in the body which taxed them.

[32] *Virginia Gazette*, March 21, 1766, quoted by McLaughlin, *Con. Hist.*, 48, note 28. McLaughlin thinks that this decision was probably the first in America if not in the world to hold that an act was void because it violated a "constitution."

internal policy, as destroying the effect of the charters. "But as the Colonies cannot make laws to extend further than their respective limits, Parliament must step in in all cases to which the legislative power of the Colonies does not extend. Parliament ought to go no farther than this: all beyond is infringing upon the domain of the colonial legislatures. From Virginia to Massachusetts this has now come to be the accepted doctrine." [33] The inclusion of Virginia indicates that the appeal is to more fundamental rights than any granted by charter, and recalls Henry's resolutions.

REPEAL OF THE STAMP ACT

When Parliament took up the protests against the Stamp Act, it was thought by most members that colonial arguments were sufficiently answered by asserting the sovereignty of the body, which as a matter of course included the power to tax subjects everywhere. It was felt that the colonists must be compelled to acknowledge this power, although it was nobody's intention to use it harshly. Grenville defended his measure by declaring that "this kingdom has the sovereign, the supreme legislative power over America," and taxation is a branch of legislation.[34] Pitt, replying to Grenville, argued on historic grounds that there was a distinction between the power of general legislation and that of taxation, and that Parliament possessed the former but not the latter where the colonies were concerned. He held also that there was a "plain distinction . . . between taxes levied for the purpose of raising a revenue, and duties imposed for the regulation of trade . . . although . . . some revenue, might incidentally arise from the latter." [35] Most members ridiculed the idea that Parliament might lay an import duty as in the Sugar Act, but not an internal tax such as the Stamp Act imposed. Led by Lord Mansfield, the chief justice, they held to the theory of virtual representation to prove that the colonies were properly represented in the House of Com-

[33] James K. Hosmer, *Life of Thomas Hutchinson*, 122, citing Hutchinson's *History of Massachusetts Bay*, III, 172.

[34] William Cobbett, *The Parliamentary History of England*, XVI, col. 101.

[35] *Ibid.* For Pitt's indebtedness to Dulaney (*infra*, Chap. VI, note 4), see Moses Coit Tyler, *Literary History of the American Revolution*, I, 111.

mons. Said the chief justice: "The British Legislature, as to the power of making laws, represents the whole British Empire, and has authority to bind every part, and every subject without the least distinction, whether such subjects have the right to vote, or whether the law binds places within the realm or without." [36] Lord Lyttleton added that this view did not preclude "the existence of inferior legislatures, with restrained powers subject to the superior legislature." [37] The liberals in general, including Burke, Chatham, and perhaps Fox,[38] agreed, but held that possession of the right did not mean that it should be exercised regardless of colonial opinion.[39]

The logical legal minds of most British statesmen were baffled by the problems presented by the new situation. They could not understand that new conditions in America changed the functioning of legal institutions, and that in turn changed psychology rendered old law obsolete. Nor could they admit, even if they grasped, the contention of the Americans that they held their liberties not by grace but by natural right.

Not unwilling to deal leniently with America yet perplexed by the unexpected uproar produced by the Stamp Act, they called Franklin before the bar of the House, evidently in the hope of getting an insight into the American mind. He told them that he believed the colonies would resist all internal taxation. Would they then also oppose external taxation? They never had, but "many arguments have been lately used here to show them that there is no difference. . . . In time they may possibly be convinced by these arguments." [40]

Whether convinced by Franklin's testimony that concessions were necessary, or moved by the protests of merchants who felt the pinch of the boycott which colonial merchants had instituted against British imports, Parliament repealed the Stamp Act at the same time proclaiming its supremacy by a Declaratory Act which

[36] Cobbett, XVI, col. 174 (Feb. 24, 1766).

[37] *Ibid.*, cols. 166–167.

[38] Randolph G. Adams, *Political Ideas of the American Revolution*, 25, and citations.

[39] Burke had no part in this debate but had made no advance beyond this position ten years later. *Cf.* his "Resolutions for Conciliation with America."

[40] Cobbett, XVI, cols. 158–159.

asserted its power to bind the colonies "in all cases whatsoever." The concrete cause of friction was thus removed, but the fundamental issue of plenary versus limited power was merely drawn more sharply. While the American public in general rested in the false sense of victory won, thinkers girded themselves against the day of renewed contention.

BIBLIOGRAPHICAL NOTE

In addition to the references cited in the footnotes in this chapter, the reader's attention is called to the following:

The book by Claude H. Van Tyne on *The Causes of the War of Independence* is an "effective summarization of the scholarly work done by others." It regards the controversy as one which aligned the liberals and conservatives in opposing camps in both countries. *Cf.* Hugh E. Egerton, *The Causes and Character of the American Revolution*, and Charles H. McIlwain, *The American Revolution, a Constitutional Interpretation.*

For the student of constitutional ideas there is much of interest in the first volume of Vernon L. Parrington, *Main Currents in American Thought*. Arthur M. Schlesinger, *Colonial Merchants and the American Revolution*, stresses the economic reasons for the dissatisfaction of Americans.

Almost epoch-making in its point of view is the essay by Andrew C. McLaughlin entitled "The Background of American Federalism," in *America and Britain*. William Seal Carpenter, *The Development of American Political Thought*, is an inquiry into the ideology of the Americans in the era of the breach with England.

VI

THE BREAKDOWN OF THE IMPERIAL CONSTITUTION

CONSTITUTIONAL DISCUSSION, 1766–1770

THE repeal of the Stamp Act was followed by a good deal of discussion of the constitutional problem. Governor Bernard of Massachusetts, an American, had already, in 1765, perceived that "the patchwork government of America will last no longer. . . . The necessity of a parliamentary establishment . . . upon fixed constitutional principles is brought on with a precipitation which could not have been foreseen a year ago."[1] It was true that the empire was, in the years following 1763, suffering for want of a clearly-defined constitutional system. The simple all-embracing creed of the advocates of parliamentary supremacy had the fatal defect of being unacceptable beyond the Atlantic.

For some time it seemed that some plan of accommodation might be devised which would be satisfactory to both disputants. The Americans argued the issue on the basis of what they conceived to be British constitutional law. They were conservative rather than revolutionary in temper. But their demands repeated the old tale of the defense of rights believed to be already theirs, when they were actually looking towards a new type of imperial organization.

In 1766 Richard Bland of Virginia tried to demonstrate that there were matters over which Parliament had no control. Certain of the king's prerogatives were, he held, independent of Parliament. One of these was his power to permit colonization.[2] In this same year Stephen Hopkins, the Governor of Rhode Island, contended that in the nature of things powers of government are capable of distribution. He pointed out that some interests are

---

[1] Channing, ed., *Barrington-Bernard Correspondence*, 99. Cited by Adams, *Pol. Ideas*, 19.
[2] *An Inquiry into the Rights of the British Colonies*, quoted by Adams, *Pol. Ideas*, 43–44. Cf. McLaughlin, *Con. Hist.*, 45, and note 24.

of a general nature, "quite out of the reach of these particular legislatures." Power over these, "every man of the least knowledge of the British constitution, will be naturally led to look for, and find it in the parliament of Great Britain. . . ."[3] His view implies that the colonial governments are on the other hand equally entitled to undisturbed exercise of the internal police power.

The latter idea emerges more clearly in a pamphlet by Daniel Dulany of Maryland,[4] who inquires whether the line may not be distinctly drawn between such acts as are necessary for "securing the Dependance [sic] of the Colonies" and such as are not—the line, in short, between the general and local police. He held, moreover, that the powers of the dependencies, once granted by the superior (Great Britain) by "express compact," limit the superior. Thus is introduced the concept of colonial autonomy. He regards the regulation of trade as a proper exercise of parliamentary authority, even if some revenue accrues incidentally, but, referring to the Stamp Act, denies the right of the "Commons of Great Britain to be thus munificent at the Expence of the Commons of America."

Thomas Pownall, sometime governor of Massachusetts, continued the discussion in *The Administration of the Colonies* (1768). He saw in the British Isles and the American colonies "one grand marine dominion," which ought "to be united into one imperium," in which the colonies would have a share in the central legislature through "knights and burgesses of their own election."[5] In later writings he advocated the establishment of a union by means of "a contractual act" which could not, "according to the law of nations, of justice and policy be altered without the consent of the parties."[6]

[3] *The Grievances of the American Colonies Candidly Examined* (London, 1766), quoted by McLaughlin, *Con. Hist.*, 41. There was an earlier edition entitled *The Rights of the Colonies Examined* (Providence, 1765).

[4] *Considerations on the Propriety of Imposing Taxes in the British Colonies* . . . (2d edn., London, 1766), quoted by McLaughlin, *Con. Hist.*, 42. (First edition appeared in October, 1765). *Cf.* Adams, *Pol. Ideas*, 70–78, *et passim*. Dulany eventually became a Tory and lost his property by confiscation.—McLaughlin, *Con. Hist.*, 42, note 20.

[5] Quoted by Adams, *Pol. Ideas*, 31.

[6] Cobbett, XVIII, cols. 326–327 (Feb. 20, 1775), quoted *ibid.*, 32.

There were other proposals of representation in Parliament, among them notably that of the Englishman, Francis Masseres, who wished to transform that body into a truly imperial legislature.[7] He also proposed the division of the subjects of jurisdiction among the superior and the subordinate legislatures, each with an exclusive sphere of activity, thus limiting the supremacy of the imperial body by reserving local control to the several component states.[8] Since such a union would derive its legality from the act of Parliament, the proposal foreshadowed the act by which the government of Canada was authorized a century later, more definitely than it did the constitutional system of the United States, which is one of powers delegated by the people themselves.

John Almon was the author of another proposal, in 1766, of a "sovereign council" composed of deputies from each province. Each "kingdom or province should continue its parliament or assembly, or whatever form of internal government it is possessed of, and defray all its expenses," and the council was not to meddle in the internal affairs of any constituent dominion, each of which was to raise its quota of troops and supplies in its own way.[9] Thomas Crowley, writing about 1770 as *Amor Patriae*, made still another suggestion of an imperial legislature, composed of delegates from all of the dominions and Ireland as well as Great Britain, in rough proportion to population. Lords were to be created also in the overseas possessions. The significant feature of the proposal was that the powers of the imperial legislature would be limited to those specified in the instrument creating it.[10] Such plans show that some Englishmen appreciated the importance of agreeing upon a system which would end the dispute "without subjugating the Americans . . . or impairing the supreme authority of" Parliament.[11]

[7] *Considerations on the Expediency of Admitting Representatives from the American Colonies to the British House of Commons* (London, 1770), cited *ibid.*, 33–34.

[8] *Ibid.*, 34.

[9] *Ibid.*, 47–48.

[10] *Ibid.*, 35–36.

[11] Words of Samuel Clay Harvey, in London *Publick Ledger*, January, 1775, quoted *ibid.*, 36–37.

THE TOWNSHEND SYSTEM

Heedless of the debate which the Stamp Act had started, Charles Townshend, as chancellor of the exchequer, proceeded in 1767 with his policy of raising a revenue by "external" taxation, that is, duties on certain enumerated articles when imported by the colonies. Commissioners were appointed to superintend the collection, and steps were taken to enforce the navigation acts by means which included the use of writs of assistance. The revenue was to be used to defray the cost of administration, support the civil governments in the royal colonies, and provide for colonial defense. The plan to provide for the support of the civil governments threatened to destroy the check which the assemblies held over the governors. In fact, every feature of the Townshend plan was obnoxious even if legal. A new period of discussion was inaugurated, the most notable contribution being the "Farmer's Letters," by John Dickinson, which appeared during 1767 and 1768.[12] The acclaim which greeted them is good evidence that they stated the American view in satisfactory terms.[13]

Dickinson acknowledged the authority of Parliament to regulate trade. "We are but parts of a whole; and therefore there must exist a power somewhere to preside, and preserve the connection in due order. This power is lodged in parliament; and we are as much dependent on Great-Britain, as a perfectly free people can be on another."[14] But he denied that Parliament could, under its power of regulating trade, impose a duty for the purpose of raising a revenue, and insisted that it had never done so. "I have looked over every statute relating to these colonies from their first settlement to this time," he wrote. "Though many of them imposed duties on trade, yet those duties were always imposed with design to restrain the commerce of one part, that was injurious to another, and thus to promote the general welfare. The raising of a revenue thereby was never intended."[15]

[12] "Letters of a Farmer in Pennsylvania," in P. L. Ford, ed., *Writings of John Dickinson.*
[13] Charles J. Stillé, *The Life and Times of John Dickinson, 1732–1808*, 90–92.
[14] *Writings*, 312.
[15] *Ibid.*

One may question the possibility of determining so certainly the intent of statutes and yet admit the immense influence of Dickinson's argument. Thenceforth there was little disposition in America to concede that Parliament possessed a power of taxation under the guise of trade regulation. Dickinson's appeal to long-established custom is also notable as characteristic of American thinking.

From the point of view of constitutional ideas, the chief significance of Dickinson's discussion is his concern with the distribution of powers among autonomous members of a composite state. Powers had been distributed, he thought, in the British empire before the adoption of the dogma of parliamentary supremacy. Under the *old* empire the colonial governments had had their share of authority. The British view that these subordinate governments existed only by sufferance meant to him that the colonies enjoyed no real freedom, however kindly the king might be, or however just the intentions of Parliament. Much less than Otis was he disposed to confide in the wisdom and justice of Parliament; much more that Otis was he disposed to demand effective means of regulating its conduct. He and other Americans desired a liberty resting on a recognized legal basis. Only those are free, he said, "who live under a government so constitutionally checked and controuled, that proper provision is made against its being otherwise exercised." [16]

As Parliament had asserted in the previous century that the king was under, not above, the law, so now Americans were applying the principle to Parliament and asserting that it too was under, not above, the fundamental law or constitution. Unfortunately, the idea of distributed powers was beyond the comprehension of the advocates of parliamentary supremacy, although some of them conceded that local government might be enjoyed by grace of Parliament so long as it seemed desirable. [17] The

[16] *Ibid.*, 356. "The only way to preserve to the Colonists their rights as British Subjects, consistent with their acknowledged subordination to the supreme Legislature of Great Britain . . . is to continue to them the same powers of Government which they have hitherto been used to, with the same Checks & no other: this is all they desire."—Cushing, *Writings of Samuel Adams*, I, 39.

[17] The doctrine of parliamentary supremacy anticipated the modern doctrine of the indivisibility of sovereignty. "In sovereignty there are no gradations," said

colonial idea went further: the control of internal police belonged to the colonies by natural right and lay outside the pale of parliamentary action. Or by another test, had not "a working practice for a hundred years" become a right?

In Massachusetts, as Otis was removed from the scene of action by illness, Samuel Adams became the protagonist of the American argument. Influenced like Otis by Locke and Vattel, he constantly reiterated the theory that the possession of property and the disposal of it are natural rights, adopted into the English constitution; that in free states the constitution is fixed, and that the supreme legislature derives its powers from the constitution and cannot change it without destroying its own foundation.[18] One of the most notable of his statements was made in the Massachusetts Circular Letter of 1768, which emphasized the view that in all free countries the governments are limited in their powers.[19] The belief that the English constitution "ascertains and limits both Sovereignty and allegiance" was widely spread as the result of the circulation of the letter.

The responses of the assemblies of the several colonies to the letter indicated a general adherence to the principles which it expressed. The British countered with a proposal to transport American agitators to England for trial, violating American ideas of justice; other measures, such as the controversy over the tax on tea and the quartering of soldiers, aggravated the strain and led to riotous acts. As a result, in the early seventies Virginia brought about the beginnings of intercolonial organization by suggesting the extension of the Massachusetts system of committees of correspondence.[20]

Dr. Johnson in *Taxation No Tyranny* (London, 1774). As late as 1838, with the American Union before them as an object lesson, many British statesmen failed to find in it any aid in solving the Canadian problem. The Duke of Wellington declared, for example, that "local responsible government [in Canada] and the sovereignty of Great Britain were incompatible."—Quoted by C. H. Currey, in *British Colonial Policy, 1783–1915*, 90.

[18] *Writings*, I, 134 *et seq*. *Cf.* E. S. Corwin, "The Higher Law Background of American Constitutional Law."

[19] MacDonald, *Select Charters*, 330–334.

[20] J. M. Leake, "The Virginia Committee System and the American Revolution."

GOVERNOR HUTCHINSON AND THE MASSACHUSETTS LEGISLATURE

In 1773 Governor Hutchinson undertook to convince the Massachusetts legislature that the doctrine of parliamentary supremacy was correct. He could see no way to draw a line between the supreme authority of Parliament and the total independence of the colonies, for, said he, there could not be two independent legislatures in one state. Such independence of legislation could exist only in the case of kingdoms united, as Scotland and England had formerly been, under one king. Under a supreme authority there could be only subordinate governments, and such was the case of the colonies.[21]

Hutchinson's logic led to the conclusion that all colonial privileges were held by grace of Parliament. In reply the council presented (by the pen of Samuel Adams possibly assisted by John Adams) a clear statement of the legal basis of distributed powers and colonial autonomy: assuming that a grant to a subordinate government is a compact, it was urged that if the grant is not violated so as to work forfeiture, "the supreme power has no rightful authority to take away or diminish it, or to substitute its own acts, in cases wherein the acts of the subordinate power can, according to its constitution, operate. To suppose the contrary, is to suppose, that it has no property in the privileges granted to it; for, if it holds them at the will of the supreme power, . . . it can have no property in them. . . . But, as in fact, the two powers are not incompatible, and do subsist together, each restraining its acts to their constitutional objects, can we not from hence, see how the supreme power may supervise, regulate, and make general laws for the kingdom, without interfering with the privileges of the subordinate powers within it?"[22] Thus the British government was held to be limited by the natural law of the obligation of contracts.

If the alternatives presented by Hutchinson are the only ones possible, the argument concluded, Massachusetts must be independent, for it cannot have been the intention of the parties to the

[21] See discussion by McLaughlin, *Con. Hist.*, 69 *et seq.*
[22] Quoted *ibid.*, 71.

compact that the colonies should be reduced to vassalage.[23] The utterance gave an ominous hint that, pushed too far, the colonies might seek actual independence as the preferable alternative.

The discussion had brought out by this time ideas which had been perhaps partially latent in 1763. Americans were becoming familiar with the concepts that the English constitution embodied natural rights and accordingly limited the powers of Parliament and king; that the only possible government in a free state is one restricted by its constitution and in practice by a system of checks and balances; that the colonies possess an indefeasible portion of governmental power. And these principles were not put forward as what *should* be, but as an interpretation of what the English constitution actually *was*. The colonists were not advocating change, but attempting to conserve what they conceived to be the existing system. It is clear both that there were elements in the actual imperial system which they wished to conserve, and concepts concerning it which were not yet actualities. If a separation took place and Americans attempted the task of establishing governments for themselves, it was inevitable that they should be profoundly influenced both by these practices and these concepts.

In contrast to these views Englishmen held that from the "state of independence of the Crown which the colonies insisted upon results the necessity of a dependence on some other power. . . . This power must be the parliament of Great Britain who hath and ought to have, a full and absolute sovereignty over all the British dominions."[24]

THE INTOLERABLE ACTS

Each lull in the dispute with England was ended by some new act the effect of which was to arouse afresh the opposition of the colonies. So the Tea Act of 1773 led to the Boston "Tea Party," which in turn induced Parliament to close the port of Boston and to pass the other "intolerable acts." These evoked a united sentiment in America. From the colonial point of view the Massachusetts Government Act was particularly inane and offensive.

[23] *Ibid.*, 72.
[24] Quoted by Adams, *Pol. Ideas*, 26, note 34.

It modified the charter, providing that the councilors should be appointed by the king, and forbidding the holding of town meetings without the governor's permission, save for the election of delegates to the assembly and other routine work.[25] This act ignored completely the colonial belief in the inviolability of charters as set out in the reply to Governor Hutchinson. Indeed it ignored the old English law of corporations as well. Still worse, it was a stupid blunder because it attempted what was a psychological impossibility. "I would not have men of a mercantile cast, every day collecting themselves together and debating about political matters," Lord George Germain is reported as saying.[26]

The other measures—the Administration of Justice Act and the Quartering Act—approximated martial law, and at least threatened resort to armed force. There was nothing in them to suggest conciliation, for Parliament deemed them necessary to vindicate its authority. The Quebec Act, unfortunately passed at the same time, with liberal intent towards the new French subjects in Canada, was offensive in the English colonies because it ignored their claims to lands west of the mountains.

REPUDIATION OF PARLIAMENT

The "intolerable acts" seemed to prove that the Americans held their privileges by a precarious tenure. None was safe under the theory of parliamentarians that they were held merely by grace. Hence many Americans were brought to the point of rejecting parliamentary authority *in toto*. The view had been growing for some time that their union with Britain was a personal one. In 1766 Hutchinson had written that, according to Massachusetts opinion, "The King . . . indeed is our Sovereign, but we have no representation in parliament, & strictly speaking, not merely those acts which lay taxes upon us, but no other acts any further than we adopt them, are binding upon us." [27] This attitude Hutchinson thought was new. "All of a sudden," he says, "we have it advanced that acts of parliament of England or Great Britain have

[25] MacDonald, *Select Charters*, 343–350.
[26] Claude H. Van Tyne, *Causes of the War of Independence*, 396–397.
[27] Gray, ed., *Quincy Reports, 1761–1772*, p. 443, quoted by McLaughlin, *Con. Hist.*, 45, note 23.

no more relation to us than acts of Parliament of Scotland had before the Union." [28] The position was not new, but was quite consistent with the utterance of Massachusetts in 1646, that the laws of England are binding only on those who live in England.

In 1766, however, according to Hutchinson's report the next year, Massachusetts still admitted that "Parliament must step in in all cases to which the legislative power of the Colonies does not extend." This view lost ground rapidly in the years which followed. If Parliament was over the whole empire, it should govern the Channel Islands, Jersey and Guernsey, which in fact it did not do, declared Franklin in 1769.[29] For America as for these islands the only bond uniting the colonies with England was the king.[30] John Adams espoused this view immediately after the controversy with Hutchinson in 1773; [31] it was in fact suggested by the governor's remark that independent legislatures could exist only under a personal union such as that between Scotland and England under the Stuarts. For Adams thenceforth Massachusetts became a kingdom of which the colonial assembly was the parliament.

The following year Jefferson rejected the authority of Parliament, holding that its acts were powers "assumed by a body of men, foreign to our constitution, and unacknowledged by our laws." [32] Even the king, in harmony with the compact philosophy, was described as "no more than the chief officer of the people, appointed by the laws, and circumscribed with definite powers to assist in working the great machine of government, erected for their use, and consequently subject to their superintendence. . . .

[28] Quoted *ibid.*, 45.
[29] John Bigelow, ed., *Complete Works of Benjamin Franklin*, IV, 309. This argument has been critically examined and expanded by a modern scholar: see Charles H. McIlwain, *The American Revolution: a Constitutional Interpretation*. Another contemporary scholar (Schuyler), however, has produced evidence showing that from the beginning Parliament did legislate on occasion for all dominions subject to the king, including the Channel Islands. Such a function was the natural result of the fact that Parliament was the outgrowth of the council, a body which was associated with the *king* rather than the English *realm*. See *supra*, Chap. I, note 6.
[30] Bigelow, *Works of Franklin*, IV, 309.
[31] See series of essays signed "Novanglus," *Works*, IV, 11–177.
[32] "A Summary View of the Rights of British America." Ford, *Writings of Jefferson*, I, 421–447.

Kings are the servants, not the proprietors of the people." [33]   No longer was Parliament to be regarded, even *ex necessitate*, as possessed of the general power of superintendence and regulation in matters which exceeded the competence of the individual colonies. Jefferson attacked the acts of trade and the system of disallowing colonial laws; he even criticised the administration of the post office as designed chiefly for the purpose of increasing the number of offices for the king's favorites.[34]

These expressions revealed a trend in American thinking which might end in revolution.   Like Locke, Jefferson stressed the origin of government in consent, the responsibility of rulers to the people, and by implication, the right of the people to alter the government. Jefferson's language is, like Locke's, democratic in its implications, and in his case the implication was supported by his desires. Neither Jefferson nor Adams intimated at this time, however, that he desired a union which would protect and guarantee the autonomy of the several "kingdoms."   The urge towards union—not only among themselves but with England—and at the same time the culmination of the attempt to define the British constitution and give it fixity of form, was shown by the Galloway Plan, presented to the First Continental Congress.

THE FIRST CONTINENTAL CONGRESS

At Virginia's call, delegates chosen during the summer of 1774 gathered in Philadelphia in September as the First Continental Congress.[35]   Various irregular methods were used in choosing the delegates. The committees of correspondence played a large part in the selection, but the legislatures had little to do with the movement because of dissolution by the governors or kindred reasons.[36]

[33] *Ibid.*

[34] Quoted by McLaughlin, *Con. Hist.*, 81–82. Madison once wrote: "The fundamental principle of the Revolution was that the colonies were coordinate members with each other, and with Great Britain, of an empire united by a common executive sovereign, but not united by any common legislative sovereign."— Gaillard Hunt, ed., *Writings of James Madison*, VI, 373.

[35] On July 7, 1773, Franklin in a letter addressed to the Massachusetts assembly suggested a continental conference to issue a united refusal to grant aids to the crown for any general war until colonial rights were recognized by the king and both houses. There was no suggestion here of governmental union.

[36] Van Tyne, *Causes of the War of Independence*, 427–428.

The congress was thus an extra-legal body, representing the dissatisfied elements. Nevertheless its members differed in the degree of their radicalism, and on the whole their instructions were not revolutionary. Rhode Island directed her delegates to discuss the principles which would "establish the rights and liberties of the Colonies, upon a just and solid Foundation." These words may be taken to express the prevailing attitude.

There was a general disposition to claim rights on all possible bases—natural law, the British constitution, the common law and the charters.[37] But there was a considerable difference of opinion as to the degree of authority to be conceded to Parliament.[38] A sub-committee of which John Adams was a member made the report which was finally accepted; it declared that the colonies were "entitled to a free and exclusive power of legislation in their several provincial legislatures . . . in all cases of taxation and internal polity, subject only to the negative of their sovereign, in such manner as has been heretofore used and accustomed."[39] Because of the necessity of some coordinating authority, it promised consent to the operation of acts of Parliament for the bona fide regulation of external commerce to promote the advantage of the whole empire, "excluding every idea of taxation, internal or external, for raising a revenue on the subjects in America, without their consent."[40] There was here no recognition of the *legal* right of Parliament to regulate trade, and how other general concerns were to be provided for does not appear. The reference to the

[37] The Declaration of Rights and Grievances adopted by the congress claimed all of the rights derived from "the immutable laws of nature, the principles of the English constitution, and the several charters or compacts." An attempt was made to enumerate the essential rights of Englishmen, in a way reminiscent of the Bill of Rights of 1689 and prophetic of the bills of rights later incorporated in the state constitutions. Among those mentioned are the right of petition and of peaceable assembly, the right to have no standing army quartered upon the people in time of peace except with the consent of the colony affected, the right of jury trial, and all rights safeguarded by the common law. The last item is in notable contrast with the seventeenth-century attitude toward the common law. One resolution declared that "they have never ceded to any sovereign power whatever, a right to dispose of either [life, liberty or property] without their consent."—MacDonald, *Select Charters*, 356–361.

[38] John Adams, *Works*, II, 374.

[39] Worthington C. Ford and Gaillard Hunt, eds., *Journals of the Continental Congress, 1774–1789*, I, 68–69.

[40] *Ibid.*

sovereign's negative has to do, presumably, with the Privy Council's practice of disallowance.

In an Address to the King it was declared that "we wish not a diminution of the prerogative, nor do we solicit the grant of any new right in our favor";[41] and in an Address to the People of Great Britain, the delegates say: "Place us in the same situation that we were at the close of the last war, and our former harmony will be restored."[42]

Thus the congress demanded recognition of the British constitution as Americans believed it stood. Such a position could threaten rebellion or revolution only as a last resort to maintain rights. The congress asserted rights, but did not propose a plan to define the legal relations and mutual powers and obligations of the various parts of the empire. Such a plan was offered by Joseph Galloway, but it was not adopted.

THE GALLOWAY PLAN

Joseph Galloway, of Maryland birth, was a resident of Philadelphia. A well-trained lawyer, he acquired a considerable fortune, partly by practicing his profession and partly through his marriage with a well-to-do Quaker woman. During the troublous years of the sixties he was a member of the provincial assembly and served for a time as speaker.[43] The inefficiency of the provincial government under the proprietorship of the Penn family, and the lack of an intercolonial union, led him to regard the presence of British troops as essential for the protection of the colonies.[44] Experience with the proprietary government inclined him to desire its replacement by the royal type, and the need of a strong and stable government led him to support the claims of Parliament—resting as it did so largely on the landed interest—as the main support of law and order.[45]

As a delegate to the First Continental Congress, Galloway took with him a copy of Franklin's plan of union of 1754.[46] The two

[41] *Ibid.*, I, 119.
[42] *Ibid.*, I, 89.
[43] E. H. Baldwin, *Joseph Galloway, the Loyalist Politician, passim.*
[44] *Ibid.*, 30.
[45] Letter to Franklin, March 10, 1768, *ibid.*, 45–46.
[46] *Ibid.*, 76, citing a writer in *Pennsylvania Gazette* for April 26, 1775.

men were close friends, and the phraseology of the plan of union which Galloway presented to the congress proves that it was based on the earlier one.

Biding his time during the early sessions and observing the trend of sentiment, Galloway realized that the denial of the authority of Parliament would leave the disunited colonies helpless to act on behalf of their common interests, or even to settle differences among themselves.[47] He noted especially the need of a power to regulate the commerce of the empire as a whole. A union was essential; but any plan which was intended as the basis of negotiation with England would have to recognize Parliament, and seek by "compact" to correct defects in the machinery of government, especially in the matter of colonial representation.[48]

Late in September Galloway arose to present his plan. "He had long waited with great patience," he said, "under an expectation of hearing some proposition which should tend to restore harmony between Great Britain and the colonies by some plan of constitution, but, to his great mortification and distress, a month had been spent in fruitless debates on equivocal and indecisive propositions which tended to inflame rather than reconcile. . . ."[49] There was "a Manifest Defect in the Constitution of the British Empire in respect to the government of the Colonies," which he hoped his plan might correct.[50] He therefore offered the following resolution: "Resolved, That the Congress will apply to his Majesty for a redress of grievances under which his faithful subjects in America labour; and assure him that the Colonies hold in abhorrence the idea of being considered independent communities on [sic] the British government, and most ardently desire the establishment of a Political Union, not only among themselves, but with the Mother State, upon those principles of safety and freedom which are essential in the constitution of all free governments, and particularly that of the British Legislature; and as the colonies from their local circumstances, cannot be represented in the Parliament of Great-Britain, they will humbly propose to his Majesty and his

[47] *Journals of the Cont. Cong.*, I, 46.
[48] *Ibid.*, 48.
[49] *Ibid.*, 44.
[50] *Ibid.*, 48.

two Houses of Parliament, the following plan, under which the strength of the whole Empire may be drawn together on any emergency, the interests of both countries advanced, and the rights and liberties of America secured." [51]

The main proposals of the plan were: A "Union between Great Britain and the colonies," with "a British and American Legislature, for regulating the administration of the general affairs of America . . . under which . . . each Colony shall retain its present Constitution and powers of regulating and governing its own internal police in all cases whatever."

A President-General was to be appointed by the king, and a Grand Council of delegates was to be chosen by the assemblies on a proportional basis. The President-General and Council were to enjoy "all the Legislative rights, powers, and authorities, necessary for regulating and administering all the general police and affairs of the Colonies, in which Great Britain and the Colonies, or any of them, the Colonies in general, or more than one Colony, are in any manner concerned, as well civil and criminal as commercial." The Council was to be "an inferiour and distinct branch of the British Legislature . . . and . . . any of the said general regulations may originate, and be formed and digested, either in the Parliament of Great Britain or in the said Grand Council . . . and . . . the assent of both shall be requisite to the validity of all such general Acts and Statutes." [52]

This project proved to be too conservative to meet the mood of the congress. Its legal basis would have been the consent of that Parliament whose authority the majority was ready to deny; more and more, American thought demanded that government should be grounded upon the authority of the people. There was criticism also of the complex plan of representation. "We are not to consent by the representatives of representatives," said one John Henry, who feared that the "American legislature" would be susceptible

[51] *Ibid.*, 49 *et seq.*
[52] *Ibid.* Italics of original omitted. The provision for concurrence of the Grand Council and Parliament is so strongly reminiscent of the relations between the Virginia assembly and the general court of the London Company as to suggest that Galloway derived his idea from the earlier practice. The present writer knows of no direct evidence that such is the case.

to bribery "by that nation which avows in the face of the world that bribery is a part of her system of government." [53]

Franklin questioned the wisdom of the proposal, not because he doubted the integrity of Americans, but because he agreed that England was corrupt, and a closer union would be undesirable. "When I consider the extreme corruption prevalent among all orders of men in this rotten old state, and the glorious public virtue so predominant in our rising country, I cannot but apprehend more mischief than benefit from a closer union." [54]

All record of Galloway's proposal was expunged from the minutes of the congress,[55] but a copy found its way to the Board of Trade which passed it on to the king with the simple comment that it was "complete in itself." Some of the royal governors viewed it with favor. The temper of Parliament would doubtless have made its acceptance impossible even if it had been approved by the congress. American writers have depreciated the merits of the scheme, perhaps in part through prejudice against the author, who when the hour of decision came remained loyal to Britain. But it was not without merit, and its legal basis was the same which was later successfully made the foundation of the Dominion of Canada. Galloway considered that, beyond the preservation of the relationship with the mother country, the chief feature was the definite separation of the powers of internal and general police, and in this feature the plan anticipated the union which was finally consumated by the independent states.

One important step towards intercolonial union was actually taken by the congress in the formation of the "Association" for the purpose of enforcing non-intercourse with England until grievances were redressed. Through local committees the Association operated effectively throughout the colonies in uniting the radicals and making them a real force in promoting the common cause.

[53] Quoted by Baldwin, *Galloway*, 64.

[54] *Works*, V, 435.

[55] Galloway presented a copy of the plan to Governor Franklin of New Jersey, which is the original of the form printed in the *Journals*. He also wrote a *Candid Examination* in which he reproduced the plan and his speech in the congress. A brief outline of the speech is given by John Adams in his diary entry of September 28, 1774. See *Works*, II, 387–389. Peter Force reprinted the plan in *American Archives* . . . 4th series, I, 905. Essential portions are reprinted in A. B. Hart, ed., *American History Leaflet*, No. 14, pp. 19–21.

PART TWO

AMERICA INHERITS THE IMPERIAL PROBLEM

VII

TRANSITION TO INDEPENDENCE

STEPS TOWARDS REVOLUTION

THE representations of the First Continental Congress seemed for a time likely to bring redress. Some of the influential English liberals desired to reach an agreement with the Americans which would define the powers of their respective governments. Burke favored a return to the régime of the days before 1763, which the colonists had repeatedly intimated would satisfy them. The influence of the merchants, who feared a renewed suspension of the colonial trade, was thrown on the side of concession, and even Prime Minister North offered a conciliatory resolution which proposed to exempt from parliamentary taxation any colony the assembly of which would engage to raise stipulated sums for imperial purposes.

Nevertheless military measures were pressed forward to meet the "rebellion" which seemed impending, and the colonies on their own part gathered military supplies and began to drill militia. Before Lord North's resolution was received by the Second Continental Congress which assembled in May, 1775, the attempt of General Gage to seize the munitions at Concord had precipitated armed conflict. The "appeal to Heaven" had been taken; the dispute had been referred to the arbitrament of arms.

North's resolution had arrived too late. Moreover, it did not abandon the parliamentary claim of power "to bind the colonies . . . in all cases whatsoever." It was therefore unacceptable to Americans who had decided that they were not subject to Parliament at all, but only to the king. The Second Continental Congress continued for some time to profess loyalty to him. To explain this anomalous attitude the Congress issued a statement which placed the blame for the violation of American rights upon the ministry. "We are reduced to the alternative of chusing an unconstitutional submission to the tyranny of irritated ministers, or resistance by force. . . . The latter is our choice, . . ." but "we mean not to dissolve that union which has so long and so happily subsisted between us. . . ." [1]

This assurance of continued loyalty was a bid for the moral support of the English Whigs, but at most it only postponed separation. Upon the news of Bunker Hill the king proclaimed that the Americans were rebels and forbade intercourse with them. A year of inconclusive fighting followed, with the direction of events veering somewhat uncertainly towards the goal of independence. But the hope of reconciliation only grew fainter, and circumstances called forth actions which were more and more difficult to reconcile with professions of loyalty. The vestiges of British authority were gradually obliterated as revolutionary organizations gained control in colony after colony, disarmed loyalists, and took steps to set up governments resting definitely upon the authority of the patriot element of the population. Thomas Paine's impassioned appeal in *Common Sense* doubtless moved men more than the calmer logic of formal resolutions and declarations. "Reconciliation is . . . a fallacious dream," he urged. "Everything that is right or natural pleads for separation. . . . Even the distance at which the Almighty hath placed England and America is a strong and natural proof that the authority of one over the other was never the design of Heaven."

As early as May, 1775, the provincial congress of Massachusetts had sought the advice of the Continental Congress "respecting the taking up and exercising the powers of civil government," thinking it likely that that body would wish to recommend some plan to be followed everywhere.[2] In reply Congress had recommended that Massachusetts proceed in accordance with the provisions of her charter as it had stood prior to the act of Parliament modifying its terms; to that act it held no obedience was due.[3] In the course of the months which followed, recommendations were made in response to the requests of other colonies, suited to the situation of each.

---

[1] "Declaration of the Causes and Necessity of Taking up Arms," MacDonald, *Select Charters*, 374–381. On the topics discussed in this chapter see Allan Nevins, *The American States during and after the Revolution, passim.*
[2] *Journals of the Cont. Cong.*, II, 77.
[3] *Ibid.*

Down to May, 1776, all of these recommendations rested upon the assumption that a reconciliation with England would sooner or later be effected. By that time, however, the hope of reconciliation had well-nigh disappeared, and Congress adopted resolutions declaring that it was necessary for each colony to suppress totally the exercise of every kind of authority under the crown and to wield all powers of government under authority of the people. Accordingly each was advised, if no such government had as yet been set up, to adopt such a plan as would, in the opinion of the representatives of the people, best conduce to the safety and happiness of their constituents and of America in general.[4]

THE DECLARATION

In this same month the "convention" which was functioning as the temporary government of Virginia not only drew up the first of the state constitutions based on the assumption of permanent separation from England, but instructed its delegates in Congress to propose and assent to a declaration that all of the colonies were free and independent states.[5] On June 7, therefore, Richard Henry Lee presented a resolution to that effect. Such a measure required unanimous support; it was not the sort of thing which a bare majority could undertake to impose upon a reluctant minority. Some time was needed to bring around the more conservative elements—those who had most to lose in case of failure, and most to fear from the popular commotions which might follow success.

In the meantime the friends of independence were able to carry a motion to appoint a committee to draft a declaration while members were making up their minds whether to accept or reject Lee's resolution. On July 1, after everything that could be said had been said a hundred times, as John Adams put it, several delegations were still to be won over. An informal vote showed that the

[4] *Ibid.*, IV, 342, 358 (May 15). The resolutions (drawn by John Adams) played into the hands of the radicals in the states who desired to popularize the state governments. *Cf.* Nevins, *Am. States,* 106 *et seq.* For contemporary discussion of a model form of state constitution see *ibid.*, 121–125.

[5] The Journal of the Virginia convention is published in Force, *American Archives,* 4th ser., VI, col. 1509–1616, *et passim.* *Cf.* H. B. Grigsby, *The Virginia Convention of 1776.* The North Carolina provincial convention had approved a proposal of independence on April 13.—Nevins, 111.

South Carolina and Pennsylvania delegates were opposed, while Delaware was divided and New York refused to vote at all. Next day, however, with New York still not voting, the resolution was adopted. Only three delegates voted in the negative. One of these was John Dickinson, who seems to have believed that the colonies should form a firm union before venturing to declare their independence.[6]

The formal Declaration drawn up by the special committee was adopted on July 4.[7] Owing to absence, Lee was not a member of this committee, but the place which would doubtless have been given to him as mover of the resolution was ably filled by Thomas Jefferson, his colleague in the Virginia delegation. To Jefferson happily had fallen also the task of preparing the draft. As might have been expected of the author of the "Summary View," the Declaration renounced all allegiance to the king, but ignored the Parliament which in his earlier paper he had described as a body "foreign to our constitution." Parliament was not referred to at all by name, but was hinted at as a usurper of power in the charge against the king that he had assented to "acts of pretended legislation." In a similar allusion the king was accused of conspiring "with others" (that is, Parliament) in wrongful acts. But Jefferson found many infractions of American rights for which the king alone was responsible.

The Declaration falls into three parts: The first sets forth principles which are said to be self-evident—that men are by nature endowed with certain inalienable rights; that government is instituted to preserve these rights, and derives its just powers from the consent of the governed, who may alter or abolish it if it proves destructive of the ends for which it was established. These principles, stated in language which is transparently a paraphrase of Locke, were the familiar doctrines which Americans had cherished from the earliest days in the New World, broadcast and intensified by the arguments addressed to the English government since 1763. Well might the Declaration refer to them as self-evident, for so

[6] McLaughlin, *Con. Hist.*, 101, note 22.
[7] *Journals of the Cont. Cong.*, V, 626. *Cf.* Herbert Friedenwald, *The Declaration of Independence, an Interpretation and Analysis;* Carl L. Becker, *Declaration of Independence, a Study in the History of Political Ideas.*

they seemed to Americans of that day. They were like axioms which need no demonstration, and were used by Jefferson as the major premise of his syllogism. For a dozen years the British constitution had been invoked in vain, as based upon them, in defense of American rights. Now America fell back upon them as fixed in nature, and above all constitutions.[8]

The second part of the Declaration was the minor premise of the syllogism. It enumerated the acts of the king, individually and in conspiracy "with others," which under Locke's definition made him a tyrant.[9]

The third part was the conclusion reached by this syllogistic style of reasoning: the king, having repeatedly violated the compact existing between him and his American subjects, had forfeited his claim to their allegiance. Consequently (in the words of the Declaration), "these united colonies are, and of right ought to be, free and independent states."

"The most important word in the Declaration," writes Andrew C. McLaughlin, is "deriving." [10] The most liberal Englishmen had been willing to concede certain privileges to Americans by grant of king or Parliament, such as that on which the autonomous rights of Canada and other self-governing dominions of the British empire rest today. However free these commonwealths may be in fact, the theory of parliamentary sovereignty underlies the legislation

[8] Richard Henry Lee declared that Jefferson copied the declaration from Locke. Other critics thought that he drew its "hackneyed" sentiments from James Otis's writings. He himself said: "Otis' pamphlet I never saw, and whether I gathered my ideas from reading or reflection I do not know. I know only that *I turned to neither book nor pamphlet while writing it.* I did not consider it as any part of my charge to invent new ideas altogether, and to offer no sentiment which had ever been expressed before." Letter to James Madison, Aug. 30, 1823.—Ford, *Writings of Jefferson,* X, 268. And again: "Neither aiming at originality of principle or sentiment, nor yet copied from any particular and previous writing, it was intended to be an expression of the American mind. . . ." To Henry Lee, May 8, 1825.—*Ibid.,* 343. These several criticisms and explanations only go to show that the principles of the Declaration were generally accepted in the revolutionary era.

Some recent writers have attempted to show that Jefferson was indebted to early Catholic fathers. See Gaillard Hunt, "Virginia Declaration of Rights and Bellarmine," and Frederick J. Zwierlein, "Jefferson, Jesuits, and the Declaration."

[9] "Tyranny is the exercise of power beyond right."—Locke, Book II, section 199. *Cf.* McLaughlin, *Con. Hist.,* 102, notes 26, 27.

[10] *Ibid.,* 103.

by which their governments were created. In 1776, such a basis did not seem adequate to Americans whose traditions harked back to Locke indeed, but even farther—to the compacts by which many of their ancestors had set up governments for themselves in the early seventeenth century. Nothing less could satisfy them now, in taking their place among the nations of the earth, than governments deriving their powers explicitly from the people over whom they were placed, rather than from any potentate or parliament posing as the possessor of inherent powers.

The Declaration of Independence is sometimes said to rest upon a philosophy which has been rejected by present-day political science. Students of institutions hold that the assumed state of nature is unhistorical. Man has never existed except as a member of some kind of society, and his individual rights have always been defined by the custom or law of his social group rather than by his own will or desire. Such facts appear to put an end to the concept of natural rights as well as to that of the original state of nature. In spite of such reasoning one cannot dismiss the experience of early Americans as meaningless, nor call the setting-up of government by them, on numerous occasions, a fiction. The theory of the compact, moreover, together with the concept of inviolable principles of right lying back of all constitutions, is inextricably woven into the fabric of our constitutional law, and must be reckoned with as an actuality. Political scientists may in time develop a terminology which will expound with greater precision the process by which the American constitutional system came into being, but for some time to come the student of constitutionalism will encounter such words as these, used by the Supreme Court a century after the passage of the Declaration of Independence: "The theory of our governments, State and National, is opposed to the deposit of unlimited power anywhere. . . . There are limitations on such power which grow out of the essential nature of all free governments. Implied reservations of individual rights, without which the social compact would not exist, and which are respected by all governments entitled to the name."[11]

[11] Loan Association *v.* Topeka (1875), 20 Wallace, 655, 663.

What these reserved rights may be, beyond those enumerated in the Constitution, it is evident the court must determine by appealing to some standard beyond and superior to the Constitution itself, and difficult to distinguish from what used to be called natural rights.

FIRST STATE CONSTITUTIONS

The adoption of the Declaration of Independence ended the period of hesitation. From this moment every man was either a Patriot or a Loyalist, and the states one by one followed the lead of Virginia in framing constitutions. By separating from Great Britain the colonists conceived that they were thrown back into a state of nature, and that the powers of government reverted to the people. The powers of the new governments should therefore emanate from the people, by virtue of new social compacts. By the word "constitution" the Americans meant, whether referring to the British government or their own, a body of principles superior to ordinary legislative enactments. The paramountcy of the British constitution had been assumed in all the arguments against the claims of Parliament to unlimited power.

By what process was the will of the people to be ascertained and introduced into a constitution? The idea of a convention had been advanced in England as early as the commotions of the middle of the seventeenth century, in a proposal that an agreement containing the fundamentals of a just government should be drawn up by a delegate body, which agreement when accepted should be above ordinary law and fix the bounds of the legislative power.[12] The procedure of the American states tended to conform to this program. The Virginia instrument was indeed framed and put in force by the provincial convention—the provisional government—without the specific authorization of the people, but step by step a more satisfactory process was evolved, including submission of the draft constitution to the voters for approval.[13] The

[12] McLaughlin, *Con. Hist.*, 109, note 8.

[13] "Jefferson always denied the power of the convention to adopt a permanent frame and intended that his draft, if adopted, should be referred to the people." —C. R. Lingley, "The Transition in Virginia from Colony to Commonwealth," 124. "Resolutions in New York and North Carolina expressed strongly the demand for a popular voice in the approval of constitutions. . . . Popular partici-

general recognition of the superiority of constitutions over statutes is shown by the fact that nine of the twelve constitutions adopted by 1778 "were drafted by legislative bodies especially empowered by their constituents to take such action."[14]   Connecticut and Rhode Island deemed it unnecessary to draw up new instruments. Their charters, although sanctioned by the king, had emanated from the people in the first place, and were essentially constitutions of self-governing republics, so that it was only necessary to proclaim in a formal way that they were henceforth to be the constitutions of free and independent states.

New Hampshire and Massachusetts were the first states to attempt the convention plan.[15]   The revolutionary government of the former adopted a temporary constitution in 1776.   But the people demanded one framed by a specially chosen body; hence the next year the legislature provided for the election of members of a convention, the work of which was to go into effect if ratified by three fourths of the voters.   This constitution was rejected; and members of the assembly of 1780 were elected with the understanding that they were empowered to support a call for a new convention.   The work of this body was also submitted to the people with the proviso of a two-thirds vote for adoption, but it was not finally ratified until it had been twice rejected and twice revised.[16]

pation was less than might have been desired because of the critical condition of affairs and of the necessity for prompt action."—W. F. Dodd, "Constitutional Convention," 425.   See McLaughlin, *Con. Hist.*, 113, and note 18 for sketch of the growth of the practice of submitting constitutions to voters.   Some action approaching submission was taken in Maryland, Pennsylvania, and both Carolinas.   The Massachusetts Constitution of 1778 was the first to be formally submitted.   *Cf.* Nevins, 126–139.

[14] W. F. Dodd, "The First State Constitutional Conventions, 1776–1783," 558. The exceptions were Virginia, South Carolina, and New Jersey.   *Cf.* Nevins, 127–129, for evidence of the slow development of the concept that a constitution, as a fundamental law, should not be drawn by the ordinary legislative body.

[15] The recommendation which Congress made to New Hampshire on Nov. 3, 1775 may have been intended to suggest a convention by the words "call a full and free representation of the people."   Similar language was used in the communications sent soon afterwards to South Carolina and Virginia.—McLaughlin, *Con. Hist.*, 107, notes 2, 3, 4, 5.

[16] Dodd, "First State Con. Conventions," 546–549.   The constitution did not become effective until June, 1784.   Meantime the Massachusetts constitution had been adopted, and the final draft for New Hampshire was "frankly based upon" it.—Nevins, 183–4.

Massachusetts went through a similar experience. In September, 1776, the House of Representatives, acting under the old charter resumed by advice of Congress in 1775, asked for a vote of the towns on the question whether the house and council should be resolved into a convention to draw up a constitution, and whether such draft should be submitted to the towns.[17] The returns showed that some of the towns objected to the proposed method and urged that a special convention be called. Among these was Concord, the town meeting of which passed resolutions declaring that the constitution should not be framed by the legislature, because "the same Body that forms a Constitution have of consequence a power to alter it." For this reason the constitution so framed could afford no security for rights as against the legislature. A "Constitution in its proper Idea intends a system of principals [sic] established to secure the subject in the Possession of, and enjoyment of their Rights & Privileges against any encrouchment [sic] of the Governing Part." [18]

In view of the objections, a committee of the legislature recommended that a convention be called, but the legislature rejected this proposal and a joint resolution again asked the voters to instruct their representatives to act with the council in drawing up the constitution. Apparently satisfied with the response, the two houses resolved themselves into a convention and framed a constitution; but when the result was submitted to the towns it was rejected, partly because of the method employed in framing it, and partly because it lacked a bill of rights.[19]

Again the legislature appealed to the voters, requesting them, if they desired a new constitution, to authorize their representatives

[17] S. E. Morison, "The Vote of Massachusetts on Summoning a Constitutional Convention." *Cf.* Nevins, 175 *et seq.*

[18] R. S. Hoar, "When Concord Invented the Constitutional Convention," *Boston Transcript,* July 3, 1917, cited by McLaughlin, *Con. Hist.,* 111, note 11. Even earlier the town of Norton had suggested a convention. Berkshire County pioneers demanded ratification by popular vote.—Nevins, 175.

[19] Morison, "Vote of Massachusetts," 242–244. Concord cast 111 votes against the constitution and none for it.—Hoar, *loc. cit.* The total vote cast stood 9,972 to 2,083.—Nevins, 177. The most notable demand for a bill of rights came from a local convention of the towns of Essex County. The "Essex Result" declared that "over the class of inalienable rights the supreme power hath no controul, and they ought to be clearly defined and ascertained . . . previous to the ratification of any constitution."—McLaughlin, *Con. Hist.,* 111, and note 13.

to summon a convention.[20] The returns being favorable, the town meetings were notified to elect delegates whose draft of a constitution should become effective when ratified by a two-thirds vote of the free male inhabitants of adult years.[21] The existing government rested upon a much narrower electorate. Under this plan the constitution was adopted in 1780.

The first aim of each of the new constitutions was to provide a frame of government, and it is noteworthy that in each state the model of the preceding colonial government was followed with such changes only as the altered situation required. Jefferson noting this fact remarked that the transition from provincial to state governments was easy, requiring little more than a formal declaration that existing powers should henceforth be vested in such and such new agencies. Connecticut and Rhode Island differed from the other states in requiring practically no changes. Americans showed little or no desire to experiment with new and untried devices; the whole contest with England was inspired by the desire to preserve institutions and laws which they conceived to be endangered by the innovations of the British government. Above all, the Revolution was directed against the external control of internal affairs; it was a fight for home rule as a natural right. But independence meant that governors, councilors, and judges could no longer receive their appointments or powers from the English crown; the authority which the crown had exercised had passed to the people of the respective states, and as they believed that the just powers of governments were delegated by the people, the new instruments of government vested the choice of all officials directly or indirectly in the voters.

To this general statement a partial exception must be made, because in every state there was a contest between the relatively conservative and relatively radical parties as to the extent to which changes should be made in the direction of democracy. The radicals showed somewhat greater inclination towards innovation, and on the whole a greater confidence in the legislative branch of gov-

[20] Morison, 245–246.
[21] H. A. Cushing, "History of the Transition from Provincial to Commonwealth Government in Massachusetts," 227–229.

ernment, especially where, as in Pennsylvania, inequities in apportionment were to be corrected and the suffrage broadened. The constitution of that state, indeed, provided for a unicameral legislature, which, although a continuance of the former provincial practice, was the more significant because the changes in suffrage and apportionment made it the agency of the radical but politically inexperienced element of the population. Relying upon elections to control the law-makers, no executive worthy of the name was instituted. Thus a wholesome check upon the legislature was lost, and within a short time Pennsylvania became an object lesson in the evils attendant upon an unbalanced government in which the legislative branch predominated.

The most considerable changes effected by the new constitutions were in the governor's status. In some of the states that officer became elective by the voters; in others the choice was to be made by the assembly. In general the office was shorn of part of its powers. Choice by the assembly tended to subordinate the executive to the legislature. In some states the governor was surrounded by an executive council, which shared and restricted his responsibility. Quite frequently he was deprived of the veto, which had been a vexatious power when used by the royal governors.

The whole series of limitations placed upon the governor reveals a suspicion of the office born of the continual friction in the royal colonies between the colonial assemblies representing popular interests and the governor representing crown interests. This suspicion was illogical when the governor's authority was no longer derived from the crown. During the early years of independence the people reposed confidence chiefly—too much as experience proved—in the elected members of the law-making body, both because in the old days they had been the champions of colonial rights and because of a tradition of legislative predominance. It took them a generation to learn that this bias was without valid foundation.

Another characteristic of the constitutions is that they were put in the form of written documents. The charters and other instruments under which all of the colonies had been ruled had served virtually as constitutions, and had familiarized the inhabitants with written schemes of government. Americans had been contending that "in every free state the constitution is fixed," as set forth in the Massachusetts Circular Letter and other documents, and had applied the doctrine even to the unwritten English constitution. The idea of fixity was much more readily associated with a written instrument. Finally, the belief that the body politic results from a social compact led naturally to the view that the articles of compact, like business contracts, should be put in writing to avoid misunderstandings and disputes.

The constitutions attempted to fix the powers and duties of each branch of the government. In theory the legislative, executive, and judicial branches were viewed as separate in personnel and functions. The doctrine of the separation of powers was well expressed in the following words of the Massachusetts constitution: "In the government of this commonwealth, the legislative department shall never exercise the executive and judicial powers, or either of them: the executive shall never exercise the legislative and judicial powers, or either of them: the judicial shall never exercise the legislative and executive powers, or either of them: to the end that it may be a government of laws and not of men." In fact, however, the separation was not so sharp. Colonial practice had included certain checks and balances such as the theory of Montesquieu called for—for example, the governor's veto, judicial review by the Privy Council, and, on the popular side, the control of finances—but the first state constitutions did not preserve as complete a mechanism. Experience presently convinced the conservative element that the reaction of American opinion against royal governors and judges had led the framers of the earlier constitutions to err in leaving the legislatures insufficiently checked. The powers of these bodies reflected the fact that they had themselves played the leading part in the framing of the constitutions. Moreover, in spite of the denial of parliamentary supremacy, American courts had imbibed after 1750, under English legal influence (due largely to the fact that increasing numbers of young Americans pursued their studies of law in the mother country), a tradition of legislative supremacy which possessed considerable vitality. The later constitutions, such as those of New Hampshire and Massachusetts, framed by conventions, laid great stress on the separation of powers and the theory of checks and balances, but since they failed to implement the checks upon the legislature, the statements of theory were of little practical effect.[22]

The constitutions of South Carolina, Virginia, New Jersey, New Hampshire, North Carolina, and New York, apparently through sheer oversight, contained no provision for amendment.[23] Those of Maryland, Delaware, and South Carolina might be amended by the legislature but not without special procedures. The Pennsylvania, Georgia, and Massachusetts instruments provided means by which the voters should have the opportunity to decide whether conventions should be called to consider changes.[24]

Following the example of Virginia, eight states adopted bills of rights as parts of their constitutions. Sometimes these were in the form of appended statements; in other cases they were incorporated with the body of the instrument. The Virginia bill of rights is an excellent summary of the contemporary ideas of the principles underlying free governments. The fundamental assumption is that men possessed rights before government was

[22] *Cf.* Locke: "Legislative neither must nor can transfer the power of making laws to anybody else, or place it anywhere but where the people have." Book II, section 142. Radical leaders believed that the legislatures would be sufficiently checked by frequent elections and the bicameral system. The Virginia constitution, although the earliest, was essentially conservative in declaring that "the legislative and executive powers of the state shall be separate and distinct from the judiciary." The Georgia convention likewise asserted that "the legislative, executive, and judiciary departments shall be separate and distinct." Nevertheless Jefferson discerned that in actuality in the Virginia constitution "all the powers of government, legislative, executive, and judiciary, result to the legislative body." "The concentrating these in the same hands," he added, "is precisely the definition of despotic government." The government Americans fought for, he said, was one "in which . . . powers . . . should be so divided and balanced among several bodies . . . as that no one could transcend their legal limits, without being effectually checked and restrained by the others."—Quoted by Nevins, 167–8. A critic of the Pennsylvania constitution similarly objected: "In the Assembly I find the most *unbounded liberty*, and yet no kind of barrier to prevent its degenerating into licentiousness"—a degeneration which soon actually took place.—*Ibid.*, 168. Paper limitations allowed legislatures to be in fact sole judges of their own powers.

It may be remarked here that the theory of checks and balances has been in part superseded, because party government requires harmony between the majority in the legislature and the executive.

[23] Dodd, "First State Con. Conventions," 559.

[24] *Ibid.*, 560–561. *Cf.* Nevins, 168–169.

formed.   As Alexander Hamilton said, the rights of man are written as with a sunbeam in the whole book of human nature. Yet the enumeration in the several bills of rights shows no such complete agreement as this sentiment might imply.   All of the constitutions nevertheless rested, like the Declaration of Independence, upon the doctrines of natural rights, the compact theory, and the derivative nature of the powers of government.

The provisions of the bills of rights were largely the principles of the English common law as expounded by Blackstone, who had brought Coke's *Institutes* up to date by incorporating the results of the English revolutions of 1648 and 1688.[25]   Some of these principles were embodied in written law for the first time in these state constitutions.   For example, although the practice of questioning a prisoner to incriminate him gradually died out in England after 1688, it was prohibited for the first time in the new state constitutions.[26]   A common provision required that procedure involving life, liberty, or property must conform to the law of the land—a provision derived from Magna Carta and anticipating the "due process" clauses of the federal Constitution.   Even Connecticut included a "law of the land" clause in her act of 1776 continuing the charter as a constitution.[27]

The political philosophy of these instruments is nowhere better set forth than in the Massachusetts constitution of 1780: "The body politic is formed by a voluntary Association of individuals; it is a social compact, by which the whole people covenants with each citizen, and each with the whole people, that all shall be governed by certain laws for the common good." [28]   "The people alone have an incontestible, unalienable, and indefeasible right to institute government, and to reform, alter, or totally change the same when their protection, safety, prosperity, and happiness require it." [29]

[25] Hannis Taylor, *The Origin and Growth of the American Constitution*, 361.
[26] *Ibid.*, 362.
[27] *Ibid.*
[28] Preamble. See Francis N. Thorpe, *Federal and State Constitutions*.
[29] Part I, Art. 7.

PERPETUATION OF MIDDLE-CLASS DOMINANCE

The philosophy of the American Revolution is apparently so thoroughly democratic that if one looked no further than these statements of theory one might easily conclude that the cause of democracy had triumphed completely.   But like Locke's language, these professions must not be taken too literally.   The Revolution was indeed a leveling movement; during the war the emigration of the Loyalists deprived the states of approximately one hundred thousand of their most intelligent and public-spirited inhabitants. Leadership fell to men of less training and experience, few of whom, outside of Virginia, belonged to the old aristocracy.   In numbers, the strength of the revolutionary party lay with the plain people, small farmers and tradesmen.   But the conservative groups were too active and influential to permit the theoretical implications of the democratic philosophy to gain their full effect. "The liberty for which they had fought . . . was the sober, intelligent, fearless liberty of our English ancestors," not the rule of "King Numbers." [30]   They were still essentially of the great middle class which had colonized America, overthrown royal autocracy, and given birth to Locke's version of the compact theory,—the class which glorified the thrift and capability of the Protestant landlord and merchant, and thought of the masses as "an inferior sort" incapable of participating intelligently and helpfully in the business of government.[31]

[30] H. C. Lodge, *Life and Letters of George Cabot*, 421.   Cf. Nevins, 139 *et seq.*, for the story of the class struggle over the state constitutions.

[31] The historian Francis Parkman writing of New England described her thus: "Politically, she was free; socially, she suffered from that subtile and searching oppression which the dominant opinion of a free community may exercise over the members who compose it"; "in defiance of the four Gospels, assiduity in pursuit of gain was promoted to the rank of a duty, and thrift and godliness were linked in equivocal wedlock."—*Pioneers of New France*, quoted by Michael Kraus, *History of American History*, 279.

The persistence of middle-class philosophy is illustrated by the views expressed by another American historian, the New Englander Richard Hildreth, who, writing about the middle of the nineteenth century, held that the merchants, large landowners, lawyers, ministers, and capitalists formed a natural aristocracy, with whom control rested "in virtue of that inherent power which superior wealth, knowledge and social position everywhere carry with them, and which no formal declaration of equality can ever take away."—*History of the United States*, III, 347.   Strangely enough, in a later work (*Theory of Politics*, New York, 1853), Hildreth expounds views which approximate those of Karl Marx.

In America, this offshoot of the English middle class, since in the New World there was no titled nobility, became the upper class or "aristocracy."

While Otis and Adams disseminated Locke's philosophy and Jefferson borrowed it in the Declaration of Independence, the frontier, finding a spokesman in Jefferson, offered a new application of the Englishman's thought in the "squatter sovereignty" doctrine: the free inhabitants of the British dominions who colonized America "possessed a right which nature has given to all men, of departing from the country in which chance, not choice, has placed them; of going in quest of new habitations, and of there establishing new societies, under such laws and regulations as to them shall seem most likely to promote public happiness." [32]

As the Revolution approached, the arguments advanced concerning colonial rights were seen to be no more applicable to the British system of domination than to that maintained by the provincial aristocracies. The revolutionary philosophy fell in exactly with the ideas of the frontier democracy, and the movement for independence became in no small part identified with a democratic movement.[33] The frontier farmers found natural allies in the hitherto disfranchised classes in the coast towns, who suddenly became of weight politically through the constant resort to mass meetings and other extra-legal organs representing the whole people. The Second Continental Congress itself was made up in considerable part of delegates chosen by irregular popular bodies, and thus reflected the liberal trend of the moment. In turn the resolution of May 15, 1776, recommending that the states adopt "such government as shall, in the opinion of the representatives of the people, best conduce to the happiness and safety of their constituents," went from the Congress to "assemblies and conventions" in the several states, which were often composed in part of persons

[32] "A Summary View," Ford, *Writings of Jefferson*, I, 427. Note the bearing of Jefferson's assertion upon the question of the force of English law in the colonies.

[33] "With the intensive preaching of majority rule and the emphasis placed on the individual . . . the arguments which had been used against English misrule were turned against minority control and misgovernment."—C. H. Lincoln, *The Revolutionary Movement in Pennsylvania, 1760–1776*, 13–14.

who had been excluded from political life under the colonial governments.[34]

Conditions favored the rise of new leaders who relied upon the people in carrying forward the patriot cause; aristocrats ceased to attend meetings where they were "sure to be outvoted by men of the lowest order"; the Pendletons and Randolphs and Galloways doubted whether insurgent radicalism was not a graver danger than British rule.[35] In Pennsylvania the reluctance of the moderates like Dickinson, Morris, and Wilson to resort to extreme measures against England allowed control to pass into the hands of the radicals who led the Scotch-Irish and German democracy of the inland counties and the Philadelphia proletariat. The moderates thus lost the opportunity to give form to the first state constitution; drawn up instead by the radical leaders and supported by solid delegations from the western counties, it was one of the most democratic constitutions of the period.[36]

In South Carolina the revolutionary movement was inaugurated at Charleston by means of mass meetings composed largely of those who had been non-voters. A general committee chosen by a mass meeting summoned the provincial congress of 1775, because it felt the need of the support of a body representing the entire colony. In this body the back country as such was allowed representation for the first time.[37] In New York and elsewhere, as in South Carolina, the unfranchised element exerted considerable influence in the early stages of the Revolution, while extra-legal machinery was being made use of to perfect the patriot organization.[38]

Thus the revolutionary movement promised for a time to become as well a great forward movement towards democracy in government and equal rights for all the people. But bills of rights,

[34] *Journals of the Cont. Cong.*, IV, 342, 358. *Cf.* the recommendations in the fall of 1775 to New Hampshire, South Carolina, *et al.*, to "call a full and free representation of the people." See *ante*, note 15. The methods by which the delegates to the First Continental Congress were chosen are briefly summarized by McLaughlin, *Con. Hist.*, 83, note 3.

[35] Carl L. Becker, *Beginnings of the American People*, 245.

[36] Lincoln, *Revolutionary Movement*, 277 *et seq.*

[37] William A. Schaper, "Sectionalism and Representation in South Carolina," 357–359.

[38] Carl L. Becker, *The History of Political Parties in the Province of New York, 1760–1776*, 275 *et passim*.

declarations that the people are sovereign, and expositions of the compact theory cannot hide the fact that while the power which the crown had held had passed to the assemblies, those bodies represented constituencies in many states not greatly changed by extensions of the franchise or reforms in the apportionment of representation. Although the new constitutions laid great stress upon democratic theory, the working systems which they provided did not fulfill the promise of the theoretical statements. In Virginia, for example, while the upper house became elective the right of suffrage in the choice of members of both houses remained as before; there was no provision for uniformity in the size of the county units of representation, nor for reapportionment, extension of the suffrage, choice of local officials by election, or even for amendment.[39] A short time after the close of the Revolution Jefferson pointed out that under the apportionment of 1780 nineteen thousand men living below the falls of the rivers "give law to upwards of thirty thousand living in" the upper parts of the state, "and appoint all their chief officers, executive and judiciary."[40]

In New Jersey the right to vote had been limited to freeholders before the Revolution, while the new constitution granted it to all inhabitants who were "worth fifty pounds proclamation money."[41] In South Carolina, where the recognition of the interior in the provincial congress of 1775 gave some promise of equal rights, only forty members in a total of 184 were allowed to the up-country,

[39] Cf. Jefferson's draft, which provided for a broad suffrage, reapportionment, amendment and religious liberty.—Ford, Writings of Jefferson, II, 7. See discussion by P. L. Ford, "Jefferson's Constitution for Virginia," and D. R. Anderson, "Jefferson and the Virginia Constitution."

[40] Writings, III, 223. Just after the adoption of the state constitution of 1776 which Jefferson criticized in the words quoted in the text, Richard Henry Lee compared the colonial government which it replaced with the corrupt class government of England. "However imperfect the English plan was," he wrote, "yet our late government in Virginia was infinitely worse. With us two thirds of the legislature, and all the executive and judiciary powers were in the same hands [hands of the same class]—in truth it was very near a tyranny, altho' the mildness with which it was executed under Whig direction, made the evil little felt."—James C. Ballagh, ed., The Letters of Richard Henry Lee, quoted by Nevins, 121. Under the constitution of 1776 each county sent two members to the legislature as in colonial times, yet the first federal census gave Berkeley County, west of the Blue Ridge, 19,713 inhabitants, while Elizabeth City County, in the tidewater, had but 3,450.—Ibid., 133.

[41] Article IV. See Thorpe, Constitutions.

although it had the majority of the white population; and the planters managed the elections so skilfully that "influential gentlemen" of English blood were chosen in every instance, no Scotch-Irish or German name appearing on the list of delegates.[42]   The temporary constitution of 1776 allowed eighteen additional members to the upland, but the suffrage requirement remained unchanged, except for the *addition* that the requisite amount of property must be possessed debt-free.   Two years later the property restrictions were slightly reduced, and, probably under the influence of current political philosophy, a promise was given that a new apportionment should be made periodically, a promise the fulfillment of which was long delayed.[43]

The contrast between theory and practice is nowhere better shown than by the much vaunted Massachusetts constitution of 1780.   After attributing all power to the people, the right to vote was confined to owners of a freehold of the annual value of three pounds, or other estate worth sixty pounds—an actual increase of about fifty per cent in the property qualification for the suffrage over the rule in the colonial period.[44]

The story of the preservation of conservative rule in Massachusetts under a constitution bearing so many aspects of a genuine charter of democracy is one which illuminates the whole history of the class contest of that era.   The formation of the Massachusetts constitution of 1780 has been called the achievement "which more nearly than any other single thing embraced the significance of the American Revolution," "because that constitution rested upon the fully developed convention, the greatest institution of government which America produced, the institution which answered, in itself, the problem of how men could make governments of their own free will."[45]   "It conclusively ended the struggle, centuries old, of enmity between government and the people; the old enemy, government, was made the servant of the politically-organized people."[46]

[42] Schaper, "Sectionalism," 357–359. The apportionment in Georgia was of the same inequitable type.—U. B. Phillips, *Georgia and State Rights*, 88, 89.

[43] Schaper, 365, 367–369. Cf. Nevins, 173–175.

[44] Part I, Art. 7. Thorpe, *Constitutions*.

[45] A. C. McLaughlin, "American History and American Democracy," 264.

[46] A. C. McLaughlin, *Con. Hist.*, 112.

This was, indeed, the theory of that constitution. The apparent reluctance of the Massachusetts legislature to call a convention to frame the constitution has been noted already. In submitting its draft to the towns, however, the convention seemed genuinely desirous of ascertaining the actual sentiment of citizens, for it requested a thorough discussion, clause by clause, not only by voters but by all adult white males, and invited a clear statement of objections from each town to any clause which proved unacceptable to the majority. If it appeared that every part was favored by a two-thirds majority in the towns, the convention requested authority to declare the instrument in force; or, lacking the required two-thirds, to alter the draft to accord with the popular will and then to proclaim it operative.

The common procedure in the towns was, first to read the draft, and then to appoint a committee to go over it and suggest changes in objectionable articles. This committee was to report its findings to a subsequent town meeting for final action. The draft was before the towns for fourteen weeks, weeks which were perhaps the darkest of the entire war period. This fact may help to account for the small proportion of the voters who attended the meetings, although another reason was advanced by opponents. The number which attended is estimated at about sixteen thousand, that is, only about one fifth of the total number of qualified voters, and far less than that proportion of the adult white males.[47] Those who did attend showed exceptional intelligence, for among the changes suggested were those which experience proved to be most needed, notwithstanding the fact that the draft was the work of such leaders as John and Samuel Adams, James Bowdoin, Theophilus Parsons, John Lowell, George Cabot, and Robert Treat Paine.[48]

After all this show of liberality, the adjourned session of the convention, when it met to canvass the returns from the towns, adopted "such principles of counting that a two-thirds majority for every article was assured in advance."[49] Objections were so dealt with

[47] S. E. Morison, "The Struggle over the Adoption of the Constitution of Massachusetts, 1780," 366; Arthur Lord, "Some Objections Made to the Massachusetts State Constitution, 1780," 55.
[48] Morison, "Struggle," 401. The chief share in framing the draft fell to John Adams.—Nevins, 179.
[49] Morison, "Struggle," 354.

that it may be doubted whether the constitution was legally ratified.[50]   Since many of the objections were directed against the
qualifications imposed upon the suffrage and the plan of apportioning representation, which favored the seaboard communities and
the well-to-do class, it appears that the methods pursued spelled
after all substantially "the victory of property over democracy." [51]

Considerable dissatisfaction followed the promulgation of the
instrument.   There was even talk of setting it aside.[52]   The reasons
for so drastic a proposal are revealed in a communication sent by
Middleboro to Plymouth, which asserted that not enough copies
of the constitution had been printed and not enough time allowed
for the townsmen to acquaint themselves with its provisions.   The
small number participating in the voting was attributed to reluctance to act hastily.   Objections were too many to enumerate, but
the plan it was alleged, would introduce "as Many Evils as Could
have Been feared from the British power."   The men of Plymouth
were appealed to "to use your utmost influence . . . in over-
throwing the said constitution . . . as a huge monster whose un-
couth and unhallowed Strides may Crush the people to a State of
abject Slavery. . . ."   The method suggested is "To Refuse To
have any Town Meeting or do any thing else in Consequence of
said frame of government." [53]

John Jay, who had a main share in the drafting of the fundamental law of New York, was of much the same mind as the
framers of the Massachusetts constitution.   The preamble of the
constitution for New York recited that "all power whatever in
the state hath reverted to the people thereof," from whom alone,
according to section one, authority is derived; but the freehold
qualifications for voting and office-holding were retained, for it
was "a favorite maxim with Mr. Jay, that those who own the
country ought to govern it." [54]   There was no provision for amend-

---

[50] *Ibid.*

[51] *Ibid.*, 401.   The criticism prepared by Joseph Hawley for Northampton is a
notable exposition of the democratic view.   See Mary Catherine Clune, "Joseph
Hawley's Criticism of the Constitution."

[52] Lord, "Some Objections."

[53] *Ibid.*, 59.

[54] William Jay, *Life of John Jay*, I, 70.   The story of the framing of the New
York constitution is told by Nevins, 158–164.   "The restriction of the electorate

ment, and Jay congratulated himself that the conservatives had succeeded in providing a "measurably centralized and measurably aristocratic" government.[55]

Even in Pennsylvania, following the democratic triumph of 1776, the conservatives carried on a campaign for constitutional revision so successfully that a modified constitution was adopted in 1790.[56] By 1784 the upland party in South Carolina was pressing for a re-apportionment as promised by the constitution of 1778. They succeeded in bringing about the meeting of a convention in which they urged the doctrines of Locke and the French philosophers in support of their demand for equitable representation; but the low country was represented on the same basis as in the existing legis-lature, and was consequently able to prevent any real reform in the new constitution of 1790.[57] Not until 1808, when the expansion of the plantation economy had almost obliterated the old geographico-economic sectionalism within the state, did the low-country party agree to surrender control of the lower house to the up-country majority, which had by that time ceased to be a menace.[58] A solu-tion was not so easily reached in Virginia; in fact, the inharmonious eastern and western portions of that state remained unequally yoked together until the Civil War. In New York, Massachusetts, and elsewhere in the East, the advent of manhood suffrage was de-layed until well along in the nineteenth century.[59]

Thus taking the country as a whole, despite the upward surge of democracy incident to the Revolution, the establishment of the constitutions left the old ruling class in substantial control in most of the states. Four states retained a freehold qualification for the

meant that none but men of large property were likely to be placed in any of the higher positions. In too large a degree the government was made of, by, and for the landholders."—*Ibid.*, 164. *Cf.* Maryland, where "the whole arrange-ment was most conservative, making it certain that the upper house would repre-sent, the wealth, position, and caution of the State."—*Ibid.*, 158.

[55] Becker, *Political Parties*, 275, 276, *et passim.* The phrase is Becker's.
[56] Lincoln, 287. *Cf.* the story of the contest as told by Nevins, 184–200. See also S. B. Harding, "Party Struggles over the First Pennsylvania Constitution."
[57] Schaper, 369–379. *Cf.* similar contest and results in Georgia.—Nevins, 202–204. In neither state was the new constitution submitted to the voters for ratifica-tion.
[58] Schaper, 407–437.
[59] John B. McMaster, *History of the People of the United States*, V, 373–394.

franchise; the others required possession of a substantial amount of personal property. The Carolinas and New Jersey required members of the legislature to be Protestants; Delaware demanded that they be Trinitarians, and Pennsylvania that they profess faith in the inspiration of the Bible. Massachusetts and Maryland excluded non-Christians from all offices.

The Revolution nevertheless released the leaven of democracy, and within another half-century its workings were to bring about equality of political privileges for all white men. The immediate effects of the democratic doctrines were not altogether happy. The philosophy of popular government and the violent overthrow of the old system of British rule weakened the bonds of society and lessened the respect felt for all governmental authority. The disorders of the years following independence may be in considerable degree ascribed to this cause. Turbulence led, in turn, to a movement of the propertied class to strengthen its control by bringing about a union of the states under a conservative constitution.

VIII

GROWTH OF UNION

EARLY PLANS

WHEN on June 7, 1776, Richard Henry Lee moved the resolution in favor of a declaration of independence he offered a second looking toward a permanent confederation. The successful prosecution of the war required united action and it was evident that the powers of Congress should be clearly defined. There was also a growing sense of a permanent community of interests which required some sort of general government. Many of the problems of peace could be dealt with for the good of all only by such a government. Thus with the prospect of independence "the problem of imperial organization crossed the ocean."[1] The perception of common interests was of course not new. Despite rivalries over boundaries and other questions, the colonies had long before learned to cooperate at times for one purpose or other. Virginia and Maryland had on several occasions even in the seventeenth century made agreements to limit the production of tobacco in order to enhance the price. At other times they had engaged in joint campaigns against the Indians, and similar actions had marked the relations of other colonies.

The most important experiment in union during the seventeenth century was the New England Confederation, formed in 1643 by Massachusetts, Plymouth, Connecticut, and New Haven. These colonies were so similar in their institutional life that before 1640 synods representing the clergy of all four were held to promote a uniform policy in church affairs. The Pequot War of the 1630's had menaced all with the same danger, and a joint campaign had shown the advantages of cooperative defense. Some disputes over boundaries and other questions had brought out also the need of an organization which could deal with matters involving conflicting interests of two or more colonies.

[1] McLaughlin, *Con. Hist.*, 118.

The outcome was a confederation with a Board of Commissioners, consisting of two men from each colony, to administer the
joint business. The vote of six commissioners was required for a
decision on any matter falling within the scope of the board's
powers. These powers included the making of war and peace, the
promotion of justice between the member colonies, and the rendi-
tion of fugitive servants and criminals. Representation on the
board being equal, the provision that contributions of men and
money for such joint undertakings as war were to be made by the
colonies in proportion to population, proved to be a fatal weakness
in the plan. As Massachusetts exceeded in population the other
three members combined, her obligations were so disproportionate
to her vote that she refused on several occasions to be bound by
the decision of the commissioners of her three associates.

At that early time the Chesapeake Bay colonies were too distant
to be thought of as possible members. Even Rhode Island, because
she pursued a different course in matters of religion, was denied
admittance. The experiment is nevertheless important because it
shows the tendency of colonies to unite as they became conscious
of the advantage of acting together. The articles of confederation
were drawn up in writing, and definitely enumerated the powers
which were to be exercised by the commissioners, thus providing
a fixed scheme of distributed powers. In both of these ways the
articles foreshadowed the Constitution of the United States. But
since the commissioners lacked authority to enforce their decision,
the system constituted in truth an alliance rather than a government.[2]

Several intercolonial congresses were held during the French
and Indian wars to plan measures against the common enemies.
These congresses were conventions of delegates, and aimed at
temporary cooperation, not permanent union; but they promoted
the growth of a common feeling and led to numerous proposals
of permanent association. Some of the plans were the work of
progressive Americans, and some came from Englishmen who were
interested mainly in simplifying the task of administering the navi-

[2] The text of the Articles of the New England Confederation may be found
conveniently in MacDonald, *Select Charters*, 94–101.

gation acts and military affairs.[3]   The culmination of this line of thinking in the colonial period was reached in the Albany Congress of 1754, called by the British government to cement friendship with the Iroquois and to concert action against the French in case of a new war.   Of this some account has already been given.

Although the Massachusetts delegation at Albany was authorized to "enter into articles of union and confederation for the general defence of his Majesty's subjects and interests in North America, as well in time of peace as of war," there was not much evidence of a widespread interest in a permanent union.   No other delegation had instructions on the point, although several individuals had formulated plans before arriving at Albany.   Among these was Franklin, of the Pennsylvania delegation.

Franklin had been for some time an advocate of union, and was probably the author of the plea which had appeared in the *Pennsylvania Gazette* in May, 1754, accompanied by a woodcut showing a snake in severed parts, each marked with the initial of a colony, and carrying the legend "Join or Die."   In 1751, referring to the Iroquois League, he had written that "it would be a very strange Thing if *Six Nations* of ignorant Savages should be capable of forming a Scheme for such an Union, and be able to execute it in such a Manner, as that it has subsisted Ages, and appears indissoluble; and yet that a like Union should be impracticable for ten or a Dozen *English* Colonies, to whom it is more necessary, and must be more advantageous; and who cannot be supposed to want an equal Understanding of their Interest." [4]

Even at the time when this letter was written he had outlined his ideas of the type of union needed by the colonies.   "Were there a

[3] On the early plans of union see *American History Leaflet*, No. 14; Bigelow, *Works of Franklin*, I, 243; II, 344, 350–375; Richard Frothingham, *Rise of the Republic*, 83–93, 107–121; Justin Winsor, ed., *Narrative and Critical History of America*, V, 611.

[4] Letter to James Parker, March 20, 1750/1, in A. H. Smyth, ed., *Writings of Benjamin Franklin*, III, 40–46.   It is said that at a conference held at Lancaster, Pa., in 1744, between chiefs of the Iroquois and delegates from Virginia, Maryland, and Pennsylvania, Canassatego, an Onondaga, urged the colonists to unite on the Indian model.   While Franklin's letter shows that the Iroquois union had attracted his attention, the New England Confederation was probably a more influential factor in his thinking.   For other possible sources of Franklin's ideas concerning union, see John B. McMaster, *Benjamin Franklin as a Man of Letters*, 161.

general Council form'd by all the Colonies, and a general Governor appointed by the Crown to preside in that Council, or in some manner to concur with and confirm their Acts, and take Care of the Execution, every Thing relating to Indian Affairs and the Defence of the Colonies, might be properly put under their management. Each Colony should be represented by as many members as it pays Sums of   Hundred Pounds into the common Treasury for the common Expence; which Treasury would perhaps be best and most equitably supply'd by an equal Excise on strong Liquors in all the Colonies, the Produce never to be apply'd to the private Use of any Colony, but to the general Service." [5]

Franklin himself tells the story of the framing of the Albany Plan. "In our way thither, I projected and drew a plan for the union of all the colonies under one government, so far as might be necessary for defense, and other important general purposes. As we pass'd thro' New York, I had there shown my project to Mr. James Alexander and Mr. Kennedy, two gentlemen of great knowledge in public affairs and, being fortified by their approbation I ventur'd to lay it before the Congress. It then appeared that several of the commissioners had form'd plans of the same kind. A previous question was taken whether a union should be established, which pass'd in the affirmative unanimously. A committee was then appointed, one member from each colony, to consider the several plans and report. Mine happen'd to be preferr'd, and, with a few amendments, was accordingly reported." [6]

The Albany Plan was an elaboration of a briefer form which Franklin had labelled "Short Hints." Analysis of the completed document shows the following features:

By act of Parliament "one general government" should be created in America, "under which . . . each colony may retain its present constitution" except as modified by the act of union;

A President General should be appointed by the crown, and a

[5] Letter to Parker. *Cf.* Hamilton's revenue system. The letter also discusses the feasibility of managing the Indian trade by establishing a system of government trading houses, thus anticipating an experiment which the federal government actually tried later. The letter contains other interesting matter, such as a discussion of the problem of German immigration.

[6] Bigelow, *Works of Franklin*, I, 243. *Cf.* Lois K. Mathews, "Franklin's Plan for a Colonial Union, 1750–1775."

Grand Council should be chosen by the assemblies of the several colonies, roughly in proportion to the money contribution of each (two to seven from each);

This body should exercise power over certain specified matters, *viz.*, (1) Indian relations—treaties, war and peace, trade, land purchases; (2) the making of new settlements and "laws for regulating and governing them till the crown shall think fit to form them into particular governments"; (3) raising and paying soldiers, building forts, equipping vessels; (4) the making of laws, the laying and levying of taxes, and the appointing of subordinate officers "for these purposes." [7]

While the authority of this proposed general government would have been derived from the act of Parliament instead of from the people, the plan anticipates the Constitution of the United States still more clearly than does the New England Confederation. It also reveals ideas current at the time of the Albany Congress. The main characteristic of the project is the attempt to distribute powers between the general government and the local governments, reserving the internal police control to the latter, and listing those matters of general police which should be placed in the hands of the Grand Council. This list is interesting, because, so far as it goes, it includes powers which were later assigned to the government of the United States. The plan embraces the ideas of a written constitution, fixity of the scheme of assignment of powers, and the limited authority of governments. It is possible that it was also intended to give to the general government the power to levy the necessary taxes for the performance of its functions, without the action of the colonial governments as intermediary agents, and to empower the courts to enforce the measures taken by the council. This interpretation is borne out by an elaboration of the project prepared by Governor Hutchinson soon after the close of the congress. According to this, tax collectors were to be appointed (by the Grand Council?) in each colony, "and all laws and orders for enforcing the payment thereof in any and every colony . . . shall be as fully and effectively observed and executed as if they

---

[7] Text in *Am. Hist. Leaflet*, No. 14. See contemporary discussion in Bigelow, *Works of Franklin*, II, 349 *et seq.*, III, 208.

had been the laws of that particular colony where any offence shall be committed, and all offences against such laws and orders shall be tried and determined accordingly." [8] Here appears the concept of enactments by a central government which have the force of law throughout the union, with the power and duty of enforcement vested in the courts, the Privy Council in England presumably serving as a supreme court. If these implications are correct, the Albany Plan was truly the embryo of "a complete Federal system." [9]

It is interesting to find that the Albany Plan was regarded as the germ of the Constitution by a writer who sent a copy of the earlier document to the *American Museum* in October, 1788. In the accompanying letter he expressed surprise that "it has lain dormant and unnoticed among all the publications on the subject of the new government. As the outlines of the plan bear so strong a resemblance to the present system it will . . . tend to convince the wavering, that the new constitution is not the fabrication of the moment, but urged upwards of thirty years ago by that great man [Franklin]." [10]

The various suggestions offered during the troublous years between 1765 and 1774 looking to some plan of imperial organization acceptable to both England and the colonies have already been discussed. The Galloway Plan was the most notable of all the proposals advanced in the hope of establishing the relations between colonies and mother country on a definite and permanent basis. It is equally significant as a link in the chain of events which at last united the American commonwealths in a permanent union. Galloway's plan, with slight changes, would have served to confederate the colonies under a scheme of distributed powers.

FORMATION OF THE ARTICLES OF CONFEDERATION

The radicals having defeated Galloway's efforts, the way was open for Franklin to make another proposal, which he presented to the Second Continental Congress on July 21, 1775, twenty-one years after his memorable work at Albany. Connections with

[8] Quoted by Rayner Kelsey, "The Originator of the Federal Idea."
[9] *Ibid.*
[10] Letter signed "A true Patriot and Federalist," quoted by Kelsey.

England having been interrupted by the outbreak of hostilities, Franklin's new plan differed from Galloway's in omitting all reference to relations with the mother country except the statement that the union was to last until a reconciliation took place, or that failing, to be perpetual. In preparing it he drew upon the Albany Plan, and even recurred to the New England Confederation.[11] It was naturally more elaborate than any previous proposal. Analysis shows the following features:

Purpose: to provide for the "common Defence . . . and general Welfare." Each colony to retain as much as it thinks fit of its own laws.

Form of government: A Congress of Delegates, elected annually, to meet in each colony in turn. Each delegate to have one vote.

An Executive Council of twelve members, chosen by the Congress, for three-year terms, divided into three groups, one group retiring each year. This Council to act in the recess of Congress.

Powers: (1) Peace and war; (2) foreign relations: sending and receiving ambassadors and entering into alliances; (3) settling disputes between colonies; (4) planting of new colonies; (5) making ordinances for the general welfare in matters which particular assemblies are not competent to deal with, *viz.:* a) general commerce; b) general currency; c) establishment of post offices; d) regulation of common forces; e) appointment of general civil and military officers; f) regulation of Indian affairs.

Apportionment: "Expenses of the union to be apportioned among the colonies according to their respective numbers of male polls between 16 and 60 years of age, each colony's share to be levied by its own legislature." Each colony to be allowed one delegate and vote in Congress for every 5,000 polls.

Amendment: Changes to be proposed by the Congress and to be in force when accepted by the assemblies of a majority of the states.[12]

No action was taken on Franklin's proposal at the time of its presentation, but Lee's resolution of the following June brought

[11] Mathews, "Franklin's Plan."
[12] Text in *Am. Hist. Leaflet*, No. 20, pp. 3–7.

the matter again before Congress. When that body decided to appoint a committee to draft a Declaration of Independence, it resolved also that there should be another "to prepare and digest the form of a confederation to be entered into between these colonies." The committee was chosen on June 12, with John Dickinson as chairman. The author of the Farmer's Letters had removed from Pennsylvania and was now a delegate from Delaware. Dickinson's committee had before it the draft which Franklin had prepared the previous summer, and using it as the basis of its work, was ready with a report on July 12.[13] The series of documents which culminated in the Articles of Confederation thus runs back with unbroken continuity to the Albany Plan.

Dickinson's draft was discussed in committee of the whole and reported back to Congress on August 20 with certain amendments. Debate proceeded slowly, for matters relating to the carrying on of the war claimed right of way, and it was not until the autumn of 1777 (November 7), some sixteen months after the presentation of the report, that a final vote was reached, under the impulse of the enthusiasm aroused by Burgoyne's surrender. Further delay occurred when the Articles were submitted to the states for approval by the legislatures, so that it was not until 1781 that they finally went into effect.

Meantime the task of managing the war and conducting other matters of general business fell upon the Continental Congress, which met in session after session between May, 1775, and March, 1781, when the Articles at last became operative. The legal status of this body has been a subject of much discussion by statesmen, historians, and students of government. Down to the Civil War the tendency in the North was to overrate its powers, as a means of combatting the arguments of southerners who held to the theory that the states continued to be sovereign even under the Constitution. The present tendency is to regard the Second Continental Congress as the successor of the Stamp Act and First Continental congresses in the work of uniting public sentiment in temporary crises. This object occasioned its first meeting, but the fact that war had begun thrust upon it a more difficult and continuous task

[13] Draft in *ibid.*, 8–16.

than the earlier bodies had faced, and from necessity it became the organ of common action or cooperation.

Since it raised and directed armies, procured the means of maintaining them, sent and received diplomatic agents, and entered into treaties with foreign countries, it performed the functions of a provisional or *de facto* government. Whether it possessed the legal authority to do what it did is perhaps a theoretical rather than a practical question. The delegates to the first session were chosen by revolutionary bodies in the states. After the organization of regular state governments the delegates were appointed by the state assemblies and were subject to their instructions. If we speak in terms of the compact theory, the people of the states did not conceive that they had surrendered any part of their rights to the Continental Congress; it was "hardly more than a meeting of the agents appointed by the state governments to make the action of the thirteen states uniform."[14] The indispensable necessity of union to meet the common danger gave its measures such force as they possessed, and whenever the people of any state found it necessary to choose between obedience to Congress and to the state government they obeyed the latter.[15] Also no state government felt itself bound by the determinations of Congress if they ran counter to its judgment. The effectiveness of congressional measures depended upon the voluntary, not obligatory, support of the states.[16]

The indefiniteness of such a union was comparable to the undefined relations of the colonies with England, and was not likely to be satisfactory as the prospect of independence drew near; hence

[14] C. H. Van Tyne, *The American Revolution*, 179–180.

[15] *Ibid.*

[16] In 1795 the New Hampshire legislature, remonstrating against the decision of the Supreme Court in the case of Penhallow *et al. v.* Doane's Administrators (3 Dallas 54), gave the following opinion on the powers of the Continental Congress previous to the adoption of the Articles of Confederation: Congress before 1781 "was merely an advisory body, chosen by the several States to consult upon measures for the general good of the whole; that the adoption of measures recommended by them was entirely in the breast of the several States or their Legislatures; that no measure could be carried into effect in any State without its agreement thereto; that the subsequent powers of Congress entirely depended upon the express grants of the State Legislatures; . . . and that the Confederation was the first act binding upon the States. . . ." Quoted by H. V. Ames, *State Documents on Federal Relations, 1789–1861*, 13.

the belief that Articles of Confederation should be carefully formulated, reduced to writing, and agreed upon. The object of
Franklin, and of Dickinson in his turn, was to decide what interests
were of common concern, and therefore suitable to be intrusted to
the care of the general government. Franklin's draft had added
some items to the list in the Albany Plan, and Dickinson's committee added a few more. As to the frame of government, nothing
more seemed feasible than to give responsibility for these common
concerns to such a body as the existing Congress, although Franklin
desired to introduce proportional representation. As a result of
the circumstances under which the Continental Congress had first
assembled, the states enjoyed equal status, each delegation casting
one vote. It had been proposed in the First Continental Congress
"to establish an equitable representation according to the respective
importance of each Colony," but the motion had been lost and the
equal vote decided upon, "the Congress not being possess'd of, or
at present able to procure proper material for ascertaining the importance of each Colony." [17] Objection was made to the decision,
and an "entry was made on the journals to prevent its being drawn
into a precedent." [18] Franklin's draft of 1775 had proposed to ap-
portion the delegates among the states according to their populations, but Dickinson, as the representative of one of the small states,
struck out this provision and inserted in his draft one continuing
equality of representation and suffrage.

Dickinson's draft did not assert that the states were sovereign.
As reported by the committee of the whole on August 20, his plan
declared that "Each State reserves to itself the sole and exclusive
regulation and government of its internal police, in all matters that
shall not interfere with the Articles of the Confederation." As the
debate proceeded, however, interstate and intersectional jealousies
were manifested which hampered agreement and led eventually to
a change of phraseology. In a letter to John Jay, written before
the plan was reported, Edward Rutledge of South Carolina char-
acterized the project as cutting too deeply into the powers of the

[17] *Journals of the Cont. Cong.*, I, 25.
[18] *Ibid.* Communication of the Connecticut delegation to Governor Trumbull,
October 10.

states. "The Idea of destroying all Provincial Distinctions and making everything of the most minute kind bend to what they call the good of the whole, is in other Terms to say that these [southern] colonies must be subject to the Government of the Eastern Provinces. . . . I am resolved to vest the Congress with no more Power than that is absolutely necessary. . . ." [19]

Writing again just before the committee of the whole reported, Rutledge said: "We have done nothing with the Confederation for some Days, and it is of little Consequence if we never see it again; for we have made such a Devil of it already that the Colonies can never agree to it." [20] In addition to his former reasons for dissatisfaction, he is evidently irritated by the constant interruption of debate, and thinks that the states would do well to choose what he calls a "special Congress" (constitutional convention) for consideration of a plan of union. "We might then stand some Chance of a Confederation, at present we stand none at all." [21]

After the report of the committee of the whole in August, 1776, debate lagged until the spring of 1777. It was resumed in April. Apparently feeling the pressing necessity of reaching a determination, Congress resolved to devote two days per week to the discussion until a conclusion was reached. It was now, apparently, that the statement was adopted which became Article II of the completed plan: "Each State retains its sovereignty, freedom, and independence, and every power, jurisdiction and right, which is not by this confederation expressly delegated to the United States in Congress assembled." Thomas Burke of North Carolina proposed the substitution of this paragraph for the original one by Dickinson, because it seemed to him that the phrasing of the original did not conform to what the states expected, but made it possible for Congress to "explain away every right belonging to the States and to make their own power as unlimited as they please." [22] After some hesitation Burke's motion was seconded by South Carolina. The chief opposition was voiced by James Wilson of Pennsylvania

[19] June 29, 1776. Edmund C. Burnett, ed., *Letters of Members of the Continental Congress*, I, 517–518.
[20] To Robert Livingston.—*Ibid.*, II, 56.
[21] *Ibid.*
[22] Letter to the Governor of North Carolina, April 29, 1777, *ibid.*, II, 345–346.

and Richard Henry Lee of Virginia. On the motion the vote stood eleven for, Virginia opposed, New Hampshire divided.[23]

Even with this change progress was difficult. As Burke wrote in May, the Congress was perplexed by the problem of "how to secure to each State its separate independence, and give to each its proper weight in the public councils. So unequaled [sic] as the States are, it will be nearly impossible to effect this; and after all it is far from improbable that the only confederation will be a defensive Alliance." [24]

The difficulty to which he referred was caused chiefly by the provisions concerning representation and the apportionment of contributions for the general treasury. Although Dickinson had dropped Franklin's provision for proportional representation, his draft called for contributions to the common treasury in proportion to population, excluding from the enumeration untaxed Indians. To this clause concerning contributions Chase of Maryland proposed an amendment making white population the basis. Property, he said, was the proper basis for estimating ability to contribute, but it was difficult to get at, and population was a "tolerably good criterion of property." Negroes, however, were property, like cattle, and should not be counted. John Adams in reply urged that slaves produced as much wealth as free laborers, and should therefore be counted if white laborers in the North were enumerated. Harrison of Virginia, maintaining that slaves were less productive than free men, suggested that two should be counted as the equivalent of one free man. James Wilson urged that the entire population was the proper basis, as otherwise the South would reap all the benefit and the North would bear all the burden of slavery. Chase's motion was lost, but the basis of apportionment was changed from population to the value of lands granted to or surveyed for any person, in the respective states, together with improvements on such land.[25]

The provision that the state delegations should have an equal vote was objected to by the representatives of the large states. As a con-

---

[23] Ibid.
[24] Letter to Governor of North Carolina, May 23, 1777, ibid., II, 370–371.
[25] Journals of the Cont. Cong., VI, 1079–1082, 1098–1106.

cession Chase proposed that votes on appropriations should be in proportion to the population of the states. Franklin, seeing in this suggestion an implied admission, remarked that if the states had an equal vote they should pay equally, as representation should be proportioned to taxation. "If [the states] have an equal vote without bearing equal burthens, a confederation upon such iniquitous principles will never last long." [26]   On the other hand, the representatives of the small states feared that their states would be reduced to vassalage unless they were protected by equality of voting. Since only matters affecting states as states could come before Congress, and since in such matters the states had an equal interest, they urged, equality of voting was the correct rule.[27]

John Adams offered quite a different view. Interests in Congress, he held, should be the mathematical representation of interests without. The purpose of the confederation was to make the people of the several states one on confederation matters. Virginia, Pennsylvania, and Massachusetts were distant from one another, and differed in products, interests and customs, and would not tend to combine against the small states, which would act with their neighbors, large or small.[28]   James Wilson, already a thorough nationalist, insisted that taxation should be levied according to wealth but that representation should be in proportion to the numbers of free men. Like Adams, he urged that "as to those matters which are referred to Congress we are not so many states, we are one large State." He believed that it was impossible to invent a case which should be for the interest of Virginia, Pennsylvania, and Massachusetts which would not be for the interest of all.[29]

To compromise this difference various amendments were offered. One proposal was to allow Rhode Island, Delaware, and Georgia one vote each, and give every other state a vote for every 50,000 inhabitants. Another would have allowed one delegate for every 30,000 people, while a third would have based representation on the amount of the contribution of each state to the general treasury. In the end the clause was left unchanged, each state being

[26] *Ibid.*, VI, 1079.
[27] See speech of John Witherspoon of New Jersey, *ibid.*, VI, 1103.
[28] *Ibid.*, 1104.
[29] *Ibid.*, 1105.

permitted to send any number of delegates up to seven, the whole delegation to cast one vote determined by the majority of its members, but to lose its vote unless at least two delegates were present.

A third issue revived an old rivalry between the colonies which by charter had received grants running westward to the Pacific and those like Pennsylvania which had definite inner boundaries—in the case of Pennsylvania, a line parallel with the Delaware River, three hundred miles distant. There had been contention between Pennsylvania and Virginia over the line between them west of the mountains even before the French and Indian War, and a clause in the Albany Plan had covertly reflected this dispute by suggesting that the council have power to reduce some of the colonies "to more convenient dimensions." Franklin's draft of 1775 expressly proposed to empower the central authority to fix disputed boundaries. The troublesome question had been raised, as soon as it became evident that independence might result from the struggle with England, by a resolution of the Virginia legislature reasserting her claim to the transmontane country included within her charter grant of 1609.[30] Other colonies had followed Virginia's lead, to the dismay of the "landless" states which had no charter basis for such claims.

Dickinson, as a former Pennsylvanian, naturally shared Franklin's views, and sought to protect the interests of these latter states, including his own state of Delaware, by reproducing Franklin's proposal of 1775, but the clause in his draft giving to Congress the power to limit the bounds of the colonies claiming lands beyond the mountains was dropped from the Articles as reported by the committee of the whole. In October, 1776, however, the Maryland legislature challenged the claims of Virginia in resolutions which, while in line with the Albany Plan's suggestions concerning new settlements, give probably the first clear expression of what must have been, by that time, under the influence of experience and the revolutionary philosophy, a common opinion as to the proper policy to be pursued in providing for the government of settlements beyond the mountains: such lands ought to be ceded

[30] William W. Hening, ed., *Statutes of Virginia*, IX, 118. Reprint in *Am. Hist. Leaflet*, No. 22, p. 2.

to Congress "to be parcelled out at proper times into convenient, free and independent governments." [31]

During the spring of 1777 the land question apparently received little if any attention while Congress was discussing the Articles. By the end of June other pressing business caused a new interruption in the debates, which were not resumed until autumn. The states were then growing restless under the unsanctioned acts of Congress, and that body feared that a reaction of opinion might prevent the consummation of a formal union unless it were accomplished without further delay. Debate was therefore resumed, and the Maryland delegation submitted a proposal "That the United States, in Congress assembled, shall have the sole and exclusive right and power to ascertain and fix the western boundary of such states as claim to the Mississippi or South Sea, and lay out the land beyond the boundary, so ascertained, into separate and independent states, from time to time, as the numbers and circumstances of the people thereof may require." The result was defeat, for the resolution received the vote only of Maryland; indeed, the large states turned the tables on her by submitting and obtaining the passage of an amendment providing that no state should be deprived of territory for the benefit of the United States.[32]

Soon after this action the Articles were committed to three members for final revision (Nov. 13), were adopted as revised (Nov. 15), and (Nov. 17) sent to the states with the understanding that each legislature, when it had approved them, should instruct its delegates in Congress to sign the engrossed copy on its behalf. Ratification by every one of the states was required before they were to be binding.

In the course of the discussion by the state legislatures numerous changes were proposed. As in Congress itself, the clauses relating to the western lands, the vote of the states in Congress, and the basis of apportioning requisitions were those most often questioned. Georgia and South Carolina would have changed the provision

[31] *Ibid.*, 3.
[32] Herbert Baxter Adams, "Maryland's Influence upon Land Cessions to the United States."

giving the "free inhabitants" of each state all of the privileges and immunities of citizens in the several states, restricting it to whites. Maryland showed similar concern over the dangers involved in the unlimited right of free Negroes to migrate from one state to another. New Jersey declared that Congress should be given the exclusive power to regulate foreign trade. In all some fifty amendments were recommended by the states and considered by Congress. No one of them was accepted by that body, although several touched points which later experience proved were of real importance.[33]

On June 26, 1778, a committee was appointed by Congress to prepare a form of ratification, and the form was reported and approved on the 27th. On July 9 the delegates from New Hampshire, Massachusetts, Rhode Island, Connecticut, New York, Pennsylvania, Virginia, and South Carolina, having been duly authorized by their respective legislatures, signed the Articles on behalf of their states. The delegates of New Jersey, Delaware, and Maryland had not yet been empowered to sign, and North Carolina and Georgia were unrepresented. A special letter was sent to these five states urging that authorization be given to their delegates, and on July 21 North Carolina complied. Georgia followed on the 24th and New Jersey on November 26, while Delaware tardily swung into line in February, 1779. Maryland, however, would not give up her fight for the land cessions, and the necessity of unanimous acceptance of the Articles gave her a great advantage. Again and again she had demanded that the lands be treated as a common possession of the states, and now she refused to ratify the Articles unless she gained her point. The other "landless" states had supported her for a long time, delaying ratification, but one by one they had given up the fight until she stood alone. As her assent was indispensable the claimant states finally yielded.[34]

This result was not obtained until Congress espoused the cause

[33] George D. Harmon, "The Proposed Amendments to the Articles of Confederation."

[34] Rhode Island, New Jersey, Pennsylvania and Delaware gave Maryland a qualified support for a time. Rhode Island and New Jersey desired to have ownership of all lands which had belonged to the crown surrendered by the states within whose charter bounds they lay, the state reserving jurisdiction.— *Journals of the Cont. Cong.*, XI, 639, 650.

of cession, and made pledges satisfactory to the claimant states concerning the future disposition of the lands. New York having passed an act on February 19, 1780, empowering her delegates to agree to "limit and restrict" her western boundaries, Congress on September 6, 1780, requested the states to remove the only remaining obstacle to the completion of the union by making cessions of their claims, and followed the plea by a resolution of October 10 promising to dispose of the ceded lands for the common benefit and to erect new settlements in the West, in due time, into new states which should be admitted to the Confederation on equal terms with the original states.[35] These pledges laid the foundation not only for the later land policy of the United States, but for the political rights of the settlers in the West, thus providing for the geographical expansion of the federal system.

As the attitude of the claimant states now assured Maryland that the cessions would be made, she authorized her delegates to affix their signatures. This was done on March 1, 1781, and on that date the Articles of Confederation went into effect.

It may be maintained that the Confederation was not fully established until the autumn of 1781, after the states had chosen new delegates. On the other hand, the Congress had been conforming to the terms of the Articles in some respects at least ever since their adoption by that body in 1777, and even regarded some provisions as binding on the states from the moment of their respective acts of ratification.[36]

ANALYSIS OF THE ARTICLES

A comparison of the frame of government provided by the Articles with those which the states had adopted shows striking differences. Not only was there no second branch of the legislature, but the separation of executive and judicial functions from that of legislation was lacking. The powers which the Articles granted

[35] "Documents Illustrating State Land Claims and Cessions," *Am. Hist. Leaflet,* No. 22.
[36] Perhaps the "Congress in existence between March and November, 1781 was simply the Second Continental Congress conforming in many particulars to the newly ratified Articles."—F. H. Garver, "The Transition from the Continental Congress to the Congress of the Confederation."

were vested in Congress, to be exercised by it or its agents. It was authorized to appoint such committees and "civil officers" as its executive business might require, and these were to perform their duties under its direction. There was the germ, but only the germ, of a judicial system in the power to provide courts "for the trial of piracies and felonies committed on the high seas," for "determining finally appeals in all cases of captures," and for the settlement of disputes between the states.

This concentration of functions in one unicameral body places the Articles in a different category from the constitutions of the states. Moreover, the latter rested on the authority of the people in each state, and created governments acting upon and responsible to them. The Articles rested upon the authority of the state governments (legislatures). Congress was responsible to them and not to the people, and did not ordinarily act upon the people. The union, as the Articles themselves declared, was a league of friendship entered into by sovereign states.

Each state legislature chose and paid its delegates in Congress, or neglected to do so as it preferred. In spite of spirited opposition, the provision had survived that the delegation of each state was to cast one vote (provided at least two delegates out of a possible seven were present). An equally divided delegation meant that the vote of the state was lost. No important measure could be adopted without the concurrence of two thirds of the delegations, that is, the vote of nine states. Amendments to the Articles, after passing Congress, required the approval of the legislature of every state.

The member states were pledged to observe certain rules of comity in their relations with one another, and to refrain from certain actions which were inconsistent with the objects of the league. Thus the free inhabitants of each state were "entitled to all privileges and immunities of free citizens in the several States," and were to enjoy freedom to come and go and carry on business in every state, while fugitives from justice were to be given up on demand of the governor of the state from which they fled. The public records of each state were to be given full faith and credit by the others.

As has been said, both Franklin and Dickinson had tried to make a list of the matters of common interest to the members of the league, and by the time Congress sent the Articles to the states in 1777 the list had grown to a very respectable length. First and foremost, naturally, among the powers of Congress, was that of "determining on peace and war." Next was the responsibility for foreign relations in general—sending and receiving ambassadors and making treaties. Then to promote uniformity for the benefit of trade, Congress was given exclusive power to fix the standards of coinage and of weights and measures. Relations with Indians "not members of any of the states" were committed to its care, likewise the postal service. The responsibility for paying the debt incurred in the War of Independence was laid upon it. Other powers were incidental to these main ones.

Some of these powers had been included in the Albany Plan, more of them in Franklin's plan of 1775. Every one of them had been wielded in colonial days by the imperial government rather than by the individual colonies. Taught by their experience while under the rule of Britain, Dickinson and his fellow members of Congress were able to make on paper a distribution of powers between Congress and the states which approached the demands of the theory of the distinction between internal and general police, reserving to each state that control over its domestic affairs which had so long been claimed as an inalienable right. Now that independence had come, that precious local autonomy was established, but Americans were turning to the task of creating for themselves a substitute for the British government in the performance of indispensable functions of general police, and the powers they were giving to Congress closely resembled those which the British government had exercised in the old days.[37]

The struggle with the mother country had nevertheless made Americans tenacious of certain views which should have been modified in their new situation. The long struggle against parliamentary taxation had grounded them in the belief that they should be taxed only by their respective assemblies. Few if any perceived as yet that taxation did not belong exclusively in the list either of

[37] A. C. McLaughlin, "Background of American Federalism."

internal or general police powers, but was instead a concurrent power, needed by both local and central governments as an essential means of carrying on their respective functions. The old objection to taxation by a body in which they were not represented was no longer pertinent, since the Congress was to be composed of delegates from the states. Habits of thought were so fixed, however, that men were disinclined as yet to give to Congress a power which had been so vehemently denied to Parliament. Consequently, instead of investing the former body with the power of taxation, the Articles only allowed it to estimate its monetary needs and then to make a "requisition" upon each state for its share of the total. The laying of taxes to raise this and all other revenues was reserved to the states respectively.

A similar error was made in regard to the regulation of commerce. This power had been one of the functions of Parliament which most colonists had for a long time admitted as a necessity, however much they disliked the working of the navigation acts. As a result of their experience with the parliamentary system the Articles gave Congress only a partial and inadequate control over commerce. It was allowed to make commercial treaties, but the right to retaliate against any foreign country which discriminated against American trade or shipping was reserved to the states, and control over interstate commerce was not so much as mentioned.

Having been sent to the states before the settlement of the land question, the Articles contained no provision for disposition of the lands by Congress, or the acquisition or government of new territories. Much worse was the dependence of Congress upon the state governments for the execution of most of its measures.

THE QUESTION OF SOVEREIGNTY

The Confederation, according to the letter of the Articles, was a league of sovereignties. But such a union did not realize the highest aspirations of thinking Americans of that epoch. For the sake of clarity a distinction should be drawn between sovereignty and autonomous control of internal police—a distinction which statesmen of the time were unable to make. The colonists' jealousy of their control over local or "internal" police had been exhibited

whenever intercolonial union was proposed, and England's interference in this sphere had led at last to armed revolt and independence.   Every project of union had carefully guarded the police
power of the constituent assemblies.   The Albany Plan contemplated "one general government . . . under which . . . each
colony may retain its present constitution" except as necessarily
modified by the act of union.   Galloway's plan was explicit in
providing that "each colony shall retain its present Constitution
and powers of regulating and governing its own internal police in
all cases whatsoever."   When the Virginia Convention instructed
its delegates in the Continental Congress, in May, 1776, to agree to
a "Confederation of the Colonies," it was with the distinct proviso
that "the power of forming Government for, and the regulation of
the internal concerns of each Colony, be left to the respective
Colonial Legislatures." [38]   Likewise the Pennsylvania Convention,
when assenting to the formation of a union, reserved "to the people of this Colony the sole and exclusive right of regulating the
internal government and police of the same." [39]

From the Albany Plan the descent of clauses reserving the control over internal police is traceable, through the Galloway proposal of 1774 and the Franklin project of 1775, to the Dickinson
draft of the next year (to pass without further notice several similar
suggestions in the period of discussion following 1765).   The sovereignty clause in the Articles as adopted marked the extreme
swing of the pendulum in this direction, but went too far.   The
error lay in the identification of autonomy in internal police with
sovereignty, an error which destroyed the significance of the concept of distributed powers.

For insistence upon reserved powers is meaningless unless set
over against the idea of powers which are surrendered.   Reserved
powers can exist only where distinct communities are joined in
some sort of political union.   At no time, either before or after the
Revolution, was complete provincial or state independence desired
by Anglo-American leaders.   The inconveniences of English rule

[38] *Journal of the Convention*, in Force, *American Archives*, 4th series, VI, col.
1524.   See also Grigsby, *Virginia Convention*, 17–18.
[39] Force, *American Archives*, 4th series, VI, col. 755.

prior to 1763 had been offset by manifest advantages, for the different parts of the empire had had some common interests, and crown and Parliament had served as organs for their management. Indeed, if some of the colonists had not felt the need of even more machinery for carrying on the common business, they would not have suggested the formation of an intercolonial union. Long before independence was gained, they were groping towards an arrangement in which general affairs would be managed by a central government and the internal police by the separate commonwealths—some scheme in which powers would be classified as "general" and "local" and assigned accordingly to the appropriate governments. Independence made union more than ever a necessity, since the British government could no longer function as an organ of intercommunity activity. Hence union came, almost inevitably, with the destruction of the only existing organic bond between the commonwealths. By 1781 the idea was taking shape "that compelling legal authority was to be exercised within given fields; one field was to belong to the national government, one to the states." [40] Such a system as this we have learned to call "federal."

The assertion of state sovereignty in the Articles gave the trend towards federalism a set-back. Although it has become the fashion to liken it to "a rope of sand," in many ways the American league went beyond all precedents. Even such a union might have worked successfully for some time if the states had gone a little further in giving power to Congress; but the lack of power to regulate commerce, to tax, and to act directly upon the people were fatal defects. [41] This is perhaps only another way of saying that a mere league fell short of the federal ideal which was slowly taking form, and for that reason proved to be only a temporary system,

[40] McLaughlin, *Con. Hist.*, 136. See H. C. Hockett, "Little Essays on the Police Power."

[41] "Originally . . . the bias in favor of local autonomy so overweighted the American constitutional system . . . that it broke down entirely, both within the states, where the basic rights of property and contract were seriously infringed, and throughout the nation at large, because from the central government essential powers had been withheld."—Edward S. Corwin, "The Progress of Constitutional Theory between the Declaration of Independence and the Meeting of the Philadelphia Convention."

destined to give way to the "more perfect union" worked out at Philadelphia in 1787.[42]

[42] Even in the Convention of 1787 delegates disagreed as to the sovereignty of the states under the Articles. The statements made on June 19 by Luther Martin, James Wilson, Alexander Hamilton and Rufus King are especially noteworthy. See Max Farrand, *The Records of the Federal Convention of 1787*, I, 322–325. One of the strongest denials of state sovereignty under the Articles was made by Charles Cotesworth Pinckney, speaking before the legislature of South Carolina on January 18, 1788. Said he: the "separate independence and individual sovereignty of the several states were never thought of by the enlightened band of patriots who framed this Declaration of Independence. . . . Let us, then, consider all attempts to weaken this Union, by maintaining that each state is separately and individually independent, as a species of political heresy. . . ."— Jonathan Elliot, *Debates in the Several State Conventions on the Adoption of the Federal Constitution* (edn. of 1853), IV, 301.

The view that the Confederation was a league of sovereign states and that the Articles were in effect a treaty is supported by the fact that certain provisions are borrowed from international law and used to define interstate relations. Thus under international law no nation has a right to demand the surrender of a fugitive by another nation unless a treaty has been made providing for extradition. The Articles, and even the Constitution, in their extradition clauses, suggest that the relations between states are akin to those between independent nations. The privileges and immunities clauses afford another illustration of the same tenor, although the latter provision of the Constitution has a long and intricate history, due largely to the difficulty of agreeing upon the applicability of the clause to the free Negro. See McLaughlin's discussion, *Con. Hist.*, 126–129.

IX

THE LEAGUE OF FRIENDSHIP

ACTUAL GOVERNMENT UNDER THE ARTICLES

THE War for Independence had been in progress for almost six years when the Articles of Confederation were ratified. During this whole period the Congress had functioned not only as a general legislature, but as the body upon which fell the responsibility of conducting military and diplomatic affairs and the attendant financial business. In the early years of its existence business was entrusted to special or permanent committees. A special committee framed the Declaration of Independence and another prepared the Articles of Confederation. The direction of the diplomatic agents in France and Spain, however, called for continuous attention, for which a standing committee of foreign affairs was required. The management of the army, the handling of finances, and other tasks of a similar continuing character were likewise assigned to permanent committees.

The labor on these committees was unremitting, and engrossed the energies of the most capable men in Congress to such an extent that the efficiency of the body as a whole suffered sadly. Important business was often neglected or postponed for long periods. It was due in part to this inefficient organization that the long delay occurred in the adoption of the Articles of Confederation, evoking Rutledge's comment that a "special congress" should be called to deal with the problem of union.

Congress slowly learned by its own painful experience the folly of overloading its members, and by the time the Articles became effective it had created departments, each headed by an expert secretary or superintendent and provided with a clerical staff. The first of these offices for executive business was that of secretary for foreign affairs, which was created by an act passed on January 10, 1781. It was followed in February by the offices of superintendent of finance and secretary at war. A secretary of marine was also

153

created, but that office was soon discontinued and its duties added to those of the superintendent of finance.[1]

The most capable incumbents of these offices were Robert Morris, who served as superintendent of finance from May, 1781, until November, 1784, John Jay, who as secretary for foreign affairs held office from 1784 until the Constitution replaced the Articles, and Henry Knox, the secretary at war, who in 1789 entered Washington's cabinet in a similar capacity. In these offices are to be found the forerunners of the departments of the constitutional period. Congress also provided itself with a presiding officer whose title of "president" was later transferred to the chief executive under the Constitution, although the duties of the two positions had nothing in common.

EMERGENCE OF A FEDERAL JUDICIARY

Unless the Albany Plan is understood as implying that the acts of the Grand Council were to be laws enforceable by the courts with the Privy Council as a tribunal of last resort, none of the early plans of union made any provision for a judicial branch. Franklin in 1775 went so far as to include among the powers of Congress that of settling disputes between colonies. Dickinson went somewhat further, and his suggestions were embodied in the Articles as adopted. A logical distribution of powers between states and federal government would have given (as the Constitution does give) jurisdiction to federal courts over all cases arising under acts of Congress, reserving jurisdiction to the state courts over cases arising under the internal police powers of the states. But the framers of the Articles had not advanced so far in their thinking, or rather still thought of the union of the states as a league instead of a government. Aware, however, of numerous disputes which had arisen between states over boundaries, and between individuals who held land by grants from different states claiming the same tracts, and conscious doubtless that the Privy Council had sometimes given judgments in such cases in the past, they assigned a somewhat

[1] *Journals of Congress* (edn. of 1823), III, 564, 575, 665. *Cf.* J. C. Guggenheimer, "The Development of the Executive Departments, 1775–1789."

similar function to Congress by a provision in the Articles.[2] However, Congress was not itself made a court for the hearing of such causes. Instead, the states concerned might by joint consent, through Congress as intermediary, choose commissioners to decide the controversy. If they failed to agree upon the composition of the tribunal, Congress was empowered to name a panel from whose members the final judges were selected by a process of alternate elimination by the parties to the dispute, and by lot, until the number was reduced to seven or nine as Congress should direct in particular cases. The majority of the judges thus chosen were to give a final decision.

This cumbrous method was actually resorted to successfully. Six disputes between states were brought before Congress, and in three cases a tribunal was chosen. Only in one case, however, did the court reach a decision. This involved an old rivalry between Connecticut and Pennsylvania over lands in the northern portion of the latter state which fell within the bounds of the Connecticut sea-to-sea charter. Sitting at Trenton in 1782, the court unanimously ruled against the claims of Connecticut.[3]

This provision of the Articles links the Privy Council with the United States Supreme Court, for when the Constitution was framed, jurisdiction in cases between states was vested in the latter. Another source of the jurisdiction of the Supreme Court is found in the English courts of vice-admiralty. The line of descent runs as follows:

When the Revolution began and the mechanism of British government in America collapsed, the vice-admiralty courts of course broke down, and the states found it necessary to supply substitutes. On a recommendation of Congress in July, 1775, Massachusetts

[2] At least nine cases of dispute between colonies had come before the Privy Council. One, Penn v. Lord Baltimore, came before an ordinary court in a way comparable to suits between two states before the Supreme Court of the United States. Looking to the Privy Council "became a real though reluctant habit. . . ."—R. G. Caldwell, "The Settlement of Inter-state Disputes." Cf. A. H. Snow, *The Development of the American Doctrine of Jurisdiction of Courts over States.*

[3] Caldwell, *loc. cit.* See also J. C. B. Davis, "Federal Courts Prior to the Adoption of the Constitution," 131 U. S., Appendix, XIX. An account of the settlement of the dispute between Massachusetts and New York is given in Payson J. Treat, *The National Land System,* 10, note 15.

(in November of that year) established a court to commission privateers and hear prize cases. On November 11 Washington recommended to Congress that it set up a federal prize court on the model of this Massachusetts court, whereupon Congress sent another recommendation to the states asking them to erect such courts and provide for appeals to Congress or to a tribunal to be created by Congress. All of the states except New York complied with this recommendation, and established admiralty courts with provision for more or less limited appeal.[4]

Illustrating the limitation of appeals, and departing from the obnoxious British admiralty precedent, the Pennsylvania act provided for a jury in prize cases, and for appeal only on questions of law. The jury's findings as to facts were to be final.

Not until appeals began to be taken from these state courts did Congress go further and provide a tribunal to hear them. At first a special committee was appointed for each, but a standing committee soon became necessary, and one was appointed on January 30, 1777, composed of five members known as the Commissioners of Appeals. At this date the Articles of Confederation had not yet been adopted, and the authority of Congress to hear appeals was found in the response of the states to the recommendation of that body that they establish their own admiralty courts. But the discussions of the months preceding the framing of the Articles had led to the inclusion in Dickinson's draft of a provision that Congress should have the sole and exclusive power of establishing courts for determining finally appeals in all cases of capture, and for the trial of piracies and felonies committed on the high seas. Ratification of the Articles gave binding force to this clause vesting final jurisdiction in Congress.

While the Articles were pending the appeal system almost broke down under the strain of the Olmstead case (to be examined more closely later), in which the Pennsylvania courts and officials, although that state had already accepted the Articles, disregarded a decision of the congressional Commissioners. The Commissioners

---

[4] J. F. Jameson, "The Predecessor of the Supreme Court." See also H. Putnam, "How the Federal Courts Were Given Admiralty Jurisdiction," and Penhallow *et al. v.* Doane's Administrators, 3 Dallas, 54.

thereupon determined to hear no more appeals until their authority was vindicated.   Although Congress with only two dissenting voices reaffirmed their powers, it had become apparent that a different type of tribunal was needed.   Under these circumstances the Court of Appeals in Cases of Capture was created in 1780.[5]

This court was modelled after the English Board of Commissioners of Appeals, a body composed of members of the Privy Council whose duty it was to hear cases carried up from the vice-admiralty courts.   The first judges were Cyrus Griffin of Virginia, William Paca of Maryland, and Titus Hosmer of Connecticut, and their salaries were fixed at $2,250 per annum.   On the adoption of the Articles an ordinance was passed to regulate the procedure of the court.   The official records have disappeared, but from private sources it has been ascertained that three sessions were held annually for awhile, one at Hartford, one at Philadelphia, and a third in Virginia.   After the war the business of the court rapidly dwindled, but it maintained a nominal existence until the new federal courts came into operation in 1789.   Its records were then turned over to the Supreme Court, and it is not unlikely that the old judges were consulted by committees of the First Congress, and that in this way the experience of the Court of Appeals had some influence upon the organization of the new federal judiciary. In all some 118 cases were disposed of by the congressional committees and the Court of Appeals, and the idea became well fixed that admiralty and maritime cases pertained to federal jurisdiction.[6] One of the most important results of the experience with this court was that its decisions were later upheld on grounds indicated above, even in cases where they had been given before the Articles were ratified by the last of the states.

FOUNDATIONS OF FEDERAL EXPANSION

The most significant acts of the Confederation were not authorized by the Articles.   In the hope of providing a sound paper currency, Robert Morris, the superintendent of finance, persuaded Congress in 1781 to charter the Bank of North America, with the

[5] Jameson, "Predecessor."
[6] *Ibid.*

requirement that it maintain a specie reserve to support its circulating paper. Amid the chaos of irredeemable paper such a corrective was badly needed, but since the Articles did not empower Congress to grant charters of incorporation, criticism was aroused which led the bank to seek a new charter from the State of Pennsylvania.

Congress was more fortunate in dealing with the public lands. Although the cessions came after the adoption of the Articles, they were made in compliance with the pledge of Congress that the lands should be disposed of for the common benefit and divided in proper time into new states for admission to the Confederation. Thus without amending the Articles the cessions carried the tacit consent of the states to the ordinances of 1784, 1785, and 1787.

The Ordinance of 1785 provided for the survey and sale of the lands, and requires no attention here. The other two acts, however, dealt with the government of new settlements and eventual statehood, and hold an important place in the history of the development of American constitutionalism, especially in its character of a union of equal commonwealths.

The idea that new settlements should be made under the supervision of the central government goes back at least to the Albany Plan of inter-colonial union, which proposed that the Grand Council should exercise the power, and "make laws for regulating and governing" the new settlements "till the crown shall think fit to form them into particular governments." Franklin's reflections upon the problem of new colonies led him to believe that the prospect of liberal government would have to be held out if settlers were to be induced to incur the hazards of the wilderness. In his own words, they would have to be allowed "extraordinary privileges and liberties." [7] The nature of these extraordinary privileges is hinted at in his suggestion that they should include the right of the pioneers to choose their own governor. Evidently colonies of the self-governing, or corporate, type, were in his mind rather than the royal province to which type the crown was attempting to reduce all of the colonial governments.

The twenty years following the Albany Congress were filled

[7] Bigelow, *Works of Franklin*, II, 474.

with projects for new colonies, and the discussions of the period gave rise to various opinions as to the most suitable kind of government for transmontane settlements.[8] The British ministry grappled with the problem and divided into friends and opponents of western expansion. Lord Hillsborough, for a time president of the Board of Trade, contended that new colonies in the interior would be too remote to be beneficial.[9] In Hillsborough's apprehensions one may perceive a presentiment of the fact that the pioneers would inevitably govern themselves in their own way, whatever forms might be imposed upon them.

As the colonial period closed Franklin, as one of the agents of the Vandalia Company, was urging a new colony in the West Virginia region, on the ground that the locality already contained a population of several thousands, who could not be governed properly from Williamsburg.[10] The Privy Council was willing to approve a grant of land to the company as a body of proprietors, provided that they would furnish bond for the payment of the salary of a governor to be appointed by the crown.[11] The outbreak of the Revolution prevented the consummation of the arrangement, and in fact transferred the whole problem of new governments in the West to Congress. The ensuing rivalry over the western lands and their cession to Congress by the claimant states as a common possession has been recounted. Out of the discussion of the land cessions emerged the promise of Congress that new states should be erected in the western territory which should possess all the rights of the original states. Congress made this pledge in asking for the cessions,[12] and Virginia repeated the provision as a condition of her act of transfer.[13] Thus equal rights for the new communities in the West were guaranteed by a compact.

This recognition of the rights of the inhabitants of the frontier

[8] *Ibid.*, 12–48. Clarence E. Carter, *Great Britain and the Illinois Country, 1763–1774*, 103–144. *Cf.* Clarence W. Alvord, *The Mississippi Valley in British Politics, passim.*

[9] Bigelow, *Works of Franklin*, V, 4.

[10] *Ibid.*, 73, 74.

[11] G. H. Alden, *New Governments West of the Alleghanies before 1780*, 28–35.

[12] *Journals of the Cont. Cong.*, XVIII, 915.

[13] *Am. Hist. Leaflet*, No. 22, p. 13. The whole question of the western lands has recently been intensively studied by Thomas P. Abernethy, in *Western Lands and the American Revolution.*

region is a more significant step in the advance of American democracy than the theoretical passages in the state constitutions. Much as Puritanism, failing of immediate success in England, found its opportunity in New England, so the unprivileged classes, suppressed by the dominant aristocrats in the original settlements, found a freer stage in the communities beyond the mountains. The turbulence and discontent of the people in the western portions of the old states showed that unwelcome restraints could not be imposed upon settlements beyond the mountains. The memorials of the inhabitants of western Virginia and North Carolina, destined later to become the states of West Virginia, Kentucky, and Tennessee, spoke eloquently even if uncouthly of the westerners' belief in their right to establish governments for themselves.[14] Only one conclusion was possible: the West would be either autonomous or independent.

Such was the intellectual climate when, following the cession of Virginia's claims, Congress took up the problem of providing a suitable government and appointed Thomas Jefferson as chairman of the committee to draft an ordinance for the purpose. His report, after some changes, was adopted as the Ordinance of 1784. This act divided the region between the mountains and the Mississippi into tracts each of which was to become a state and enter the Union with full rights when its population equaled that of the least populous of the original states. There were eighteen of these divisions. Previous to statehood the inhabitants were to enjoy limited self-government under the supervision of Congress.

This ordinance was passed before the cessions were completed, and before any of the areas into which it proposed to divide the West had acquired enough inhabitants to qualify for admission as a state. Consequently it never became operative, and was superseded in 1787 by the more famous Northwest Ordinance, so called from the fact that it applied only to the region between the Ohio and Mississippi rivers, which the states had ceded by that date. The region south of the Ohio was left to be organized when the claimant states should have relinquished their claims to it.

[14] Frederick J. Turner, "Western State-making in the Revolutionary Era." *Cf.* Theodore Roosevelt, *The Winning of the West*, II, 398–399.

The Ordinance of 1787 provided that the Northwest should be divided eventually into not more than five nor fewer than three states. While the process of occupation was in its early stages, government was to be in the hands of officials chosen by Congress, but as soon as five thousand free adult males had removed to the territory, the qualified voters were to elect a house of representatives. In this second stage Congress was to continue to name the governor, and was also to appoint the members of an upper house, or council, from a list of persons nominated by the representatives. This plan was much like that of colonial Massachusetts under the second charter. A delegate to sit in Congress without a vote reminds one of the colonial agent. The ordinance shows the temper of the times in its property qualifications for voting and office-holding during the territorial régime, and in its inclusion of a bill of rights of the same type as those contained in the state constitutions.

Under the plan laid down in this ordinance, with minor modifications, the whole wide space of the continent was destined to be occupied, as additional areas were brought under the flag by purchase or conquest, and the westward movement called for government in the new regions. Experience as subjects of Britain undoubtedly influenced the members of Congress in shaping this territorial, or as it might appropriately be called, this colonial, system. In effect if not in words the ordinance asserted that Congress possessed the right to control the internal police of dependencies, and provided for the active exercise of this control during the first stages of settlement. The theoretical basis of this power was not the compact philosophy on which the state constitutions rested; it was much closer akin to the theory of parliamentary supremacy. In a country where all government professedly derived its authority from the people, the apology for the claim that Congress possessed sovereign authority over the inhabitants of territories was that necessity demanded it and that the territorial status was temporary.

The temporary character of the territorial status was indeed the respect in which the American colonial system differed from that of contemporary England. She held her colonies in permanent subordination. It was this inferiority of status, associated with her refusal to recognize the autonomy of the colonies in domestic concerns, that drove them to the separation. By contrast, the American plan held before the settlers on the western frontiers the prospect of early admission to all the privileges of partnership in the Union, for the ordinance, repeating the pledge of Congress, promised that whenever any one of the divisions of the Northwest attained a population of sixty thousand souls it should be admitted to the Union forthwith, on terms of full equality with the original states. Although it remained for the future to clarify the meaning of the words "full equality," this equality of new and old states is one of the unique features of American constitutionalism, and it goes far to explain the strength of the bonds of union.

CONFLICT OF OPINION CONCERNING THE WEST

The plan of administering the government of the frontier settlements, with the promise of eventual membership in the Union, did not yield universal satisfaction. Men of liberal mind regarded the territorial status as one of degraded dependence in which a part of the population was deprived of some of the essential liberties of Americans.[15] Some of the conservatives, on the contrary, would gladly have denied statehood to the westerners. The two attitudes have persisted throughout our history, and many citizens in our times—true heirs of British eighteenth-century imperialism—still favor holding acquired territory in permanent dependence.[16]

From the very beginning the prospect of new states possessing equal rights in the Union with the original ones was disliked by the heirs of British tradition, as a menace to the control which they had so far enjoyed in the separate states, and desired to continue in the Confederation. In these divergent policies concerning western settlements is to be found another phase of the incipient class struggle in America, disguised somewhat by the partial geograph-

[15] See, for example, the opinion expressed by James Madison during the debate over the admission of Tennessee, in which he declared that the territorial status was a "degraded situation," lacking "a right essential to freemen—the right of being represented in Congress."—*Annals of Congress*, 4 Cong., 1 sess., 1308–1309.

[16] See discussion in H. C. Hockett, *Western Influences on Political Parties to 1825*, 53–54, and footnotes. The attitude of leading Federalists in the early nineteenth century is discussed, *ibid.*, 68 *et seq.*

ical segregation of the opposing groups. The contest at first threatened to deprive the new regions of the equality promised by the ordinances of 1784 and 1787, but eventually resulted in the triumph of political democracy and the overthrow of many of the features of middle-class government. This in turn proved to be only a phase of a long-drawn-out struggle in which political democracy has found itself worsted time and again by its old antagonist in the new guise of capitalism.[17]

There is no lack of evidence of the apprehension with which the growth of the West was regarded by the conservatives in the older communities. Timothy Pickering, for example, opposed plans in 1785 to extinguish the Indian title to lands in the Ohio Valley on the ground that they would be occupied by "lawless emigrants." [18] In both North and South there were persons who were doubtful of the wisdom of disturbing the balance of political power by admitting new states. Apprehensions of this supplied one reason for reducing the number of prospective states from the eighteen contemplated by the Ordinance of 1784 to the three to five mentioned in the Ordinance of 1787.[19] In 1785 a Virginia member of Congress informed Washington that certain unnamed eastern gentlemen were uneasy over "the consequences which may result from the new states taking their position in the Confederacy," apparently wishing "that this event may be delayed as long as possible." [20] These views were symptoms of a feeling which was to result in a sharp contest in the Constitutional Convention between the delegates who favored equality for the new states and those who wished to repudiate the pledge which Congress had repeatedly given.

[17] "We may trace the contest between the capitalist and the democratic pioneer from the earliest colonial days."—Frederick J. Turner, "Social Forces in American History," 227.

[18] Justin Winsor, *The Westward Movement*, 270.

[19] J. A. Barrett, *Evolution of the Ordinance of 1787, passim.*

[20] Letter of William Grayson, April 15, 1787, quoted by George Bancroft, *History of the Formation of the Constitution of the United States of America*, I, 425. Grayson may have referred to Rufus King, who was his associate on the committee which framed the Land Ordinance of 1785. From other sources King is known to have held such views.

FAILURES OF THE CONFEDERATION

The efforts of Congress to manage the country's business in accordance with the provisions of the Articles of Confederation present a dismal record. The history of these failures concerns us only as they served to prove the inadequacy of the Articles and to point the way to necessary changes. The Articles were deficient, as experience proved, at exactly those points where there was crucial need of a competent government, namely in dealing with foreign nations, in handling the public debt incurred in the Revolutionary War, and in the actual power to carry legitimate measures into execution.

Independence had freed American trade from the irksome restrictions of the navigation system in intercourse with non-English countries. But the people of the states naively hoped that England could be persuaded to make a treaty continuing the old free intercourse with all parts of the empire which they had enjoyed as British subjects. Instead, as foreigners, they found their vessels excluded from the West Indies, and subjected to discriminating charges in the ports of the British Isles. John Adams, sent to England in 1785, could make no headway in negotiating a trade agreement. The ministers refused to make a commercial treaty because of alleged breaches of the treaty of peace, and intimated that they doubted whether under the Articles the states would be bound by any treaty entered into by Congress.

This doubt was well founded, and the lesson was not lost on Adams. His reports to the secretary for foreign relations indicated that no progress could be expected unless Congress were empowered to impose restrictions upon foreign vessels such as American ships were subjected to abroad.

In France Jefferson fared little better. Concessions granted during the war were withdrawn when peace was made. Like England, France now applied her navigation system to the new nation. Spain's course was similar. The effort to reach an understanding with her was peculiarly humiliating. John Jay, secretary for foreign affairs, began negotiations with the Spanish minister Gardoqui in 1786, asking for a treaty of commerce, the establishment of the boundary between Spanish West Florida and the United States at the line claimed by the latter, and the recognition of the right of Americans to navigate the Mississippi through the Spanish territory near its mouth. In return he had practically nothing to offer, not even the threat of closing American ports to Spanish vessels. At most he could only attempt to purchase a part of the concessions asked for by surrendering his demand for others. Accordingly he asked the permission of Congress to propose to Gardoqui that the United States would forbear for a term of twenty-five years or more her insistence upon the right to navigate the river, provided a satisfactory commercial agreement were obtained. This proposal failed, Congress instead of casting the nine votes required for its approval, favoring it by a vote of only seven to six.

Jay's proposal to relinquish the claim to the navigation of the Mississippi was construed as part and parcel of the indifference of the East towards western interests. James Monroe believed "that Jay and his party in Congress are determined to pursue this business as far as possible, either as the means of throwing the Western people and territory without the government of the United States and keeping the weight of population and government here [in the East], or of dismembering the Government itself, for the purpose of a separate confederacy." [21]

The failure of Jay's efforts not only left Spanish relations in a most unsatisfactory posture, but enabled malcontents in the Kentucky and Tennessee settlements to engage in intrigues which threatened the secession of that region. The root of the difficulty was the lack of power in Congress to provide for the welfare of the westerners, and they, with pardonable indignation, were tempted to question the value of their connection with the eastern states.

The incapacity of the government in these diplomatic efforts was conspicuous, but it did not follow that commerce was prostrated for want of government patronage. On the contrary the later years of the Confederation brought increasing prosperity.

[21] Letter to James Madison, August 14, 1786, quoted by Charles Warren, *The Making of the Constitution*, 25. See *infra*, 202 et seq.

The foreign demand for American products was growing, and they found their way indirectly into countries with which no treaties had been made. Commerce also enjoyed a promising beginning in the Pacific, and before many years had passed Yankee skippers were second only to the English in the ports of China. Ships from New England developed the fur trade on the northwest coast of America, making Canton the market for their cargoes, and bringing home in return the products of the Far East. The American cities along the Atlantic shared in the profits of these ventures. Even the import trade with England increased by leaps and bounds; it jumped from approximately one-twelfth of the total British exports in 1788 to about one-fifth six years later.

For this improvement credit could hardly be given to the government. The mercantile class became increasingly convinced, however, that with more adequate powers Congress could do a great deal to advance its interests, and that such fostering care was preferable to leaving commerce to grow from natural causes alone, or under state protection. For want of a common regulating authority indeed a good deal of confusion existed, due to the rivalries of the states. Through the town of New York passed the trade not only of the Hudson Valley but of the adjacent parts of Connecticut and New Jersey. Through Philadelphia passed another part of New Jersey's external commerce, creating a situation which led Madison to liken that state to a cask tapped at both ends.[22] The duties collected by New York, largely on the commerce of these neighbor states, were sufficient to defray a substantial part of her own expenses, thus lightening the tax burdens of the great landlords and giving them an interest opposed to the surrender of the customs to Congress. As a rule goods of the growth or produce of one state were exempted from import duties by all the others, but Virginia and Maryland exacted export duties, some states demanded greater tonnage duties from vessels of other states than from their own, and in a few cases tariff legislation took on the character of retaliatory acts aimed at neighboring states.[23]

[22] Preface to his notes on the debates in the Constitutional Convention, written many years after the notes were taken.—Farrand, *Records*, III, App. A, CCCCI, 542.
[23] A. A. Giesecke, *American Commercial Legislation before 1789*, 134–139.

It was in fact the need of uniform commercial regulations that brought about the first of the series of conventions which culminated in the one which framed the Constitution.

The confusion in financial matters was even greater than in trade. It was out of the question for Congress to attempt the redemption of the worthless continental currency issued during the war. Still less was it possible to check the paper money craze which drove some of the states into further issues of irredeemable paper. Morris and his advisers could not establish a specie circulation in a country which was almost destitute of the money metals, although they devised the decimal system of coinage which is still in use. Their chief effort in the direction of a sound currency was to utilize the scanty supply of specie as a reserve for the support of a paper circulation, through the operations of the Bank of North America. The burden of the war debt, however, was one under which the superintendent of finance struggled in vain. Morris described his situation as that of a man charged with the direction of the finances of a country pressed by creditors but under "a government whose sole authority consists in the power of making recommendations." [24] Finding himself unable to make headway, he resigned, not wishing, he said, to be a "minister of injustice." [25]

A part of the public debt was payable to France, Holland, and Spain for money loaned to Congress during the Revolution. A larger portion was represented by certificates issued in payment of soldiers' wages or for supplies for the army. Many certificates had been issued to the actual producers of food, or to the owners of grain, wagons, horses, and cattle seized under pressure of military necessity. Those original holders of certificates who were able to keep these evidences of the sums due them were fortunate; in most cases poverty compelled the receivers to sell them to speculators who, buying at a heavy discount, could afford to take the risk of non-payment.

The government needed money, first of all, to meet its own

[24] Letter to B. Franklin, Jan. 11, 1783, in Francis Wharton, ed., *The Revolutionary Diplomatic Correspondence of the United States*, VI, 203.
[25] McLaughlin, *Con. Hist.*, 140.

current expenses. Next came the interest on the debt, especially the portion owed abroad. After that would have come, had there been funds, the principal of the domestic debt. To provide for these needs the resources afforded by the Articles were requisitions on the states and new loans. The sale of public lands promised to become in time another source of income.

Experience soon showed that requisitions on the states would not yield the sums needed. During the first two years under the Articles Congress asked for $10,000,000 and received less than $1,500,000. During the entire period of the Confederation the amount realized from requisitions barely met the government's operating expenses, leaving nothing over to be applied to interest on the debt. Some new loans were obtained and the proceeds used in paying the most pressing of the interest obligations, but by 1790 arrearages ran into the millions. The net result was an actual rise of the debt in time of peace because the government lacked the power of taxation.[26]

PUBLIC DISORDERS

To the conservative class whose idea of a proper government was one which could promote enterprise and provide for the payment of the public obligations as well as protect property, life and liberty, a few years under the Articles were sufficient to prove the existing Confederation a failure. All of these great objects seemed to be endangered by the violent disposition shown by certain dissatisfied elements of the population. The collapse of the continental currency, the depreciation of the certificates of indebtedness, and the fall of prices which followed the peace increased the economic burdens of many persons who had incurred debts while high prices prevailed, and furnished the chief motive for the de-

[26] The difficulties experienced by Congress in obtaining money from the states under the requisition system are illustrated by the case of New Jersey. When that state approved the Articles, it insisted that Congress should be given the exclusive power to regulate foreign trade. The demand grew out of resentment at the power of New York and Pennsylvania to collect a revenue on imports which were to be consumed in New Jersey. Since nothing came of the demand for amendment of the Articles, the state legislature resolved in 1786 not to pay its quota until the states consented to the federal impost. Congress sent a committee which sought in vain to persuade New Jersey to comply with the requisition.—Francis N. Thorpe, *Constitutional History of the United States*, I, 279.

mand for the issue of legal tender paper by the states. The advocates of paper money included the rural classes which had both before and during the Revolution sought to reform government along democratic lines. They had the moral support of the wage-earners of the towns who could not vote. In spite of the restricted suffrage, this inflationist party was strong in all of the states. It triumphed in seven, and in several others was defeated only because of the regulations which preserved the rule of the propertied minority.

Suffering from economic conditions, angered by the retention of undemocratic provisions in the new state constitutions, and thwarted by these provisions in their efforts to change laws regarding currency and debts which they thought were conceived in the interests of the property-owning class, the radicals adopted views which the conservatives believed to be dangerous. The philosophy by which rejection of the British authority had been justified was susceptible of being carried to extremes. If governments derived their just powers from the consent of the governed, what obedience did these hard-pressed debtors owe to a government controlled by their oppressors? The wealthy merchants and money-lenders were the very men who controlled the legislatures, and lawyers and judges seemed to be their allies and agents in enforcing laws passed for their protection, at the expense of human rights. Where were the much-vaunted checks and balances which prevented tyranny? For the masses the state governments took on more or less the appearance of mechanisms for their exploitation by the minority.

The limits of the revolutionary philosophy had not been defined. Under such circumstances it tended to violence where there seemed to be no other means of redressing grievances, fancied or real. Revolution had been the final resort of Patriots who could not otherwise combat the arbitrary rule of Parliament and king. Tom Paine's philosophy appealed to the debtor element, and contained even more dynamite than that of Thomas Jefferson, for it perpetuated the ancient feeling that government is the natural enemy of man rather than his servant. Like Rousseau, who declared that man, although created free was everywhere in chains, Paine

asserted that "government, like dress, is the badge of lost inno-
cence; the palaces of kings are built on the ruins of the bowers of
Paradise." [27]

The triumphant paper-money party in Rhode Island passed a
legal-tender law under which arose one of the earliest cases involving the right of courts to pass upon the constitutionality of acts of
legislation.[28]   In Massachusetts the inflationists, defeated at the
polls, rose in insurrection in 1786.   Farmers in the barren hill
country of the frontier counties, under the lead of Daniel Shays,
a veteran of Bunker Hill, broke up court sessions at Northampton
and Worcester engaged in the trial of debt cases.   From the United
States arsenal at Springfield they tried to take arms, and for a
while the town was under siege.

The chief grievances of which Shays and his followers complained were the provisions of the state constitution which made
the senate the representative of wealth (and hence indifferent to
the needs of the people), and the swarms of lawyers "who have
been more damage to the people at large, especially the farmers,
than the common, savage beasts of prey."   Among other changes
they demanded the amendment of the constitution to eliminate the
senate, the removal of the capitol from the aristocratic atmosphere
of Boston to a region more congenial to the farmers, reduction of
taxation through sale of the state lands in Maine, and payment of
the national debt by import and excise taxes in place of direct taxes
on lands and polls.[29]

To modern ears there is nothing very shocking in these demands,
and even at the time there was widespread sympathy with the

[27] Quoted by McLaughlin, *Con. Hist.*, 138.
[28] See *post*, 176–177.
[29] Contemporary newspapers devote much space to the Shays Rebellion. See
the citations by Warren, *Making of the Constitution*, 30, note; also Warren's discussion.   The earliest full account of the episode is the work of George R.
Minot, *History of the Insurrections in Massachusetts*.   His volume reflects the
inability of the dominant class to understand the disposition of the unfortunate
farmers.   For a long time historians followed Minot and perpetuated his bias.
This is true of Hildreth, the temper of whose history is Federalist; of Fiske, for
whom advocacy of paper money was an unpardonable sin; and of McMaster,
although to a less extent.   See account by the last-named in *History of the
People of the United States*, I, 288 *et seq.*   For a more sympathetic account see
Julian Aronson, "The 'Forgotten Man' of Yesterday."

"rebels." But conservatives everywhere took alarm, not perhaps so much at their program as because the resort to violence seemed to prove the turbulent disposition of the people and the need of a general government capable of protecting the states against domestic violence. Redress of grievances was less thought of than the necessity of repression. Congress had been unable even to defend its own property when Shays attacked the Springfield arsenal. Conservatives became much concerned also about the sanctity of contracts, which legal-tender and relief laws menaced, and began to feel that the power of the states should be checked.

DEFECTS IN STATE GOVERNMENT

Shays's Rebellion was one of the chief factors in uniting conservative opinion on a country-wide basis, by arousing the fears of property owners. In a paper written in the spring of 1787, on the "Vices of the Political System of the United States," James Madison stressed the "want of guarantee to the States of their constitutions and laws against internal violence." [30] Liberal that he was, he shows for the moment a distrust of democracy. Viewing the paper money legislation and many other "unjust" laws of the states, he asks what is to keep a majority [of the voters] from infringing the rights of a minority, and suggests that a remedy may be found in an enlargement of the geographical basis of the government. A large republic would make more difficult the combination of dangerous factions. A central government with power to nullify state legislation would give the responsible element a check upon sporadic outbreaks of dangerous tendency, and involve "the least possible abridgement of the State sovereignties." The control of the central government over "the internal vicissitudes of State policy and the aggression of interested majorities on the rights of minorities and individuals" would, he thought, be a "happy effect." [31]

The proposal to give Congress a veto upon state legislation is evidently an adaptation of the royal disallowance. The essay is chiefly notable as showing that while reformers did not wish to

[30] Quoted by Edward S. Corwin, "Progress of Constitutional Theory," 534.
[31] *Ibid.*, 535.

destroy the autonomy of the states, they thought of the state governments as needing reform quite as much as that of the Confederation.[32] In fact, the two problems were only phases of the one great problem of the proper make-up of both local and general governments as parts of a confederated system.

EMERGENCE OF JUDICIAL REVIEW

Within a few years the concentration of executive, legislative, and judicial functions in Congress came to be felt as a serious defect in the plan of confederation, especially as the sentiment grew that the union should be, not a mere alliance, but a real government. But as has been noted, even the states, under the early constitutions, did not have at the beginning a real separation of powers. In the colonial governments the legislative body had usually exercised judicial functions also, and while the state constitutions vested the judicial powers in distinct tribunals, there was a lack of clear definition of the relations between legislature and court.

Obviously the judiciary could hardly check the legislature so long as the two functions were vested in the same body. The complete separation of the branches of government according to function was therefore one prerequisite for the emergence of the practice of judicial review. Another was a sufficiently clear grasp of the concept to warrant its translation into action. British history, as we have seen, afforded no clear-cut example of a decision in which a court held an act of Parliament void on the ground of conflict with the common law, the principles of natural justice, or any other "superior" law; and it must be remembered that the rulings of the Privy Council against the validity of colonial statutes were, legally, judgments as to the powers of corporations. Neither Locke, Blackstone, nor Montesquieu advanced the theory of judi-

[32] See quotation from Madison's essay in *Federalist, post,* 175–176. Even Jefferson called the state governments under control of the "rag-money" party, "elective despotisms."—*Notes on Virginia,* quoted by Corwin, "Progress of Constitutional Theory," 519. See Corwin's article for other criticisms of the state governments. In view of Jefferson's later attitude towards the federal courts his opinion at this time is not to be overlooked. Criticising the proposal to give Congress a negative on state legislation, he wrote to Madison, June 20, 1787: "Would not an appeal from the state judicatures to a federal court in all cases where the act of Confederation controlled the question, be as effectual a remedy, and exactly commensurate to the defect?"—Ford, *Writings of Jefferson,* IV, 391.

cial review. Locke, indeed, says that legislatures should not exercise the judicial authority, and Montesquieu holds that the merging of the two functions would make law-makers of judges and give them arbitrary power. Blackstone on the contrary upholds the judicial function of Parliament in certain cases.[33] The American belief in the English origin of the doctrine seems to rest upon Lord Coke's dictum, and the unsoundness of his precedents has already been noted. Otis's argument, being derived from Coke, of course added nothing to its validity.

The debt of America to England for this doctrine is therefore slight. Its emergence is associated with the misconceptions of Coke and Otis, and with the Privy Council's function of judging of the legislative powers of the colonies as corporations; the elevation of these to the plane of political commonwealths is another factor. These influences were the prelude to a new development which first became possible under the state constitutions. Stress should probably be placed on the interpretation that here is another example of the development of old germs, in a new soil or amid new surroundings, into a virtually new legal institution.

The truth seems to be, as hinted above, that while the concept of judicial review certainly took form in the mind of Otis and perhaps others, the idea lacked the proper soil for growth until the American state constitutions vested legislative and judicial functions in separate branches of government. The theory of checks and balances was a corollary of that of the separation of powers, and in current thinking was closely associated with the preservation of liberty. But the theory of checks and balances could be, and was, maintained before judicial review was conceived of as an appropriate check.[34]

Actual resort to the judicial check on legislation came about by slow degrees. Despite the repudiation of parliamentary supremacy, Americans trusted their assemblies unduly because they had been the champions of colonial rights during the contests with England. Moreover, law-makers and judges were alike deeply

[33] Corwin, *loc. cit.*, 524, 525.

[34] *Cf.* Dickinson's assertion that only those are free "who live under a government so constitutionally checked and controuled, that proper provision is made against its being otherwise exercised."—*Writings*, 356.

imbued with the Blackstonian tradition of legislative preëminence.

This fact is well brought out by the case of Rutgers *v.* Waddington, in New York mayor's court, 1784, in which the court observed: "The supremacy of the Legislature need not be called into question [by this decision]; if they think fit positively to enact a law, there is no power which can controul them. When the main object of such a law is clearly expressed, and the intention is manifest, the Judges are not at liberty, although it appears to them to be unreasonable, to reject it: for this were to set the judicial above the legislative. . . ."[35] This is the practice of the English courts of justice, from which we have copied our jurisprudence, as well as the models of our internal judicatories."

The approach to the new doctrine was facilitated by a shift of attitude towards constitutions which took place in the years of the Confederation. In the revolutionary era Americans had regarded the English constitution as something which embraced the immutable principles of natural law. After independence, while the state constitutions were also thought of as explicitly incorporating such principles, the former view yielded somewhat to the idea that a constitution represents an act of legislation by the sovereign people, who thereby fix the metes and bounds of governmental authority, and especially the legislative authority. Such a philosophy is much more favorable to the rise of the practice of judicial review than the earlier. On the face of things, it is a much simpler matter to compare an act of legislation with a written constitution than with a vague, undefined set of principles known as natural law. It is much simpler for the court to say: "Here are the principles by which the sovereign people have ordained that government shall be carried on. It is our duty to follow this fundamental law rather than any statute which oppugns it."

[35] The words omitted relate to Blackstone's tenth rule for construing statutes where the object is not expressed with unmistakable clarity by the law. "Throughout the Revolution the Blackstonian doctrine of 'legislative omnipotence' was in the ascendant."—Corwin, *loc. cit.,* 517. Coxe says that by this decision "Blackstone's tenth rule for construing statutes in England under an unwritten constitution was . . . adopted bodily by a court of New York under a written constitution."—*Essay on Judicial Power,* quoted by Boudin, I, 57. The point here is the recognition by the New York court of the doctrine of legislative supremacy, and the adoption of the same rule which denied to British courts the power to declare acts of Parliament unconstitutional.

Viewing the constitutions as superior *law* to which acts of assembly must conform, the state courts began to find themselves occasionally almost compelled to choose between statute and constitution where the two seemed contradictory. Especially was this true when the state legislatures began to disregard constitutional limitations. The necessity of some check upon the legislative power then became painfully evident. No longer subject as they had been before the Revolution to the crown and its agencies the royal governor and the Privy Council, under constitutions now which did not implement the statements of the theory of checks and balances, and controlled in some of the states by inexperienced "popular" parties, the legislatures were guilty of excesses which called for the application of new restraints.

Madison wrote most pointedly of this need. Said he, referring to the state constitutions: "In no instance has a competent provision been made for maintaining in practice the separation [of powers] delineated on paper." "The legislative department is everywhere extending the sphere of its activity and drawing all power into its impetuous vortex. . . . The conclusion which I am warranted in drawing is, that a mere demarcation on parchment of the constitutional limits of the several departments, is not a sufficient guard against those encroachments which lead to a tyrannical concentration of all the powers of government in the same hands." [36]

In other words, Madison perceived that some workable device, one which could check the legislature, was required for the maintenance of the separation of powers which was provided for on paper. As such a mechanism he suggested the congressional veto of state legislation. Although he desired the separation of the legis-

[36] Paul Leicester Ford, ed., *The Federalist*, essays Nos. 47 and 48. No. 49, doubtfully attributed to Madison, continues the discussion of the excessive influence of the legislatures. The Pennsylvania legislature was a gross offender. See Nevins, 189–192. A movement was on foot in Virginia as early as 1784 for revision of the constitution of 1776. Madison was already at that time aware of the defect of that constitution in that the lack of provision for interpreting it except by the legislature left that body unchecked.—*Ibid.*, 195. R. D. Spaight criticized the North Carolina constitution in 1787 on the ground that there was no "sufficient check to prevent the intemperate and unjust proceedings of our legislature."—*Ibid.*, 204. Similar opinions were directed against the constitutions of other states.

lative, executive and judicial departments, he seems to have been slow to perceive that judicial review was exactly such a check as he was seeking; and the universal omission of any express provision for it in the state constitutions is strong presumptive evidence that the concept had not definitely emerged in the consciousness of statesmen when the state constitutions were drawn up. Nevertheless one must look to the Confederation period for the beginnings of the *practice* of judicial review as distinguished from the origin of the *concept*.

It has been customary for historians to recite several cases which were heard in state courts previous to the framing of the federal Constitution, as evidence of the acceptance of the doctrine of judicial review. The most that can be learned from the meager records still extant is that the doctrine was taking shadowy form here and there. Some of the supposed decisions and opinions are of questionable historicity. Thus in 1780, in the case of Holmes *v.* Walton, the supreme court of New Jersey is supposed to have refused to recognize the validity of an act of the legislature providing for the trial of certain classes of cases by a jury of six, on the ground that the constitution of the state contemplated (by implication) a twelve-man jury. That there ever was such a decision seems doubtful, since six-man juries were in regular use in the state until a new constitution was adopted in 1844.[37]

Quite different is the case of Trevett *v.* Weeden (1786), in which an act of the Rhode Island legislature for the enforcement of the laws making paper money legal tender was challenged. As counsel for the defendant, James M. Varnum attempted to prove that the act of the legislature should be disregarded by the court on the ground that it was in conflict with superior law and consequently void. By superior law Varnum meant not merely the constitution of the state (the charter granted by Charles II), in which there was no express stipulation concerning the point at issue; he appealed also to Magna Carta, invariable custom, natural law, and the law of God. Loose as was this concept of the law which he urged the legislature must not transgress, Varnum's ar-

[37] Austin Scott, "Holmes *v.* Walton, the New Jersey Precedent." *Cf.* Boudin, I, 531 *et seq.*, especially 552.

gument was an unmistakable appeal for the exercise of judicial review. "The judiciary," he declared, "have the sole power of judging of laws . . . and cannot admit any act of the legislatures as law against the Constitution." [38]

That same year James Iredell, in North Carolina, in the case of Bayard *v.* Singleton, likewise asserted that the constitution of a state is the *fundamental* law, and declared that judges must take care that acts of assembly which they undertake to enforce are warranted by the constitution, adding that, "if the power of judging rests with the courts their decision is final." [39]

THE ARTICLES AS FUNDAMENTAL LAW

While the evil of legislative omnipotence was calling into use in the states the check of judicial review and suggesting to Madison the need of a congressional brake on state action, the necessity of a union which could act effectively was giving birth to the theory that the Articles were fundamental law, that acts of Congress authorized by them were paramount to state legislation, and even that Congress possessed the implied power of coercive action to carry its measures into effect. The last power if established would have served in itself as a check upon the evil of "excessive concentration of power in the hands of the legislative departments" in the states, which was often so used as to thwart the functions of Congress.[40] To gain any additional grant of power, however, by amendment of the Articles required the assent of every one of these same legislatures, and on every attempt of the kind one or more of them held out. The resort to the theory that some powers were implied (in spite of the assertion in the Articles that the states retained every power not *expressly* granted) became under these circumstances a counsel of desperation.

The validity of the charter of the Bank of North America was defended by James Wilson on the broad ground that any power which could be exercised only on a national scale must belong to

---

[38] Corwin, "Progress of Constitutional Theory," 526. On Varnum see Coxe, *op. cit.*, 281 *et seq.* Cf. Peleg W. Chandler, *American Criminal Trials*, II, 281 *et seq.*, and McMaster, *History*, I, 330–340, 392–393.
[39] Corwin, 526.
[40] *Ibid.*, 528.

Congress, because, being beyond the actual competence of the state legislatures, it could not be "retained by the states" since they never possessed it; and for the same reason it could not be delegated.[41]

Hamilton, in Rutgers *v.* Waddington, argued that an act of the New York legislature was void because it was contrary to the law of nations, the treaty of peace, and the *Articles of Confederation.* In his manuscript notes he wrote: "Though in relation to its own citizens local laws might govern, yet in relation to foreigners those of the United States must prevail. It must be conceded that the Legislature of one State cannot repeal a law of the United States." [42]

In a report to Congress in October, 1786, John Jay urged that "when . . . a treaty is constitutionally made, ratified, and published by Congress, it immediately becomes binding on the whole nation, and superadded to the laws of the land, without intervention, consent or fiat of state legislatures." [43] He urged that state courts should enforce the treaty in cases involving rights of individuals, and that the state legislatures should be estopped from legislation adversely affecting treaties.[44] Congress unanimously endorsed this view, and most of the state legislatures seemed ready to regard treaties as binding upon them. The North Carolina Supreme Court, moreover, in the case of Bayard *v.* Singleton, held that "the Articles of Confederation are a part of the law of the land unrepealable by any act of the general assembly" of the state.[45]

The theory that the Articles constituted law cognizable by courts might if acted upon have transformed the character of the Confederation and brought about a real government. Coercive operation on individuals without intervention of state legislatures was

[41] *Ibid.,* 528, 529. *Cf.* Margaret C. Klingelsmith, "Two Theories in Regard to the Implied Powers."

[42] Corwin, 530.

[43] Quoted *ibid.,* 531.

[44] The British ministry was refusing at this time to make a treaty with the United States, on the ground that it did not appear from the Articles that Congress had power to make a treaty which the states would be bound to observe. Jay's recommendation should be read in the light of such cases as Rutgers *v.* Waddington and Bayard *v.* Singleton, which involved state acts of confiscation of royalist property and the rights of individuals as affected by the provisions of the treaty of peace with England and these laws.

[45] Corwin, 531.

needed also to attain this object.   Even this power might have been gained by Congress in time, through general recognition that it was indispensable.   Madison, indeed, reasoned later that there had been from the first a power of direct action on individuals under the provisions relating to captures, piracy, the post office, coinage, weights and measures, Indian trade, conflicting land claims under grants of different states, and above all, courts martial in army and navy.[46]   The amendments proposed but not adopted relating to customs and the regulation of commerce would have carried, similarly, extensions of the power of action on individuals.   However, the advance in constitutional theory during the Confederation era had little effect on the actual practice of government.   It was only in the new Constitution which was about to be framed that this thinking was to produce results.

[46] Essay No. 40 in *Federalist*. *Cf.* his similar statement in the Federal Convention: Farrand, *Records*, I, 447.

X

THE MOVEMENT FOR MORE PERFECT UNION

INTRODUCTORY

FROM the preceding chapter it can be seen that the years of the Confederation, while marked by many failures in the functioning of governments, both state and general, nevertheless brought clarification of the problems of federalism. Even the painful experiences of the period revealed the defects of the existing system and thus aided in determining the remedies to be applied. Some of these defects were, indeed, perceived almost from the moment of the drafting of the Articles, and discussion of their merits and faults accompanied the debates over their adoption and continued in increasing volume until they were superseded. Many men were active in this discussion—Washington, Hamilton, Jefferson, Madison, Jay, Lee, Randolph, Pelatiah and Noah Webster, Stephen Higginson, and a host of lesser celebrities, both in and out of Congress. Between July 6, 1780 and Nov. 30, 1785, Washington alone wrote at least twenty-two letters to twenty different correspondents, dealing with the need of government reform.[1] The men engaged in the agitation pointed out defects, suggested the additional powers required, and considered the ways and means of obtaining them. As a consequence, these leaders came to substantial agreement as to the changes to be sought. The idea that the powers of the states should be carefully distinguished from those assigned to the general government was accepted by all participants in the discussion.[2] They laid special stress upon

[1] Warren, *Making of the Constitution*, 12, note 1, enumerates twenty-two letters and calls it a "partial list."

[2] "Power to govern the Confederacy, as to all general purposes, should be granted and exercised."—John Jay to Gouverneur Morris, Sept. 24, 1783, quoted by Warren, *Making*, 13. Writing from France, Jefferson said that "the politics of Europe rendered it indispensably necessary that with respect to everything external we be one nation firmly hooped together; interior government is what each State should keep to itself."—To Madison, October 8, 1786. W. C. Rives, *Life and Times of James Madison*, II, 31, quoted by Warren, 46. Again he wrote: "To make us one nation as to foreign concerns and keep us distinct in

the necessity of giving Congress three additional powers—those of taxation, commercial regulation, and coercion. They perceived also that there was need of some means of maintaining the supremacy of the laws of Congress over those of the states in matters entrusted to the care of the general government. This was perhaps a corollary of the power of coercion, but there was no very definite vision as to how it should be implemented. The extravagant legislation of some of the states and the prevalent social disorders suggested the need of checks on the part of the general government upon the licentious tendencies of state legislatures, especially in the direction of paper money issues and the impairment of the obligation of contracts. Some felt that a bicameral body should be substituted for the one-house Congress, and that legislative, executive and judicial powers should be separated and vested in three distinct branches of government.

If these changes could not be brought about by resort to the process of amendment prescribed by the Articles, a general convention was favored as a possible means of obtaining them. A convention would be a suitable body to prepare a plan for thoroughly revising the government, while Congress could present proposals of change only piecemeal. Some desired that the proposals of a convention should be passed upon by the voters in the several states instead of by the legislatures, thus basing the revised government on the consent of the people as required by the political philosophy of the time.

Thus through discussion the views of statesmen were brought to a focus. This in itself took time and hung to a degree upon the march of events. But the success of the reform movement required much more than a focussing of opinion. The efforts of Congress to obtain amendments even of the most obvious necessity were balked sometimes by the stubbornness and selfishness of single states. Congressional jealousy of the prerogatives granted by the Articles in the matter of initiating amendments proved to be an obstacle in the way of calling a convention. The ignorance

domestic ones, gives the outline of the proper division of power between the general and particular Governments."—To Madison, Dec. 16, 1786, quoted by Warren, 47.

and inertia of the masses, and their fears, not wholly baseless, of the establishing of aristocratic dominance through the creation of a stronger central government, created no end of trouble. For several years in consequence of all these difficulties, the Confederation limped along, becoming constantly more ineffectual, until it threatened to fall to pieces. As its feebleness became increasingly apparent, the diversity of sectional interests played their disruptive part, threatening the dissolution of the confederacy and the formation of several regional unions. European powers looked on, vulture-like, awaiting the breakup to profit by the failure of Americans in the experiment at self-government. Looking backward, it seems almost miraculous that the leaders of the movement for a stronger union succeeded in overcoming so many difficulties.

Writing six months before the Articles became operative through Maryland's ratification, Alexander Hamilton proposed the calling of a convention of all the states with authority to give Congress adequate powers to meet all public exigencies.[3] He thought that "the Confederation . . . should give Congress a complete sovereignty; except as to that part of internal police which relates to the rights of property and life among individuals, and to raising money by internal taxes. It is necessary that everything belonging to this should be regulated by the State Legislatures. Congress should have complete sovereignty in all that relates to war, peace, trade, finance, and to the management of foreign affairs . . . laying prohibitions on all the articles of export or import; imposing duties, . . . and applying to their own use, the product of these duties . . . ; of coining money; establishing banks . . . ; transacting everything with foreign nations; making alliances, offensive and defensive, treaties of commerce, etc., etc." He also advocated giving Congress power to raise revenues by means of poll and land taxes, and the sale of public lands.

This letter shows that Hamilton desired a sharper discrimination between the internal police powers reserved by the states and the general powers of the Confederation. Under the "complete

[3] To James Duane, Sept. 3, 1780, in Gertrude Atherton, *A Few of Hamilton's Letters*, 90 *et seq.*, quoted by Harmon, "Proposed Amendments," 21.

sovereignty" of Congress he would place, in addition to the matters already covered by the Articles, full power to regulate foreign commerce and ample powers of taxation. What he means by "complete sovereignty" is not explained, but the phrase suggests that he believes Congress should be enabled to enforce its legislation. If so, this early letter covers all three of the main points persistently urged by the reformers during the following years.

The month before Hamilton's letter was written delegates from the New England states had met at Boston and urged that adequate powers be granted to Congress; and before the close of the year 1780 another gathering of delegates from these states and New York, at Hartford, had declared that "all governments suppose the power of coercion." [4]

THE PROBLEM OF COERCIVE POWER

In operation, the need of coercive power was first felt acutely because of the inability of Congress to obtain money from the states under the requisition system. Article 13 provided that "Every State shall abide by the determinations of the United States in Congress assembled, on all questions which by this confederation are submitted to them." Like the clauses in the state constitutions concerning the separation of powers, this article was a mere paper obligation, lacking sanction or mechanism for giving it effect. Perceiving this, William Henry Drayton, a member of the assembly of North Carolina, had proposed as early as January 20, 1778, while the Articles were pending before the states, that they be amended so that if a state violated them Congress might declare that state under the ban and proceed against it in arms until it "paid due obedience." Thereupon it should be restored to the full benefits of the Confederation.[5]

[4] Harmon, "Proposed Amendments," 22.

[5] Hezekiah Niles, *Principles and Acts of the Revolution*, quoted by Warren, *Making*, 8, note 2. Drayton was chief justice of the state, and an ardent defender of state sovereignty. He opposed the adoption of the Articles and drew up a plan of his own. He did not, he said, desire "any confederation that gives Congress any power that can with propriety be exercised by the several states." He would have required the vote of eleven states for any important legislation, since otherwise "the most important transactions in Congress may be done contrary to the united opposition of Virginia, the two Carolinas, and Georgia, states possessing more than one-half of the whole territory of the Confederacy. . . . If

On the very day on which the Articles were ratified Congress was listening to the report of a committee which had been instructed to consider the question of additional powers. This committee, composed of the three Jameses—Madison of Virginia, Duane of New York, and Varnum of Rhode Island—held that Article 13 implied that Congress possessed power to enforce the terms of the Confederation against any state which did not abide by them. To act on this theory, however, would have been rash; hence the committee recommended that Congress seek an amendment authorizing the use of "the force of the United States . . . to compel any delinquent State to fulfill its Federal engagement, by restraining its vessels, merchandise, and trade." [6]

From one committee to another this vital matter was passed along until August 22, when a report was presented setting forth the requisites for making the Confederation adequate for the purposes for which it was created. In the long list of needed powers was that of distraining the property of any state delinquent in meeting its quota of money or men. No action was taken on the report.[7]

The earliest comprehensive project for a new constitution was drawn up by Pelatiah Webster, who published on February 26, 1783, a pamphlet entitled *A Dissertation on the Political Union and Constitution of the Thirteen United States*. The author proposed that Congress should have power to do all those things which are necessary for the general welfare but which are beyond the competence of the states singly. This would include, of course, power to regulate commerce. Congress should, moreover, have the powers of taxation and coercion. Webster carefully pointed out the necessity of a sanction for all laws. "No laws of any State, whatever," said he, "which do not carry in them a force which extends to their effectual and final execution, can afford a certain or a sufficient security to the subject." He would have Congress

things of such transcendent weight may be done notwithstanding such an opposition, the honor, interest and sovereignty of the South are in effect delivered up to the care of the North."—Harmon, "Proposed Amendments," 14–18.

[6] *Journals of the Cont. Cong.*, March 1, 1781. *Cf.* same for March 6, May 2, July 20, and August 22, 1781; August 5, 1782; April 18, 1783. See reprints of committee reports in *Am. Hist. Leaflet*, No. 28.

[7] *Ibid.*, 4–7.

possess the right to use force against any state which resisted national legislation.   Still more significant was the suggestion, in crude form, of direct action on individuals.   Any person who disobeyed the "supreme authority" should be haled before Congress for trial and punishment.   Webster desired also to see Congress made a bicameral body.   Suggestive as it was, especially as to the compulsive action of the federal government on individuals, Webster's pamphlet seems not to have attracted much attention at the time.[8]

Two years later Noah Webster, the great lexicographer, made his contribution to the agitation for an improved plan of government.   "In the first place," he urged, "there must be a supreme power at the head of the union, vested with authority to make laws that respect the states in general and to compel obedience to these laws. . . .   There must be a supreme head, clothed with the same power to make and enforce laws, respecting the general policy of all the states, as the legislatures of the respective states have to make laws binding on those states, respecting their own internal police. . . .   Let the several states, as to their own police, be sovereign and independent. . . .

"The general concerns of the continent may be reduced to a few heads. . . .   Such a power would not abridge the sovereignty of each state in any article relating to its own government.   The internal police of each state would be still under the sole superintendence of its legislature. . . .

"The ninth article recites the powers of Congress, which are perhaps nearly sufficient to answer the ends of our union, were there any method of enforcing their resolutions. . . .   A law without a penalty is mere *advice;* a magistrate without the power

[8] Extract from the *Dissertation* in *Am. Hist. Leaflet,* No. 28, pp. 7–11.   There has been quite a controversy over the influence of Webster's pamphlet.   Hannis Taylor, in various writings, has maintained that he was the real author of the Constitution.   With the possible exception of the proposal that government should operate directly on individuals, however, there is nothing in his pamphlet that had not appeared elsewhere and earlier, although nowhere perhaps had all of his proposals been previously brought together.   No direct evidence has been produced to show that members of the Constitutional Convention were familiar with the *Dissertation,* although Taylor makes out a rather plausible circumstantial case.   The only conclusion warranted at present is that Webster summarized ideas that were "in the air."

of punishment is a *cypher*. Here is the *great defect* in the articles of our federal government." [9]

Spurred perhaps by such comments out of doors and certainly pushed on by the handicaps under which it worked, Congress continued through committees to study the problem of its powers. On August 14, 1786, Charles Pinckney of South Carolina reported for one such committee a new plan for enforcing acts of the Confederation government. The proposal was that Congress be authorized "to institute a federal judicial court for trying and punishing all officers appointed by congress for all crimes, offenses, and misbehavior in their offices, and to which court an appeal shall be allowed from the judicial courts of the several states in all causes wherein any question shall arise on the meaning and construction of treaties entered into by the United States with any foreign power, or on the law of nations, or wherein any question shall arise respecting any regulations that may hereafter be made by congress relative to trade and commerce, or the collection of federal revenues pursuant to powers that shall be vested in that body, or wherein questions of importance may arise, and the United States shall be a party, provided that the trial of the fact by jury shall ever be held sacred, and also the benefits of the writ of *habeas corpus;* provided, also, that no member of congress or officer holding any other office under the United States shall be a judge of said court, and the said court shall consist of seven judges." [10]

Characteristically, Congress took no final action on this proposal, which of course never came before the states. But from the date of this report can be traced a growing tendency to think of a federal judicial system as an agency in enforcing the laws of the Union. The very next month Rufus King remarked that to give

[9] *Sketches of American Policy*, 30–48 *et passim*. Extract in *Am. Hist. Leaflet*, No. 28, pp. 21–24.

[10] George Bancroft, *History of the Formation of the Constitution*, II, 374–377. Extract in *Am. Hist. Leaflet*, No. 28, pp. 26–30.

The report of Pinckney's committee advocated the addition of a long list of powers to those already possessed by Congress. The chief of these were: 1. To regulate interstate and foreign trade; 2. To appoint, in the last extremity, assessors and collectors if any state persistently refused to meet its requisitions. If such federal officials should be resisted, the final remedy was to consider the conduct of the state "an open violation of the federal compact"; 3. To create a federal court; 4. To provide for securing the attendance of members of Congress.

Congress the power to regulate foreign and domestic commerce "will run deep into the authorities of the individual States, and can never be well exercised without a Federal Judicial." [11]

This use of the judiciary was associated with the demand for the separation of government into the usual three departments.   In King's letter just quoted he wrote: "Let there be a Federal Government, with a vigorous Executive, wise Legislature, and independent Judicial."   John Jay had urged four days after the report in Congress, that the "three great departments of sovereignty should be forever separated, and so distributed as to serve as checks on each other." [12]   Jefferson was like-minded.   To Madison he wrote in December, "To enable the Federal head to exercise the power given it to best advantage, it should be organized, as the particular ones are, into Legislative, Executive, and Judiciary." [13]   Again, in February, 1787, Jay wrote: "There is one [change] which I think would be much for the better, viz.: to distribute the Federal sovereignty into its three proper departments of Executive, Legislative, and Judicial; for that Congress should act in these different capacities was, I think, a great mistake in our policy." [14]

Washington was among the first to perceive the necessity of coercive power.   Throughout the years of the Confederation he dwelt constantly on the theme that if the powers of Congress were not enlarged "anarchy and confusion must ensue."   In 1783 he addressed a circular letter to the governors of the states, in which he declared that "it is indispensable to the happiness of the individual states, that there should be lodged somewhere a supreme power to regulate and govern the general concerns of the confederated republic, without which the Union cannot be of long duration." [15]   These words, so strikingly like those used by Noah Webster in 1785, were reiterated by Washington time and again. In 1786 he wrote: "I do not conceive we can exist long as a nation without having lodged somewhere a power which will pervade

[11] To Jonathan Jackson, Sept. 3, 1786. Quoted by Warren, *Making*, 19–20.
[12] To Jefferson, August 18, 1786. *Ibid.*, 46.
[13] Dec. 12, 1786. *Ibid.*, 47.
[14] To John Adams, Feb. 21, 1787. *Ibid.*, 42.
[15] Worthington C. Ford, ed., *The Writings of George Washington*, X, 258.

the whole Union in as energetic a manner, as the authority of the State Governments extends over the several States." [16]

Washington fully appreciated the fact that a law without a sanction is no law; and, like Madison, he thought that the state legislatures were in need of restraint. "Thirteen sovereign, independent, disunited States [legislatures]," he wrote, "are in the habit of discussing and refusing compliance with [requisitions] at their option. . . . If you tell the Legislatures they have violated the treaty of peace and invaded the prerogatives of the Confederacy, they will laugh in your face." [17]   But how to provide a coercive system was puzzling. "I have my doubts," said Washington, "whether any system, without the means of coercion in the sovereign, will enforce due obedience to the ordinances of a General Government. . . . But what kind of coercion, you may ask. This indeed will require thought, though the non-compliance of the States with the late requisition is an evidence of the necessity." [18]

Madison, wrestling with this problem, came to the conclusion, as already noted, that Congress must be given a veto upon acts of legislation by the states. To Washington he wrote that "a negative in all cases whatsoever on the legislative acts of the states" was absolutely necessary. Without it "every positive power that can be given on paper, will be evaded and defeated." In this same letter he favored the separation of the legislative, executive and judicial departments.[19]

Thus the need of coercive power supplied a continuing motive for revision of the Articles of Confederation. Even men like

[16] To John Jay, August 1, 1786. *Ibid.*, XI, 53–54.
[17] *Ibid.*
[18] To Madison, March 31, 1787. Warren, *Making*, 43–44.
[19] April 16, 1787. Jared Sparks, ed., *The Writings of George Washington*, IX, 516–519. This letter is especially noteworthy, because it reveals the ideas with which Madison came to Philadelphia for the Convention the next month, and shows that in broad outline he had in mind already the principles which became the fundamental features of the Constitution. *Cf.* letter to Jefferson, March 19. The new features which Madison had in mind were: (1) ratification of the new Constitution by the people rather than by state legislatures; (2) a negative by the national legislature upon acts of the state legislatures; (3) proportional instead of equal representation of states; (4) separation of the three departments of the federal government.

Richard Henry Lee, who had already made himself conspicuous as a jealous defender of the sovereignty of the states, came to the point of conceding its necessity. Almost at the moment of the meeting of the Philadelphia Convention, concerned over the failure of states to meet the requisitions of Congress, he wrote that if they refused to pay, "no form of government whatever, short of force, will answer. . . ." "Do you not think," he asked his correspondent, "that it ought to be declared, by the new system, that any State act of legislation that shall contravene, or oppose, the authorized acts of Congress, or interfere with the expressed rights of that body, shall be *ipso facto* void, and of no force whatever?" [20]

The friends of strong government, however, had learned that mere paper declarations would not suffice. "Powers delineated on paper cannot alone be sufficient," wrote Stephen Higginson. "The Union must not only have the right to make Laws and requisitions, but it must have the power also of compelling obedience thereto, otherwise our federal Constitution will be a mere dead letter." [21]

Madison clung to his belief in the necessity of a congressional veto on state legislation up to the moment of the meeting of the Convention. But the alternative, or additional, check of judicial action was gaining favor. From Jefferson, to whom he had written his views, he received in reply the inquiry: "Would not an appeal from the state judicatures to a federal court in all cases where the act of Confederation controlled the question, be as effectual a remedy, and exactly commensurate to the defect?" [22] When Madison received this letter the Convention had already begun its work, and to that body fell the task of implementing provisions for the compulsive operation of federal law.

THE QUESTION OF REVENUE

In so far as the delinquencies of the states consisted of failures to meet their quotas under the requisitions of Congress, an alternative to coercion lay in the possibility of authorizing Congress to raise its own revenue; and this, since the source would inevitably

[20] To George Mason, May 15, 1787. Kate M. Rowland, *Life of George Mason, 1725–1792*, II, 105 *et seq.*
[21] To Henry Knox, Feb. 8, 1787. "Letters of Stephen Higginson," 745.
[22] Letter of June 20, 1787. Ford, *Writings of Jefferson*, IV, 391.

be a duty on imports, involved in turn the regulation of commerce. These three interrelated questions already confronted Congress when the Articles became effective, on March 1, 1781. A month before, that body had sent an amendment to the states asking power to levy a duty of five percent ad valorem on all imports.

This was the so-called Five Percent Amendment. Congress resolved, on February 3, 1781, "that it be recommended to the several States as indispensibly [sic] necessary, that they vest a power in Congress to levy for the use of the United States a duty of five per cent advalorem at the time and place of importation upon all goods wares and merchandizes of foreign growth and manufactures [sic] which may be imported into any of the said States from any foreign port Island or plantation after the first day of May 1781, except arms ammunition cloathing [sic] & other articles imported on account of the United States or any of them: . . . Also a like duty of five per cent on all prizes and prize goods condemned in the court of Admiralty of any of these States as lawful prize.

"That the monies arising from the said duties be appropriated to the discharge of the principal & interest of the debts already contracted or which may be contracted on the faith of the United States for supporting the present war.

"That the said duties be continued until the said debts shall be fully & finally discharged." [23]

This amendment failed as the result of rejection by the single state of Rhode Island (November 1, 1782). Three reasons were assigned for her action: The hardship which duties would impose on commercial states, especially Rhode Island; the dislike of collection by federal officers; the danger to liberty involved in allowing Congress to collect and expend a revenue for which it would not be accountable to the constituent states.[24] In addition it may be surmised that Rhode Island did not wish to lose the income which she had been deriving from imports destined for use in neighboring states.

Efforts to persuade Rhode Island to adopt a more cooperative course were abandoned when news reached Congress that the Vir-

[23] *Am. Hist. Leaflet*, No. 28, pp. 2–3.
[24] Bancroft, *Hist. of Const.*, I, 43.

ginia legislature had withdrawn its assent to the amendment.   For
this action Richard Henry Lee was responsible.   Patrick Henry's
principle, adopted nearly twenty years before, that the people of
Virginia could be taxed only by their own assembly, retained so
much of its vitality that the assembly now resolved that "the permitting any power other than the general assembly of this
commonwealth to levy duties or taxes upon the citizens of this
state within the same is injurious to its sovereignty, may prove
destructive of the rights and liberty of the people, and, so far as
congress may exercise the same, is contravening the spirit of the
confederation." [25]

In 1782, while the Five Percent Amendment was before the
states, Robert Morris, the superintendent of finance, in a letter to
the governors of the states, urged that Congress be empowered to
lay excise, poll, and land taxes in order to discharge the public
debt.   He desired to have a specific tax levied on each hundred
acres of land, regardless of value.   This feature probably led to
the rejection of the whole plan when it was taken up in Congress,
as the North Carolina members opposed the land tax as "insuffer-
ably unequal." [26]   Early the next year Hamilton renewed in Congress the discussion of the five percent proposal, with a proviso
designed to meet the objections of Rhode Island.   The collectors,
he suggested, should be inhabitants of the state in which they
exercised their duties, and approved by the state, although they
were to be nominated by, accountable to, and removable by Congress.   In addition to the impost he proposed a land and house
tax.[27]

Hamilton's propositions were introduced on March 20, 1783.
On the 28th of the month a committee proposed to amend the
eighth article concerning requisitions upon the states in such a
way as to substitute population for land as the basis of apportionment.   All free inhabitants were to be counted for this purpose,
plus three-fifths of all other inhabitants except untaxed Indians.
The measure revived the contest preceding the adoption of the

[25] *Ibid.*, quoting Hening, *Statutes*, XI, 171.
[26] Harmon, "Proposed Amendments," 23–24.
[27] *Ibid.*, 24.

Articles by Congress, but was at length adopted and became a part of a new amendment which was sent to the states in April.[28]

This Revenue Amendment proposed that for a period of twenty-five years specific duties should be collected on certain enumerated articles of import, and that a five percent ad valorem duty should be levied on all other imports, the revenue to be applied solely to the principal and interest of the public debt. The collectors were to be appointed by the states in which their duties were to be performed but to "be amenable to & removable by" Congress alone. If any state neglected to make the appointments after due notice, the selection was to devolve upon Congress. A new feature was a provision that during the twenty-five year term each state should provide special taxes for raising its proportion of a total of $1,500,000 annually, to be used in discharging the principal and interest of the debt. The apportionment was to be made according to the new rule of population including three-fifths of the slaves.[29]

Soon after Congress sent the Revenue Amendment to the states Washington expressed his mind in characteristically vigorous fashion. The action of his own state in cancelling its ratification of the Five Percent Amendment was not forgotten when he declared: "To suppose that the general concerns of this Country can be directed by thirteen heads, or one head without competent powers, is a solecism, the bad effects of which every man who has had the practical knowledge to judge from, that I have, is fully convinced of; . . . For Heaven's sake, who are Congress? are they not the creatures of the People, amenable to them for their conduct, and dependent from day to day on their breath? Where then can be the danger of giving them such Powers as are adequate to the great ends of Government, and to all the general purposes of the Confederation (I repeat the word *general*, because I am no advocate for their having to do with the particular policy of any state, further than it concerns the Union at large)?"[30]

[28] *Ibid.*, 24–25.
[29] *Am. Hist. Leaflet*, No. 28, pp. 12–15.
[30] To Dr. William Gordon, July 8, 1783. Ford, *Writings of Washington*, X, 275, 277–8. The immediate occasion of the letter was the proposal to hold a general convention to suggest changes in the Articles.

At the end of three years only two states had accepted the Revenue Amendment, although seven others had indicated that they might do so if certain changes were made. Four states had made no response. A committee of Congress considered the changes proposed by the states and reported that the proposals of 1783 were "freer from well-founded exceptions than any which the wisdom of Congress can devise." It was the duty, therefore, of the state legislatures to accede, "as the sole means, in their judgment, of preserving the sacred faith of the Confederacy." Further reliance upon requisitions would be dishonorable and dangerous. "After the most solemn deliberation . . . the committee are of opinion that it has become the duty of Congress to declare most explicitly that the crisis has arrived when the people of these United States, by whose will and for whose benefit the federal government was instituted, must decide whether they will support their rank as a nation by maintaining the public faith at home and abroad; or whether, for want of . . . a general revenue . . . they will hazard not only the existence of the union, but of those great and invaluable privileges for which they have so arduously and. so honorably contended." [31]

Congress accepted the report and declared that the states must surrender to it the power of establishing a revenue system. Under this urging all of the states yielded except New York, whose refusal wrecked this final effort. Thus another critical problem was laid on the doorstep of the Convention of 1787.

THE PROBLEM OF COMMERCE

Mention has been made of the fact that while the Articles of Confederation were pending, New Jersey desired an amendment to give Congress the exclusive power to regulate foreign trade. This desire was due to her peculiar position—like a cask tapped at both ends, as Madison described it. Just before the Articles went into effect one of her representatives in Congress—Witherspoon—renewed this proposal, introducing a resolution which declared "that it was indispensably necessary" that Congress should have this power. Nothing came of the motion, and later (1786) the

[31] Harmon, "Proposed Amendments," 25–26, 43–44.

state refused to meet the requisitions of Congress unless her demand was met.

The plan of taxation proposed by Hamilton in August, 1781, included the control of trade by means of a "moderate tax," and from that moment taxation and trade regulation were closely associated. The plans of government drawn up by individuals like the two Websters, no less than the reports of committees in Congress, included both powers as necessary for the proper functioning of the central government. In the field of foreign relations there was abundant evidence of the need of giving Congress control over trade. When the British issued an order in council on July 2, 1783, excluding American vessels from the West Indies, the legislature of Virginia passed an act authorizing Congress, so far as one state could do so, to adopt retaliatory measures.[32]

On April 30, 1784, Congress submitted to the states a Commerce Amendment. Pointing out that "unless . . . vested with powers competent to the protection of commerce, they can never command reciprocal advantages in trade; and without these our foreign commerce must decline & eventually be annihilated," Congress "recommended to the legislatures of the several States" that they "vest the United States in Congress assembled for the term of fifteen years with power to prohibit any goods wares or merchandize from being imported into or exported from any of the States in vessels belonging to or navigated by the subjects of any power with whom these States shall not have formed treaties of Commerce," and to prohibit the subjects of such powers from importing into the United States any goods not the produce or manufacture of their own countries.[33]

In spite of the predicament in which John Adams found himself in his efforts to obtain a treaty of commerce with England, and in spite of the inglorious failure of John Jay in his negotiations with the Spanish minister Gardoqui, this amendment fared no better at the hands of the state legislatures than the earlier proposals.

In the agitation for more power over commerce James Monroe played an important part. As a member of Congress he proposed

[32] *Ibid.*, 36.
[33] *Am. Hist. Leaflet*, No. 28, pp. 20–21.

(on a day which cannot be ascertained) an alteration in the ninth article to give Congress the exclusive power to regulate both inter-state and foreign commerce, and to lay "such imposts and duties upon imports and exports, as may be necessary for the purpose," all such duties to be collected under the authority and to accrue to the use of the state in which the same may be payable.[34] This proposition was referred, on March 28, 1785, to a committee of which Monroe was chairman. It reported in favor of the amend-ment, but after discussing the matter on July 13 and 14 Congress took no action.

At about this time Monroe drew from Madison the statement that "experience has confirmed what reason foresaw, that" trade "can never be . . . regulated" with effect "by the states acting in their separate capacities. They can no more exercise the power separately, than they could separately carry on war, or separately form treaties of alliances or commerce." [35]

The lack of treaty agreements with foreign nations was felt and deplored by the merchants, both in the North and South, and ef-forts were made by them to obtain favorable action. Those of a number of the coast towns of Virginia memorialized the legislature in 1785, and Governor Bowdoin of Massachusetts, at the request of Boston merchants, urged the legislature to consent to the neces-sary addition to the powers of Congress.

These events were followed by the report of the committee of Congress, on August 14, 1786, whose recommendation of a federal court has already been noted. In this again was taken up the rec-ommendations concerning commerce which had been sent to the states in the Commerce Amendment, and repeated with some variations in the report of Monroe's committee the previous sum-mer. Congress had formed the habit of talking instead of acting, and again went no further than the discussion of the report.

MOVEMENT FOR A CONVENTION

By this time the imbecility of Congress and the failure of all the amendments which had been submitted to the states indicated

[34] *Ibid.*, 25.
[35] Rives, *Madison*, II, 14, quoted by Harmon, 37.

that some new path would have to be found if the country was to get out of its difficulties.   Hamilton had suggested a general convention in his letter to Duane in 1780, and two years later (July 21, 1782) had persuaded the New York legislature to request Congress to call one.   Congress seemed as incapable of taking action on this proposal as on the committee reports which so frequently came before it.   By individuals, newspapers, and legislatures, however, the plan was more and more favored.   Governor Bowdoin endorsed it in his recommendations to the Massachusetts legislature in 1785, and sent a letter to the President of Congress and to each of the state governors urging its adoption.   Following his example the legislature instructed the state's delegates to attempt to persuade Congress to issue a call.   This the delegates did not do, considering the moment inopportune because other measures looking towards betterment of conditions were engrossing attention.[36]

Meantime Virginia and Maryland, having some joint problems connected with the navigation of Chesapeake Bay and the Potomac River, sent commissioners to Washington's home at Mount Vernon, at the end of March, 1785, to try to effect an agreement.   Such a meeting ignored a provision of the Articles which required the consent of Congress to all agreements between two or more states. Nevertheless the commissioners formed a plan which contemplated uniform import duties, regulations of commerce, and currency in the two states.

When the report of this conference was presented to the Maryland legislature, it accepted the proposals as to uniformity (Dec. 5, 1785), and suggested that Pennsylvania and Delaware be invited to join in the agreement with Maryland and Virginia.   News of this action reached the legislature of the last-named state before it had accepted the report of the commissioners.   It had been discussing the still-pending Commerce Amendment, and Madison had argued the cause of a stronger government so warmly that he had aroused some feeling against himself.   In the Maryland proposal he perceived the possibility of bringing about a general meeting to consider the problem of commerce, and cleverly managed to have the invitation for such a convention issued by the Virginia assembly

[36] Harmon, 38.

(Jan. 21, 1786) without appearing himself as the author of the idea. The proposed meeting was to be held at Annapolis, Md., in September. The invitation ignored Congress, but that body was itself considering a motion for a convention, although afflicted with its usual inability to reach a decision. William Grayson, one of Virginia's delegates, reported this fact and his own hesitation: "It is contended that the present Confederation is utterly inefficient, and that if it remains much longer in its present State of imbecillity [sic] we shall be one of the most contemptible Nations on the face of the earth:—for my own part I have not made up my mind . . . whether it is not better to bear the ills we have than fly to others that we know not of. I am however in no doubt about the weakness of the foederal [sic] Government."[37]

Many persons hoped that the Annapolis convention would lead to something more than a commercial agreement. Jay thought it should have a wider purpose,[38] and King seemed perplexed because he could not discover that Madison contemplated anything more than a trade pact.[39] Higginson thought that the regulation of commerce was only the ostensible aim of the meeting, and that it was intended to include political objects, if indeed these were not its principal aims. The fact that so few of the delegates were interested in commerce led him to this conclusion.[40] Grayson thought that even if the eastern delegates contemplated only commercial regulation, Virginia should propose the consideration of all the problems of the Union.

Madison was convinced that many persons wished to convert the Annapolis meeting into a "plenipotentiary Convention for amending the Confederation." He shared their desire, he admitted, but confined his views to commercial reform because he had little hope of accomplishing anything more.[41]

At least nine states appointed delegates to go to Annapolis, but only five were represented on the day set for the opening of the conference. No such rump gathering could pretend to be a gen-

---

[37] To Madison, March 22, 1786. Hunt, *Writings of Madison,* II, 403, note.
[38] Warren, *Making,* 16.
[39] *Ibid.,* citing Mass. Hist. Soc. *Proceedings,* XLIX (1915).
[40] To John Adams, July, 1786. "Letters," 734 *et seq.*
[41] Letter to Jefferson, Aug. 12, 1786. Warren, 22.

eral convention, and after waiting three weeks the delegates decided to adjourn after sending out another call. Although it is not known who the schemers were, there is ground for the suspicion that those on the inside did not intend that the meeting should do anything more than promote the movement for a convention authorized to deal with the whole problem of government. Such was the opinion of M. Otto, the representative of France in the United States, who informed his government that some of the delegates purposely delayed their arrival in order to give the leaders at Annapolis a pretext for adjournment.[42] Alexander Hamilton was in all probability one of the leaders in the design, for, although he was not a member of the committee which prepared the report of the conference, he is said to have drafted it.[43]

A copy of this report was sent to the legislature of every state and to Congress, with the suggestion that the states "use their endeavours to procure the concurrence of the other States, in the Appointment of Commissioners to meet at Philadelphia on the second Monday in May next, to take into Consideration the situation of the United States to devise such further Provisions as shall appear to them necessary to render the Constitution of the Federal Government adequate to the exigencies of the Union; and to report such an Act for that purpose to the United States in Congress Assembled, as when 'agreed to by them and afterwards confirmed by the Legislatures of every State' will effectually provide for the same."[44]

Before the close of the year Virginia, New Jersey, and Pennsylvania had taken steps to prepare for the Convention. North Carolina followed in January, 1787, Delaware and New York in February, Georgia and South Carolina in April, Maryland in May. New Hampshire delayed the choice of delegates until June, after the Convention had assembled. Rhode Island did not choose delegates at all.

Congress refused for a time to take any action, although a com-

[42] Letter to Vergennes, Oct. 10, 1786, in Bancroft, *Hist. of the Const.* II, App., 399–401, reprinted in A. B. Hart, ed., *American History told by Contemporaries*, III, 185–187.
[43] Warren, 23.
[44] Reprinted in Johnson, *Readings*, 96–98.

mittee reported that a convention should be called. Finally (Feb. 21, 1787), on motion of Rufus King, it recommended a convention in terms which ignored the Annapolis movement but set the same time and place. Members thus saved their own pride. According to this action, the Philadelphia Convention was to meet for the "sole and express purpose of revising the articles of confederation," and of reporting to Congress such alterations as should "render the federal constitution adequate to the exigencies of government, and the preservation of the union." Thus the status of the Philadelphia Convention was officially designated as a body advisory to Congress.

The year of the Annapolis Convention was that in which Shays's Rebellion occurred. This event undoubtedly stimulated the sentiment in favor of a stronger government, although Madison believed that even such disturbances found their roots in the commercial situation. "A continuance of the present anarchy of our commerce will be a continuance of the unfavorable balance on it, which, by draining us of our metals, furnishes pretext for the pernicious substitution of paper money, for indulgences to debtors, for postponement of taxes. In fact most of our political evils may be traced to our commercial ones, as most of our moral may be to our political." [45]

Knox thought that the Rebellion caused "men of reflection" to determine "to endeavor to establish a government which shall have the power to protect them in their lawful pursuits, and which will be efficient in all cases of internal commotions or foreign invasions," [46] and Higginson believed that whereas sentiment had previously favored extensions of the power of Congress over commerce, there was now a desire for "increasing powers of Congress . . . generally." [47] Jay feared, on the contrary, that the continuance of disorder would produce an unrepublican reaction.[48] "The best citizens," he asserted, "naturally grow uneasy and look to other systems." [49] "I am told," wrote Washington, "that even respect-

[45] To Jefferson, March 18, 1786. Warren, 16.
[46] To Washington, October, 1786. *Ibid.*, 31.
[47] To Knox, Nov. 25, 1787. "Letters," 743.
[48] To Washington, June 27, 1786. Warren, 17.
[49] To Adams, Nov. 17, 1786. *Ibid.*, 18.

able characters speak of a monarchical form of government without horror." [50] He thought, however, that the New England states
showed an indifference towards the Annapolis convention which
indicated that the recent disorders had not convinced them of the
need of a competent government.[51]

HOPES AND FEARS

Even with the Philadelphia Convention assured, and its main
objects agreed upon,[52] no one could be sanguine of its success. Jay
expected little good from a convention of delegates selected by the
state legislatures. He favored popular conventions in each state
to choose delegates to a general convention which should have
power to alter the Articles. If any alterations were made, they
should be "deducible from the only source of just authority—the
People." [53] Knox and Higginson wanted the Philadelphia Convention to submit its work to special state conventions:[54] Madison
agreed that ratification of changes should be the work of the people
instead of the legislatures.

Madison found "men of reflection much less sanguine as to the
new than despondent as to the present system." [55] "The difficulties
which present themselves are . . . almost sufficient to dismay the
most sanguine," but "the mortal diseases of the Constitution" compel the most timid to face the difficulties.[56] "The nearer the crisis
approaches," he wrote a little later, "the more I tremble for the
issue." The difficulties as he summarized them were: to get the
concurrence of the Convention; next, to obtain the approbation of
Congress; and finally, to procure the sanction of the states. So

[50] To Jay. *Ibid.*
[51] To Humphreys, Nov. 4, 1786. *Ibid.,* 33.
[52] Otto advised his government as early as April 10 that the Convention would
concern itself "with the adoption of a new plan of confederation, to give Congress coercive powers, considerable imposts, an army, the right to regulate exclusively the commerce of all the states."—Letter to Montmorin, in Farrand,
Records, III, 16. Farrand prints numerous documents which prove that these
objectives were commonly understood by the public.
[53] To Washington, Jan. 7, 1787. Warren, 36. By "the people" Jay of course
meant only the enfranchised element.
[54] Knox to Benjamin Lincoln, Jan. 28, 1787. *Ibid.,* 37. Higginson to Knox,
Feb. 8 and 13, 1787. "Letters," 745, 750.
[55] To Edmund Pendleton, Feb. 28, 1787. Warren, 45.
[56] To Jefferson, March 19, 1787. *Ibid.,* 47.

many chances of miscarriage would lead to despair, he thought, if the alternative were less formidable.[57]   He recognized that "the diversity of opinions and prejudices and of supposed or real interests among the States renders the issue totally uncertain." [58]

King thought that "what the Convention may do at Philadelphia is very doubtful. . . . My fears are by no means inferior to my hopes." [59] Edward Carrington doubted whether the Convention "will be productive of any immediate effects." [60] Jay was not "sanguine in my expectations." [61] Humphreys had "heard few express any sanguine expectations concerning the successful issue of the meeting," [62] and urged Washington not to attend lest his reputation suffer through its failure. Franklin was fearful that if the gathering "does not do good, it must do harm, as it will show that we have not wisdom enough among us to govern ourselves; and will strengthen the opinion of some political writers, that popular governments cannot long support themselves." [63] William Livingston did not think that Americans exhibited "the virtue that is necessary to support a republican government." [64]

When Madison spoke of the "probable diversity of opinions and prejudices and of supposed or real interests among the States," he touched upon a cause of great concern. Since 1783 there had been much talk of breaking up the Confederation into several smaller ones. Letters and articles in newspapers both North and South pointed out the divergent conditions and interests in the several sections, and expressed doubts as to whether they could ever be reconciled within one union. Divisions were proposed according to climate and other natural conditions, "whose effect no

[57] To Pendleton, April 22, 1787. *Ibid.*, 50.
[58] To James Madison, Sr., April 1. *Ibid.*, 47, note.
[59] To Theophilus Parsons, April 8. *Ibid.*, 52. King had never been an ardent advocate of a convention, doubting whether such a gathering could accomplish anything that Congress could not do. Previous to the action of Congress calling the Philadelphia meeting he had opposed a convention because the Articles gave Congress the exclusive right to initiate amendments. John Adams and John Jay were of much the same opinion. See letters of Adams to King, June 14, 1786, and King to Adams, Oct. 2, 1786.
[60] To Jefferson, April 24. *Ibid.*, 53.
[61] To Jefferson, April 25. *Ibid.*
[62] *Ibid.*, 64, and note.
[63] To Jefferson, April 19. *Ibid.*, 52.
[64] To Elijah Clarke, Feb. 17, 1787. *Ibid.*, 40.

positive law ever can surpass. The religion, manners, customs, exports, imports and general interest of each being then the same, no opposition arising from differences in these (as at present) would any longer divide their councils." [65]

The notion of several confederacies received an impetus from Jay's negotiations with Gardoqui over the navigation of the Mississippi. Monroe believed that it was the purpose of Jay and his party either to force the West out of the Confederation or to form a separate northern confederacy. He reported to Jefferson that Jay and his friends had "held in this city Committees for dismembering the Confederacy, and throwing the States eastward the Hudson into one government." [66]

That Monroe's belief was not wholly unfounded may be inferred from the words of Theodore Sedgwick of Massachusetts to Caleb Strong. After saying that no advantage could come to New England from the proposed convention at Annapolis, he wrote: "It well becomes the Eastern and Middle States, who are in interest one, seriously to consider what advantages result to them from their connection with the Southern States. They can give us nothing as an equivalent for the protection which they derive from us, but a participation in their commerce." [67] Said Stephen Higginson: "In their habit, manners, and commercial interests, the Southern and Northern States are not only very dissimilar, but in many instances directly opposed." [68] General Benjamin Lincoln did not see, in view of the conflict of sectional interests, "how we shall surmount the evils under which we now labor, and prevent our falling into the utmost confusion, disgrace, and ruin, but by a division." Safety might be secured "by a firm alliance between the divisions." [69] Dr. Benjamin Rush added his testimony that "some of our enlightened men who begin to despair of a more complete union of the States in Congress have secretly proposed an Eastern Middle and Southern Confederacy, to be united by an alliance

[65] Quoted by Warren, 30.
[66] *Ibid.*, 25. *Cf.* Charles Warren, "The Mississippi River and the Treaty Clause of the Constitution."
[67] Warren, *Making*, 27.
[68] To John Adams, Dec. 30, 1785. "Letters," 704.
[69] Warren, *Making*, 26.

offensive and defensive. These Confederacies, they say, will be united by nature, by interests, and by manners, and consequently they will be safe, agreeable, and durable. The first will include the four New England States and New York. The second will include New Jersey, Pennsylvania, Delaware and Maryland; and the last Virginia, North and South Carolina and Georgia." [70] Bingham of Pennsylvania avowed his own desire for several confederacies. [71]

The sentiment in favor of dissolving the Confederation seems to have increased rather than diminished as the time for the Convention drew near. A letter appeared in many newspapers questioning whether three allied republics would not be better than one general government, [72] and one writer proposed that Massachusetts invite the New England states to meet, leaving "the rest of the Continent to pursue their own imbecile and disjointed plans." [73]

Much of this disunion sentiment was, as Madison suggested, a matter of prejudice. Men were prone to speak slightingly of residents of other states. Elbridge Gerry of Massachusetts was of the opinion that the Virginians had too great a sense of their own importance. [74] Nor was he particularly friendly towards the neighboring state of Connecticut—"the D[evi]l," he said, "is in that State." [75] Ephraim Paine of Vermont, having failed to obtain advantages for his state at the hands of Congress, spoke of the southern members as "nabobs" who "behave as though they viewed themselves a superior order of animals when compared with those of the other end of the Confederacy." [76]

Washington was not much concerned over the fear of monarchy. [77] Madison believed that the great body of the people were not disposed either to submit to anti-republican changes nor to a division of the Confederation. [78] With reference to the latter possibility John Adams wrote, "the most shortsighted must perceive

[70] To Dr. Richard Price, Oct. 27, 1786. *Ibid.*, 27–28.
[71] *Ibid.*, 28.
[72] *Ibid.*, 29.
[73] *Ibid.*, 29, note 2.
[74] To Rufus King, May 9, 1785. King *Life and Correspondence*, I, 96.
[75] To same, May 27, 1785. *Ibid.*, 101.
[76] Bancroft, *Hist. of Const.*, II, 264.
[77] To Madison, March 31, 1787. Warren, 43–44.
[78] To Edmund Pendleton, Feb. 28, 1787. *Ibid.*, 45.

such manifest danger, both from foreign Powers and from one another, as cannot be looked upon without terror." [79]

To Madison the danger of several confederacies seemed more
real than that of monarchy, and a possibility in case the Convention
failed.   He hoped therefore that the danger would rouse all "real
friends of the Revolution to exert themselves in favor of such an
organization of the Confederacy as will perpetuate the Union, and
redeem the honor of the Republican name." [80]

Amid such uncertainties the day of the meeting approached.

[79] To Jay, May 8, 1787. *Ibid.*, 54.
[80] To Pendleton, Feb. 28, 1787. *Ibid.*, 45.

XI

FORMATION OF THE CONSTITUTION

THE PHILADELPHIA CONVENTION

ON Monday, May 14, 1787, George Washington recorded in his diary: "This being the day appointed for the Convention to meet, such members as were in town assembled at the State House, but only two States being represented, viz. Virginia and Pennsylvania, agreed to attend at the same place tomorrow." Delegates drifted into Philadelphia slowly, assembling daily and adjourning for want of a quorum, until Friday, May 25, when a majority of the states were found to be represented. Thereupon the Convention organized. Upon motion of Robert Morris of the Pennsylvania delegation, Washington was unanimously chosen as the presiding officer. Franklin, the only possible rival, was to have made the nomination, but bad weather and ill health confined him to his home. Major William Jackson, who had assisted Henry Knox, the secretary of war, was made secretary but proved to be incompetent for the task. Fortunately James Madison, conceiving that a report of the debates would be of great future value, and possibly conscious of Jackson's incapacity, set himself the task of taking his own notes. Choosing a favorable position in the hall, he attended the sessions with the utmost diligence, and succeeded in preserving a surprisingly full and accurate record of the proceedings.[1]

Having examined the credentials of delegates and appointed a

[1] See Madison's own account in Farrand, *Records*, III, 550. This work under Farrand's editorship is the chief collection of source materials for the Convention. The events leading to the meeting and the work of the Convention are treated briefly by the same author in *The Framing of the Constitution*, and *The Fathers of the Constitution*. Robert L. Schuyler gives a parallel account in *The Constitution of the United States*. Charles Warren, *The Making of the Constitution*, gives a day by day record composed of newspaper comments, extracts from diaries and letters of delegates, portions of the journal, and notes of members. Valuable for factual content rather than for interpretation are the earlier accounts: George Bancroft, *History of the Formation of the Constitution of the United States* and George Ticknor Curtis, *History of the Origin, Formation, and Adoption of the Constitution of the United States*.

committee to draft rules of procedure, the Convention adjourned to meet at 10 o'clock on Monday, May 28.

At this opening session there were present twenty-nine delegates from seven states. Others came later, increasing the total of actual attendants to fifty-five, representing every state except Rhode Island. In all seventy-four delegates were appointed. Some declined to attend, and many others attended irregularly; the average number of delegates present throughout the sessions was only about thirty. The personnel as a whole was unquestionably of extraordinary caliber. Enthusiastic contemporaries called it "an assembly of demigods." Passing by other flattering comments of friends of the movement, one may note the judgment of the French chargé, that "if all the delegates named for this Philadelphia Convention are present, one will never have seen, even in Europe, an assembly more respectable for talents, knowledge, disinterestedness and patriotism than those who will compose it." [2] In a day when higher education was the privilege of the few, about one half of the delegates were college graduates. By profession they were physicians, planters, merchants and lawyers, the last occupation accounting for more than half of the total. Most of the members were comparatively young men, only twelve of the fifty-five being over fifty-four years of age, while six were under thirty-one. Yet the large majority had seen public service of some kind, and hardly a man was not known throughout the Confederation.

Standing admittedly at the head of this list of notables was General Washington, revered as the savior of his country. He had hesitated to accept appointment as a delegate, not because friends feared the failure of the Convention and consequent injury to his prestige, but because of "a rheumatic complaint in my shoulder . . . at times I am hardly able to raise my hand to my head. . . ." [3] As the date for the meeting drew near friends had changed their advice and urged that the weight of his influence was essential to the success of the Convention and its proposals. Yielding his personal preferences to these solicitations, Washington finally decided to go to Philadelphia, and all the evidence indicates that his

[2] Otto to Montmorin, April 10, 1787, in Farrand, *Records*, III, App. A, III, 15.
[3] To Randolph, March 28. Quoted by Warren, *Making*, 66.

endorsement was a chief if not an indispensable factor in winning the acceptance of the new Constitution.

The contribution of the veteran Franklin was of a similar kind. Too burdened by the weight of years (he was now eighty-one and a sufferer from the gout) to take an active part in debate, his sobriety of judgment and unfailing tact more than once carried the Convention through dangerous crises.[4]

The men who spoke most frequently were Gouverneur Morris and James Wilson of Pennsylvania, James Madison and George Mason of Virginia, Roger Sherman of Connecticut, and Elbridge Gerry of Massachusetts. One of the most significant generalizations concerning the personnel of the gathering is that, with a few exceptions, its members were in temper and philosophy distinctly of what we have described as the middle class (in America, the upper class).[5] The Convention contained no representatives of the wage-earning and small-farmer classes which were responsible for Shays's Rebellion and the Rhode Island inflation program. More than forty of the fifty-five delegates were at one time or other holders of securities which were sure to be enhanced in value by the creation of a government capable by taxation of establishing the public credit. Their traditions were those of the propertied class, and they came to Philadelphia to establish on a national scale the control of their own class as they had already done in most of the states. They felt that many of the evils of the times were due, as Gerry put it, to an "excess of democracy." They were keenly conscious of the defective form and powers of the general government and of the abuses of government in the states. Even the most liberal of them—men like Madison—regarded the paper money craze as a delusion and wished to render the states harmless when their governments fell into the hands of ignorant and incompetent

[4] On the delegates see Farrand, *Framing*, Chap. II, and Warren, *Making*, Chap. II. William Pierce, one of the members from Georgia, recorded his impressions of many of his colleagues. His sketch is one of the chief sources for later appraisals; it is found in Farrand, *Records*, III, App. A, CXIX, 87–97. Charles A. Beard has made a remarkable analysis of the economic interests and political philosophy of the delegates. See *An Economic Interpretation of the Constitution*.

[5] Beard develops this middle-class character of the framers fully in the work just referred to.

men. Like Locke, with a few exceptions they believed that the preservation of order, the protection of life and liberty, and especially the safeguarding of property rights, were the chief ends of government.

While the Virginia delegates were awaiting the arrival of a quorum, they made good use of the opportunity to confer about the agenda of the Convention.[6] The result was a set of resolutions, which were drawn up ready for presentation whenever the Convention should be prepared to take up business. As soon as the report of the committee on rules was made and adopted (a process which occupied the session of May 28 and a part of that of May 29),[7] these resolutions, variously known as the Randolph plan, the large-state plan, and the Virginia plan, were presented to the Convention by Edmund Randolph, who as governor of Virginia was the ranking head of the state delegation. The drafting of these resolutions is doubtless attributable mainly to Madison, as they conform closely to the ideas advanced in his correspondence during the months preceding. No individual, however, deserves exclusive credit for the authorship, as the resolutions really summarized the ideas on which the leaders of the movement for a stronger central government were united. The essential propositions were those which any one of a number of men would have drafted.[8]

Randolph presented the Virginia resolutions on May 29, supporting them at some length in a speech in which he analyzed the defects of the existing system. The Convention then resolved itself

[6] George Mason wrote to his son, on May 20, saying: "The Virginia deputies (who are all here) meet and confer together two or three hours every day, in order to form a proper correspondence of sentiments. . . . These and some occasional conversations with the deputies of different States, and with some of the general officers of the late army . . . are the only opportunities I have hitherto had of forming any opinion upon the great subject of our mission. . . . Yet . . . I have reason to hope there will be greater unanimity and less opposition, except from the little States, than was at first apprehended. . . ." Farrand, *Records*, III, 23. Cf. Madison to Noah Webster, Oct. 12, 1804, *ibid.*, 409.

[7] In addition to simple rules of order, the regulations provided for secret sessions. The rule in voting which obtained in Congress was tacitly accepted, although some of the large-state delegates had seriously considered making a stand in favor of a change which would give them a voice in the Convention in proportion to their importance.

[8] For full text see Farrand, *Records*, I, 20–22. Reprinted in Johnson, *Readings*, 104–107.

into a committee of the whole, to meet next day, for informal preliminary consideration of the propositions.

The deliberations in committee of the whole were continued until June 14, by which time it was evident that delegates from some of the smaller states were dissatisfied with the trend of the discussion. These requested an adjournment for a day to allow them to draw up a plan more in keeping with their desires. The adjournment was agreed to, and on June 15 William Paterson of New Jersey laid before the Convention the plan which the small states wished to substitute for the Virginia project.[9]

Both sets of resolutions were now referred to the committee of the whole and for three days more the discussion was continued in committee. On June 19 a vote of the states showed that seven preferred the Virginia plan, which was thereupon reported to the Convention with certain amendments and elaborations which had been agreed upon in committee. Thenceforward the debates were carried on in Convention.[10]

The preference shown for the Virginia resolutions did not mean that the views of the small-state party were wholly rejected. On the contrary, the friends of the two sets of resolutions agreed at many points.[11] Thus both groups believed that Congress should be

[9] Text in Farrand, *Records*, I, 242–245. Reprinted in Johnson, 107–109.

[10] For convenient reference the following chronology of the Convention is given:

1) Preliminaries, May 14–29.
2) First Period, May 30 to June 19, in committee of the whole.
3) Second Period, June 19 to July 26. Convention discusses report of committee of the whole. In this period occurs the great crisis over apportionment, and the great compromise is reached.
4) Recess, July 26 to August 6, while committee of detail works.
5) Third Period, August 6 to September 17. Convention discusses report of the committee of detail, committee on unfinished parts is appointed and reports. Committee on style at work September 8 to 12. Examination of report of committee on style, and finishing touches, September 13 to 17. Adjournment sine die, September 17.

[11] Besides the Virginia and New Jersey resolutions two other sketches of a new government were presented to the Convention. On May 29, after Randolph had spoken, Charles Pinckney of South Carolina, one of the youngest of the delegates, "laid before the House the draught of a federal Government" which he seems to have prepared before coming to Philadelphia. This was referred to the committee of the whole, along with the Virginia resolutions, but it was not at any time mentioned in the debates so far as the extant records show. There is evidence that it was drawn upon more or less by the committee of detail, but all

empowered to lay taxes and regulate commerce. They agreed likewise that the general government must be enabled to enforce its laws; both plans authorized the use of armed force against any state which failed to perform its duties as a member of the union. Both plans also contemplated separate legislative, executive, and judicial departments. As to restraints on the states, the Randolph resolutions, carrying out Madison's idea, proposed that the national legislature should be empowered "to negative all laws passed by the several States, contravening . . . the articles of the Union," while the Paterson resolutions proposed to make measures of the general government the supreme law of the states, and to bind the state courts to uphold them even as against state laws. The latter plan, moreover, authorized the national executive to enforce national measures against disobedient individuals as well as states.

These points on which the two groups substantially agreed covered the main objectives of the Convention. As Madison put it just after the Convention adjourned, its objects were to blend stability and energy and the republican form in the general government, and at the same time to trace the proper line of demarcation between it and the state authorities. Although there was unanimous agreement as to these ends, he said, the means of attaining them admitted of infinite diversity of opinion.[12]

The most serious clash of opinion arose over a matter which from our point of view seems to be of minor importance. The sponsors of the Randolph resolutions desired a Congress of two houses, and, representing the larger states, they were determined not to continue the equal representation of states which obtained under the Articles. They demanded that in both houses the number of delegates from each state should be apportioned according to its population or

copies were lost and many years later a preliminary draft of the Constitution by the committee of detail was mistaken for the original of the Pinckney plan. The misconception gave rise to a problem in historical criticism which was not solved until the present century. See Farrand, *Records,* index under Pinckney plan.

On June 18, while the Virginia and New Jersey plans were being compared in committee of the whole, Alexander Hamilton declared that he was unfriendly to both, especially that of New Jersey, and presented his own sketch, not as a proposition for consideration, but only "to give a more correct view of his ideas." —*Ibid.,* I, 282–293.

[12] Quoted by Warren, *Making,* 742. *Cf.* Robert L. Schuyler, "Agreement in the Federal Convention."

contribution to the common treasury. Although the opposing group preferred to retain the one-house Congress, holding that the real defect was its want of adequate powers, they were willing to accept the bicameral arrangement provided that, to protect the smaller states, equal representation was continued in at least one chamber. The rejection of this proposal almost broke up the Convention, but that unhappy termination was averted by a compromise. It was agreed that the equality of states should be retained in the upper house while proportional representation according to population should be adopted in the lower. To this was added the provision that all bills for raising or appropriating money should originate in the lower branch, thus giving the large states the control of the public purse.

The agreement that the states should be represented in the lower house in proportion to population raised a critical issue, between those which had slaves and those which did not. Should slaves be counted as part of the population? Yes, said the southern delegates; No, said those from the North. But the two groups exchanged positions when a rule was sought for levying direct taxes, and another compromise was effected by which it was agreed that three-fifths of the slaves should be counted for both purposes. Apparently a happy solution of a vexatious problem at the time, the "three-fifths" compromise became later the source of much discontent.

These compromises indicate that many adjustments were necessary to assure all sections and groups that their interests would be duly protected in the new union. Among these adjustments was the agreement of southern delegates that Congress should have power to regulate commerce by a bare majority vote on condition that it should not prohibit the slave trade before 1808, tax exports, or give any preference to the ports of one state over those of another. Some differences of opinion were evaded rather than settled, by the use of clever phraseology which might be construed to support either of the contending views. Thus it was agreed that "Congress may admit new states into this Union," leaving it uncertain whether Congress might prescribe the conditions of admission.

Both sets of resolutions merely stated the principles on which the new government should be formed; neither presented them in the form of a draft of a constitution. The essential agreement on basic principles made it easy and time-saving, as soon as the Convention had adopted the major compromises, to turn over to a committee the task of putting the evident desires of the body into appropriate form. For this purpose a committee of detail was appointed near the end of July.

Much of the committee's work was almost mechanical. That is to say, the Convention having decided upon a government with "compelling legal authority" over general concerns, it was left to the committee to clothe that government with familiar attributes. From the state constitutions were borrowed the provisions relating to legislative procedure, privileges of members, and powers and functions of the executive. Substantially all of these can be traced back to the practice of the colonial governments, and most of them to earlier English usage.[13] The committee also transcribed from the Articles the powers of the old Congress, added the powers over taxation and commerce which were so evidently necessary, and arranged all of this matter in logical form, divided into articles and sections. This draft, reported on August 6, was then discussed by the whole Convention, and after some further modifications, was signed on September 17.

Ever since the Albany plan had recognized the possibility of drawing a line between the powers assignable to the general government and those which the states should retain, the promoters of union, as we have seen, had cherished the concept of distributed powers. The Articles of Confederation had included in the powers of Congress nearly all that the theory indicated should be given to it, but the assertion of state sovereignty and the withholding of compelling authority had practically nullified this action. The Philadelphia Convention returned to the concept of distributed powers and carried it out more consistently, but it was able to add only a few items of a general character which were not already embraced by the Articles. Provisions concerning taxation, com-

---

[13] The debt of the Constitution to the practice of the states and colonies is the theme of Sydney G. Fisher, *The Evolution of the Constitution*.

mercial regulation, and compulsory authority, of course, led the new list, followed by clauses relating to naturalization, bankruptcy, patents, copyrights, and the punishment of counterfeiting.

The new Constitution conformed closely to the theory of separation of powers. The legislative, executive, and judicial functions were vested in independent and coordinate branches of government, with the intent presumably that they should check and balance one another. Congress was empowered to impeach executive officers and judges, the President was given a veto upon acts of the legislature, the two houses acted as mutual checks, and the Senate held a check upon the executive in the making of treaties and appointments. In spite of this evidence of unwillingness to rely upon the "demarcation on parchment of the constitutional limits of the several departments," there was no provision authorizing the judiciary to hold acts of Congress void. This omission is not easy to explain. The doctrine of judicial review may not yet have been clearly grasped by the delegates in general, although some were aware of the fact that courts had exercised the function in the states. Remarks made in the course of debate show that a number of the leading members regarded the power as inhering in courts under a written constitution. The omission of all reference to the matter, however, enabled later critics of the court to charge that the exercise of this function was a usurpation.

Nevertheless the Constitution gave the judicial branch a place of great importance in the new system. Under the Articles it had been rudimentary, with a jurisdiction restricted to a few specified causes. The framers of the Constitution were wise enough to perceive that the legislative and judicial authority of the federal government should be coextensive; in other words, that under the scheme of distributed powers, its authority on the judicial side should extend to all cases arising under legislation resulting from the powers assigned to it. In the Constitution this purpose was indicated by the declaration that the judicial power of the United States should "extend to all Cases in law and equity arising under this Constitution, the Laws of the United States, and Treaties made . . . under their Authority." Other clauses enumerated certain cases about which, even under this inclusive principle, there might be doubt. Out of the supreme law clause of the Paterson resolutions, moreover, the Convention evolved the declaration that "This Constitution, and the Laws of the United States which shall be made in Pursuance thereof; and all Treaties made, or which shall be made, under the Authority of the United States, shall be the supreme Law of the Land; and the Judges in every State shall be bound thereby, any Thing in the Constitution or Laws of any State to the Contrary notwithstanding." Read in conjunction with the jurisdiction clause, this provision became the support later of the contention that the federal government, through its judicial branch, is the judge of its own powers.

One of the most significant aspects of the judiciary as established under the Constitution is found in its relation to the "compelling legal authority" of the general government. The idea of employing armed force against states, which appears in both the Randolph and the Paterson resolutions, was soon discarded because it was seen to be the equivalent of civil war. Besides, the federal idea called logically for a general government resting, like the state governments, on persons, and operating directly on individuals within its peculiar sphere of authority. Clearly, then, federal law, like state law, should ordinarily be enforced by courts. Only in case of insurrection so formidable as to defy these was it desirable to employ military force. This latter contingency was cared for by giving Congress the power to provide for calling out the militia to execute its laws and suppress insurrections against the authority of the Union. Here, too, individuals and not states were the objects against which the use of force was contemplated. A danger, unforeseen at the time, lay in the fact that individuals might claim to act as state officials and not as private citizens of the United States. When that issue arose, the United States found it convenient to ignore the claim that the use of force against such individuals was equivalent to the coercion of states, and to deal with the recalcitrants as insurrectionary citizens.

Congress was also empowered to authorize the use of the militia to repel invasion. The United States was enjoined to protect every state against invasion, and upon request, against domestic disorder, and to guarantee to each state a republican form of government.

The provision that the United States should aid the state against domestic violence *upon request*, protected the latter against meddlesome interference with its internal police, but, of course, did not prevent federal action within any state to maintain United States laws and carry on federal functions. With all this solicitude for state autonomy, however, the Constitution imposed some new restrictions upon the states. While these restrictions aided in clarifying the respective spheres of the general and state governments, they reflect distinctly the disposition of the conservative class to clip the claws of the radicals. The chief of these provisions deprived the states of the power to emit bills of credit, make anything but gold and silver legal tender in payment of debts, or pass bills of attainder, ex post facto laws, or laws impairing the obligation of contracts.

At every turn the Constitution reflected the lessons of experience and embodied the principles which Americans had long followed in practice or for which they had contended. But the statesmanship of the fathers naturally failed to anticipate the future; indeed at several points it did not even deal adequately with existing conditions. Beyond the mountains were vast expanses awaiting settlement which the states were in process of transferring to Congress. In this very summer while the Convention was in session the old Congress passed an ordinance organizing the Northwest Territory. Yet the Constitution was silent on the question of acquiring new territory, and as to that already in possession, merely authorized Congress "to dispose of and make all needful Rules and Regulations respecting" it "or other Property belonging to the United States." This clause apparently referred to the "territory" only as property, that is, as land belonging to the public which Congress was to sell, yet here or nowhere is the constitutional warrant for government by Congress of the people in the territories prior to the erection of new states. The lack of clear definition of the powers of Congress at this point was fraught with serious future peril to the Union.

Almost equally unfortunate was the failure to define citizenship. The term had seldom been used by Americans, who before independence had been "subjects" of the king of England. "Citizen" was adopted as a more appropriate designation for the inhabitants of a free republic, and promptly appeared in the usage of the states. The duality of the system of government under the new Constitution implied duality of citizenship, and in the Convention men began to speak of themselves as citizens of their states and also of the United States. If a definition of citizenship had been inserted in the Constitution it would have prevented a great deal of controversy.

The Articles had provided that "the free inhabitants of each of these States, paupers, vagabonds, and fugitives from justice excepted, shall be entitled to all privileges and immunities of free citizens in the several States." In this provision "free inhabitants" and "free citizens" seem to be synonymous terms. Slightly changed in wording, the provision was carried over into the Constitution with the reading "The Citizens of each State shall be entitled to all Privileges and Immunities of Citizens in the several States." It seems likely that the word "citizen" was intended to exclude the "paupers, vagabonds and fugitives from justice" mentioned in the earlier document. But the language of the Articles clearly gave free Negroes the privileges and immunities of citizens. Did the words used in the Constitution deny citizenship to this class of free inhabitants, and deprive them of these privileges?

As has been noted, some of the southern states had taken exception to the phrasing of this clause of the Articles, and the changed wording of the Constitution made it possible to maintain that free Negroes were not citizens.

This problem attracted no attention in the Convention, but when it emerged some years later, the determination not to recognize free Negroes as citizens nullified all efforts to define citizenship, to enumerate the privileges and immunities pertaining to it, or to distinguish between state and United States citizenship. Indeed, it required eventually the Civil War to solve the problems connected with citizenship.

Proposals to give Congress power to build roads and canals and to grant charters to corporations engaged in interstate activities were voted down in the Convention. Larger authority to regulate industry of more than local scope would have been of the utmost importance a century later, but the framers could not foresee the industrial expansion of the future, and the small-scale enterprises of 1787 seemed to fall within the police control of the states. Interstate activities were supposed to be adequately covered by the power of Congress to regulate commerce "among the several States"—a phrase which until recently has invariably been understood as meaning "*between* the several States," but which some now contend was intended by the framers to cover commerce *throughout* the United States.

Aware of the impracticability of dictating the precise means by which the powers of the general government were to be carried into execution, the framers authorized Congress "to make all Laws which shall be necessary and proper" for that purpose; and, aware of the certainty that experience would reveal the desirability of adding to, taking from, or otherwise modifying the provisions of the Constitution, several methods of amending it were set forth. The chief of these—the one employed for the first twenty amendments—required the affirmative vote of two thirds of the members of both houses of Congress followed by the approval of the legislatures of three fourths of the states. The provision for amendment marks a vast advance in the theory and practice of popular government since Locke's day. Remembering that the philosopher saw no remedy for abuses in government short of revolution, one can appreciate Jefferson's comment, that "we can surely boast of having set the world a beautiful example of a Government reformed by reason alone, without bloodshed." [14] Up to this time Jefferson himself had believed that a revolution was necessary every two or three decades to clear away accumulated injustices. The possibility of making changes peacefully and by legal means left little excuse for recourse to the "ultimate remedy," if the new mechanism proved to be a workable device for expressing the deliberate will of the "sovereign people."

The Convention, in assigning general powers to the new government, acted on the theory that all powers not delegated to that government were reserved to the states or people. The omission of the word "expressly," which had been used in the Articles, left

[14] Letter to Edward Rutledge, July 18, 1788.

room, however, for the development of the implications of the "necessary and proper" clause; and carried along with the very idea of government, it seems, were other powers which were not enumerated because they are inherent in all governments. An example of such a power, assumed to belong to the federal government although nowhere mentioned in the Constitution, is that of eminent domain. Certain phrases, moreover, served as open doors for the entry into our constitutional law of whole codes of principles which the Constitution did not set forth in detail. Such doorways the power "to define . . . Offences against the Law of Nations," and "to make Rules for the Government and Regulation of the land and naval Forces," proved to be. The restriction (in the fifth amendment) that no person should be deprived of life, liberty, or property without "due process of law" virtually adopted the English common law as a code limiting federal action. Of similar character was the prohibition of "cruel and unusual punishments" (eighth amendment).

As has been intimated, the delegates did not intend to establish a democratic government. The rejection of the idea of direct election of the President was due in part to the belief that the voters were incapable of making a wise choice; this in the face of the fact that the voters were a privileged class from which the masses were excluded. The Senate, designed to represent the states as such, was equally expected to be a bulwark of the conservative class, and for both reasons the choice of senators was entrusted to the state legislatures. The Convention discussed the property qualifications which should be required for federal office-holding, but did not place them in the Constitution because it seemed wiser to leave the decision to Congress.

The aristocratic temper of members was strikingly evident when future statehood for the western settlements was under discussion. In every colony the dominant class had had difficulty with the democratic population of its frontier. Shays's Rebellion was only the latest of a long series of contests running back at least to Bacon's Rebellion of 1676, between the ruling class and the back-country people of Virginia who believed that they were treated unfairly. Far from being dissipated by these struggles, class prejudices were perpetuated by them and were thoroughly alive among the members of the Convention. Gouverneur Morris, averring that "property is the main object of Society," and that "the Busy haunts of men not the remote wilderness, is the proper School of political Talents," urged that "the rule of representation ought to be so fixed as to secure to the Atlantic States a prevalence in the National Councils," [15] and so many delegates agreed with him that they cast the vote of four of the nine states in favor of such discrimination. It was not dislike of discrimination, in all probability, that caused its failure, so much as its impracticability. As James Wilson pointed out, "this jealousy misled the policy of Great Britain with regard to America. . . . Like consequences will result on the part of the interior settlements, if like jealousy and policy be ours." [16]

Wilson's logic was convincing even to those who did not wish to grant equal rights to new western states. In his own view policy and right united, for "he could not agree that property was the sole or primary object of government and society. The cultivation and improvement of the human mind was the most noble object." Moreover, he held that "the majority of the people wherever found ought, in all questions, to govern the minority. If the interior country should acquire this majority, it will not only have the right, but will avail itself of it, whether we will or no." [17]

Wilson ranks with James Otis and Thomas Jefferson as one of the great democrats of the formative period of the Republic. Beside him, in the Convention, should be placed George Mason and James Madison. Wilson's utterance was, indeed, prophetic of the time to come when new western states would democratize the nation. The Constitution itself made this possible, without its being intended, by providing that "the House of Representatives shall be composed of members chosen every second year by the People of the several states, and electors [voters for members of this house] in each state shall have the qualifications requisite for electors of the most numerous Branch of the State Legislature." This rule, in effect allowing the legislature of each state to fix the qualifications of voters for representatives, automatically democratized

[15] Farrand, *Records*, I, 533–34.
[16] *Ibid.*, I, 605.
[17] *Ibid.*

the national lower house as the states adopted manhood suffrage. The choice of presidential electors was democratized by a similar process. By these means the frontier influence gradually broke down the traditional aristocratic type of government which most of the framers intended to perpetuate in the Constitution, for without exception western communities, as they became states, rested their governments on a broad popular basis. A generation after the adoption of the Constitution the old states were compelled under stress of competition with the new, to liberalize their own practices.

RATIFICATION OF THE CONSTITUTION

At the request of the Convention the Confederation Congress transmitted a copy of the Constitution to the legislature of each state to be submitted to a delegate convention chosen expressly for the purpose of ratifying or rejecting it, with the proviso that it was to become effective for the ratifying states when nine had acted favorably. Although there were other reasons for adopting this plan of ratification, at least some of the framers favored it as a resort to the people, the ultimate source of authority. The method conformed to the compact theory, but whether the people of the United States were thought of as forming the compact by agreement among themselves as members of one great community, or as members of separate political bodies, cannot be determined. This question, like many others, did not come sharply to the front until a later time.

Nor can it be decided whether the people at large favored or opposed the Constitution. Since the ballot was so restricted, any attempt to arrive at popular opinion is almost pure conjecture. Even the views of the voters can be inferred, and that uncertainly, only from those of the delegates whom they sent to the state conventions. However, as the members of the state legislatures which chose the delegates to the Philadelphia Convention were elected by the same groups of voters who sent delegates to the ratifying conventions, the Constitution was both framed and ratified by representatives of the same elements of the population.[18] The sharp

[18] Cf. Beard, *Economic Interpretation, passim.* In Chap. IX he discusses the popular vote.

division which presently appeared between its supporters and critics must therefore be regarded as a division within the ranks of the enfranchised, propertied class, rather than one between the Haves and the Have Nots.

The Constitution was pending before the country from September, 1787, until June of the next year, when the ninth state—New Hampshire—ratified. Discussion pro and con was rife throughout these months—in fact it did not cease with the ninth ratification, since four states were still to act. The rule of the Convention had forbidden delegates to divulge what was going on in the sessions, but adjournment was followed immediately by numerous communications to their correspondents telling what had been done and giving their judgment on it. Some of them also made reports to their state legislatures.

Within a few weeks essays began to appear in the newspapers or in the form of pamphlets for general distribution.[19] Richard Henry Lee, of Virginia, who had introduced the motion in June, 1776, favoring the declaration of independence, was one of the ablest of the critics, while Hamilton, Madison and Jay took first rank on the affirmative side with the papers since known collectively as *The Federalist*. The final discussions took place in the state conventions.[20]

It cannot be said that the framers themselves entered the period of debate with enthusiasm for the results of their efforts. So many

[19] The most important of these essays have been collected by Paul L. Ford and reprinted in two volumes entitled *Pamphlets on the Constitution . . . 1787–1788*, and *Essays on the Constitution . . . 1787–1788*.

[20] The standard collection of debates in the state conventions is the work of Jonathan Elliot, ed., *Debates in the Several State Conventions on the Adoption of the Federal Constitution, . . . together with the Journal of the Federal Convention*. Standard secondary accounts are given by Bancroft, *History of the Constitution*, Part IV, and Curtis, *Constitutional History of the United States*, II. For a briefer account from a more modern point of view see Andrew C. McLaughlin, *The Confederation and the Constitution*, Chap. XVIII.

Special studies have been made of ratification in a few states. The most notable of these studies are: Samuel B. Harding, *The Contest over the Ratification of the Federal Constitution in the State of Massachusetts*, J. B. McMaster and F. D. Stone, *Pennsylvania and the Federal Constitution, 1787–1788*, and Joseph B. Walker, *A History of the New Hampshire Convention . . . 1788*. Orin G. Libby, *The Geographical Distribution of the Vote of the Thirteen States on the Federal Constitution, 1787–1788*, supports the theory that the frontier settlements were aligned against the coast on the issue of ratification.

mutual concessions had been necessary in order to achieve agreement (several delegates in fact refused to sign the completed document) that no one felt that the ideal system had been attained. "The wisdom of the Convention was equal to something greater," said William Pierce of Georgia, "but a variety of . . . circumstances . . . made it impossible to give [the plan] any other shape or form." "I wish," wrote Washington, two days after returning to Mt. Vernon, "the Constitution which is offered had been made more perfect; but I sincerely believe it is the best that could be obtained at this time." In like vein wrote many others: Nicholas Gilman of New Hampshire described the Constitution as "the best that could meet the unanimous concurrence of the States in Convention; it was done by bargain and compromise, yet notwithstanding its imperfections, on the adoption of it depends (in my feeble judgment) whether we shall become a respectable nation, or a people torn to pieces by intestine commotions and rendered contemptible for ages." [21]

To most of the framers the wise course seemed to be to ratify promptly and make such changes later as experience should prove to be desirable. The provision for amendment made this procedure entirely feasible. Said Washington: "As a Constitutional door is opened for amendment hereafter, the adoption of [the Constitution], under the present circumstances of the Union, is in my opinion desirable." And again: "The people . . . can . . . decide with as much propriety on the alterations and amendments which are necessary, as ourselves. I do not think we are more inspired, have more wisdom, or possess more virtue, than those who will come after us." To him the Constitution was not an infallible charter drawn up by supermen to guide the nation through all future years, but a law which should be shaped and adapted to the needs of an ever-changing society. In like manner Jefferson's faith in the people made him confident that they would correct evils if and when they arose. The hopes of these and other great statesmen of the era were built, not upon belief in the perfection of the instrument of government, but upon faith in the people.

Men who had not attended the Philadelphia Convention and

[21] For these and other similar comments see Warren, *Framing*, 733 *et seq.*

whose first knowledge of the provisions of the Constitution was gained after its adjournment were not so sure that the new plan should be adopted without some preliminary changes. Lee expressed a common opinion when he wrote: "This Constitution has a great many excellent regulations in it, and if it could be reasonably amended would be a fine system. . . . It is certainly the most rash and violent proceeding in the world to cram thus suddenly into men, a business of such infinite moment to the happiness of millions."

This difference—whether to ratify and later amend or to amend before ratifying—turned out to be the practical difference between Federalists and Antifederalists; for most of the divergences of view which came to light during the months of debate, like those which had appeared in the Convention, concerned the ends sought less than the means of attaining them. There were, to be sure, extremists who preferred the existing system. Some of these disliked to have the states relinquish the power to tax imports; some feared that the new government would abandon the claim to the navigation of the Mississippi River which was vital to West and South; in each section there were men who feared the consequences if other sections gained control of the government—conditions in the several parts of the country were too diverse, they thought, to admit of regulation by any body of men without harm to some one; some could not grasp the theory of distributed powers or believed that it was not workable, and that the new system would result in the consolidation of all of the states under one government.

Most of the Antifederalists, however, were merely dissatisfied with the checks worked out by the Convention and demanded additional safeguards to prevent consolidation, or to protect sectional interests or the rights of states and individuals. For this reason the contest echoed the debates in the Convention. Unfortunately, the lifting of the ban of secrecy had not been followed by publication of the record of proceedings and doubters were ignorant of the reasons for its decisions. Consequently much old straw was threshed over. Some of the southern states, fearing that the provisions concerning the regulation of commerce and the making of treaties would place them at the mercy of an eastern majority, renewed the demand for a two-thirds vote in both houses for restrictions on commerce—a demand which had been made and met by concessions in the Convention.

A persistent protest was directed at the elegibility of the President for a second term. The Convention had devoted a vast amount of thought to the problem of the executive and yet in the end had taken rather ill-advised action. In the early stages of discussion, when it was expected that this official would be chosen by Congress, it had seemed wise to give him large powers but to deny him a second term in order to prevent intrigue for reelection. When later the electoral college was hit upon, the removal of the danger of intrigue led the framers to withdraw the rule against reeligibility, but without any reduction of executive powers. To the Antifederalists this combination of large power with an unlimited possibility of reelection seemed to provide a primrose path to monarchy, and they asked for a correction here, by way of an amendment limiting the executive to a single term.

Objections were made also to the great powers of the Senate, which, besides being a branch of the legislature, shared with the President the powers of appointment and treaty-making, and acted as a court for the trial of impeached officials. Being chosen by the state legislatures instead of the voters, the Senate seemed to give a distinctly aristocratic character to the whole system. The provision for choosing federal judges by appointment rather than election pointed in the same direction.

Probably no demand for amendment was of more basic importance than that which dealt with safeguards of personal liberty. In vain the Federalists urged that as the new government would possess only delegated powers it would have none which could threaten individual rights: in vain did they urge that an attempt to list powers not delegated might be misconstrued as conferring any which might inadvertently be omitted in the enumeration. The Constitution actually contained several provisions which were of the nature of a bill of rights; such were those regulating the suspension of the privilege of the writ of habeas corpus, prohibiting bills of attainder and ex post facto laws, defining treason, and guaranteeing jury trial. The Antifederalists demanded more stipulations of the kind, and an explicit statement, besides, that the powers not granted to the United States were reserved by the states.

Hardly a provision of the Constitution escaped criticism, although like the framers the ratifiers overlooked several serious omissions. Some of the objections seem trivial and even foolish in the perspective of history, yet many were by no means unreasonable. Nor were the Antifederalists by any means the stupid and unprincipled men which old-time historians with Federalist leanings have called them. They formed a rather more liberal group than the Federalists, and while they seemed to trust to the perfection of the instrument of government more than to the capacity of the people to correct evils, the amendments they desired tended to preserve cherished liberties won in England through the Revolution of 1688 or protected by the principles of the common law. They were at a disadvantage because they were demurring to a positive program which promised a distinct improvement upon existing conditions; failure to accept it threatened disunion and confusion as the alternative. Besides, the general confidence in Washington's judgment was worth a hundred arguments. The Antifederalists therefore allowed themselves to be persuaded—by narrow margins in some states—to ratify the Constitution without previous changes, but with the assurance of the Federalist leaders that the matter of amendments would be taken up by the new government as soon as it was organized.

One of these leaders was James Madison. Following his election to the First Congress he took more than one hundred proposals which had emanated from the state conventions, compressed the more important suggestions into a series of resolutions, and introduced them into the House of Representatives in June, 1789. Seventeen passed the House; the Senate rejected two, combined others, and returned twelve to the lower chamber. The House concurring, they were transmitted to the states, where ten won acceptance.[22]

[22] A list of one hundred twenty-four amendments proposed by the state conventions is given in H. V. Ames, *Proposed Amendments to the Constitution*, 307–310. For the history of the action taken by Congress on these proposals, see *Ann. of Cong.*, 1 Congress. Francis N. Thorpe gives a full account in *Constitutional History of the United States*.

To all intents and purposes these first amendments are a part of the original Constitution, since their adoption was the direct result of agreements made during the ratification contest. The first eight constitute a bill of rights, guaranteeing the liberties of the individual—religious liberty, trial by jury, freedom of speech, etc.— against interference by the federal government. Subsequent history was to give abundant evidence of the wisdom of the Antifederalists in insisting upon them; to that much maligned group the friends of liberty owe a belated acknowledgment. The ninth and tenth amendments assert the existence of non-delegated powers which are reserved to the states or people. The tenth, designed to protect the rights of the states by declaring that "the powers not delegated to the United States by the Constitution, nor prohibited by it to the States, are reserved to the States respectively, or to the people," became the corner stone of the doctrine of strict construction.

ANALYSIS OF THE FEDERAL SYSTEM

When the plan of government was completed in 1787 thoughtful persons were sufficiently conscious of its defects to be skeptical of its success. Nearly half a century later, after doubt had been dispelled by actual experience, a notable study of the American system was made by a Frenchman, Alexis de Tocqueville, who visited the United States during Andrew Jackson's presidency. He described it as resting on a "wholly new theory," which he thought might "be considered a great discovery in modern political science."

"The United States of America," he wrote, "do not afford the first or the only instance of a confederation. . . . In studying the constitutions of [other confederacies] one is surprised to see that the powers with which they invested the federal government are nearly the same with those awarded by the American Constitution to the government of the United States. . . . Nevertheless, the federal government of these different states has always been as remarkable for its weakness and inefficiency as that of the American Union is for its vigor and capacity. . . . In all the confederations which preceded the American Constitution of 1789, the allied states for a common object agreed to obey the injunctions of a federal government; but they reserved to themselves the right of ordaining and enforcing of the laws of the union. . . . The American States which combined in 1789 agreed, that the Federal government should not only dictate the laws, but should enforce its own enactments. . . . In America the subjects of the Union are not States, but private citizens. . . . Its force is not borrowed, but self-derived and it is served by its own civil and military officers, its own army, and its own courts of justice." [23]

The use of the term "federal" to designate this novel type of government was unfortunate, for previous to 1789 the words "federation" and "confederation" had been interchangeable. In the foregoing pages this double usage of "federal" has doubtless confused the reader. The defenders of the Constitution, during the ratification contest, referred to it as "federal" for tactical reasons; but the continued use of the word gave a new connotation to the old term. De Tocqueville had deplored the fact that "the new word which ought to express this novel thing does not yet exist." Years afterwards German scholars, adepts at word-coining, introduced the term *Bundesstaat* to express the new meaning, while *Staatenbund* continued to stand for a confederation of the old type. This German contribution to the terminology of political science came too late to aid Americans, who had long since become habituated to the use of the word "federal" as descriptive of their government. Hence it is necessary to analyze this American so-called federal system in order to comprehend the connotation of the term since 1789.

The American federal system consists, then, of (1) a government possessing legislative, executive, and judicial powers in those matters which pertain to the interests of the country as a whole (the "general police"), (2) superimposed upon a group of states to each of which is reserved full legislative, executive, and judicial authority over matters relating to its own domestic affairs ("internal police"), (3) resting, through representation, direct or indirect, upon the electorate of the country as a whole as the state governments rest upon their local electorates, (4) acting upon its

[23] *Democracy in America*, I, 198 *et seq.*

individual citizens directly as the states do on theirs, and (5) hold-ing its powers under a written Constitution in which they are formally enumerated.

More briefly, the American federal system is a dual system of government, with a fixed scheme of distributed powers, each gov-ernment possessing coercive authority in matters entrusted to it, and resting upon a representative basis.

It has been shown that all of these elements may be traced to the experience of Americans while the colonies were a part of the British Empire. But they did not exist in this combination in British imperial practice. There was in that system, in practice, a scheme of distributed powers, but it lacked the representative basis as well as the fixity which goes with a written constitution.[24] These two elements of the American Constitution were partly the outgrowth of ideas developed as the result of conflict with the British. The American system was new in the sense that it was a synthesis of ideas and practices which had not previously been com-bined.

The old claim of local autonomy in matters of internal police was at the very basis of the scheme of distributed powers, and the writ-ten form of the Constitution was intended to guarantee the stabil-ity of the assignment. It is not quite accurate to say, however, that all governmental authority was parcelled out by the Constitu-tion between the states and the federal government. The tenth amendment alludes to powers which are not allotted to either, but are reserved to the people. Certain powers, moreover, are common to the governments of both states and nation. The fol-lowing diagram will aid in making the scheme of distribution clear.

In explanation of this diagram the tenth amendment may be paraphrased as follows: All powers not granted to the United States by the Constitution are reserved (1) to the respective states if they partake of the nature of internal police, unless the Con-stitution expressly withholds them; (2) to the people of the United States if they partake of the nature of general police. It should be noted that the concurrent powers are means to ends rather

[24] The debt of the Constitution to the British imperial system is the subject of a penetrating study by Professor Andrew C. McLaughlin entitled "The Back-ground of American Federalism."

than ends in themselves; for example, the reason for collecting money is to enable government to function and coercion is for the purpose of making its authority effective. Even the smallest government unit, such as a school district, must be able to levy taxes. The revolutionary patriots, by associating taxation indissolubly with representation, obscured the necessity of parliamentary taxa-

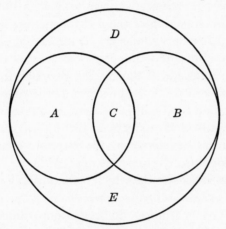

DIAGRAM ILLUSTRATING DISTRIBUTION OF POWERS

Outer circle represents the totality of governmental powers.
A. Represents the powers expressly delegated to the United States. Examples: To make war and treaties and regulate interstate and foreign commerce.
B. Represents the powers reserved to the states respectively. Examples: To care for the health, morals, and public welfare of the people of the state by laws dealing with domestic relations (husband and wife, master and servant, etc.), contracts, crimes, torts, education, sanitation.
C. Represents concurrent powers. Examples: taxation, coercion.
D. Represents powers prohibited to both states and federal government (reserved by the people). Examples: *ex post facto* legislation, violation of due process (applied to states by XIV amendment).
E. Represents powers prohibited to states, but neither prohibited nor expressly delegated to the United States. Examples: issue of bills of credit, impairment of contracts, purchase of foreign territory.

tion if Parliament was to perform general police duties. Logically they should have been represented in a body which could tax them for imperial purposes. Their suggestion that each colony would collect its quota of tax money for the general treasury under a system of requisitions went unheeded; but when they themselves put the plan to the test of experiment under the Articles of Confederation it utterly failed to work. That they had learned their lesson is proved by the constitutional provisions for both federal and state taxation, each for its own legitimate functions.

In saying that the power to tax is enjoyed concurrently by the states and the United States it must not be overlooked that the incidence of taxation is not quite the same in the two cases. The grant to the United States is subject to certain limitations which have been noted, and in practice the federal authority has relied largely upon import duties, which the states are not permitted to levy.

In a system of distributed powers the question naturally arises as to where sovereignty resides. The fact that each government was given exclusive authority within its own sphere led contemporaries to speak commonly of sovereignty as divided. It is difficult to discover just what they meant by sovereignty, but in recent times the concept of divided sovereignty has ceased to be acceptable. Moreover a truly sovereign community possesses both internal and general police powers and when associated with like communities the union is an alliance or league. But the communities which formed the American Union jealously retained their control over internal police and at the same time acquiesced in the exercise of the general police by a body which represented all of them and acted compulsively upon their citizens. Under such a system the characteristics of a league disappear, and with it, logically, the idea of state sovereignty. "Autonomous" seems to be a more suitable term to describe the status of the members of such a union; but since this autonomy of states cannot be violated by the federal authority, the latter can no more be called sovereign than the state. Perhaps the most consistent view of a matter which must remain debatable is that in adopting the Constitution the portion of the people in each state which possessed political rights entered into an agreement with the like groups in the other states by which as individuals they formed a new body politic. The Constitution thereupon became an expression of the will of this sovereign body, allocating certain powers to the states and certain others to the federal government, and withholding some from both.

PART THREE

THE ESTABLISHMENT OF THE CONSTITUTION

XII

LAUNCHING THE SHIP

ORGANIZING THE GOVERNMENT

WHEN formal notice reached Congress that the ninth state had ratified the Constitution, it took steps to prepare for the new régime. The first Wednesday in January, 1789, was fixed as the time for choosing presidential electors, and the first Wednesday in February as the day for casting their ballots. The first Wednesday in March was set for the meeting of Congress, with New York as the place.

It was April before a quorum of members arrived in New York and the houses organized. The Constitution empowered the House of Representatives to choose its own presiding officer, or "Speaker," but assigned the duty of presiding over the Senate to the Vice-President. To act until the result of the electoral vote should be known the Senate chose a president *pro tempore*.

As soon as the work of internal organization had been done the houses turned to the business of counting the electoral vote. The constitutional provision for the choice of President gave each state a number of electors equal to the sum of its representatives and senators, to be chosen as its legislature might prescribe. Several methods were used in the first election: three states used the general ticket; in five the legislatures made the choice; the rest divided the state into districts and allowed the voters in each to choose one elector. The first of these methods eventually became universal, but for many years the second was generally used. New York lost its vote in 1789 through a disagreement in the legislature as to the best method of choosing electors.

The electors met in their own states on the day appointed and each voted for two persons, one at least a nonresident of the state. The Constitution did not provide that one of these should be designated for the presidency, the other for the vice-presidency. From each state a certified list of the votes was to be sent to the president of the Senate, who was to open them in the presence of both houses. If a majority of the electors had voted for the same man he was to be the President. In case of a tie, or of no person having a majority, the House of Representatives was to choose one of the five leading candidates, each delegation voting as a unit to preserve the equal influence of the small states as under the Confederation. After the President was chosen the candidate having the next largest electoral vote was to become Vice-President. In case of a tie vote for the second place the choice devolved upon the Senate.

This cumbrous machinery had given the Convention much satisfaction. It was expected to serve as a kind of nominating device, since it was not anticipated that electors would often coincide in their judgment sufficiently to cast a majority vote for one man. Hence the choice was expected to come to the House rather regularly. The framers of the Constitution failed to foresee the effect which the rise of political parties would have upon this system. The provision worked so badly that it was modified within a few years by the twelfth amendment. In the first election, however, no difficulty was encountered, for Washington's name was found upon the ballot of every elector. Their second votes were scattered among several men, but John Adams had more than any other candidate, although less than half of the total number.

The work of the First Congress was second in importance only to that of the Constitutional Convention. The Constitution was but a framework or skeleton which awaited the action of Congress to give it life. Its provisions were not self-executing, but needed legislation to put them into effect. The decisions involved were momentous, for they set precedents of almost constitutional force.

The Constitution alludes only incidentally to executive departments. In Article II, section 2, paragraph 1 there is a provision that the President "may require the Opinion, in writing, of the principal Officer in each of the executive Departments, upon any Subject relating to the Duties of their respective Offices." Paragraph 2 of the same section permits Congress to vest appointments to inferior offices "in the President alone, in the Courts of Law, or in the Heads of Departments."

This assumption that there would be executive departments, together with the silence as to their number, functions, and relations, threw upon Congress the decision as to what offices were needed, and the task of legislation to create them and define the duties of the officials. In the course taken Congress was to some extent guided by the experience of the Confederation period. On July 27, 1789, an act was passed creating the department of foreign affairs. A few weeks later the head of this department was given the duty of preserving the laws passed by each session of Congress, and in consequence, his department was renamed the department of state. In August the war department was established with supervision over both army and navy, and in September the act was passed which established the department of the treasury.

In the appointment of the heads of these departments, known as "secretaries," the clause of the Constitution governed which provides that the President "shall nominate, and by and with the Advice and Consent of the Senate, shall appoint Ambassadors, other public Ministers and Consuls, Judges of the Supreme Court, and all other Officers of the United States, whose appointments are not herein otherwise provided for, and which shall be established by law." [1] Washington first offered the post of secretary of state to John Jay, the associate of Franklin and Adams in the diplomacy of the Revolution, and secretary of foreign affairs during the Confederation. The choice was a fitting one, as Franklin had passed the age for active service and Adams was Vice-President. When Jay declined Washington turned to Jefferson, the agent of the United States in France. For the war department he chose Henry Knox, of Massachusetts. This was a virtual continuation in office, since Knox held the corresponding post under the Confederation. Hamilton became secretary of the treasury and Edmund Randolph, attorney-general. [2]

The Constitution was not clear as to how appointed officials should be removed. In the case of judges, whose tenure of office according to the Constitution is good behavior, it was fairly clear that the proper procedure was by impeachment. The question whether the same method should apply generally to cases of removal was raised by the bill for the creation of the department of

[1] Art. II, sec. 2, paragraph 3.
[2] The office of attorney-general was provided for by the Judiciary Act of 1789.

foreign affairs. That bill as drawn provided that the secretary should be "removable by the President." A motion to strike out this clause brought forth a debate during which several views were set forth as to the proper method of making removals. Alexander White of Virginia held that since the Senate shared the power of appointment it ought to share likewise the power of removal. Some believed that Congress should pass legislation prescribing how removals should be made. Others contended that the only method of making removals contemplated by the Constitution was by impeachment. Madison reasoned that the secretaries had duties of an executive nature, and that as the President was chief executive, he could not properly perform his duties unless these officials were regarded as his subordinates, responsible to him, and therefore dismissible by him. If the President abused this power, he himself could be punished by impeachment. To share the power with the Senate would be to abolish "that great principle of unity and responsibility in the executive department, which was intended for the security of liberty and the public good." [3]

Madison's view prevailed, perhaps largely because of the confidence which members generally felt in the character of Washington as President. The clause in question was replaced by another to the effect that "whenever said principal officer shall be removed by the President" the chief clerk should perform his duties; the point of the change lying in the fact that the original reading seemed to imply that the power of removal was conferred upon the chief executive by legislative act, while the substitute reading allowed it to appear that the power inhered in the President. The view of White was to recur at various later epochs, notably under Presidents Jackson and Johnson.

As in the case of the executive departments, the Constitution left much to the discretion of Congress in giving form to the judicial branch. The Convention had found the nucleus of a federal judiciary in existence, and as an evidence of the root from which the new system sprang there was included in the Constitution a provision which pointed back to the admiralty courts of the colonial

[3] For this debate see *Ann. of Cong.*, 1 Cong., 1 sess., 473–521, 616–631, *et passim*. Extracts are reprinted in Johnson, *Readings*, 168–177.

era, for it extended the judicial authority of the United States "to all Cases of admiralty and maritime jurisdiction." Moreover, imbued with the idea that the "National Legislature ought to be empowered . . . to legislate in all cases to which the separate states are incompetent"—a clause in the Virginia resolutions—the Convention, as has been pointed out, had perceived that the scope of the federal judicial power should be coextensive with that of the the law-making body, and had decided that it should extend to "all cases, in law and equity, arising under this Constitution, the laws of the United States, and treaties made . . . under their authority." It had determined also that "the judicial Power of the United States shall be vested in one supreme Court, and in such inferior Courts as the Congress may from time to time ordain and establish." [4]

This last provision had been agreed upon by the Convention only after much discussion and difference of opinion. Whenever the question of the judiciary had arisen members had divided on the desirability of inferior federal courts. One group, led by Madison, insisted that there must be a complete federal system, while the other faction held with equal tenacity to the view that the state courts would answer every need of lower jurisdiction, saving the right of appeal in cases involving federal law to the United States Supreme Court. The phraseology adopted was a compromise; unable to agree, the two factions by the wording adopted had passed the dispute along to be dealt with by Congress. The Constitution enumerated, however, the classes of cases in which the jurisdiction of the Supreme Court should be original but left to Congress the determination of the jurisdiction of whatever inferior courts might be created, and the fixing of the conditions governing appeals.

In the First Congress the old question of inferior courts therefore necessarily arose again, and after a lively contest an act was passed which was a new compromise.

The Judiciary Act of September 24, 1789, determined that the supreme bench should consist of a chief justice and five associates, and that the court should hold two sessions each year. Thirteen inferior tribunals, called district courts, were created, one for each

[4] Art. III, sec. 1.

of the eleven states which had ratified the Constitution plus one each for the Maine district of Massachusetts and the Kentucky district of Virginia. For each district court a single judge was provided, and these courts were grouped in three circuits for which there were no distinct judges; a session of the circuit court was held in turn in each district of the circuit by the judge of that district and two justices of the Supreme Court. As few cases were expected to come before the highest tribunal, it was thought not to be unfair to require each justice to make the round in one circuit annually.

These provisions represent the desires of the faction which insisted upon a complete system of federal courts. But in deference to the demands of the opposing faction it was agreed that under certain circumstances cases involving federal law might be heard in state courts as well as in inferior federal tribunals. In effect, federal jurisdiction was shared with the state courts, which were taken into the federal system by the arrangement, although under the Constitution federal jurisdiction might have been reserved exclusively to the courts of the United States. The compromise was a clumsy one fraught with danger, since it obscured the distinction between two jurisdictions. Section twenty-five of the act provided for appeals from the decisions of state courts which failed to uphold federal law. In time the very group which had contended for the use of state courts became dissatisfied with the workings of the plan of appeals and denounced it as unconstitutional. Apparently forgetting that the state courts were a part of the federal system, they insisted that appeals could not be taken beyond the highest court of the *same* jurisdiction (meaning the supreme state tribunal), and thus sought to prevent the review by the Supreme Court of cases decided by the state judiciary.[5]

The appeal provision of the Judiciary Act, which rested on the supreme law clause [6] of the Constitution, made the Supreme Court

[5] See *infra*, Chap. XVIII.

[6] "This Constitution, and the Laws of the United States which shall be made in Pursuance thereof; and all Treaties made, or which shall be made, under the Authority of the United States, shall be the Supreme Law of the Land; and the Judges in every State shall be bound thereby, any Thing in the Constitution of any State to the Contrary notwithstanding."—Art. VI, par. 2.

the final interpreter of the Constitution and laws of Congress, even in disputes between the states and federal government over their respective powers. However, this clause taken literally laid the duty of upholding the supremacy of federal law upon the *state* courts. Critics were therefore able to argue that the Judiciary Act went beyond the Constitution in assigning this function to the Supreme Court, even on appeal. The alternative which they advocated gave no assurance that the interpretation of the supreme law would be uniform throughout the United States, but it fitted the theory that the Union was a confederation of sovereign states.[7]

On September 24, 1789, the same day on which he penned his signature to the Judiciary Act, President Washington sent to the Senate his nominations of justices. He had given much thought to the selection, and had found himself perplexed by the number of well qualified men. He had been urged to appoint John Rutledge of South Carolina or Robert R. Livingston, the Chancellor of New York, as chief justice. James Wilson of Pennsylvania ventured to offer himself for that post. Washington did in the end decide to appoint Rutledge and Wilson to the bench as associate justices, but the chief position was bestowed on John Jay. As the other associates he named William Cushing of Massachusetts, John Blair of Virginia, and James Iredell of North Carolina. The ages of these men ranged from thirty-eight to fifty-seven years. All had distinguished records, and four had filled high judicial offices in their own states; their appointments were received with marks of public approval. The court met for the first time on Monday, February 1, 1790.[8]

[7] Information concerning the framing of the Judiciary Act of 1789 is meager. Oliver Ellsworth of Connecticut had much to do with it. He perceived that to give jurisdiction to the state courts over federal cases would take them into the federal system, necessitating many appeals from the highest state courts to the supreme United States tribunal, and foresaw that such appeals, by placing the state courts in a subordinate situation and subjecting their decisions to frequent reversals, would hurt their pride. Because of the insistence of the state party, however, he was willing to "divide the ground with them," and leave it optional with the parties in litigation to select their court, thinking this compromise would lessen the danger of future dissatisfaction. See letter to Judge Richard Law, in William Garrott Brown, *The Life of Oliver Ellsworth*. There is much of value in Charles Warren, "New Light on the History of the Federal Judiciary Act of 1789." For the text of the act see *U. S. Statutes at Large*, I, Chap. XX.

[8] Charles Warren, *The Supreme Court in United States History*, I, Chap. I.

THE RELATIONS OF THE THREE DEPARTMENTS

The inaugural address of the President has no other constitutional basis than the provision in Article II, section 3, that "He shall from time to time give to the Congress Information of the State of the Union, and recommend to their Consideration such Measures as he shall judge necessary and expedient." [9] Washington referred to the above passage and mentioned the need of amendments to the Constitution, but beyond that confined his inaugural address to expressions of appreciation of the confidence and esteem of the country and devout wishes for the favor of Providence upon it. The precedent which he set of making an address at the beginning of his term has persisted without interruption to the present.

The same passage forms the warrant for the annual and special messages to Congress, but fixed no procedure to be followed, apparently leaving the time to be determined at the discretion of the President, but suggesting neither a written message nor a speech delivered in the presence of the houses. Upon the occasion of his first message, Washington sent a messenger to the houses notifying them that he was ready to make a communication. Thereupon the House went to the Senate chamber and the President appeared and delivered an address. The House then returned to its own chamber, went into committee of the whole, passed a resolution in favor of an address in reply, appointed a committee to draft it, adopted its report, sent a committee to ascertain when the President would be pleased to receive the House, and at the time set went in a body to his residence, where the speaker presented the address and the President made a reply. This cumbrous, time-consuming ceremonialism was distasteful to the Republicans, but the annual message continued to be delivered as an address until Jefferson became President. He adopted the plan of sending the message in written form declaring that he did so principally out of regard for the convenience of the legislature, economy of their time, and relief from the embarrassment of immediate answers on subjects not fully discussed.

[9] The documentary history of the preparations for Washington's inaugural is to be found in James Richardson, comp., *Messages of the Presidents*, I, 42–57. Extracts are reprinted in Johnson, *Readings*, 151–156.

In recent years there has been a recurrence to the spoken address in place of the annual written message. President Wilson took the lead in this departure from custom, and his example has been followed by his successors. In explanation of the revival of the original practice, Wilson said that the executive and legislature should not deal with each other as "inhabitants of different planets." Of course there was no revival of the old ceremonialism of replies and counter replies.

From the presidency of Washington on, written messages were employed whenever special business called for communication with either house.

The meaning of the phrase "recommend to their Consideration" has been held to be equivalent to the power of initiating legislation. While, of course, it does not give the President the right to introduce a bill upon the floor of either house, bills are, as a matter of fact, not infrequently drawn by executive officials and introduced through the regular committees. The President and his subordinates often exercise an important influence over legislation through informal conference with leaders in the houses, sometimes to the extent of cooperating in the drafting of bills. The significance of the power of recommendation depends largely upon the chief executive's capacity for leadership.

The Convention at one time contemplated the creation of a council of advisers to be associated with the President, but in the end decided it would be better to give some of the functions of an executive council to the Senate. Such functions had been frequently enjoyed by the upper houses of colonial legislatures and were exercised by some of them under the state constitutions. In Article II, section 2, paragraph 2, therefore, the President's power to make treaties and appoint officers was made dependent upon the advice and consent of the Senate.

Washington soon faced the problem of the method by which this advice and consent was to be obtained, and left a memorandum of his first tentative conclusions. The time, place, and manner, he thought, should be determined by the President at discretion. Whenever a suitable executive chamber should be provided, the Senate should attend the President there, at least when the business concerned appointments. When treaties were in hand, as they partook more of the nature of legislation, the President might visit the Senate chamber. Possibly, he thought, a chamber might be provided for joint business of both kinds, and he foresaw that experience might indicate the wisdom of oral discussion in some cases and written communications in others; but on the whole he was of the opinion that the Senate should accommodate their rules to the desires of the President.[10]

The Senate also considered the question of procedure in executive session, and apparently thought, like Washington, that some joint business might be presented orally, for on August 21, 1789, the body passed a resolution to the effect that when the President visited the chamber, he should occupy the Vice-President's chair, while that officer took one upon the floor. The resolution provided also that the Senate should meet the President elsewhere if summoned to do so, and that, in all cases, votes should be taken *viva voce*.[11]

The first occasion for an attempt at consultation arose from the necessity of submitting for the Senate's "advice and consent" a treaty which the war department had made with the Creek Indians. Washington went to the Senate chamber accompanied by Secretary of War Knox, because he was acquainted with all of the details and could give any information which senators might require. The incident is related from the point of view of a senator, by William Maclay, of Pennsylvania, who confided his impressions to his journal. The treaty was read, he tells us, but the noise in the street was so great that he could barely make out that it was something about Indians. Vice-President Adams then proceeded at once to put the question on the first article. As no one seemed ready to speak, Maclay reluctantly acted upon a hint from Morris, and spoke to the effect that the Senate should inform itself more fully on the business before voting. "I cast an eye at the President of the United States. I saw he wore an aspect of stern displeasure." At length Maclay moved postponement until Mon-

[10] Ford, *Writings of Washington*, XI, 418–419. Reprint in Johnson, *Readings*, 160–161.
[11] Ford, *op. cit.*, XI, 419, note. Reprint in Johnson, 161.

day, and when the motion was carried, the papers submitted by the President were, after some discussion, referred to a committee. Thereupon the President "started up in a violent fret. 'This defeats every purpose of my coming here,' were the first words that he said. . . . We waited for him to withdraw. He did so, with a discontented air. Had it been any other than the man whom I wish to regard as the first character in the world, I would have said, with sullen dignity." On Monday the President returned and the business was concluded. Yet, said Maclay, "a shamefacedness, or I know not what, flowing from the presence of the President, kept everybody silent." [12]

Washington did not repeat the attempt to obtain the advice and consent of the Senate while he was himself present, but thereafter submitted executive business by special message, allowing the Senate to deliberate at its leisure. In view of the prominent part which he had taken in thwarting the President's evident desire in the above episode, Maclay was surprised to receive soon afterwards an invitation to dinner, and could not escape the impression that it was designed in some way to influence his political conduct. But, he declared, "I am convinced all the dinners he can now give, or ever could, will make no difference in my conduct." The failure of the Senate to function satisfactorily in personal consultation with the President has probably lessened its influence over foreign relations. In practice the President carries on negotiations with other governments until a treaty is agreed upon. The Senate is not consulted until the completed treaty is submitted, and at that stage modification or rejection is difficult. It has become more or less

[12] Edgar S. Maclay, ed., *Journal of William Maclay*, 128–133. Extract in Johnson, 162–167. John Jay had visited the Senate on May 25, 1789, before the new secretary of state had been appointed. His errand was the presentation of a consular convention negotiated by Franklin and concluded by Jefferson. This was the first bit of international business done by the Senate, as successor to the old Confederation Congress, under which this particular negotiation had been begun. Jay told the Senate that the old Congress had specifically promised to ratify a convention such as he submitted, and the Senate raised no objection. Some agreements with Indian tribes made under similar conditions were presented to the Senate during this period of transition from the old to the new order, but in spite of the explanation that the treaties were made according to instructions given by Congress, the Senate was disposed to look into the facts in each case before giving its approval.

customary for the President or the secretary of state to consult informally the chairman of the Senate committee on foreign affairs, but even his concurrence in negotiations falls far short of "advice and consent". of the Senate.

Even if the Senate had functioned satisfactorily as an advisory body, the scope of its advice was limited to appointments and treaties. Its failure to meet the President's need of a council and the broad scope of the problems which he had to face led him to look elsewhere. Since the Constitution authorized him to "require the Opinion, in Writing, of the principal Officer in each of the executive Departments, upon any Subject relating to the Duties of their respective Officers," [13] it was clear that the secretaries were intended to act as advisers, individually, at least, concerning the business of their departments. As early as 1790 Washington called upon the secretaries for written opinions; but he did not consider that he was forbidden to go beyond the limits mentioned in the Constitution, and soon made it his habit to call the three secretaries and the attorney-general into conference on important business relating to the work of any of the departments, in addition to asking them for written opinions as needed.

The first meeting of these advisers as a group took place, however, in the absence of the President. On April 4, 1791, Washington wrote to the secretaries suggesting that they hold a consultation in case any important matter arose during his absence, and notify him in case his presence seemed to be required. The four men did meet and Jefferson sent to the President a report of the discussion.

Washington did not confine his requests for advice to these four officers. In authorizing the meeting of 1791 he had suggested that the Vice-President might be called in. A little later, when the bill incorporating the United States Bank was pending, he requested Madison, then a member of the House of Representatives, to draft a veto for his use in case he decided against signing the measure. Again, preceding the first actual veto, he consulted Madison as well as his secretaries. In 1793, he requested the opinion of the judges of the Supreme Court on a legal problem connected with

[13] Art. II, sec. 2, par. 1.

our treaties with France. Such consultation of judges by the executive was provided for by some of the state constitutions, notably that of Massachusetts, but the United States judges did not think that it was proper for them to give an opinion upon a question of law unless the issue were presented in the form of a suit. Their refusal tended to make the attorney-general the chief adviser on legal questions.

Apparently the first occasion on which the President and cabinet met together for consultation was in March, 1792. The House of Representatives, desiring to investigate the defeat of St. Clair by the Indians of the Northwest, passed a resolution which indicated the possibility that the secretary of war might be called into conference with a House committee, and that officer was in fact asked to supply papers connected with the campaign. The meeting of the cabinet was called to consider the course to be pursued under these circumstances.

Many of the chief problems of the administration arose in the field of foreign relations, and Jefferson felt aggrieved because the President asked for the opinions of Randolph, Knox and Hamilton as well as his own, especially as he showed a disposition to follow Hamilton's advice. One of the most significant of the measures discussed by the cabinet in these early days, however, fell within the province of the secretary of the treasury, giving Jefferson the opportunity to attack the constitutionality of his rival's pet project of establishing the United States Bank.

Such was the origin of the cabinet. Unknown to the Constitution, it was the creation of Washington. The term "cabinet" came gradually into use, but does not appear in any act of Congress before 1907. Its members rank in the order of the creation of their offices, the secretary of state being consequently the ranking member. The importance of the institution is indicated by the fact that the law determining the succession to the presidency, in the event of the death or disability of both President and Vice-President, devolves it upon cabinet officials in the order of their rank.

The vitality of this pseudo-constitutional device springs, first of all, from the need of a body advisory to the chief executive. A second factor in its utility is the necessity of executive coherence. Gradually it became a body held together by a common loyalty. Washington's experience taught him the disadvantage of bringing into the official group a man whose political tenets did not accord with administration policies. The rise of political parties made it impossible for opponents such as Hamilton and Jefferson had been to sit in the same cabinet. When Jefferson became Vice-President, he refused to attend meetings of the cabinet, which previous Vice-Presidents had done at times, because of his perception of the necessity of executive unity. He was of the opinion, moreover, that his functions were legislative rather than executive in nature. From that time until quite recently the Vice-President has not attended cabinet meetings. The principle has been long accepted that a cabinet member who cannot publicly support the measures formulated therein as those of the administration must retire. Madison's argument in favor of removal of executive officials by the President alone rested upon the need of agreement on policy in the official family.[14]

The Convention had not doubted the necessity of giving the President a veto. Its first use came late in 1791. Article I, section 7, paragraph 2 of the Constitution reads:

"Every Bill which shall have passed the House of Representatives and the Senate, shall, before it becomes a Law, be presented to the President of the United States; If he approve he shall sign it, but if not he shall return it, with his Objections to that House in which it shall have originated, who shall enter the Objections at large on their Journal, and proceed to reconsider it. If after such Reconsideration two thirds of that House shall agree to pass the Bill, it shall be sent, together with the Objections, to the other House, by which it shall likewise be reconsidered, and if approved by two thirds of that House, it shall become a Law. . . . If any Bill shall not be returned by the President within ten days (Sundays excepted) after it shall have been presented to him, the Same shall be a law, in like Manner as if he had signed it, unless the Congress

[14] The most important discussions of the cabinet are: H. B. Learned, *The President's Cabinet*, and Mary L. Hinsdale, *A History of the President's Cabinet*. Both of these works contain helpful bibliographies on the subject.

by their Adjournment prevent its Return, in which Case it shall not be a Law."

In England the crown's veto on acts of Parliament had long been obsolete, there having been no instance of its exercise since the days of Queen Anne, but in America this executive power had been kept alive, and made odious, by the royal governors, and it was freely predicted that no President would ever venture by its use to thwart the will of Congress. A piece of careless legislation enabled Washington to employ the negative without arousing resentment.

In November, 1791, on the basis of the census of 1790, the House of Representatives passed a bill apportioning representation in that body at the rate of one member for every 30,000 inhabitants. This figure, used as a divisor, left large fractions in certain of the northern states, and in the Senate an amendment was adopted giving representation to these fractions when in excess of 15,000. The House accepted the change and the bill came to Washington, who hesitated. Although Jefferson had submitted his opinion, in writing, that the bill was unconstitutional, Washington held it till the tenth day. On that day, still undecided, he again consulted Jefferson, expressing the fear that as the vote in Congress had shown a sectional alignment, a veto might be construed as "taking side with a southern party." Supported by the advice of Randolph and Madison, in addition to Jefferson's, he finally vetoed the bill, the three advisers drafting the message by his request.[15] The objections offered were constitutional: "First. The Constitution has prescribed that Representatives shall be apportioned among the several States according to their respective numbers; and there is no one proportion or divisor which, applied to the respective numbers of the States, will yield the number and allotment of Representatives proposed by the bill.

"Second. The Constitution has also provided that the number of Representatives shall not exceed one for every thirty thousand . . . and the bill has allotted to eight of the States more than one for every thirty thousand."[16]

Upon reconsideration in the House of Representatives the vote

[15] Ford, *Writings of Jefferson*, I, 192. Reprint in Johnson, *Readings*, 157.
[16] *Ann. of Cong.*, 2 Cong., 1 sess., 539–541. Reprint in Johnson, 157–159.

stood, Yeas 23, Nays 33. "And so the said bill was rejected, two-thirds of the House not agreeing to pass the same."

The veto was well received. Jefferson noted that "a few of the hottest friends of the bill expressed passion, but the majority were satisfied, & both in and out of doors it gave pleasure to have at length an instance of the negative being exercised." The South was satisfied because the veto favored that section, and the North was satisfied because the Federalists desired to have the veto made effective. A new bill was now passed by both houses allotting one representative for every 33,000 inhabitants.

Some difference of opinion existed in these early days as to the proper limits upon the use of the veto, the Republicans inclining to a restricted use, the Federalists to liberality. In his opinion on the United States Bank Bill, Jefferson wrote: "The negative of the President is the shield provided by the constitution to protect against the invasions of the legislature: 1. The right of the executive. 2. Of the Judiciary. 3. Of the States and State legislatures. . . . Unless the President's mind on a view of everything which is urged for and against this bill, is tolerably clear that it is unauthorized by the Constitution; if the pro and the con hang so even as to balance his judgment, a just respect for the wisdom of the legislature would naturally decide the balance in favor of their opinion." Hamilton's view was much less circumscribed for he believed that the veto was properly applicable to measures which the President considered objectionable for any reasons whatsoever.

Very little use was made of the veto power before Madison's presidency. John Quincy Adams had no recourse to it, but Jackson employed it systematically, vetoing twelve bills. Grover Cleveland earned the nickname of "the veto President" by vetoing more than three hundred bills, mostly private pension acts. Except under Andrew Johnson, only some half-dozen measures, in total, have been passed over the veto.

In 1792 arose the question of the right of the houses to call on department heads for papers. The occasion was the investigation by the House of Representatives, already mentioned, of St. Clair's defeat by the Indians in the Northwest Territory. A cabinet meeting was held on March 31 and a second one April 2, and the unanimous decision was that calls for papers were proper, and that the executive should respond unless public injury would result; but at the same time it was held that calls should be addressed to the President and not to department heads. These decisions were interpretations of the constitutional provisions already referred to, permitting the President to "require the Opinion, in writing, of the principal Officer in each of the Executive Departments, upon any Subject relating to the Duties" thereof, and authorizing him "from time to time to give to the Congress Information of the state of the Union."

By the acts creating the departments of state and war, the secretaries were directed to perform such duties as the President should entrust to them. The treasury was not, like these, called an executive department. In the cabinet discussion Hamilton pointed out that by the act creating the treasury department it was made more directly subject to Congress than the other departments. The act made it the duty of the secretary of the treasury to "digest and prepare plans for the improvement and management of the revenue and for the support of the public credit and make reports and give information to either branch of the legislature, in person or in writing as may be required, respecting all matters referred to him by the Senate or House of Representatives, or which shall pertain to his office."

Jefferson's interpretation of Hamilton's remark was that he would like to "place himself subject to the house when the Executive should propose what he should not like, & subject to the Executive when the house should propose anything disagreeable." [17] Nevertheless, the exceptional position of the treasury department was admitted, and in 1801 Gallatin wrote: "the invariable practice has been to call for financial information directly on the Treasury Department . . . and for information respecting Army, Navy or State Department, the application is always to the President, requesting him to direct, &c." Gallatin also questioned whether the exception "was not introduced . . . in order to give Mr. Hamilton a department independent of every executive control. It may be

[17] Ford, *Writings of Jefferson*, I, 189–190. Reprint in Johnson, 184–186.

remembered that he claimed under those laws the right of making reports and proposing reforms, &c., without being called on for the same by Congress." In Gallatin's opinion "this was a Presidential power, for by the Constitution the President is to call on the Departments for information, and has alone the power of recommending." [18]

THE CONSTITUTION AND FOREIGN RELATIONS

While the people of the United States were wrestling with the problems incident to the effort to organize an effective government under the Constitution, Frenchmen were in the throes of a revolution which overthrew the ancient monarchy and set up a republic. With the monarchy the United States had made treaties of alliance and of amity and commerce. The news that the republic was sending a minister to the United States to replace the representative of the overturned monarchy created a problem which Washington had to confront, and which called for consideration by the cabinet. All of the members thought that the new minister should be received, but there was a difference of opinion as to whether the treaties were still in effect. The treaty of alliance, dating from 1778 when France went to war with England to secure America's independence, bound the United States to defend France's West Indian possessions "forever." This promise was peculiarly embarrassing, since France was again at war with England, and Washington, moved by a strong sense of the necessity of keeping his infant country at peace, decided, with the support of the cabinet, to issue a proclamation of neutrality. The word "neutrality" was not used, but the proclamation announced that the United States was at peace with all the warring European powers, and warned Americans against acts of hostility towards any of them.[19]

The President evidently believed that the alliance was defensive only, and that the United States was under no obligation to protect the French islands in a war in which he regarded France as the

[18] Gallatin to Jefferson, November, 1801, in Henry Adams, ed., *Writings of Albert Gallatin*, I, 66–67. Reprint in Johnson, 186–187. See Edward C. Mason, "Congressional Demands upon the Executive for Information."

[19] *American State Papers, For. Rels.* I, 140. Reprinted in MacDonald, *Select Documents*, 112–114.

aggressor. Jefferson, believing that the alliance was still in force, disliked the proclamation in spite of the fact that he had consented to it. He thought that if the proclamation had been withheld, the United States might have obtained some advantage from one or other of the belligerents as the price of neutrality.[20] As he thought the matter over he persuaded himself that the President's statement that the country was at peace was equivalent to a declaration that it would not go to war. Since the power to declare war was entrusted to Congress, the President's utterance took on, in Jefferson's mind, the character of an encroachment upon the legislative branch.[21]

The evidence of discontent with the proclamation was sufficient to lead Hamilton, writing as "Pacificus," to come to the defense of the President. Although to Hamilton "executive power" under the Constitution was to be understood as that pertaining to the executive in England except as qualified by the provisions of the American fundamental law, the point of significance for the discussion of 1793 was his exposition of the view that at any given moment it is within the power of the President to declare what the existing law is, subject, of course, to the power of Congress to change the law whenever it may choose to do so.[22]

At Jefferson's instigation Madison replied to Hamilton under the pen name of "Helvidius." He succeeded only in maintaining that "Pacificus" derived his concept of executive powers from the prerogatives of English royalty, a concept of such broad implications that if admitted, "no citizen could any longer guess at the character of the government under which he lives." [23]

This discussion of the President's powers was followed by a much more serious controversy over the part of the House of Representatives in treaty-making. That the framers of the Constitution did not turn out a perfect instrument of government is evident

[20] Letter to Madison, June 23, 1793. Ford, *Writings of Jefferson*, VI, 338.

[21] "A declaration of neutrality was a declaration there should be no war, to which the Executive was not competent."—*Ibid.*

[22] John C. Hamilton, ed., *The Works of Alexander Hamilton*, VII, 76–117. As to presidential proclamations, see James Hart, *The Ordinance Making Powers of the President.*

[23] James Madison, *Letters and Other Writings*, I, 611–654.

in many ways. A troublesome ambiguity which vexed the country for many years is found in the provisions relating to the making of treaties. The power to make treaties is vested in the President "by and with the advice and consent of the Senate," and treaties, along with the Constitution and laws of Congress, are the "law of the land." However, all legislative power is declared to be vested in a Congress consisting of "a Senate and a House of Representatives." Does or does not a treaty become a part of the law of the land without the participation of the House of Representatives? To the House, moreover, is assigned the right to originate all bills for raising revenue, and appropriations can be made only by "law." Is a treaty a law in the sense that it can appropriate money without the participation of the House? Or if President and Senate make a treaty involving the payment of money, is the House bound to make the appropriations required to give it effect? Finally, does the House have the right to judge of the merits of a treaty and by withholding its assent to appropriations to give it effect, hold the power virtually to nullify it? [24]

These questions arose first in connection with the treaty negotiated with England by John Jay and ratified by the Senate in special session in June, 1795. Some months later Washington, having received notice of ratification by the English government, issued a proclamation announcing that it was the law of the land. In due time he sent a copy to the House, since the carrying out of the agreement required an appropriation.

The terms of the treaty were disliked by the Republicans. At

[24] The several provisions of the Constitution on which the questions discussed in the text turn are as follows: The President "shall have Power, by and with the Advice and Consent of the Senate, to make treaties, provided two thirds of the Senators present concur."—Art. II, sec. 2, par. 2.

"This Constitution, and the Laws of the United States which shall be made in Pursuance thereof; and all Treaties made, or which shall be made, under the Authority of the United States, shall be the supreme law of the Land. . . ."—Art. III, par. 1.

"All legislative Powers herein granted shall be vested in a Congress of the United States, which shall consist of a Senate and a House of Representatives."—Art. I, sec. 1.

"All Bills for raising Revenue shall originate in the House of Representatives. . . ."—Art. I, sec. 7, par. 1.

"No Money shall be drawn from the Treasury, but in Consequence of Appropriations made by Law. . . ."—Art. I, sec. 9, par. 7.

the time they possessed a majority in the lower chamber, and their course was foreshadowed when the legislature of Virginia proposed an amendment to the effect that no treaty with a stipulation involving powers vested in Congress should become the law of the land until the House as well as the Senate had approved it.

The first act of the House after receiving the President's communication was to call upon him for the papers relating to the negotiation.[25] Washington consulted his cabinet, and with their approval refused to comply with the request, on the ground that it did not appear that the papers related to any functions of the House unless it contemplated his impeachment.[26] The representatives now adopted a resolution asserting that when a treaty depends for its execution on legislation by Congress, it is the right and duty of the House to deliberate on the expediency of carrying the treaty into effect, and to act according to their judgment of what is for the public good; and that, in calling upon the executive for papers it is not necessary to state the purpose for which they are wanted.[27]

In support of this contention the chief argument was presented by Albert Gallatin of Pennsylvania. He held that the House had full discretion and might give or refuse the cooperation necessary to give effect to the treaty. He did not claim for it a share in the treaty-making power, but a check upon it. If treaties could become the law of the land without action of the House, the President and Senate could "absorb all Legislative power." [28]

Jefferson praised this exposition as worthy of a place in the *Federalist*. Hamilton, who was now in retirement, advised the President, on the contrary, that the House had neither moral nor legal right to refuse to execute a treaty: no moral right because the treaty pledged the public faith; no legal right because it was law without the action of the House. Washington informed the House, in the message refusing the call for papers, that his opinion

[25] For the House debate, which ran with interruptions from March to May, 1796, see *Ann. of Cong.*, 4 Cong., 1 sess., 426–772 *et passim*. Extracts are reprinted in Johnson, 197–205.

[26] *Ibid.*, 202–204.

[27] *Ibid.*, 205.

[28] *Ann. Cong.*, 4 Cong., 1 sess., 464 *et seq*. Reprinted in Johnson, 198–201.

on the matter had been formed while a member of the Constitutional Convention, during which, he said, a proposition that no treaty should be binding on the United States which was not ratified by law had been explicitly rejected.

So far as Jay's treaty was concerned, the outcome of the dispute was a victory for the Federalists, due largely to a famous oratorical effort of Fisher Ames. The bill making the appropriation passed by the small margin of 51 to 48. But the constitutional issue was not settled by this vote; in fact, it was to come up again and again until eventually the treaty-making power, recognizing that the House could not be coerced, conceded that a treaty touching matters delegated to the legislative control of Congress must in practice receive the approbation of both houses.[29]

No proposal to amend the Constitution at this point has ever won serious consideration, and the working arrangement mentioned renders it unnecessary. The history of this compromise is a good illustration of the rise of what may be called the *usages* of the Constitution. These are practices which to all intents and purposes have become an essential part of the constitutional system. The existence of a body of such customs makes it impossible to understand this system merely by reading the Constitution.[30]

[29] J. M. Mathews, *The Conduct of American Foreign Relations.* The growth of federal authority in later years was promoted by the liberal interpretation of the treaty-making power: see Chap. XIV of the present volume; also E. S. Corwin, *National Supremacy,* Chap. VI. In recent years the treaty-making power has been held to warrant the making of treaties which in turn sustain legislation which would otherwise be unconstitutional. See Missouri *v.* Holland, 252 U. S. 416 (1920), known as the migratory bird case.

Among the more useful studies of the treaty-making power and foreign relations in general, besides those already mentioned, are: Samuel B. Crandall, *Treaties, their Making and Enforcement;* Henry St. George Tucker, *Limitations on the Treaty-Making Power under the Constitution of the United States;* Philip Quincy Wright, *The Control of the Foreign Relations of the United States.*

[30] Herbert W. Horwill, *The Usages of the American Constitution.*

XIII

THE NATURE OF THE CONSTITUTION
AND THE UNION

THE BEATIFICATION OF THE CONSTITUTION

IN the foregoing pages the story of the framing and adoption of the Constitution has been told as if the participants were guided throughout the whole process by cool reason and judgment. To regard their action in this light would be to miss the significance of the psychology which soon made loyalty to the Constitution more a matter of sentiment than of reason. It has been wisely said that "popular government, like monarchy, rests on fiction and lives by expedients. It suffices that the fiction be accepted and the expedient happy."[1] It is true that Federalists and Antifederalists engaged in a sharp contest, but doubts about the new instrument of government speedily gave way to general enthusiasm. As Woodrow Wilson once wrote, "the divine right of kings never ran a more prosperous course than did the unquestioned prerogative of the Constitution to receive universal homage."[2] This phenomenon, whether resting on judgment or sentiment, goes far to explain the success of the Constitution. The early years of the new government were years of unexampled prosperity, and Oliver Wolcott was probably correct in his judgment that amidst such conditions "it must be a very bad administration which overturns a government."[3]

The rise of the "tradition" of the Constitution was due in part to the conscious propagandism of the men who worked for its ratification. By cleverly appropriating the name "federal" which their opponents had first (and more fittingly) used to designate

[1] Anatole France, quoted by Frank I. Schechter, "The Early History of the Tradition of the Constitution," 708.

[2] Quoted *ibid.*, 719. This remarkable phenomenon was first discussed by Hermann E. von Holst, who referred to it as "the canonization of the Constitution." See the *Constitutional and Political History of the United States*, I, Chap. II. The best study of it is the article by Schechter. See also Edward P. Smith, "Movement towards a Second Constitutional Convention in 1788."

[3] Schechter, 721, quoting George Gibbs, *Memoirs of the Administrations of Washington and John Adams*, I, 58.

their own group, the nationalists adopted a term which properly stood for decentralization and state supremacy. The voters were more or less confused by this strategy, and the critics of the Constitution were made to appear as enemies of progress and the public welfare. Although the leaders in the Convention offered the results of their work with some diffidence, conscious rather of its defects than its merits, and although the friends of ratification used "steam-roller" tactics to obtain favorable action in some of the states,[4] the whole movement for the new Constitution was represented as a deliberate exercise of reason and choice on the part of a free people, unexampled in the history of the world. Said James Wilson in the Pennsylvania convention: "Government . . . has hitherto been the result of force, fraud or accident. . . . America now presents the first instance of a people assembled to weigh deliberately and calmly, and to decide leisurely and peaceably, upon the form of government by which they will bind themselves and their posterity."[5]

Wilson was doubtless sincere; he believed that America was proceeding in accordance with the dictates of the compact philosophy which she professed. Truly popular government having nowhere come into existence as yet, the fact that perhaps not more than five percent of the population of America voted for members of the ratifying conventions did not present the inconsistency to contemporary minds that it does to ours. On the contrary, America's course was expected to challenge the approval of foreign nations and to enlighten the world. In November, 1787, just before the Pennsylvania convention assembled, the *Connecticut Gazette* declared: "We anticipate the praise with which the new federal government will be viewed by the friends of liberty and mankind in Europe. The philosophers will no longer consider a republic as an impracticable form of government; and pious men of all denominations will thank God for having provided in our Federal Constitution an ark, for the preservation of the justice and liberties of the world. . . ."[6]

[4] See Beard, *Economic Interpretation*, Chap. VIII.
[5] Quoted by Schechter, 723.
[6] Quoted *ibid.*, 724.

Religiously-minded America was, as hinted in this quotation, prompt to associate the new movement with the guidance of Providence. Even Franklin the rationalist fostered this tendency by saying, in one of his last writings: "I must avow I have so much faith in the general government of the world by Providence, that I can hardly conceive a transaction of such momentous importance to the welfare of millions now existing, and to exist in the posterity of a great nation should be suffered to pass without being in some degree influenced, guided and governed by that omnipotent, omnipresent and beneficial Ruler, in whom all inferior spirits live, and move, and have their being." [7]

From this position that God was on the side of the framers it was not a long step to the belief that Antifederalists were atheistic obstructionists. "A minister of the gospel, through the medium of our paper," reported the *New Haven Gazette and Connecticut Magazine*, "begs leave to ask, whether men can be serious in regard to the Christian religion, who can object to a government that is calculated to promote the glory of God, by establishing peace, order and justice in our country—and whether it would not be better for such men to renounce the Christian name, and to enter into society with the Shawanese or Mohawk Indians than to attempt to retain the blessings of religion and civilization with their licentious ideas of government." [8]

These appeals to religious prejudice were associated with the parade and pageantry which so often weigh heavily with the unthinking masses. The news that ratification had been achieved was made the occasion of public celebrations which may very well have aroused enthusiasm even among the ninety-five percent of the people who did not vote. In Philadelphia James Wilson repeated to the crowd at such a celebration what he had said in the state convention—that adoption of the Constitution signified "a people free and enlightened, establishing and ratifying a system of government, which they have previously considered, examined and approved." [9] Similar scenes were enacted in nearly all centers

[7] Bigelow, *Works of Franklin*, IX, 439, quoted by Schechter, 719.
[8] Issue of Oct. 12, 1787, quoted by Schechter, 728.
[9] Quoted by Schechter, 718.

of population. The effects of such methods are evidenced by such hard-headed witnesses as John Quincy Adams. When the delegates who had attended the Massachusetts convention returned to Newburyport with the news that the state had ratified, he tells us that "the mob huzza'd and one would have thought that every man from the adoption of the Constitution had acquired a sure expectancy of an independent fortune." [10]

During the prosperous years of the early nineties, orators were prone to attribute the good times to the beneficent influence of the Constitution, overdrawing the hard times of the Confederation period to heighten the contrast. Said Richard Bland Lee: "I will only mention the stimulus which agriculture has received. In travelling through the various parts of the United States, I find fields, a few years ago, waste and uncultivated, filled with inhabitants and covered with harvests; new habitations reared, contentment in every face, plenty on every board, confidence is restored, and every man is safe under his own vine and his own fig tree, and there is none to make him afraid. To produce this effect was the intention of the Constitution, . . . and it has succeeded." [11]

Apparently only cool observers were able to resist the myth-making forces. Of course there were many of these. William Maclay, one of the first senators from Pennsylvania, who feared that the Constitution would "turn out the vilest of all traps that was ever set to ensnare the freedom of an unsuspecting people," discounted the fulsome praise which identified the adoption of that instrument with the passing of the night. These "declamatory gentlemen," he said, "paint the state of the country under the old . . . congress, as if neither wood grew nor water ran in America before the happy adoption of the new Constitution." [12] A Boston dissenter wrote that "the populace of Boston are regulated by their big men. . . . They have had a great fulsome parade at the ratification. . . . However, all these manoeuvres will not answer; they may serve to please children, but freemen will not so easily be gulled out of their liberties. . . . I would not be surprised if

[10] *Diary*, 94, quoted by Schechter, 710, note 13.
[11] *Ann. of Cong.*, 3 Cong., 261–262, quoted by Schechter, 720.
[12] Quoted *ibid*.

the people from Georgia to New Hampshire would rise and crush the real authors and promoters of this system of arbitrary power."[13]

But men of critical mind did not determine the currents of thought, and no popular uprising followed the setting up of the new government. A turning point in opinion seems to have come with the adoption of the first group of amendments. The Antifederalists now began to pose as friends of the Constitution, and indeed, soon outdid the Federalists themselves in their professions of loyalty, claiming to be the only true supporters of the Constitution in its real intent. They overlooked or disregarded the evidence that the framers did not intend to establish a popular form of government; and with the rise of political parties, the Republicans under Jefferson's lead assumed that the Constitution was a charter of liberty, deriving its authority from the popular will. It thereupon became the professed purpose of the Republicans to prevent the Federalists from diverting the government, in practice, from its charted course.

Thus if the Federalist leaders were clever in creating a popular tradition concerning the origin of the Constitution, Jefferson and his friends were no less clever in claiming for themselves the custody of this tradition. To Jefferson the Federalists became enemies of democracy and foes of the Constitution who were able to give the government an abnormal direction by capitalizing the prestige of Washington. Holding such views he was not above assisting the poet Philip Freneau to publish an opposition newspaper by giving him a clerkship in the state department. Not yet was the rule of cabinet unity established. Washington hinted strongly that the action violated the proprieties, but Jefferson refused to take the hint, believing that Freneau was doing a useful service by checking an administration which was "fast galloping into monarchy."

Towards the end of the first decade Jefferson explained his position and conduct. "The Republicans," he wrote, "through every part of the Union, say, that it was the irresistible influence and popularity of general Washington played off by the cunning Hamilton, which turned the government over to anti-Republican

[13] Quoted *ibid.*, 719.

hands, or turned Republicans chosen by the people into anti-Republicans. . . . But still I repeat it, this is not the natural state. Time alone would bring round an order of things more correspondent to the sentiments of our constituents. . . . A little patience and we shall see the reign of witches . . . pass over, and the people recovering their true right, restoring the government to its true principles." [14]

HAMILTON AND JEFFERSON

One might suppose that the purpose of a written Constitution was to chart a clear and unmistakable course for government to follow. Most of the framers undoubtedly thought of the discretionary action of the several branches of the government as narrowly limited by the principles of the written document. If experience showed that changes were desirable, they could be made by methods providently defined in the instrument itself. As a matter of fact, the Constitution was of a neutral tint, making it possible for two parties to "profess an attachment to and a reverence for" it "as their guide," and yet to "differ in opinion as to the modes and measures manifesting their attachment and veneration, and reciprocally charge each other with designs to warp, subvert and destroy the Constitution itself." [15] In a word, the instrument did not commit the government beyond cavil either to aristocracy or democracy, nationalism or particularism. Instead, the character of the administration was certain to be determined by the *interpretation* of the Constitution by its administrators, and the interpretation in turn would result from the political philosophy of those administrators.

Of all the defects which the Constitution displays under modern critical analysis, the most serious is this neutral character at critical points. The causes of most of the constitutional difficulties of the whole period previous to the Civil War were, (1) that it did not clearly indicate whether the Union which it formed was a con-

[14] To John Taylor, June 1, 1798. Ford, *Writings of Jefferson*, VII, 263–265, quoted by Schechter, 712.

[15] Schechter, 713, quoting Charles Pettit's pamphlet of 1800 entitled *An Impartial Review of the Rise and Progress of the Controversy between the Parties Known by the Names Federalists and Republicans.*

federation of sovereign communities or one sovereign community with subdivisions each of which possessed autonomous control over its internal police; and (2) that it did not indicate unmistakably how the scheme of distributed powers was to be maintained—that is, in case of a dispute between a state or states and the federal authority as to the allocation of a particular power, by what organ or agency of government the dispute was rightfully to be decided. These uncertainties opened a wide door for differences of interpretation.

These reflections bring into view the truth that our actual constitutional system has been determined hardly more by the words of the fundamental law than by the interpretations of statesmen. The list of the men who have helped in the shaping of this system is a long one, but a few names stand out preeminently. Among these the earliest are the great rivals, Alexander Hamilton and Thomas Jefferson, who as chiefs of the first political parties to take form after the adoption of the Constitution, epitomize in their own thinking two rival philosophies of government which have competed during many generations of American life.

Alexander Hamilton, native of the island of Nevis, came to New York in 1772, at the age of fifteen. Within another fifteen years this precocious youngster won recognition as one of the intellectual lights of the infant republic. As secretary of the treasury in Washington's cabinet his financial program, by aligning men as supporters or opponents, marks the beginning of the Federalist and Republican parties. This program was quite consonant with the philosophy of government which he had set forth in the Constitutional Convention when he presented his plan for the government of the United States.

"All communities divide themselves," he said, "into the few and the many. The first are the rich and well born, the other the mass of the people. The voice of the people has been said to be the voice of God; and however generally this maxim has been quoted and believed, it is not true in fact. The people are turbulent and changing; they seldom judge or determine right. Give therefore to the first class a distinct, permanent share in the government. They will check the unsteadiness of the second, and as they cannot receive any advantage by a change, they therefore will ever maintain good government. Can a democratic assembly who annually revolve in the mass of the people, be supposed steadily to pursue the public good? Nothing but a permanent body can check the imprudence of democracy." [16]

While thus betraying his lack of confidence in the people at large, Hamilton did not advocate their complete exclusion from government. "Give all power to the many, they will oppress the few. Give all power to the few, they will oppress the many. Both, therefore, ought to have the power, that each may defend itself against the other." "In his private opinion . . . the British Government was the best in the world; and he doubted much whether anything short of it would do in America." [17] He did not hope that his ideas would be adopted, but he believed that a proper government should provide for a Senate and executive with tenure of office during good behavior and chosen by the electoral system instead of directly by the voters. His idea of the Senate was derived from the English House of Lords, which he thought was "a noble institution. Having nothing to hope for by a change and a sufficient interest by means of their property, in being faithful to the national interest, they form a permanent barrier against every pernicious innovation whether attempted on the part of the Crown or of the Commons." As for the states, he would have reduced them virtually to administrative subdivisions.[18]

That Hamilton's political philosophy followed closely middle-class English theory is sufficiently evident from these statements. The Constitution of 1787 fell far short of providing the basis for such a government as he desired, but he took office with the intention of making it serve as such a basis so far as possible, by his method of construing its meaning. This intention is evident in all of his measures as secretary of the treasury. Recognized as the leading spirit in the administration, his whole scheme of practical politics favored the moneyed interests and allied the government with the financiers, merchants, manufacturers, and specu-

[16] Farrand, *Records*, I, 299 *et seq.*
[17] *Ibid.*, 282–293.
[18] *Ibid.*, 288.

lators. These were an influential section of the group which had established the Constitution, and without their active support Hamilton saw no hope of successful government. They were the rich and well born whose influence was essential to check the unsteadiness of the masses. Under his guiding genius the Federalist party became the party of the great majority of the old ruling class, especially in the northern states.

If Hamilton incarnated the spirit of the old dominant class which had derived its political creed from England, Jefferson personified no less that New-World spirit born of the frontier. Himself a son of the Virginia border, his philosophy of the state was permanently influenced by his early environment. The tendencies thus imparted to his thought were intensified by his later study of political philosophy, and his residence in France during the early days of the revolution which began in 1789 brought him into contact with theories which confirmed his own conclusions concerning the conditions conducive to human welfare and happiness. Principles which Rousseau and his fellows arrived at by dint of abstract reasoning, Jefferson held as naturally as if he had breathed them in with the air of the Virginia piedmont. It was fitting that the man who adopted Locke's creed to form the philosophical justification of revolution hurled by the western part of the British world against the eastern, should later accept its democratic implications literally as leader of the inland farming democracy in its contest with the American heirs of British tradition.

Jefferson's political creed, like Hamilton's, was the reflex of his philosophy of society. He believed that a simple agricultural economy afforded the best basis for a free state, because it fostered individualism and equality. Such a society American conditions made possible for a long time to come, with its "immensity of land courting the industry of the husbandman." A complex industrialism with workshops and wage labor he did not wish to encourage, because it tended to destroy self-reliance and equality of condition among men, and to introduce the class antagonisms which had led to the oppression and debasement of the people of the Old World. Commerce he favored to a limited extent as the means of exchanging the surplus of an agricultural country for the manufactures of the overcrowded countries of Europe, and hence as a means of keeping manufactures with their corrupting influences away from our shores. The ships for the carrying trade, with the navies required to protect them, he preferred to let the European nations supply. In such an Arcadian society the functions of government would be at a minimum, the need of taxation slight, and individual freedom and liberty at the maximum.[19]

The relation of Jefferson's concept of the ideal society and government to his early surroundings and to the life of the class whose spokesman he was is as obvious as the antecedents of Hamilton's thought. He has been, very appropriately, called a "backwoods statesman." But while he identified the cause of good government with the predominance of the agricultural class, as opposed to the capitalistic interests led by Hamilton, his democracy had certain limitations. He was not ready to advocate manhood suffrage except as associated with land ownership, but he would have had lands granted from the public domain to all adult males.[20]

---

[19] In a famous passage Jefferson paid his tribute to the tillers of the soil in the following terms: "Those who labor in the earth are the chosen people of God, if ever He had a chosen people, whose breasts He has made His peculiar deposit for substantial and genuine virtue. . . . Corruption of morals in the mass of cultivators is a phenomenon of which no age nor nation has furnished an example. It is the mark set on those, who, not looking up to heaven, to their own soil and industry, as does the husbandman, for their subsistence, depend for it on casualties and caprice of customers. Dependence begets subservience and venality, suffocates the germ of virtue, and prepares fit tools for the designs of ambition. This, the natural progress and consequence of the arts, has sometimes perhaps been retarded by accidental circumstances; but, generally speaking, the proportion which the aggregate of other classes of citizens bears in any State to that of its husbandmen, is the proportion of its unsound to its healthy parts, and is a good enough barometer whereby to measure its degree of corruption. While we have land to labor, then, let us never wish to see our citizens occupied at a workbench, or twirling a distaff. Carpenters, masons, smiths, are wanting [needed] in husbandry; but, for the general operations of manufacture, let our workshops remain in Europe. It is better to carry provisions and materials to workmen there, than to bring them to the provisions and materials, and with them their manners and principles. The loss by the transportation of commodities across the Atlantic will be made up in happiness and permanence of government. The mobs of great cities add just so much to the support of pure government as sores do to the strength of the human body." "Notes on Virginia," written in the winter of 1781–1782. Ford, *Writings of Jefferson*, III, 268–269.

[20] See his draft of a constitution for Virginia, 1776, in Ford, *Writings of Jefferson*, II, 7, and discussion of it by Ford in the *Nation* for August 7, 1890 and D. R. Anderson in *Am. Hist. Rev.*, XXI, 750–754.

He never overcame his distrust of the working class of cities, for he believed that "when we get piled upon one another in large cities, as in Europe, we shall become as corrupt as in Europe, and go to eating one another as they do there." [21]   Thus he appears to be less the apostle of a complete democracy than the champion of a society of Arcadian simplicity not unlike that made actual on the frontier.   There is little here to suggest Marxism.   Jefferson developed no theory concerning the relations of classes in an industrial society; he sought instead to avoid the growth in America of such a society.   The background of his thinking was the frontier.   Yet even so one must recognize in his philosophy an attitude towards the masses which under different conditions might have resulted in something like Marxism.

Believing that the ideal government would be wise and frugal, that it would "restrain men from injuring one another," but beyond that "leave them . . . free to regulate their own pursuits of industry and improvement, . . . and not take from the mouth of labor the bread it has earned," [22]   Jefferson's program for government was largely negative or *laissez faire*.   In the Federalist period he appears in national politics as the opponent of policies conceived in the interest of the capitalist class—the advocate of restoration of the government to the democratic simplicity which it seemed to him was intended by the Constitution.[23]

Thus the philosophies of these two men tended on the one side towards strongly centralized aristocratic or plutocratic government, on the other towards the utmost autonomy in the states and popular if not democratic government.   A clash over concrete measures was inevitable.   Yet in the critical months of 1787 and 1788, while changes of government were so much under discus-

---

[21] Letter to Madison, Dec. 20, 1787, Ford, *Writings of Jefferson*, IV, 479.

[22] Inaugural address of 1801. *Ibid.*, VIII, 4.

[23] Jefferson as President was supported by the southern planters, as a class, most of whom had favored the formation of a stronger government. They could not follow Hamilton because some of his measures were directly contrary to their interests. They had little liking for Jefferson's agrarian creed, however; the union of the small farmers and the planters in southern Republicanism was artificial. During Jefferson's presidency the aristocratic section was much in evidence in Congress and elsewhere, and the President held their support by avoiding undue stress upon democratic principles.

sion, both men expressed views which they rejected later. Experience under the state constitutions did not warrant the confidence that either the states or the federal government would scrupulously heed mere "parchment restrictions"; and while the Constitution was still pending the need of additional checks and balances was considered by both men. In essay number 26 of the *Federalist* Hamilton declared that the state legislatures "will always be not only vigilant but suspicious and jealous guardians of the rights of the citizens against encroachments from the federal government, will constantly have their attention awake to the conduct of the national rulers, and will be ready enough, if anything improper appears, to sound the alarm to the people, and not only to be the VOICE, but, if necessary, the ARM of discontent."

Reflection led Hamilton to add that the federal courts would check Congress if it passed unwarranted legislation. Instead of thinking of the legislative body as the final judge of its own powers, he said, it is more rational "to suppose that the courts were designed to be an intermediate body between the people and the legislature, in order, among other things, to keep the latter within the limits assigned to their authority. The interpretation of the laws is the proper and peculiar province of the courts. A constitution is, in fact, and must be regarded by the judges, as a fundamental law. It therefore belongs to them to ascertain its meaning, as well as the meaning of any particular act proceeding from the legislative body. If there should happen to be an irreconcilable variance between the two, that which has the superior obligation and validity ought, of course, to be preferred; or, in other words, the Constitution ought to be preferred to the statute; the intention of the people to the intention of their agents." [24]

Hamilton admitted that there was "not a syllable in the [Constitution] which *directly* empowers the national courts to construe the laws"; the function he thought was "deducible . . . from the general theory of a limited Constitution." If this power was abused by the judges, it could be checked by instituting impeachments against them.[25]

[24] Ford, ed., *Federalist*, No. 81.
[25] *Ibid.*

In this elucidation Hamilton considered only the relation of the federal courts to congressional legislation. He said nothing about the cognate function of judging of the compatibility of state acts with federal authority, that is, of the courts as preservers of the scheme of distributed powers. Oddly enough Jefferson endorsed this latter function before Hamilton accepted it, for writing to Madison in the spring of 1787, he said that such a process was preferable to Madison's plan of giving Congress a negative on legislation by the states.[26] The actual measures of the Hamiltonian party soon turned his thoughts to what seemed to him to be the greater need of protecting the reserved rights of the states, and the possibility of checking encroachments thereon through action by the states. Whether consciously or not, he borrowed the doctrine which Hamilton had set forth in essay number 26 of the *Federalist*, and became its foremost champion.

Defensive action by the state legislature or some other agency of the people of a state fitted well into the concept of the Union as a confederation of sovereign communities. The federal government's measures, however, savored rather of the rival theory. In spite of its concessions to the state's rights faction in Congress, the Judiciary Act of 1789 rested on the strong government theory. It was not long before the champions of the rival theory found an opportunity to announce their opposing doctrine.

THE DOCTRINE OF SENTINELSHIP

If the Supreme Court was not to be accepted as the final interpreter of the law, what was to be done in case of a dispute between a state and the federal government? Hamilton had predicted that the state legislatures would be vigilant guardians of the rights of citizens against encroachments by the federal government, and as fate would have it, one of his own measures as secretary of the treasury supplied the provocation for the first protest. In January, 1790, as part of his plan for establishing the public credit, he proposed that the federal government should assume the debts of the states. These debts, he reasoned, had been incurred in the common struggle for independence and were a just charge upon the common

[26] See *supra*, Chap. IX, note 32.

treasury. The plan was also a part of his program of enlisting men of wealth and intelligence in supporting the federal government. Assumption would cause them to look to it as the source of income on their investments. This policy, which tended to foster a moneyed interest, encountered stiff resistance in Congress. Comparatively few southerners had capital for speculative investments in government securities, and their representatives blocked the project for a time.

When the act was finally pushed through the opposition to it was renewed in the state legislatures, several of which adopted resolutions denouncing it. Virginia had particular reason to dislike the measure, because she had already paid off her state debt. James Monroe in the Senate and Madison in the House presented the state's resolutions declaring the act repugnant to the Constitution. The Virginia House of Delegates drew up also a memorial to Congress setting forth its objections. It was dangerous and impolitic, said this address, to foster a moneyed interest in an agricultural country; it would in time either prostrate agriculture or bring about a change in the form of government which would destroy liberty. Moreover, the Constitution gave Congress no authority to assume the debts of the states, and every power not granted was withheld. "As the guardians then of the rights and interests of their constituents, as *sentinels* placed by them over the ministers of the federal government, to shield it from their encroachments, or at least to sound the alarm when it is threatened with invasion, they can never reconcile it to their consciences, silently to acquiesce." [27]

From a phrase in the· memorial this doctrine has come to be known as the doctrine of "sentinelship." Based on the tenth amendment with its assertion of reserved rights and delegated powers, it marked the first step in the development of the theory that the state—not the federal courts—is the judge of the constitutionality of acts of Congress where the interests of the state are touched. In its ultimate development the theory led to nullification and secession. By the time this memorial was prepared Hamilton had perceived the tendency of his own former view and now repudiated it. Writing to John Jay he called the Virginia protest

[27] Ames, *State Docs.*, 4–7. Italics supplied.

"the first symptom of a spirit which must either be killed or will kill the Constitution of the United States." [28]

IMPLIED POWERS

In the case of the assumption act the protest of Virginia was of no slight significance, although Congress did not alter its course. Another of Hamilton's financial measures caused quite as violent a controversy in Congress, and was of quite as permanent significance because it led to the formulation of the theory of implied powers. Congress was necessarily, in the first instance, the judge of its own powers, subject to the presidential veto, an adverse court decision (if Hamilton's theory was acted upon), or to the protest, even if ineffectual, of the states.

On December 14, 1790, Hamilton laid before the House of Representatives a report which proposed that it should charter a Bank of the United States. The institution was to be owned privately (although the government might hold stock) but managed according to conditions laid down in the charter. Hamilton's alleged purpose in making this recommendation was, in the first place, to provide a sound circulating medium. The paper money of the Confederation period was disappearing and the Constitution forbade further issues by the states. Owing to the scarcity of specie, however, the state governments were under strong temptation to charter banks of issue without requiring that their paper be safely backed by reserves of gold and silver, and the multiplication of unregulated banks was likely to flood the country with depreciated notes unless steps were taken to prevent it. The establishment of a great central bank with branches throughout the nation, pledged to redeem its notes on demand, would supply the channels of trade with a sound currency. The secretary of the treasury urged also that such a bank would "be of the greatest utility in the operations connected with the support of the public credit," especially by aiding the government in obtaining loans, while through its branches it would facilitate the collection of taxes and the transfer of funds from one part of the country to another.[29]

[28] H. P. Johnston, ed., *Correspondence and Public Papers of John Jay*, III, 405.
[29] *Am. St. Papers, Finance*, I, 67–76. Extract in MacDonald, *Sel. Docs.*, 67–76.

Hamilton's bill passed the Senate without a division, although the criticism was voiced that it created a monopoly. In the House a violent opposition developed, both on economic and constitutional grounds. The friends of state banks disliked the idea of a central institution with a monopoly of special privileges; its utility and convenience were questioned, and it was feared that the state banks would be destroyed. Besides, such an institution would give the moneyed class another opportunity for investment and tend to create what today would be called a money trust.

The constitutional argument against the bill was presented most cogently by Madison. He was unable to find in the Constitution any grant to Congress warranting the incorporation of a bank. It was not included, he said, in the power to tax, for that power could be used only to carry out the enumerated powers. To say that the power to borrow included that of creating conditions favorable to borrowing would involve a dangerous latitude of construction. If such reasoning were permissible the power to declare war would include that of raising armies; yet the latter was separately enumerated, which indicated that the grant of some powers was not intended to carry others by implication. The necessary and proper clause, he admitted, authorized Congress to choose the means of carrying the specified powers into execution, but its choice of means was limited to those which were indispensable if the enumerated powers were to be made effective.

The taxation clause to which Madison referred is the first paragraph of section 8, Article I, of the Constitution, which reads "The Congress shall have Power to lay and collect Taxes, Duties, Imposts and Excises, to pay the Debts and provide for the common Defence and general Welfare of the United States." Madison's rendering made it mean that Congress has power by taxation to raise the money needed (1) to pay the debts and (2) perform the other functions covered by the list of enumerated powers, the phrase "general welfare" being only a brief way of indicating these.[30] This was the narrowest possible interpretation of the clause. If it were held to mean that Congress has power: (1) to lay and collect taxes; (2) to pay the debts; (3) to provide for the general welfare, the enumera-

[30] *Ann. of Cong.*, 1 Cong., 2 sess., 1894 *et seq.*

tion of powers would be needless, since the last of the three co-ordinate phrases would be an all-inclusive formula. Needless to say, this interpretation has never won serious advocates. Within a few decades a third interpretation gained general acceptance; it fell between these two extremes and made the taxation clause mean that Congress may collect and spend money for the purpose of paying the public debt and for any other purpose which would promote the general welfare, even if not specifically included in the enumeration of the powers of the general government.

However, the discussion of Hamilton's bank turned less on this provision than on the necessary and proper clause. When the bill passed Congress and came to President Washington for approval he asked for the opinions of the members of the cabinet. Jefferson, the secretary of state, followed Madison's reasoning closely. He found no mention of the power to incorporate a bank among those enumerated. The general welfare clause limited the raising and spending of money to the purposes defined by the grant of powers to the government, adding nothing to the grant. As to the power of Congress "to make all laws which shall be necessary and proper for carrying into execution" the powers of the general government, he urged that since "they can all be carried into execution without a bank[,] a bank . . . is not necessary, and consequently is not authorized. . . . The Constitution allows only means which are 'necessary,' not those which are merely convenient for effecting the enumerated powers." The Constitution restrains Congress "to those means without which the grant of power would be nugatory." [31]

As the bank measure had originated in the treasury department, Washington submitted Jefferson's opinion to Hamilton for rebuttal. The gist of his answer lies in his interpretation of the necessary and proper clause. Jefferson does not deny, he says, that some powers are delegated by implication. The reason why there are such powers is that they serve as means "of carrying into execution . . . the specified powers. . . ." He could not accept the doctrine that the Constitution confines Congress to those means without which the grant would be nugatory. On the contrary, "the only question must be . . . whether the mean . . . has a natural relation to

[31] Ford, *Writings of Jefferson*, V, 285–287. Extract in MacDonald, 76–81.

any of the acknowledged objects or lawful ends of the government. . . . If the *end* be clearly comprehended within any of the specified powers, and if the measure have an obvious relation to that *end*, and is not forbidden by any particular provision of the Constitution, it may safely be deemed to come within the compass of the national authority." "The powers contained in an instrument of government . . . ought to be construed liberally in advancement of the public good. . . . It will not be contended . . . that the clause in question gives any new or independent power. But it gives an explicit sanction to the doctrine of implied powers." [32] Hamilton recognized also a class of non-enumerated powers which he called "resultant" powers. While implied powers were the *means* of carrying enumerated powers into execution, resultant powers were the *consequence* of powers enumerated or implied. An illustration of the latter (not used by Hamilton) would be the power to govern the people of an acquired territory. If the acquisition of territory is warranted by the Constitution, the power to govern its inhabitants is a necessary result.

Although Hamilton's influence was fundamental in other ways also, the doctrine of implied and resultant powers is perhaps his chief contribution to our constitutional system. His principles of construction supplied an element of elasticity which made it possible to adapt the fundamental law to the changing needs of a rapidly growing nation, without many formal changes of wording. A rigid framework, incapable of such adaptation, must soon have been destroyed by the vital forces of the growing organism. The doctrine of implied powers has been by many regarded, not as the means of destroying the Constitution, as Jefferson feared, but of preserving it. In theory the process of construction has not changed it, but only brought out what was inherent.

But the theory that construction has not changed the Constitution is a legal fiction, and the historian is interested in fact. In view of the lack of agreement as to what the original intent of the Constitution was, the Hamiltonian principles of interpretation assisted in making it in practice what he and his associates wished it to

[32] Hamilton, ed., *Works of Alexander Hamilton*, IV, 104–138. Extract in Mac-Donald, 81–98.

be. Jefferson regarded it as akin to the charter of a corporation, to be, like such a charter, construed strictly, and changed only by the authority which granted it in the first place. Resort to the amending process, which he advocated, although almost impossibly cumbrous in operation, would have tended to prevent changes not endorsed by the sentiment of the people at large; while Hamiltonian construction made it comparatively easy for selfish minority groups to gain a dominant influence. It must be remembered, however, that Jefferson himself, when he came to the head of the government, was unable to adhere consistently to his theory of strict construction.

THE VINDICATION OF COERCIVE POWER

The passage of the act for the assumption of the state debts called for increased revenue. It would have been easy to obtain the funds by changing the general tariff rates, but Hamilton preferred to recommend an excise on distilled liquors and an increase of the duty on imported spirits. Like his other financial measures, the excise was inspired partly by political considerations. It seemed to him wise to establish the precedent of federal authority in the field of internal taxation under a popular President, lest non-action should be construed as indicating that the right should not or would not be exercised. He apparently had in mind also the importance of making the power of the new government felt by the individualistic farmers of the western frontier. Along the border from Pennsylvania southward the making of whiskey had become an important industry. Separated from the coast markets by the mountains, the transportation of grain was out of the question, and the farmers would have been without a market if they could not have converted their crop into the portable and comparatively valuable form of distilled spirits. The same conditions which kept their grain out of the coast towns kept eastern goods from reaching them, so that they were hardly touched by the tax on imports. Naturally they resented the excise, which seemed to single them out as subjects for special taxation, and reminded them of the internal taxes with which England had goaded the colonists to revolution. Even in passing the act Congress was not without apprehensions of the results. Many persons felt, with Jefferson, that the law was "an infernal one."

The resentment of the people of southwestern Pennsylvania soon took the form of active resistance. Meetings were held in which defiance was urged, and revenue officers began to be threatened with personal violence. At length, in 1794, when warrants were issued for the arrest of some of the agitators who were destroying the property of persons who had complied with the law, actual bloodshed occurred, and the malcontents began to gather under arms.

These events afforded Hamilton and his friends an opportunity to demonstrate the fact that at the head of the country was no longer the imbecile Confederation Congress, which faltered in the face of Shays's Rebellion, but a government which could deal with insurgency.

Up to the time when the opposition threatened to reach the stage of insurrection Congress had enacted no legislation to meet such an emergency. But since the Constitution empowered it "to provide for calling forth the Militia to execute the Laws of the Union, suppress Insurrections and repel Invasions," [33] both houses took up, in April, 1792, a bill to give this clause effect.

The Constitution contemplated the use of force in three distinct contingencies: (1) in case of an insurrection against the federal authority; (2) in case a state, threatened by internal disorder, called for aid; and (3) in case of invasion by a foreign foe. Congress proposed to provide for all three contingencies in the same act, and so far as the second and third were concerned the bill aroused no opposition. The words "Congress may provide" indicated that it was not the intent of the Constitution to confine the power of calling out the forces to Congress itself, which might not be in session when an emergency developed, but to authorize it at its discretion to delegate the power to some other branch of the government. There was some wrangling as to where it should be vested, but the rather obvious solution was reached that the executive was the fittest official for the function. The act as passed authorized the President, in case of invasion or imminent danger

[33] Art. I, sec. 8, par. 15.

of invasion, to call forth such numbers of militia of the state or states near the seat of danger as he might deem necessary. In case of an insurrection against the government of a state, he was empowered to take similar action upon request of its legislature, or of the governor in case the legislature could not be convened.

These decisions were to give rise to much controversy between states and nation in future, but in 1792 the chief criticism of the bill was directed against the proposal to use force to "execute the Laws of the Union." The enforcement of the obnoxious excise law was, of course, in contemplation. Said one member: "Mild and equitable laws will not be resisted and I hope that objectionable laws will be repealed and not enforced by martial law." A number of members desired to strike out the part of the bill concerning the suppression of insurrections. "It was for the purpose," it was contended, "of calling out the military . . . in case an old woman was to stick an excise officer with a broomstick."[34] In the end the President was given the same power to call out the militia as in the other two contingencies, but with the proviso that, before having recourse to actual force, he must have received from one of the associate justices or a district judge of the United States information of an insurrection too formidable to be met by ordinary judicial processes, and must then have issued a proclamation to the insurgents warning them to disperse peaceably. The use of the militia might be continued, if necessary, until the end of thirty days after the beginning of the next session of Congress.[35]

The intent of this section of the law was to enable the militia to assist the judiciary. The forces were to be employed only when "the laws of the United States shall be opposed, or the execution thereof obstructed, in any state, by combinations too powerful to be suppressed by the ordinary course of judicial proceedings, or by the powers vested in the marshals." Thus the act preserved the English tradition of strict subordination of the military to the civil arm of government—a tradition in marked contrast with that of continental Europe.

While Congress was by this legislation placing the administration

[34] *Ann. of Cong.*, 2 Cong.
[35] *Stat. at Large*, I, 264.

in position to enforce the excise, it was making concessions to the malcontents by lightening the tax. They, however, responded by increased violence, and Hamilton, in the summer of 1794, urged the President to proceed energetically to suppress the disorders. Although the attorney-general did not think that the use of force was necessary, Washington issued a proclamation on August 7 reciting the acts of the rioters and the conciliatory measures of Congress, as well as the statute authorizing him to call forth the militia, and the fact that James Wilson, an associate justice of the Supreme Court, had notified him of combinations too powerful to be suppressed by the ordinary processes of the court, calling upon the insurgents to disperse on or before the first day of September, and summoning militia from Virginia, Maryland, Pennsylvania, and New Jersey to be ready to march at that time if the warning were not heeded.[36]

So great was the sentiment against repressive measures that the governor of Pennsylvania had to speak publicly in order to secure the quota of men called for from his state. Hamilton himself feared that the troops might refuse to march against the insurgents. But commissioners were sent ahead of the troops to persuade the malcontents to disband, and when the forces arrived no armed opponents were to be found. Some of the leaders were arrested and two were convicted of treason, but having vindicated the national authority Washington showed clemency and pardoned them. Although the whole incident revealed little understanding of the grievances of the western inhabitants, the demonstration of the government's ability to meet rebellion with overwhelming force was complete and produced a new respect for the federal power.

The act of 1792 was limited in duration; but in 1795 a new act was passed, in almost identical terms, and without limitation.[37] It was on the statute books in 1861 and was the basis of the first measures of President Lincoln in dealing with the southerners who through acts of secession disavowed their obligation to obey federal laws.

[36] Richardson, *Messages*, I, 158–160. Extract in Johnson, 188–191.
[37] *Stat. at Large*, I, 424.

XIV

THE NATURE OF THE CONSTITUTION
AND THE UNION (*Continued*)

THE FEDERAL JUDICIARY IN OPERATION

THE function of the federal judiciary as a checking and balancing factor in the constitutional system has two aspects. First, there is the question of its relation to the national legislature, and the problem of its right to judge of the constitutionality of acts of Congress; and second, there is the question of its right to maintain (according to its own judgment) the distribution of powers as between states and the federal Union by passing on the compatibility of state statutes and court decisions with the supreme law of the land.

It cannot be said that Hamilton originated the theory that it is the right of the federal courts to judge of the constitutionality of acts of Congress. The genesis of the concept has already been studied. As applied to the government under the Constitution the idea was a carry-over from the Confederation period during which we have seen it emerge in some of the states as a phase of the system of checks and balances under a written constitution. The fact that the federal Constitution, like those of the states, contained no specific provision for the exercise of this function may mean that the delegates had not attained a consensus of opinion on the point; or it may mean that the majority of them assumed that the duty was inherent in the courts under a written constitution. It is probably impossible to prove which if either of these views is correct. It is certain, however, that many persons held opinions similar to those set out in Hamilton's comment in the *Federalist*. While his essay became better known than these other expressions, it was not the earliest utterance of the kind.

In the Virginia ratifying convention John Marshall, consistently with his later principles when chief justice, said that if Congress "were to make a law not warranted by any of the powers enumerated, it would be considered by the judges as an infringement of

the Constitution which they are to guard. . . . They would declare it void." [1]   In the same convention Patrick Henry, although
an Antifederalist, said that it was "the highest encomium on this
country, that the acts of the legislature, if unconstitutional, are
liable to be opposed by the judiciary." [2]   Ellsworth, in Connecticut,
spoke to similar effect,[3] and others could be mentioned as doing
likewise.

Since a new union was in process of formation, contemporaries
seem to have thought even more of the second phase of the problem
of the judiciary. W. R. Davie, for example, in the North Carolina
convention, said: "The Constitution might be violated with impunity by particular states—if there were no power in the general
government to *correct and counteract* such laws. This great objective can *only* be safely and completely obtained by the instrumentality of the federal judiciary." [4]   Charles Pinckney, in the
South Carolina legislature before the calling of the ratifying convention, said that it would be the task of the judiciary "to keep
state judicials within their . . . limits whenever they shall attempt
to interfere with" federal power.[5]

Opinions such as those of Davie and Pinckney formed the basis
for the inclusion in the Judiciary Act of 1789 of the twenty-fifth
section concerning appeals. Reflection makes plain to the modern
student, also, that courts in general, state as well as federal, could
not operate at all without finding it necessary to decide frequently
whether acts of legislation were consistent with the higher law of
the state or federal constitutions. To claim for the Supreme Court
of the United States the right to judge of the constitutionality of
both state and congressional enactments was only to concede to it
the same power as other courts enjoyed. There was this difference: *the Supreme Court was in practice made the final authority*.

So far as congressional legislation is concerned, the power
claimed for the courts was not exercised for fifteen years after
the adoption of the Constitution. The trend of judicial thought

[1] Elliot, *Debates*, III, 553.
[2] *Ibid.*, III, 325.
[3] *Ibid.*, II, 196.
[4] *Ibid.*, IV, 155.
[5] *Ibid.*, IV, 257.

was none the less made gradually evident. In 1792 Congress passed an act which directed the circuit courts to examine applications for pensions. Chief Justice Jay, Associate Justice Cushing, and District Judge Duane in circuit court for the New York district, formally recorded their opinion that neither the legislative nor the executive branch of the government could constitutionally assign to the judiciary any duties but such as were properly judicial. However, on the theory that the law created them commissioners for the purpose, they proceeded to act.

Associate Justices Wilson and Blair, and District Judge Peters, of the circuit court for the Pennsylvania district, refused to act under the law of 1792, upon the application for a pension by one William Hayburn. Contemporary statements show that this refusal was viewed as a decision that the law of Congress was unconstitutional. This so-called first Hayburn case was not, however, properly speaking, a judicial case, for the opinion of the judges was not rendered in a suit.[6]

The attitude of the judges seems to have pleased the Republicans. Freneau's *National Gazette* quotes "a correspondent" as saying that the Pennsylvania decision "affords just hope that not only future encroachments [by legislature or executive] will be prevented [by the judiciary], but also that any existing law of Congress which may be supposed to trench upon . . . constitutional rights . . . will . . . undergo a revision; particularly that establishing a National Bank." [7]   The general attitude of the Federalists was the reverse, for they seem to have feared that the courts would fail to give Congress much-needed support, and instead, by declaring acts invalid, would strengthen the states and proportionately weaken the national government. Of this fear Fisher Ames wrote: "At best, our business is uphill and with the aid of our law Courts, the authority of Congress is barely adequate to keep the machine moving; but when they condemn the law as invalid, they embolden the States and their Courts to make many claims of power which, otherwise, they would not have thought of." [8]

[6] See Max Farrand, "The First Hayburn Case."
[7] Warren, *Supreme Court*, I, 70–74.
[8] *Works*, I, quoted *ibid.*, 76.

Attorney-General Randolph, alarmed by the refusal of the judges to proceed on Hayburn's application under the pension act, filed a motion before the Supreme Court for a mandamus to compel them to do so. The court divided equally on the question of the propriety of this procedure, and before any further action could be taken Congress modified the statute. This episode is known as the Second Hayburn Case. Meanwhile all of the judges except Wilson decided to construe the statute as authorizing them to act, not as judges, but as unofficial commissioners. The episode closed with no nearer approach to a judicial decision against a congressional statute.[9]

Although not applied specifically to the powers of the judiciary in relation to acts of Congress, Justice Paterson in 1795 stated in vigorous terms the general doctrine of the function of the courts in voiding unconstitutional acts. The case before him in the United States circuit court for Pennsylvania involved a statute of that state.[10] Said he:

"I take it to be a clear position that if a legislative act oppugns a constitutional principle the former must give way and be rejected on the score of repugnance. I hold it to be a position equally clear and sound that in such a case it will be the duty of the court to adhere to the constitution, and to declare the act null and void."

The case of Hylton v. United States [11] involved the question whether a carriage tax laid by Congress was a direct tax or not. If the Supreme Court had held that it was a direct tax, it could hardly have avoided ruling that it was contrary to the constitutional requirement that direct taxes must be apportioned among the states according to population, since Virginia had more carriages in proportion to her population than any of the other states. The court decided that the tax was in the nature of an excise and thus avoided the issue of constitutionality. Said Samuel Chase, in rendering the decision, "It is unnecessary for me at this time to determine whether this Court constitutionally possesses the power to declare an act of

[9] Warren, *Sup. Court*, I, 77–80.
[10] Van Horne's Lessee v. Dorrance, 2 Dallas 304. William Paterson, the champion of the New Jersey plan in the Constitutional Convention, was appointed associate justice on March 4, 1793.
[11] 3 Dallas 171 (1796).

Congress void." [12]   The same justice shortly afterwards summed up
the opinion of the legal profession by declaring that "it is indeed
a general opinion, it is expressly admitted by all this bar, and some
of the judges have individually in the circuits decided, that the
Supreme Court can declare an act of Congress unconstitutional and
therefore invalid, but there is no adjudication of the Supreme Court
itself upon the point. Altho' it is alleged that all acts of the legislature [Congress?] in direct opposition to the prohibitions of the
Constitution would be void, yet it still remains a question where
the power resides to declare it void." [13]

Chase's utterance was a comment "by the way," not required for
the decision of the case before the court. The eighteenth century
ended, therefore, with no official pronouncement of the court upon
the scope of its powers in relation to unconstitutional legislation:
this notable occurrence did not take place until the tribunal under
John Marshall as chief justice decided the case of Marbury *v.*
Madison, in 1803.

Turning to the second aspect of the court's functions we find a
different story. Within two years after the establishment of constitutional government the federal courts began to hold state
statutes invalid. The first instance occurred in May, 1791, the
United States circuit court holding that an act of the Connecticut
legislature was an infringement of the terms of the treaty of peace
with England. A year later (June, 1792) Chief Justice Jay, Associate Justice Cushing, and District Judge Henry Marchand, holding the session of the circuit court for Rhode Island, held void an
act of that state as violating the constitutional provision against impairing the obligation of contracts. So far as appears, these decisions aroused no protest on the part of the states or the friends of
state's rights. [14]   Other cases followed in rapid succession. That of
Van Horne's Lessee *v.* Dorrance has already been mentioned, since
it led to the statement by Associate Justice Paterson of the prin-

[12] In this case the court held that only capitation and land taxes could be classified as direct taxes. A century later it changed its ruling in Pollock *v.* Farmers'
Loan & Trust Co., 157 U. S. 429 (1895). Chase had received his appointment to
the bench in January, 1796.
[13] Cooper *v.* Telfair, 4 Dallas 14 (1800).
[14] Warren, *Sup. Court,* I, 65–68.

ciple of judicial determination of the constitutionality of legislation. In 1796, in Ware *v.* Hylton,[15] the court again set aside an act of a state on the ground that it conflicted with the provisions of the treaty of peace, the state involved being Virginia. For many years this case was thought to be the first instance of voidance of a state statute on the ground of repugnance to federal law, but recent scholarship has revealed the earlier cases noted above.[16]

Notwithstanding the fears of the Federalists which the justices on circuit in Pennsylvania aroused by the refusal to examine pension claims, the federal courts quite consistently supported the authority of the central government during these formative years. In one of the most notable cases of the period the Supreme Court upheld the validity of the admiralty jurisdiction of Congress during the Revolution.

It will be recalled that the British courts of vice-admiralty were replaced, soon after the Revolution began, by courts created by the states. This action was taken upon the recommendation of the Second Continental Congress in 1775, that the states provide for the trial of prize cases, with an appeal to Congress or a tribunal to be erected by it. All of the states acted upon this recommendation, although some of them, notably Pennsylvania and New Hampshire, permitted appeals only on questions of law. Congress at first made use of committees to hear these appeals, but in 1780 set up the Court of Appeals in Cases of Capture. Meantime the Articles of Confederation had been drafted but not yet adopted; they provided that Congress should have the sole and exclusive power to establish courts for determining finally appeals in all cases of capture.

Soon after the appointment of the committee of Congress, a privateer owned by citizens of New Hampshire but commissioned by Congress captured a British brigantine. The New Hampshire court condemned this vessel as lawful prize and refused to allow an appeal. The congressional committee nevertheless received and granted a petition for a hearing of the case, and in 1783 the Court

[15] 3 Dallas 199.
[16] Much of the credit for bringing these early cases to the attention of students is due to Charles Warren, in his work on the *Supreme Court.*

of Appeals reversed the decision of the New Hampshire court. Here the matter rested until after the adoption of the Constitution and the establishment of the new federal judiciary, which inherited the jurisdiction of the old Court of Appeals. To the federal circuit court of New Hampshire came, therefore, in 1793, an application for the enforcement of the decree of the old court. Carried finally to the Supreme Court, under the title of Penhallow *et al., v.* Doane's Administrators, the case was decided in 1795 and the appellate jurisdiction of the United States courts was upheld.[17]

Although the action of federal courts up to this time in voiding state legislation had evoked no serious opposition, the overruling of the decision of the New Hampshire court provoked more than one remonstrance from the legislature of that state, on the ground that previous to the adoption of the Articles of Confederation in 1781 Congress was "entirely dependent on the good-will or the resolves of the several States"; hence the law of New Hampshire relating to prizes, "prior to an express grant to Congress," was "final in every way concerning the capture of vessels by this State, or citizens thereof, from the British, the enemy we were then engaged with in war." "The confederation was the first act binding upon the States which was not expressly agreed to by them individually." Hence they "resolve not to submit the laws, made before the existence of the present government by this (then independent state) to the adjudication of any power on earth, while the freedom of the Federal Government shall afford any constitutional means of redress."[18]

While the government was still in its infancy the court found itself compelled to enter into an analysis of the nature of the Union, and thus became a pioneer in attempting to clear up the other fundamental uncertainty imposed upon the nation by the framers of the Constitution. This attempt on the part of the judiciary to expound the character of the constitutional compact arose from the suit of Chisholm *v.* Georgia.[19] In 1792 a man named Chisholm, executor of a citizen of South Carolina, brought suit in the United

[17] 3 Dallas 54.
[18] Ames, *State Docs.*, 11-15.
[19] 2 Dallas 419.

States Supreme Court to enforce a claim against the State of Georgia.[20] He relied upon the provision of the Constitution which includes in the jurisdiction of the United States cases "between a State and Citizens of another State."[21] The Antifederalists had challenged this clause in the state ratifying conventions but had been assured by Federalists that it would never be construed so as to permit the citizen of one state to sue another state. Statesmen of the first rank took this stand. John Marshall, the later chief justice, said in the Virginia convention that it was "not rational to suppose that the sovereign power should be dragged before a court. The intent is, to enable states to recover claims of [against] individuals residing in other states. . . . If an individual has a just claim against any particular State, is it to be presumed that, on application to its Legislative, he will not obtain satisfaction?"[22] A similar view was set forth by Hamilton in the *Federalist*. "It is inherent in the nature of sovereignty," wrote the latter, "not to be amenable to the suit of an individual without its own consent."[23] Madison explained that the clause would merely enable a state to sue citizens of other states.[24] Chisholm's action against Georgia came as a rude shock to persons who had relied on such representations.

The case came up at the August term, Edmund Randolph, the attorney-general, representing the plaintiff. As no one appeared on behalf of the state, Randolph moved that judgment be entered for the plaintiff unless the defendant was represented by counsel at the February term, 1793, or showed due cause for failure. In December a resolution was introduced into the Georgia House of Representatives declaring that this suit "if acquiesced in by this State would not only involve the same in numberless law-suits for papers issued from the Treasury thereof to supply the armies of the United States, and perplex the citizens of Georgia with perpetual taxes . . . but would effectually destroy the retained sover-

[20] Warren, *Sup. Court*, I, 91–104.
[21] Art. III, sec. 2.
[22] Elliot, *Debates*, III, 555.
[23] Number 81. Most of the states have made provision for suits against themselves, although some of them did not do so until recently. See Thorpe, *Con. Hist.*, II, 270, note.
[24] Elliot, *Debates*, III, 533.

eignty of the States, and would actually tend in its operation to annihilate the very shadow of State government, and to render them but tributary corporations to the government of the United States." The State of Georgia would therefore not be bound by the decision of the Supreme Court but would regard it as "unconstitutional and extrajudicial." The resolution further suggested an amendment explaining the true meaning of the Constitution.[25] Apparently this resolution was not adopted, but at the February term a written remonstrance was presented by the state, refusing to accept the rôle of defendant on the ground that as a sovereign it could not be sued without its consent. The court thereupon considered Randolph's motion, heard his argument, and decided that unless Georgia appeared on the first day of the next term judgment by default should be entered against her. This was tantamount to holding that the clause of the Constitution in question gave the court jurisdiction in cases where a state was party defendant at the suit of an individual citizen of another state. The decision was unheeded by Georgia, hence judgment was finally rendered in favor of Chisholm. Before any steps could be taken to enforce it the movement for the eleventh amendment took the matter out of the court's control.

It was the consideration of the argument that the sovereignty of a state gives it immunity from suit that called out the judges' comments on the nature of the Union. Said Chief Justice John Jay: "Every State Constitution is a compact made by and between the citizens of a State to govern themselves in a certain manner; and the Constitution of the *United States* is likewise a compact made by the people of the *United States* to govern themselves as to general objects, in a certain manner. . . . The sovereignty of the nation is [in] the people of the nation, and the residuary sovereignty of each state [is] in the people of each State. . . ." The people of the United States, "acting as sovereigns of the whole country," established a "Constitution by which it was their will, that the State Governments should be bound, and to which the

---

[25] Ames, *State Docs.*, 7–11. A year later the lower house passed an Act Declaratory of the Retained Sovereignty of the State in which the death penalty was decreed against any person attempting any levy against the state by authority of the United States. This proposal failed in the Senate.—*Ibid.*, 9–11.

State Constitutions should be made to conform." Although Jay here evidently thinks of sovereignty as divided between the people of the states and the people of the United States, there is no admission of the idea, developed five years later by Jefferson in the Kentucky Resolutions, that the Constitution is a compact made by the *states* in their *corporate* capacity, that is, as bodies politic. His idea is much nearer to the theory that sovereignty resides in the people of the United States, from whom both state and federal governments derive their powers.

As for such sovereignty as the state possessed being incompatible with suability, Jay reasoned that since the Constitution permitted *all* the people of a state to sue another state, "it plainly follows that suability and State sovereignty are not incompatible." If the Constitution really meant to limit the jurisdiction of the United States, in "controversies between a State and citizens of another State," to those in which the state was plaintiff, he thought it "inconceivable that it should have attempted to convey that meaning in words . . . so incompetent."

Justice James Wilson's concurring opinion was similar in tenor; he held that the Constitution itself "shows that the people of the United States intended to form themselves into a nation," so far as national purposes are concerned. The citizens of Georgia formed a part of the "people of the United States," and as such did not surrender to the state the sovereign power in affairs relating to the purposes of the Union. As to these "Georgia is not a sovereign state."

From the decision of the majority Justice Iredell dissented on the ground that the American states were the heirs of British sovereignty, and that under the common law the sovereign cannot be sued.[26]

While the case was pending the governor of Georgia recommended that the legislature request the other states to join in obtaining an amendment prohibiting such suits.[27] Meantime actions had been brought against Massachusetts, New York, Maryland,

---

[26] Iredell's interpretation of British law and precedents is refuted by William D. Guthrie, "The Eleventh Article of Amendment."
[27] Ames, *State Docs.*, 8–9.

Virginia, and South Carolina, so that Georgia's proposal struck a responsive chord. The stand taken by the court appears to have caused general surprise and dismay; several states by resolution denounced the doctrine of suability, and Massachusetts took measures through her senators and representatives to initiate an amendment declaring the true intent of the clause. The appropriate resolution was introduced in the Senate on February 20, 1793.[28] About a year later, having passed both houses, the amendment was submitted to the states and on January 8, 1798, President Adams announced that it had become a part of the Constitution.[29] As adopted it reads: "The judicial power of the United States shall not be construed to extend to any suit in law or equity, commenced or prosecuted against one of the United States by citizens of another State, or by citizens or subjects of any foreign State."

Conflicting views as to the suability of a state by an individual had been expressed in the Constitutional Convention. Some persons had expected the provision to be changed during the consideration of the first group of amendments.[30] Failing this, the eleventh amendment, conforming to prevalent sentiment, was regarded as an interpretation by the amending power of the true meaning of the Constitution which had been misconstrued by the court. The action was in effect a rebuke to the court, which suffered loss of prestige in consequence. In the course of the years which followed, the amendment itself was subjected to the interpretation of the judiciary and as a result its scope was gradually restricted within narrow limits. The non-concurrence of the public with the court's decision concerning the suability of a state had no bearing upon its exposition of the nature of the Union. That nationalistic exposition was challenged in a different way.

FORMULATION OF THE COMPACT THEORY

If Jefferson shared the hope of Republicans, in 1792, that the federal courts would maintain the rights of the states by voiding acts of Congress, he had abandoned that hope by 1798. The steady

[28] *Ann. of Cong.*, 2 Cong., 2 sess., 651–652, 656; 3 Cong., 1 sess., 25, 30, 225.
[29] *Ibid.*, 5 Cong., 1 sess., 483.
[30] Guthrie, "Eleventh Amendment."

support of federal authority by the judicial branch had by that time taught him to look elsewhere for the defense of state's rights, and he turned to the doctrine, contained in germ in· the theory of sentinelship, that the state itself was the judge of what powers it had relinquished to the federal government and what powers it had retained. The immediate occasion for formulating the doctrine was given by the measures of the Federalists, in 1798, when the country was threatened with a war with France. By a new naturalization law they extended the period of residence required before foreigners could become citizens from five to fourteen years. By a second law called the Alien Act, the President was authorized to order the departure of any foreigner whom he deemed dangerous to the peace and safety of the country. If he did not obey, he was upon conviction liable to imprisonment. This act was to run for two years only, but a third one, the Alien Enemies Act, was to be in effect during war if it occurred. It gave the chief executive extraordinary powers to deport resident subjects of any country with which the United States engaged in war, and to prescribe the restraints to which they should be subjected if allowed to remain in America. The final number of this series of measures, the Sedition Act, not only provided for the punishment of persons who conspired together to impede the operation of federal laws, but forbade any person to write, print, or utter any "false, scandalous, and malicious" statement "against the government of the United States, or either house of the Congress of the United States, or the President of the United States, with intent to defame . . . or to bring them . . . into contempt or disrepute." [31]

To the first of these laws the Republicans objected on grounds of policy. To the other three they objected on the ground that Congress did not possess the power to pass them, and in so doing had violated the Constitution. The Sedition Act they held to be a violation of the first amendment, by which Congress is forbidden to abridge the freedom of speech or of the press; the Alien Act they thought was incompatible with the provision which forbade Congress, prior to 1808, to refuse admission to any persons

---

[31] Text of these acts will be found in *Stat. at Large*, I, 566–569, 570–572, 577–578, 596–597. Reprints are in MacDonald, *Sel. Docs.*, 137–148.

whom any of the existing states wished to admit; the Alien Enemies Act deprived persons of liberty without due process of law.

From cases which came before the courts it was evident that, as usual, the judges would enforce the enactments of Congress.[32] The discontent of the Republicans was so great that some of them were even ready to abandon the Union. John Taylor of Virginia suggested to Jefferson that the time had come to calculate the relative advantages of a southern confederacy, but the latter rejected the idea of secession, confident that the Federalists had committed a blunder which would result in the overthrow of the rule of the "witches" at the approaching presidential election.[33]

From this point of view, the Republican problem was how to make an effective appeal to the voters. Party platforms and the other devices now so familiar in election campaigns were as yet undreamed of. Hence as a means of publicity it was decided to draft resolutions denouncing the obnoxious laws, and to obtain their passage by the legislatures of some of the states. Such resolutions would be certain to attract wide attention. Under Jefferson's inspiration Madison drew up one set of resolutions for this purpose, which the Virginia assembly passed. Concealing his authorship from the public, since he was at that time Vice-President, Jefferson himself drafted another set, which was introduced in the Kentucky legislature by his friend John Breckinridge, and passed by a large vote after slight changes had been made in the wording.[34] But the resolutions were more than a denunciation of the

[32] For these cases see Frank M. Anderson, "Enforcement of the Alien and Sedition Acts." See also Claude G. Bowers, *Jefferson and Hamilton*, Chap. XVII. Bowers's account is graphic but somewhat biassed.

[33] It was at this time that he wrote the letter cited *supra*, Chap. XIII. Ford in an editorial note indicates that perhaps Taylor's letter, correctly understood, did not suggest secession.

[34] For Jefferson's draft see H. A. Washington, ed., *The Writings of Thomas Jefferson*, IX, 464–471. Reprints of the resolutions as passed are in *Am. Hist. Leaflet* No. 15, pp. 17–21, Johnson, *Readings*, 228–235, and MacDonald, *Sel. Docs.*, 149–155.

It was at first proposed that Jefferson's resolutions should be presented in the legislature of North Carolina, but the elections in that state did not prove to be favorable enough to the Republicans. Kentucky was thereupon chosen. On October 11, 1798, in a letter to Mason, Jefferson wrote that he fancies some legislatures will take strong ground on the Alien and Sedition Acts; the laws, he thinks, are an experiment to see what Americans will stand, and are only a beginning with monarchy as the goal.—Ford, *Writings of Jefferson*, VII, 283. About

Alien and Sedition Acts for campaign purposes. Their permanent significance lies in the fact that they rest upon a theory of the Union which the Republicans, and Jefferson especially, were putting forward as the rival of the nationalistic theory which the Federalists and the federal judiciary were developing.

As in the case of the Assumption Act, state legislatures in passing these resolutions were assuming that it was their duty to judge of the constitutionality of congressional legislation. In this instance more elaborate statements were offered of the grounds on which the legislatures rested their right to challenge the acts of the federal government. This right arose, according to the Kentucky Resolutions, from the nature of the Union. The several states had formed it by a compact "under the style and title of a Constitution for the United States," and had set up a general government to which they had delegated certain definite powers, each state reserving the residuary mass of right to its own self-government. If at any time the general government assumed undelegated powers, therefore, its acts were void. "To this compact each State acceded as a State and is an integral party, its co-States forming, as to itself, the other party:" . . . "the government created by this compact was not made the exclusive or final judge of the extent of the powers delegated to itself; since that would have made its discretion, and not the Constitution, the measure of its powers; but . . . as in all other cases of compact among parties having no common Judge, each party has an equal right to judge for itself, as well of infractions as of the mode and measure of redress."

In the original draft the eighth resolution read: "Where powers are assumed which have not been delegated, a nullification of the act is the right remedy," and the document concluded with an expression of the hope that "the co-States . . . will concur in declaring these acts void and of no force, and will each take measures

1820 the son of Breckinridge, the reputed author, asked Jefferson to disclaim the authorship, which John Taylor had imputed to him. Jefferson then admitted his part. On the whole topic see E. D. Warfield, *The Kentucky Resolutions*, and F. M. Anderson, "Contemporary Opinion of the Virginia and Kentucky Resolutions."

The Virginia Resolutions are printed in Madison's *Letters and Other Writings*, IV, 506–507; reprinted in MacDonald, 155–157. See also Warfield, *op. cit.*, 179–185 and Anderson, *loc. cit.*

of its own for providing that neither of these acts . . . shall be exercised within their respective territories." As changed by Breckinridge this section was toned down to instructions to the representatives of the state in Congress to work for the repeal of the obnoxious acts in the next session; and after the words "no force" in the final resolution, the reading was changed to "and will unite with this commonwealth in requesting their repeal at the next session of Congress." Either Breckinridge himself did not approve of the original resolutions, or he feared that opinion in the legislature would not support them.

For once Jefferson was in agreement with Hamilton, at least in seeing that the Constitution had not provided a judge to decide disputes between a state and the general government. From that point they parted company. Hamilton while admitting that "there is not a syllable in the Constitution which directly empowers the national courts to construe the laws," thought that the right was deducible from "the general theory of a limited Constitution." Jefferson, on the contrary, had come to believe that to recognize this function of the federal courts would in effect make "the government created by the compact . . . the . . . judge [of] its [own] powers." Evidently he feared that the judicial branch of the federal government would always support the legislative department to the detriment of the claims of states.

In the Virginia Resolutions Madison declared that "in the case of a deliberate, palpable, and dangerous exercise of . . . powers not granted by the said compact, the States, who are parties thereto, have the right and are in duty bound to interpose for arresting the progress of the evil, and for maintaining within their respective limits the authorities, rights, and liberties appertaining to them." The conclusion was an appeal to the other states to join Virginia in declaring the acts "unconstitutional, not law, void, and without effect."

Madison's resolutions were introduced by John Taylor, and before passage the clause beginning "not law" was stricken out and a statement substituted expressing the hope that the co-states would join in proper measures of cooperation to preserve the rights and liberties of the people.

The Kentucky and Virginia Resolutions were sent to the legislatures of all of the other states, in the hope that they would draw
forth concurring resolutions.   One or both houses in every legislature north of Mason and Dixon's line replied to one or both sets,
but in every case the character of the replies was determined by
Federalist majorities.   The debates attending the passage of the
replies, however, bring out the views of the Republican minorities
in these assemblies.

Without exception the resolutions in reply expressed emphatic
disapproval of the Kentucky and Virginia Resolutions.   The Pennsylvania House asserted that a declaration by a state legislature that
an act of the federal government is void is a "revolutionary
measure."   The replies also endorsed the Alien and Sedition Acts
as constitutional and expedient, and generally asserted that the
federal judiciary is the proper authority to pass on the constitutionality of acts of Congress.

Strangely enough, the compact theory was passed by unchal-
lenged by all of the states except Vermont.   The reply of that state
summarized the Kentucky Resolutions as teaching "that the states
constituted the general government, and that each state as a party
to the compact has an equal right to judge for itself as well of the
infractions of the Constitution, as of the mode and measure of redress."   Vermont asserted that this doctrine was false, although
true under the old Confederation.   She maintained on the contrary
that "the people of the United States formed the federal constitution, and not the states, or their Legislatures.   And altho' each state
is authorized to propose amendments to the constitution, yet there
is a wide difference between assuming or inviting, a power to dictate or control the General Government." [35]

The failure of the other states to protest against the compact
theory has been interpreted to mean that it was generally accepted.
The argument from silence is not convincing, especially as the co-
states were intent upon defending the Alien and Sedition Acts and
the functions of the federal courts.   It must be remembered, too,
that the maintenance of the judicial function was itself, with some,

[35] For replies of the states see Ames, *State Docs.*, 15–26, and Anderson, "Contemporary Opinion."

equivalent to an avowal of the theory of the Union which the compact theory was intended to supplant.

While the Republican minorities in the Federalist states accepted the view that the states individually were parties to the federal compact, they disclaimed "any intent to justify an opposition, in any manner or form whatever, to the operation of any act of the union." Disliking the Alien and Sedition Acts, they approved the protest against them without accepting the remedy advocated by Jefferson and Madison. They opposed the resolutions in reply chiefly because they endorsed acts which the Republicans regarded as inexpedient and unconstitutional.

After the publication of the first set of Kentucky Resolutions, George Nicholas joined with Breckinridge in issuing a pamphlet in which they denied that Kentucky entertained any thought of seceding from the Union, or of making improper opposition to federal legislation. Merely impolitic laws, they declared would be obeyed, and unconstitutional laws would be opposed only by appealing to the *real laws*. This statement, uncertain as its meaning was, may have served to allay any local apprehension lest Kentucky go too far, and the election in Kentucky may perhaps be regarded as a ratification by her people of the first set of resolutions.

In Virginia copies of the resolutions of 1798 were widely distributed and acted upon pro and con in the various counties according to their political complexion. The Federalist minority in the legislature prepared a protest against the resolutions, of which John Marshall was alleged to be the author. It made no criticism of the remedy proposed for usurpation. The most elaborate Federalist appeal was a pamphlet signed "Plain Truth." The writer held that the resolutions pointed towards disunion, and denied the compact theory, saying that the state governments were no more parties to the compact than the general government, but that both were in some respects agents of the people. Neither government was either party or creator, the people only being competent to create. In this the Union differed from the Confederation. The Constitution was sanctioned by the people assembled in their respective states.

The Virginia Federalists in general charged that the Republicans were seeking to dissolve the Union, while the Republicans denied any such intent. In the state election the Republicans won but the Federalists made slight gains.

The leaders in Virginia and Kentucky thought that the replies of the states called for notice. In Kentucky the discarded portion of Jefferson's draft was now taken up and with some changes incorporated in 1799 in a new set of resolutions which asserted that the sovereign states have a right to judge of infractions of the Constitution, and that nullification by those sovereignties is the proper remedy. It is noteworthy that the plural, "sovereignties" is used, while Jefferson's draft seems to mean that a single "sovereignty" can "nullify." [36]

The Virginia legislature examined the replies of the co-states, and Madison, as chairman of a special committee, submitted a report in 1800 which recommended reaffirmation of the doctrines of 1798. Federalist counter-resolutions were voted down, 98 to 57. Madison explained that the word "states" in the former resolutions meant "the people composing those political societies, in their highest sovereign capacity." Thus the people of each state, and not *en masse*, ratified the Constitution and were the parties to it. The Federalists did not combat this view. The report reasserted the right of the states to "interpose" their authority in case of violations of the compact, but disavowed advocacy of any other than strictly constitutional means.[37]

The statements of 1799–1800 called forth no comment from the co-states. They appeared at about the time of Washington's death, and were overshadowed in interest by that unfortunate event. They were not even officially communicated to the other states. In New York, Alexander Addison replied to Madison, accepting his definition of "state," but arguing that it does not follow, "because the *parties* to a compact must be the judges whether it has been violated, [that] the legislatures of each state are the judges whether the constitution has been violated." Addison did not perceive that his argument tended to justify the right of judgment by the *people* of the individual states, acting in their "highest sover-

[36] MacDonald, 158–160. Johnson, 235–236.
[37] For Madison's report see his *Letters and Other Writings*, IV, 515–555.

eign capacity," a conclusion worked out by Calhoun thirty years later.

It is impossible to determine just what Jefferson and Madison meant when they used the words "nullification" and "interposition." They both, indeed, offered explanations many years later, but they may have erred in their memory of their former views. Jefferson wrote to Justice Johnson, in 1823, to the effect that the ultimate arbiter in judging of infractions of the Constitution is the people of the Union assembled in convention at the call of Congress or of the legislatures of three-fourths of the states; *i.e.*, a federal constitutional convention is the ultimate judge when two parts of the government come into conflict in interpreting the Constitution.[38]

Although about 1830 Madison explained that it had not been his intention to assert the right of an individual state to annul an act of the federal government or withdraw from the Union, it was difficult to make the words of the resolutions appear so innocent, or to explain away the fact that Jefferson had said that *each party*, which could only mean each state individually, had the right to judge for itself both of infractions of the Constitution and of the mode and measure of redress. Calhoun made the obvious meaning of the words the basis of the doctrine of nullification which he evolved in 1828.[39]

The immediate effect of the resolutions of 1798 was to extricate the Republican party from its French entanglement and enable it to pose as the champion of individual and state's rights. In the election of 1800 the Republicans made the utmost of the denunciation of the Alien and Sedition Acts, and the election may be regarded as a repudiation of them, although it is not so clear that it was an endorsement of the compact theory of the Union. The permanent significance of the resolutions is that they gave definite form for the first time to the concept of the Constitution as a

[38] Letter of June 12. Washington, *Works of Jefferson*, VII, 422. *Cf.* 298.

[39] For Madison's interpretation of the doctrines of 1798 and his comment on nullification see his letters as follows: To J. C. Cabell, Sept. 7, 1829 (Hunt, *Writings*, IX, 346–348), Edward Livingston, May 30, 1830 (Madison's *Letters and Other Writings*, IV, 80), Edward Everett, August 28, 1830 (Hunt, IX, 383 *et seq.*), Andrew Stevenson, February 4, 1833 (*Letters*, etc., IV, 269 *et seq.*).

compact made by mutual agreement of states as bodies politic. The resolutions gave new life to the belief in state sovereignty, and from this time forward it showed great vitality. Federalist New England adopted it during the troublous years culminating in the War of 1812, it was the foundation of South Carolina's attempt at nullification in 1832, and even the resort to secession in 1861 was a logical consequence of the doctrines promulgated in 1798. For the next two decades, however, these doctrines are of historical significance chiefly in demonstrating the need of an impartial umpire in disputes between the states and the general government.

XV

JEFFERSON IN POWER

THE TWELFTH AMENDMENT

JEFFERSON'S administration faced several constitutional questions at the very outset. One of these concerned the method of choosing the President. Among the developments which the framers of the Constitution failed to foresee was the rise of political parties and the rôle they were to play in the operation of constitutional government. Parties as the delegates knew them had been factional divisions of evil influence, and they heartily hoped to be rid of them in the new order. The first result of their rise was the breakdown of the original plan of choosing the chief executive.[1] The method which the Convention adopted was hailed with satisfaction at the moment, because it seemed to solve a perplexing problem. The plan was a com-

---

[1] "Each State shall appoint, in such Manner as the Legislature thereof may direct, a Number of Electors, equal to the whole Number of Senators and Representatives to which the State may be entitled in the Congress: but no Senator or Representative, or Person holding an Office of Trust or Profit under the United States, shall be appointed an Elector.

"The electors shall meet in their respective States, and vote by ballot for two Persons, of whom one at least shall not be an Inhabitant of the same State with themselves. And they shall make a List of all the Persons voted for, and of the Number of Votes for each; which List they shall sign and certify, and transmit sealed to the Seat of the Government of the United States, directed to the President of the Senate. The President of the Senate shall, in the Presence of the Senate and House of Representatives, open all the Certificates, and the Votes shall then be counted. The Person having the greatest Number of Votes shall be the President, if such Number be a Majority of the whole Number of Electors appointed; and if there be more than one who have such Majority and have an equal Number of Votes, then the House of Representatives shall immediately chuse by Ballot one of them for President; and if no person have a Majority, then from the five highest on the List the said House shall in like Manner chuse the President. But in chusing the President, the Votes shall be taken by States, the Representation from each State having one Vote; A quorum for this Purpose shall consist of a Member or Members from two-thirds of the States, and a Majority of all the States shall be necessary to a choice. In every Case, after the Choice of the President, the person having the greatest Number of Votes of the Electors shall be the Vice-President. But if there should remain two or more who have equal Votes, the Senate shall chuse from them by Ballot the Vice-President."—Constitution, Art. II, sec. 1, par. 2, 3.

promise between the large and small states. The electoral college was expected to operate as a kind of nominating body, since it was not anticipated that the votes of electors would normally be concentrated sufficiently to effect a choice. Hence the eventual choice would ordinarily fall to the House of Representatives. As the weight of the states in the electoral college would be in proportion to "federal numbers," the advantage in this body would lie with the large states; but when the balloting took place in the House the provision that each state should cast one vote would give the small states equal weight with the large. It was expected that each elector would cast his vote according to his personal judgment of the fitness of the candidate. Finally, since the "runner-up" in the balloting for President was to become the Vice-President, it was certain that the latter would be a man of presidential caliber.

Party divisions were quite distinct by the end of Washington's first term, and it was becoming evident that success in elections depended upon united support of party candidates. Hence arose the party caucus of congressmen as a means of nominating them, and more or less pressure began to be brought to bear on electors to support the caucus nominees. Following the election of 1796 Burr complained of the failure of the Republican electors to support him equally with Jefferson, and virtually made it a condition of his acceptance of the vice-presidential candidacy in 1800 that they be pledged to do so. Thus the right of the elector to vote at discretion gave way to the moral obligation to support the regular party candidates.

Washington's great personal prestige secured for him the unanimous vote of the electors in 1789 and 1792, but the "second" votes were scattered in the former year among twelve persons, and in 1792 among five. Thirteen received ballots in 1796, and while Adams had a majority over Jefferson, his Republican opponent, the latter led the Federalist vice-presidential candidate and in consequence won the second office.

The failure of the electors of the majority party to concentrate on their second candidate was thus responsible for the election to the vice-presidency of the minority party candidate for the chief office. An equal vote for the second name would prevent a recurrence of this calamity, but the resulting tie would create as great an evil, since it would throw the election into the House. Separate ballots for the two positions would, however, avoid both dangers.

Such considerations were behind the resolution offered on January 6, 1797, by William Smith of South Carolina, in the House of Representatives.[2] It proposed an amendment which would require the electors to designate their choice for the respective offices. This resolution was ordered printed but no further action was taken upon it. Two or three times during 1799 and 1800 similar proposals were made, but Congress showed little interest in the change.

The election of 1800 proved to be the turning point. The equal support given to Jefferson and Burr produced the inevitable tie and threw the election into the House; there the Federalists were strong enough to prevent a choice until the thirty-seventh ballot, while intrigues were carried on to bring in Burr as President in place of Jefferson. This experience produced a sharp demand for a modification of the Constitution. Vermont, New York, and North Carolina made known to Congress their desire for a change. The support of the proposal was bi-partisan; the New York resolutions, fathered by the Federalist Hamilton, were presented to Congress by the Republican Clinton. The House by a large majority passed a resolution favorable to the amendment, but on May 2, 1802 it failed in the Senate by one vote.

Under the stimulus of action by more states, the House again passed a resolution on October 28, 1803 providing that electors should cast separate ballots for President and Vice-President. Representatives of the small states objected, on the ground that the original plan was adopted to quiet the fears of these states. The Senate made an additional change by reducing the number of names to come before the House from five to three, and again representatives of the small states objected, urging that there was more likelihood of the success of a small-state candidate if the choice were made from the larger number. Under the proposed

[2] *Ann. of Cong.*, 4 Cong., 2 sess., 1824.

amendment, they thought, the large states could easily combine and would always bring their candidates before the House. With five names, moreover, the small states had a better chance for the vice-presidency, the incumbent of which office was the "heir apparent." The change would violate the compromise and alter the vital principle of state equality protected by the federal compact.[3]

The small-state men were defending an interest which parties rendered fictitious, but some of the Federalists opposed the amendment on better grounds. Perceiving that it favored the majority party, which was likely for some time to be that of the Republicans, they centered their fire upon the effects of the proposed change. Gouverneur Morris foresaw that it would become the bait with which to catch the vote of a doubtful state. Others feared that it would be the means of bringing second rate men into the presidency by way of the second office. White of Delaware predicted that the effect would be to give the western states within a few years power to choose both officials. Dana of Connecticut proposed to abolish the vice-presidency.

The 22 to 10 vote by which the Senate adopted the amendment was two thirds of the members present but not of the entire membership. Grasping this straw the Federalists maintained that the Constitution required a two-thirds vote of the full membership, while the Republicans asserted that two thirds of the members present had been deemed sufficient on previous occasions.[4]

Final action by Congress came in December, 1803. The Republicans were anxious for ratification before the presidential election of the next year. For this acceptance by thirteen states was necessary, and ratifications came in so rapidly that on September 25, 1804 the secretary of state announced by proclamation that the amendment had become a part of the Constitution. The legislatures of three Federalist states—Massachusetts, Connecticut, and Delaware—refused to ratify, holding the amendment to be unwise, impolitic, and "unconstitutional." [5]

[3] *Ann. of Cong.*, 8 Cong., 1 sess., *passim.*
[4] In the National Prohibition Cases, 253 U. S. 350 (1920), the Supreme Court held that the two-thirds rule meant two thirds of the members present.
[5] On this amendment see Lolabel House, *The Twelfth Amendment.* On this and other amendments consult Ames, *Proposed Amendments.*

The twelfth amendment was the constitutional recognition of the existence of political parties.[6] Even as changed the electoral system has not worked well; it is like a fifth wheel of a vehicle. Many alternative methods have been suggested. Of these popular election of the President has never gained great favor, because it is felt that the states as such ought to be factors in any method used. This, at least, the electoral system provides for. The change most favored by Congress would divide the states into districts, in each of which one elector would be chosen, with two additional electors-at-large. The distribution of the electoral vote among the states in proportion to the vote in each for each candidate is perhaps the fairest plan, but legislators have been more interested in party success than in justice.

In practice, amendment of the Constitution has proved to be very difficult. Although the number of proposed changes has run into the thousands, far less than one percent have been adopted.

[6] The text of the amendment is as follows: "The Electors shall meet in their respective states, and vote by ballot for President and Vice-President, one of whom, at least, shall not be an inhabitant of the same state with themselves; they shall name in their ballots the person voted for as President, and in distinct ballots the person voted for as Vice-President, and they shall make distinct lists of all persons voted for as President, and of all persons voted for as Vice-President, and of the number of votes for each, which lists they shall sign and certify, and transmit sealed to the seat of the government of the United States, directed to the President of the Senate;—The President of the Senate shall, in the presence of the Senate and House of Representatives, open all the certificates and the votes shall then be counted;—The person having the greatest number of votes for President, shall be the President, if such number be a majority of the whole number of Electors appointed; and if no person have such majority, then from the persons having the highest numbers not exceeding three on the list of those voted for as President, the House of Representatives shall choose immediately, by ballot, the President. But in choosing the President, the votes shall be taken by states, the representation from each state having one vote; a quorum for this purpose shall consist of a member or members from two-thirds of the states, and a majority of all the states shall be necessary to a choice. And if the House of Representatives shall not choose a President whenever the right of choice shall devolve upon them, before the fourth day of March next following, then the Vice-President shall act as President, as in the case of death or other constitutional disability of the President. The person having the greatest number of votes as Vice-President, shall be the Vice-President, if such number be a majority of the whole number of Electors appointed, and if no person have a majority, then from the two highest numbers on the list, the Senate shall choose the Vice-President; a quorum for the purpose shall consist of two-thirds of the whole number of Senators, and a majority of the whole number shall be necessary to a choice. But no person constitutionally ineligible to the office of President shall be eligible to that of Vice-President of the United States."

The required two-thirds vote in both houses of Congress plus a majority in the two houses of three fourths of the state legislatures is almost impossible of attainment under ordinary conditions. Partly as a result of the difficulty of obtaining amendments, the growth of the constitutional system has come mainly through interpretation of the fundamental document by Congress and the courts.

PROBLEMS CONCERNING THE JUDICIARY

The Judiciary Act of 1789 had entrusted the work of the circuit courts to the district judge sitting with two justices of the Supreme Court. From the beginning this itinerant duty of the justices was odious to them, and besides, the legal profession regarded it as bad practice for the same judges to sit in cases when appealed to the Supreme Court, which they had heard in the lower courts. The justices protested in 1792 against the requirements of the statute, and at about the same time the attorney-general gave an adverse opinion on this provision of the law. The onerous duty on circuit fell with especial weight upon elderly men in the days of primitive transportation; Gouverneur Morris remarked that the work required "less the learning of a judge than the agility of a post-boy."

In 1793 Congress modified the law to the extent of permitting one justice to sit with the district judge, but this modification was not regarded as sufficient, and several times the President recommended that further relief be given. In 1799 President Adams insisted that repeal of the requirement of itinerant duty was "indispensably necessary." Any such change involved creation of a new class of judges for the circuit courts. A bill for the purpose introduced in that same year was not acted upon; but it was revived in December, 1800, after the defeat of the Federalists, and became the basis of an act passed early in 1801.

The new act excused the justices of the Supreme Court from all circuit duty and decreased their number to five. More district courts were provided, especially to care for newly settled areas, and the number of circuits was increased to six, each with its complement of judges. The act called for a total of sixteen new judges and some additional attorneys and marshals, at a total cost of somewhat less than fifty thousand dollars.

The Republicans had disliked the federal judicial system from the beginning. It was distasteful to them to have federal justice brought close to the people, as an alternative to that of the states. If the citizen of one state wished to sue his debtor in another state, the courts of the latter were open. The Republicans preferred to have such jurisdiction exercised by the state courts, and this the act of 1789 permitted. But under the Constitution the jurisdiction of the United States also extended to such cases, as well as to all others where it might be claimed that federal law was involved; under the concurrent jurisdiction which the act of 1789 gave to state courts and to the lower federal courts, the Republicans believed that the federal tribunals would gradually absorb all business. Senator Maclay was not alone in holding that the act of 1789 set up an "infernal system."

The prompt rallying of the friends of state's rights to carry through the eleventh amendment following the Chisholm decision is an evidence of the tendency of the elements unsympathetic with the courts to come together in the Republican party, and the assertion of the Virginia and Kentucky Resolutions of 1798 that the states were the judges of the constitutionality of acts of Congress was the alternative which the leaders of that party advanced in opposition to the view of Hamilton and the Federalists that the courts were the proper interpreters of the Constitution.[7] As has already been noted, the Republican discontent extended to the method of selecting the justices by appointment and their tenure during good behavior, which would ordinarily mean life tenure. They disliked the system also because it relieved the judges, as they believed, of all sense of responsibility to the people. In the states it was their policy to favor election of judges for limited terms.

Much as the Republicans disliked the system, it was too firmly established, when they came to office following the election of 1800, to be attacked as a whole. But Jefferson found in the Judi-

[7] This view was urged by the Federalist states in their replies to the Virginia and Kentucky Resolutions. See Anderson, "Contemporary Opinion."

ciary Act of 1801 a vulnerable point. To the Republicans this legislation was clearly partisan, designed to entrench their defeated opponents in the judiciary. There is no doubt that the Federalists had made haste to pass the bill in order that President Adams might make the appointments before quitting office. Referring to these new judges, Jefferson's first message called them "excrescences on the judiciary," and asserted that there was a universal demand for the repeal of the law. As evidence that there was no need of expanding the third department, he submitted statistics showing the small amount of business handled by the courts.

On January 8, 1802, Senator Breckinridge moved the repeal of the act of 1801 on the ground that the new courts were expensive and unnecessary.[8] The repeal bill passed the Senate on February 3. In the House the Federalists contended that since the constitutional tenure of federal judges was during good behavior, to deprive them of office by repealing the act was a violation of the Constitution. Said Bayard of Delaware, "What is the sum of this notable reasoning? You cannot remove the judge from the office, but you may take the office from the judge. . . . If your Constitution cannot resist reasoning like this, then indeed is it waste paper." Favoring repeal, Giles of Virginia maintained that the office did not become the vested property of the judge, and must be held subject to the judgment of Congress as to whether its continuance benefits the people—a position which, notwithstanding Bayard's attempted *reductio ad absurdum*, was sound, Congress having the same discretion in abolishing inferior courts as it has in creating them.

Giles also charged that the act was passed for partisan purposes and that appointments under it had been made contrary to the spirit of the Constitution, which forbids the appointment of members of Congress to offices created during their terms. Three or four members had, in fact, been appointed to fill positions made vacant by promotion of the former incumbents.

The House passed the repeal bill on March 3.[9] The law previously in force was revived, but near the end of April the Republi-

[8] *Ann. of Cong.*, 7 Cong., 1 sess., *passim.*
[9] W. S. Carpenter, "Repeal of the Judiciary Act of 1801."

cans enacted their own measure, increasing the number of associate justices of the supreme bench to six. The net result of the legislation was to restore the circuit duty of the justices, an arrangement which was not again interfered with until 1867. The law of April also postponed the next session of the Supreme Court to February, 1803, for the purpose, according to some authorities, of preventing the Supreme Court under John Marshall from declaring the abolition of the circuit courts unconstitutional.[10]

This question of the power of the Supreme Court to hold an act of Congress void had been a notable feature of the debate on the repeal bill. The Federalist members had very clearly claimed the right for the court. Senator Mason of Massachusetts had stressed the necessity of a judiciary independent of both executive and legislature, "because the duties which they have to perform, call upon them to expound not only the laws, but the Constitution also; in which is involved the power of checking the Legislature in case it should pass any laws in violation of the Constitution."

The chief denial of this argument came from Senator Breckinridge. "My idea of the subject," said he, "is, that the Constitution intended a separation of the powers vested in the three great departments, giving to each exclusive authority on the subjects committed to it. That these departments are co-ordinate. . . . That those who made the laws are presumed to have an equal attachment to, and interest in the Constitution; are equally bound by oath to support it, and have an equal right to give a construction to it. That the construction of one department of the powers vested in it, is of higher authority than the construction of any other department; and that, in fact, it is competent to that department to which powers are confided exclusively to decide upon the proper exercise of those powers: that therefore the Legislature have the exclusive right to interpret the Constitution, in what regards the law-making power, and the judges are bound to execute the laws they make. For the Legislature would have at least an equal right to annul the decisions of the courts. . . ."[11] To this

[10] *Ann. of Cong.,* 7 Cong., 1 sess., 1332.
[11] *Ann. of Cong.,* 7 Cong., 1 sess., 178 *et seq.* In the First Congress Madison had expressed a similar opinion. "I acknowledge," he said, "in the ordinary course of Government, that the exposition of the laws and constitution devolves

Gouverneur Morris replied: "If this doctrine be sustained . . . what possible mode is there to avoid the conclusion that the moment the Legislature of the Union declare themselves supreme, they become so? . . . The sovereignty of America will no longer reside in the people, but in the Congress, and the Constitution is whatever they choose to make it."

MARBURY V. MADISON

The powers of the judiciary were asserted by the Supreme Court itself a few months after this debate. The act which the Republicans repealed in 1802 was not the only one which the Federalists had passed just before they lost control of Congress and the executive: another had authorized the appointment of a number of justices of the peace for the District of Columbia. Adams made the appointments so late in his term that it was said he had sat at his desk until midnight on March 3 signing the commissions. In fact some of them had not been delivered when Jefferson took office. He, thinking it "indecent" for Adams to show such eagerness to put men into office to serve under a successor, instructed Madison, the secretary of state, not to deliver the commissions. Marbury, one of the "midnight" appointees, therefore applied to the Supreme Court at the December term, 1801, for a rule requiring Madison to show cause why a mandamus should not issue directing him to deliver the commission. The rule was granted but Madison ignored it, whereupon (1803) Chief Justice Marshall gave the opinion of the court on the motion for the mandamus.[12]

The chief justice's opinion dealt with the issues in the case in such a remarkable way as to arouse the suspicion that he was looking for an opportunity to assert the right of the court to pass upon the powers of the other departments. Despite many assertions that

upon the Judiciary. But, I beg to know, upon what principle it can be contended, that any one department draws from the constitution greater powers than another, in marking out the limits of the powers of the several departments? . . . If the constitutional boundary of either be brought into question, I do not see that any one of these independent departments has more right than another to declare their sentiments on that point."—*Ibid.*, 1 Cong., 1 sess. For Jefferson's view see letter to Judge Spencer Roane, Sept. 6, 1819, in Washington, *Writings of Jefferson*, VII, 134–135. Reprinted in Johnson, 252–253.

[12] Marbury v. Madison, 1 Cranch 137.

the courts could judge of the constitutionality of acts of Congress, there had not been up to this time a decision of the Supreme Court itself maintaining the doctrine. Recent discussions amounted to a challenge to the court to declare itself at the first opportunity.

Marshall inquired, (1) whether Marbury had a right to his commission, and answered in the affirmative; (2) whether the laws afforded him a remedy for the violation of his right, and again returned an affirmative answer. Finally, he asked whether he was entitled to the remedy for which he had applied. This, he said, depends upon the nature of the writ applied for and the power of the court. Finding that the writ of mandamus was a remedy properly suited to the case, he reached the question of the power of the court.

Examining the wording of the Judiciary Act of 1789, which authorized the Supreme Court to "issue writs of mandamus . . . to any courts appointed, or persons holding office, under the authority of the United States," he compared it with the Constitution, which distributes the judicial authority between the Supreme and inferior courts, giving original jurisdiction to the former in certain specified cases and in all others restricting it to the hearing of appeals. In the Marbury case, therefore, for the court to take jurisdiction it was necessary that it either fall within the original jurisdiction or come to the court on appeal.

As the case did not meet either of these tests, some authorities believe that the chief justice might have made this question of jurisdiction the first object of his inquiries, and might at this point have dismissed it for want of jurisdiction. There was in the act of 1789 no clear intent to give the court power to issue a mandamus except in the circumstances which Marshall indicated, but he chose to see in the act a grant of authority not warranted by the Constitution: "the authority . . . given to the supreme court," he said, "by the act establishing the judicial courts of the United States, to issue writs of mandamus to public officers, appears not to be warranted by the constitution. . . ."

Having thus created the desired setting it became "necessary to inquire whether a jurisdiction so conferred can be exercised." Declaring that government is established by the will of the people, who organize it and assign to the several departments the powers they are to exercise, the alternatives arise that either "the Constitution controls any legislative act repugnant to it," or "the legislature may alter the constitution by an ordinary act." If the former be true the act is not law; if the latter, "written constitutions are absurd attempts, on the part of the people, to limit a power in its own nature illimitable."

Since the former alternative is evidently the correct one as the court sees matters, and an act contrary to the Constitution is not law, does it nevertheless bind the courts? This question also calls for a negative answer, for "it is emphatically the province and duty of the judicial department to say what the law is. . . . If both the law and the constitution apply to a particular case, so that the court must either decide that case conformably to the law, disregarding the constitution, or conformably to the constitution, disregarding the law, which of these conflicting rules governs the case? . . . If . . . the courts are to regard the constitution, and the constitution is superior to any ordinary act of the legislature, the constitution, and not such ordinary act must govern the case to which they both apply."

The Republicans generally were enraged by Marshall's decision. They saw in it an assertion of judicial supremacy which was quite incompatible with their doctrine of the independence and coordinate standing of the three branches of government. They forgot the theory of checks and balances, to which they had adhered on occasion. However, the refusal of the courts to be bound by acts which they deemed unconstitutional is not to be considered as an assertion of superiority over Congress. It arose in fact from the separation of departments. As Gouverneur Morris pointed out, the independence of the judicial branch would be a fiction if the judges were bound to give validity to every congressional act.

However, the clear-cut contradiction between act and Constitution which Marshall hypothesized was likely to occur rarely. It did not exist even in the Marbury case. Not until 1857 was the court again to hold an act of Congress unconstitutional (in the Dred Scott decision), and in that case again the issue was dragged in unnecessarily. As a matter of fact, within a few years criticism of the Supreme Court by Jefferson and his friends was to rest, not on its proneness to void acts of Congress, but on the quite contrary tendency to uphold acts of legislation which involved latitudinarian construction of the Constitution. Even in 1803, Jefferson did not complain so much of Marshall's voidance of a part of the Judiciary Act as of his arrogant attitude towards the executive. The courts, Jefferson admitted, must decide whether act or Constitution applies in a case properly before it. But the Marbury case, he held, called for no expression of the kind from the Supreme Court, because it was not within the jurisdiction of the tribunal, as Marshall himself ruled; moreover the issuance of the commission demanded by Marbury was a matter falling within the discretion of the executive department, and the whole discussion of his rights was a gratuitous "lecture" on the duties of the President.[13]

By 1803 Jefferson had definitely rejected the idea that the federal courts were the proper judges of the distribution of powers either between states and nation, or between the several branches of the federal government. Disputes over such questions formed the germ of what came to be known as "political cases."

IMPEACHMENTS

Marshall's exposition of the right and duty of the Supreme Court to disregard statutes which it deems contrary to the Constitution had great and permanent significance. Nonetheless, the Marbury decision is a landmark in the party strife between Republicans and Federalists. It was in effect a reply to the action of the Republicans in repealing the Judiciary Act of 1801. The restoration of the circuit court duty of the Supreme Court justices so outraged their feelings that Marshall proposed to his colleagues

[13] Warren, *Sup. Court*, I, 264–266. The discussion of the power of the courts to declare acts of legislation unconstitutional has produced a voluminous literature. Besides Warren's work, the following are among the more important contributions: Charles A. Beard, *The Supreme Court and the Constitution*; Edward S. Corwin, "Marbury v. Madison and the Doctrine of Judicial Review"; Brinton Coxe, *Essay on Judicial Power and Unconstitutional Legislation*; Charles G. Haines, *The American Doctrine of Judicial Supremacy*; Andrew C. McLaughlin, *Foundations of American Constitutionalism*, Chap. V. See also A. J. Beveridge, *Life of John Marshall*.

that they refuse to act and "risk the consequences." Associate Justice Samuel Chase departed from the path of propriety so far as to inform a federal grand jury at Baltimore that the repeal had shaken the independence of the federal judiciary to its foundation. Although he trusted to the virtue of the "people" to restore it, he decried universal suffrage. It would "rapidly destroy all protection to property, and all security to personal liberty; and our republican constitution [would] sink into a mobocracy, the worst of all possible governments." The Republicans of course were responsible: "The modern doctrines by our late reformers, that all men in a state of society are entitled to enjoy equal liberty and equal rights, have brought this mighty mischief upon us." [14]

The attitude of the judges led many Republicans to believe that the repeal of the act of 1801 should be followed by other measures to discipline the courts. In some of the states judges were removable by the governor upon the joint address of the two houses of the legislature, but under the Constitution of the United States impeachment was the only method of removing a judge unless the office itself was abolished. The Republican leaders therefore cast about for a plausible occasion to turn the machinery of impeachment against the Federalists entrenched in the judiciary. [15]

---

[14] *Ann. of Cong.*, 8 Cong., 2 sess., 673–676.

[15] The parts of the Constitution which relate to impeachment are the following:
"The President, Vice-President and all civil Officers of the United States, shall be removed from Office on Impeachment for, and Conviction of, Treason, Bribery, or other high crimes and misdemeanors."—Art. II, sec. 4.
"The Judges, both of the Supreme and Inferior Courts, shall hold their Offices during good behavior."—Art. III, sec. 1.
"The Senate shall have the sole Power to try all Impeachments. When sitting for that Purpose, they shall be on Oath or Affirmation. When the President of the United States is tried, the Chief Justice shall preside; and no Person shall be convicted without the Concurrence of two thirds of the members present.
"Judgment in Cases of impeachment shall not extend further than to removal from office, and disqualification to hold and enjoy any Office of honor, Trust or Profit under the United States; but the Party convicted shall nevertheless be liable and subject to Indictment, Trial, Judgment and Punishment according to Law."—Art. I, sec. 3, pars. 6, 7.
The machinery of impeachment was first invoked against William Blount, a senator from Tennessee. He had engaged in a plot for a filibustering expedition against Spanish territory on the lower Mississippi in violation of the neutrality laws, and had been expelled from the Senate by vote of that body. Afterwards he was charged with "high crimes and misdemeanors" by the House of Representatives.—*Ann. of Cong.*, 5 Cong., 1 sess., 44; 2 sess., 498. (*Continued next page.*)

It was not long before a scapegoat was found in the person of Judge John Pickering, of the New Hampshire federal district court. In February, 1803, at the very time when the Supreme Court was hearing Marbury's plea, President Jefferson sent a special message to the House of Representatives accompanied by documents showing that Judge Pickering was guilty of habitual drunkenness and profanity while upon the bench. The House thereupon took steps to bring the accused before the Senate to answer charges of malfeasance and unlawful conduct in handling a case, and with being a man of loose morals and intemperate habits. In the language of the Constitution, these offences amounted to "high crimes and misdemeanors." [16]

The Senate summoned Pickering to appear for trial on March 2, 1804. Meantime his son petitioned for a postponement of the trial to give him time to collect evidence to show that at the time of the alleged crimes the judge was insane. Robert G. Harper, heard as agent for the petitioner, showed conclusively that the impeached

The case came before the Senate for hearing on December 17, 1798. Blount's counsel pleaded that he was not liable to impeachment because he was no longer a senator; and moreover, that even while a senator, he was not a civil officer of the United States within the meaning of the Constitution. By a vote of 14 to 11 the Senate acquitted the accused, apparently on the ground that a senator is not a civil officer of the United States, thus setting a precedent in favor of the doctrine that members of both houses are exempt from impeachment.—*Ann. of Cong.,* 5 Cong., 3 sess., 2245.

Each house is the judge of the qualifications of its own members and possesses the power to expel members. The term "civil officer" does not include members of Congress, since they are not commissioned by the President.

The Blount case suggests the question whether resignation is a bar to impeachment. This issue was raised in 1876, in the case of W. W. Belknap, Grant's secretary of war. Having been detected in corrupt transactions he resigned, but the House impeached him. His counsel pleaded that he was not an officer of the United States at the time of impeachment, but by a vote of 37 to 29 the Senate overruled the plea that by resignation he had escaped liability to impeachment. This was not a two-thirds vote. On final vote he was acquitted, as more than one third of the senators believed that the Senate lacked jurisdiction.—See Robert Wild, "Belknap Impeachment Trial." Resignation should be no bar to impeachment, since punishment may include disqualification for holding office in future, as well as removal. Besides, since impeachment lies for other than criminal offences, process in criminal court is no remedy for such offences and if resignation bars impeachment there is no remedy. On impeachment in general see Alexander Simpson, Jr., *A Treatise on Federal Impeachments.*

[16] *Ann. of Cong.,* 8 Cong., 1 sess., 315–367. See McMaster, *History,* III, 165–167, for account of Pickering's conduct in the case of the ship *Eliza.* On the trial see Henry Adams, *History of the United States,* II, 143–149.

man was insane, and urged "that to constitute any crime a vicious will is necessary, and that a man insane cannot be put upon his trial." This evidence placed the Republican leaders in a dilemma. They were forced either to maintain that insanity was no bar to impeachment or to drop the case. But if insanity was not a bar to impeachment, it followed that an insane man could be guilty of "high crimes and misdemeanors" in the constitutional meaning of the words; that is to say, these words as used in the Constitution must have a wider meaning than in ordinary law, where they denote indictable offences.

The Republicans split on this dilemma. The Virginians were willing to give the Constitution a broad meaning and hold that impeachment did not imply criminality in the ordinary legal sense. The northern Republicans, however, were not willing to give up the view that impeachment is a criminal process, and in this they had the support of the Federalists. Nevertheless some who could not conscientiously vote that the conduct of the insane Pickering amounted to high crimes and misdemeanors agreed that he should be removed from office, and decided that they could consistently vote that he was "guilty as charged." Out of a total of 34 senators only 26 voted, several being absent and some withholding their voices. The result stood 19 to 7, that for removal from office 20 to 6.

As a precedent the case is confusing. The managers of the prosecution failed to make a consistent statement of their position, yet it seems clear that they held any misbehavior showing unfitness for office to be a misdemeanor in the constitutional sense. Hence while insanity barred criminal action against Pickering it did not bar impeachment. Only by some such broad doctrine is it possible to protect the public, for there are many forms of unfitness which do not bring officials within the range of a grand jury's action. However, when the conservative ground is abandoned there is grave risk of a latitudinarianism which would permit impeachment for mere differences of political opinion or errors in judgment. This danger was pointed out by Senator White during the trial. The procedure followed would, he said, warrant removing anyone from office; every officer would be "at the mercy of Congress."

Having dealt successfully with Judge Pickering's case the Republicans moved forward. The conduct of Judge Chase had been peculiarly offensive to them. In addition to his harangue to the Baltimore grand jury, he had browbeaten certain persons when on trial a few years before under the Sedition Act of 1798. But no act of his could be called a violation of law, and to impeach him charges must rest on a latitudinarian construction of the Constitution. In spite of the opposition of several Republican senators the administration faction resolved to try the dubious experiment. Their party counted twenty-five of the senators and the Federalists nine. It was certain, of course, that all of the Federalists would vote for acquittal. If three Republicans failed to vote for conviction the impeachment would miscarry, and five votes were uncertain.

The trial began early in 1805. Of the eight articles of impeachment the most important were those which charged that Chase had acted in the sedition trials "in a manner highly arbitrary, oppressive, and unjust," and that he had addressed the Baltimore grand jury in a "highly indecent, extra-judicial" manner "tending to prostitute the high judicial character with which he was invested to the low purposes of an electioneering partisan." None of the articles alleged an infraction of law.[17]

The counsel for the defense excelled their opponents in ability. They maintained consistently that an offense to be impeachable must be indictable in law, and tried to drive the prosecution to take the contrary position, knowing that several of the Republican senators would not vote for conviction on broad grounds. The House managers, however, failed to take a consistent stand, and sadly bungled the whole matter. When the vote was taken on March 1, the question on each article was put in the following words: "Is Samuel Chase guilty or not guilty of a high crime or misdemeanor as charged in the article just read?" This form, although not quite as ambiguous as that used in the Pickering case, allowed each senator to define terms for himself. Twenty-three votes were needed for conviction, but the highest number voting

[17] *Ann. of Cong.*, 8 Cong., 2 sess., 85–88. *Cf.* Warren, *Sup. Court*, I, 273–282, 289–297. On the Chase impeachment see Adams, *History*, II, Chap. X.

"guilty" on any count was 19. This vote was polled on the charge concerning the speech at Baltimore.

The members of the administration faction were extremely disappointed at this collapse of their assault on the judiciary. Jefferson himself admitted years later that resort to impeachment had proved to be "a mere scarecrow." Success in the Chase trial, it seems, would have been followed by the impeachment of Marshall, probably for his method of handling the Marbury case. Senator John Quincy Adams, at all events, wrote to his father that "the assault upon Judge Chase . . . was unquestionably intended to pave the way for another prosecution, which would have swept the Supreme Judicial Bench clean at a stroke." [18] Allowance must be made for Adams's habit of listening to the gossip of the corridors; but rumor went so far as to indicate that Jefferson had in mind, as Marshall's successor, Judge Spencer Roane, of Virginia. The trend of constitutional development during the next twenty-five years, if Roane had reached the chief-justiceship, forms an interesting subject of speculation!

These early cases left the theory of impeachment unclarified. The trend towards a liberal interpretation of the constitutional provisions, imparted in the Pickering case, was somewhat checked by the outcome of the Chase trial. Later experience, however, established a reasonably liberal interpretation of the term "misdemeanor" so that, in the words of Chief Justice Taft, "there is now no difficulty in securing the removal of a judge for any reason that shows him unfit." [19]

THE LOUISIANA PURCHASE

For many years Thomas Jefferson had believed that the time would come when the United States would expand beyond the Mississippi River. The vast Province of Louisiana, stretching westward to the Rocky Mountains, had been held by Spain since 1763. But the interest of Americans in the region, prior to Jefferson's presidency, was hardly that of possible settlers. Rather it was due to jealousy of the control which Spain exercised over the navi-

[18] Quoted in Warren, *Sup. Court*, I, 294–295.
[19] "The Selection and Tenure of Judges," 432.

gation of the Mississippi, a situation which threatened the hold of the United States upon her own territory between the Appalachians and the river. No one was more aware of this danger than Jefferson. While secretary of state, in 1790, a prospect of war between England and Spain had aroused his fear that the possession of Louisiana and the Floridas might fall to the former. It was to the interest of the United States to have Spain retain her possessions rather than that they should pass into the hands of a more powerful nation.

A decade later France forced Spain to return to her the transmississippi country which she had once owned. For years she had played upon Spain's fears of American encroachments, urging her to retrocede a province which only the strong arm of France could defend. When Bonaparte became First Consul his interest in reviving his country's colonial empire led him to embrace the project of recovering Louisiana, and in 1800 by false promises he regained the province by the treaty of San Ildefonso. Being at war with England, he feared to let the mistress of the seas know of his acquisition until he had occupied New Orleans. His plans encountered delay, however, and before the army reached New Orleans a truce which had given him the opportunity to prepare the expedition was about to be ended by a new period of war.

Meantime rumors of the cession reached Jefferson and revived his apprehensions of a strong power at the mouth of the Mississippi. To Robert R. Livingston, the American minister in Paris, he declared his views on the transfer in terms which threatened an alliance of the United States with England when war broke out afresh. Not long afterwards, came news that the Spanish officials at New Orleans had withdrawn commercial privileges granted to Americans by a treaty of 1795. Before this tangle could be smoothed out the people of the West, expecting the French legions and aroused to frenzy by the closure of the Mississippi, were on the point of attacking New Orleans. To quiet them Jefferson instructed Livingston to negotiate for a tract at the mouth of the river sufficient to insure unmolested enjoyment of navigation and transshipment of cargoes to ocean-going vessels, and dispatched Monroe, who was popular in the West, as special envoy to assist Livingston.

Before his arrival in France, Napoleon, faced with the certainty of the rupture of the peace, decided to dispose of what he could not hold. On April 11, 1803, Talleyrand, his minister of foreign affairs, while discussing with Livingston the sale of the Isle of Orleans, suddenly asked, "What would you give for the whole of Louisiana?" Once assured that the question was asked seriously, the only difficulty was to agree on the price; the treaty was ready for signing when Monroe arrived.

The negotiation for New Orleans had been started with the understanding that if it succeeded the purchase would require the express sanction of a constitutional amendment.[20] Therefore, when the news of the cession reached Jefferson he took up with his advisers the matter of an amendment and called a special session of Congress to meet in October. Article III of the treaty promised that "The inhabitants of the ceded territory shall be incorporated in the Union of the United States, and admitted as soon as possible, according to the principles of the Federal Constitution, to the enjoyment of all the rights, advantages, and immunities of citizens of the United States; and in the meantime they shall be maintained and protected in the free enjoyment of their liberty, property, and the religion which they profess." To Breckinridge Jefferson wrote, with this article in mind, "the Constitution has made no provision for holding foreign territory, still less for incorporating foreign nations into our Union." The executive, he thought, had properly seized the opportunity to advance the good of the country, but in making the treaty it had done what the Constitution did not authorize. Like the executive, Congress should, after ratifying the treaty and passing the measures to give it effect, "throw themselves on their country for doing for them unauthorized, what we know they would have done for themselves had they been in a situation to do it." He believed that the "nation" would not disavow the act, and by appealing to it for the amendment the lines of the Constitution would be all the more strongly marked.[21]

In his desire for an amendment the President found himself

[20] Everett S. Brown, *The Constitutional History of the Louisiana Purchase, 1803-1812.*
[21] August 12, 1803. Ford, *Writings of Jefferson*, VIII, 244-246.

alone. Advisers thought it wiser to avoid an expression of public opinion, since rejection of the amendment would stamp the acquisition as unconstitutional. The treaty-making power, it was urged, included that of acquiring territory. Reluctantly Jefferson yielded. To consider the grant of power to make treaties as boundless, he reasoned, and to assume powers by construction, was to make blank paper of the Constitution. He thought it important "to set an example against broad construction, by appealing for new power to the people." Nevertheless he found it possible to "acquiesce with satisfaction" in the contrary opinion of his friends, and to decide to "do *sub silentio* what shall be found necessary." [22] To decide in this fashion was, in the words of one modern critic, to deprive the Constitution "of all restraining and conservative force; to make the official oath to support it a meaningless formality; and to deprive the fundamental law in the popular, as well as in the official mind, of all sense of sanctity." [23]

Constitutional issues were, however, not to be covered by the soft mantle of silence, for when the special session of Congress met the Federalists were vehement in their denunciation of the treaty on the ground that it was both impolitic and unconstitutional to acquire territory with a promise that it should be incorporated into the Union.[24] Although they were not so inconsistent as to deny that territory might be acquired by treaty, even without an amendment, they saw in the promise of incorporation a pledge of future statehood. Upon this provision they centered their attack. The fear of eclipse by the South and West lay behind their constitutional arguments. In the House their fundamental objection was frankly stated by Uriah Tracy of Connecticut, who declared that "the relative strength which admission gives to a Southern and Western interest is contradictory to the principles of our original Union." "This would be absorbing the Northern states, and rendering them as insignificant in the Union as they ought to be, if by their own consent the measure should be adopted." As to the constitutional question, Gaylord Griswold of New York

[22] To W. C. Nicholas, Sept. 7, 1803, *ibid.*, 247; to Breckinridge, *ibid.*, 474.
[23] Thomas M. Cooley, "The Acquisition of Louisiana," 160.
[24] *Ann. of Cong.*, 8 Cong., 1 sess.

argued that the power to admit new states was restricted to those carved from the original territory, and was vested in Congress, not in the treaty-making organ of the government: its power was exceeded, in his opinion, by the promise to admit Louisiana as a state. Roger Griswold of Connecticut admitted that "a new territory and new subjects may undoubtedly be obtained by conquest and by purchase," but held that "neither the conquest nor the purchase can incorporate them into the Union. They must remain in the condition of colonies and be governed accordingly." The treaty pledge to admit Louisiana assumed, he thought, that the President and Senate might at will admit any foreign nation into "this copartnership without the consent of the States."

In the Senate Timothy Pickering also admitted the right to acquire territory by conquest or purchase and to govern it as a dependent province, but denied that incorporation could be effected by the President and Senate in a treaty, by Congress under its power to admit new states, or even by means of an ordinary amendment. "In like manner as in a commercial house, the consent of each member would be necessary to admit a new partner into the company," so the admission of a new state formed from acquired territory would require the assent of every individual state.

During the debate Gouverneur Morris, who was not in Congress at the time, was asked for his opinion as to the status of acquired territory, since, as a member of the federal Convention, he had prepared the final draft of the Constitution. In reply he wrote: "Can Congress admit, as a new State, territory, which did not belong to the United States when the Constitution was made? In my opinion they can not. I always thought that, when we should acquire Canada and Louisiana, it would be proper to govern them as provinces, and allow them no voice in our councils." [25]

The Republicans on their part vigorously defended the constitutional power to acquire territory which the Federalists did not dispute, stressing especially the implications of the power to make war and treaties. They denied, however, that the promise to incorporate Louisiana into the Union meant statehood; that ques-

[25] Jared Sparks, *Life of Gouverneur Morris*, III, 192.

tion, they insisted, was not at issue. Senator Taylor of Virginia gave a lucid explanation of the pledge of incorporation, maintaining that "the words are literally satisfied by incorporating [the inhabitants] into the Union as a territory." If the promise meant statehood, he reasoned, there would be no occasion for the additional provision that the inhabitants should be admitted as soon as possible "to the enjoyment of all the rights, advantages, and immunities of citizens of the United States"; the intent was to give citizenship to the people of the *territory*, since statehood would confer it without further words. "Being incorporated in the Union as a Territory, and not as a State a stipulation for citizenship became necessary. . . ." Nicholas, like Taylor, declared that the treaty did not promise statehood. If it was to come later, it would be conferred in accordance with the "principles of the Constitution."

The vote in the Senate on ratification of the treaty stood 26 to 5. In accordance with the Republican theory of the rights of the House, Jefferson desired that the treaty be passed on by that branch also, and there the vote stood 90 to 25. All of the negative votes were cast by Federalists, and 17 of them represented New England states.

In this debate the Federalists laid the ground work for imperialism. Morris's opinion was quite in harmony with his stand in the Constitutional Convention against the admission of new states to equal status with the original members of the Union, and foreshadowed the acquisition and government of dependencies by the United States a century later. The situation presented a serious dilemma either horn of which was destructive of the Virginia theory of the Constitution: acquired territory must eventually be formed into states or held permanently in dependence. If the former alternative were chosen the original union was ended; if the latter, the United States was headed towards empire. The second horn was consistent with Federalist theory; it meant that the states had established a government which could hold the rest of the "world in despotic control, and which bought a foreign people as it might buy cattle, to rule over them as their owner." The Republicans chose the former: eventual statehood was in harmony with Jeffersonian liberalism, and many years later the Supreme Court ruled (in the Dred Scott decision) that under the Constitution statehood was necessarily the ultimate status of acquired territory. But Jefferson and his colleagues could not escape the consequences of their choice, for with the Louisiana treaty the old union ceased.

Notwithstanding their imperialism, the Federalists suddenly became strict constructionists when they considered the powers of Congress in dealing with the new territory. In fact, the two parties made a curious exchange of positions. Article VII of the treaty accorded certain privileges to French and Spanish ships; vessels of those lands coming directly from their home countries or their colonies, loaded only with the produce or manufactures thereof, were to "be admitted during the space of twelve years in the port of New Orleans, and in all other legal ports of entry within the ceded territory, in the same manner as the ships of the United States coming directly from France or Spain or any of their colonies, without being subject to any other or greater duty on merchandise, or other or greater tonnage than that paid by the citizens of the United States." During the debate Gaylord Griswold had challenged this article as a violation of the constitutional prohibition of any preference "by any regulation of Commerce or Revenue to the Ports of one State over those of another." To this Nicholson had made the startling answer that Louisiana was not a state, but was "in the nature of a colony whose commerce may be regulated without any reference to the Constitution."

In a special message dated October 23, President Jefferson requested Congress to make "such temporary provisions . . . as the case may require" for the government of the new acquisition.[26] The bill which was reported to carry out this recommendation emanated from the executive department, and rested on the doctrine of Nicholson that Louisiana was a dependency which could be governed without any reference to the Constitution. Writing long afterwards, Senator Thomas H. Benton described it as "a startling bill, continuing the existing Spanish government; putting

[26] Brown, *Louisiana Purchase*, Chaps. VI–VIII.

the President in the place of the King of Spain; putting all the
territorial officers in the place of the King's officers, and placing
the appointment of all these officers in the President alone without
reference to the Senate . . . a mere emanation of Spanish despotism." [27]

The bill provided that immediately upon ratification of the
treaty the President should take possession of the territory, and
that all military, civil, and judicial powers exercised by the government of Louisiana should rest in the appointees of the President.
When the Federalists objected that it conferred unconstitutional
powers on the President, the Republicans developed the doctrine
suggested by Nicholson in the former debate.   Said Caesar A.
Rodney, "Congress have a power in the territories which they
cannot exercise in the States, . . . the limitations of power found
in the Constitution are applicable to States and not to territories."
Thus the term "United States" was made to mean two things:
the states united, and the states and territories taken together composing the geographical domain of the American people: and thus
the Republicans added their contribution to the theoretical ground-
work of imperialism.

This first bill for Louisiana was passed by a party vote and became law on October 31.   Governor Claiborne of Mississippi Territory was made governor also of Louisiana as soon as it was received from the French in December.   Four weeks after the passage
of this first act a second bill, drawn by Madison in cooperation
with the President, was introduced in the Senate by Breckinridge.
It divided Louisiana into two parts at the thirty-third parallel.
The northern part, named the District of Louisiana, was placed
temporarily under the government of Indiana Territory.   For the
southern part, denominated the Territory of Orleans, a government
was provided consisting of a governor and council of thirteen
members, to be appointed by the President from the property-
holders resident in the territory, without the advice and consent
of the Senate.   The governor possessed the legislative power, the
council merely accepting or rejecting his measures: it was called

[27] Adams, *History*, II, 119, quoting Benton's Examination of the Decision of the
Supreme Court in the case of Dred Scott, 55.

and dismissed at his pleasure. Jury trial was required only in capital cases and in civil suits involving more than $20.

Some Republicans joined the Federalists in attacking these proposals. Campbell of Tennessee declared that the measure established a despotism and did not give the inhabitants any of the rights to which the treaty entitled them, nor indicate when they would be granted. John Quincy Adams proposed a resolution asserting that no constitutional power existed to tax the people of Louisiana without their consent, but only three senators voted with him on the motion. The great majority of senators believed that the people of the territory were not ready for self-government of the American type, and passed the bill, on February 18, 1804, by a vote of 20 to 5. The House made some changes of a liberal character, but the only one to which the Senate agreed limited the act to one year.

Within the year Americans who had migrated to Louisiana protested so vigorously against the continuation of the autocratic government that Congress was quite ready to abandon it. In 1805, consequently, a third act gave Orleans the usual type of territorial government, the immediate model being supplied by the Territory of Mississippi. Among the settlers from the states was Edward Livingston, brother of the negotiator of the treaty of cession, who came from New York and made for himself a permanent name in the history of the region by his codification of the law derived from the Spanish and French régimes.

Massachusetts, where the secession sentiment was strong, foreseeing that the admission of new states and the extension of slavery would result in the decline of the political influence of New England, proposed an amendment to the Constitution for apportioning direct taxes and representation in the House according to the respective numbers of free inhabitants in the several states. Pickering presented the amendment in the Senate, while Massachusetts communicated it directly to the other states to draw out their sentiment. All but two answered promptly condemning the proposal.[28]

The Republicans believed that the real purpose was to feel out

[28] McMaster, *History*, III, 44–47.

public opinion with disruption of the Union in view. New England continued to favor the change, however, and renewed the proposal on various later occasions.

If it cannot be said that the stretch of power involved in the purchase of Louisiana and the legislation which followed gave the death blow to the theory of strict construction, it is true that these acts dealt the theory a blow in the house of its friends which permanently impaired its vitality. A precedent had been set which henceforth overshadowed all appeals to the old Jeffersonian doctrine of extending federal authority only by amending the Constitution.

The question of the constitutional powers of the federal government in relation to acquired territory was to arise again and again in many forms with the passing years. In The American Insurance Company v. Canter,[29] a case growing out of the purchase of Florida, decided by the Supreme Court in 1828, John Marshall for the court affirmed the power to acquire territory under the war and treaty-making clauses of the Constitution, and suggested that the right to govern such territory was a necessary result. He derived the power to govern also from the clause which gives Congress authority "to make all needful rules and regulations respecting the territory and other property belonging to the United States." If possible, even more significant for the future was his opinion that the internal police regulations of acquired communities remained unchanged until altered by the "newly created power of the state," that is, the government of the nation to which the territory was ceded. In his own words, "the same act which transfers their country, transfers the allegiance of those who remain in it; and [that part of] the law, which may be denominated political, is necessarily changed, although that which regulates the intercourse and general conduct of individuals, remains in force until altered by the newly created power of the state." This pronouncement meant that Congress possesses the power to regulate the internal police of territories; the point was to become a bone of contention between the sections when the slavery issue became acute.

[29] 1 Peters 511.

XVI

FEDERAL AUTHORITY VERSUS STATE'S RIGHTS

THE OLMSTEAD CASE

SERIOUS as had been the protest of New Hampshire in the case of Penhallow *v.* Doane, it created no such crisis as that caused by Pennsylvania in the so-called Olmstead case.[1] In 1778, Gideon Olmstead and three other men, while captives on a British vessel bound for New York with supplies for the troops stationed there, managed to get possession of the vessel and were bringing it into port when it was captured by a Pennsylvania cruiser. The state court condemned the prize and awarded a part of the proceeds of the sale to the crew of the captor and to the state. Olmstead appealed to Congress, but the state denied its jurisdiction since its own law did not permit appeals on questions of fact. Although Congress with only two dissenting votes affirmed the powers of its commissioners, the marshal of the Pennsylvania court disregarded the decision of the congressional tribunal and paid the proceeds of the sale of the prize to the judge of the state court. He in turn delivered the money to the state treasurer, David Rittenhouse, taking his personal bond for repayment if later it became necessary to account for it to the Court of Appeals.

Rittenhouse held the money as his personal property, since the state did not relieve him of his bond, and upon his death the securities in which he had invested it came into the hands of two daughters who were his heirs and executrices. The decision of the Supreme Court in the New Hampshire case in 1795 asserting that the federal district courts had power to execute the decisions of the old Court of Appeals in Cases of Capture, encouraged Olmstead to sue the executrices, and in 1803 he obtained a judgment against them. At this point the state legislature required that the

---

[1] Ames, *State Documents*, 45–52; McMaster, *History*, V, 403–406; Hampton L. Carson, "Pennsylvania's Defiance of the United States"; Warren, *Sup. Court*, I, 366–388.

money be turned into the state treasury and empowered the governor to use the militia if necessary to prevent the federal marshal from serving a writ of execution. Under these circumstances Judge Peters, of the United States district court for Pennsylvania, did not attempt to execute the judgment of his court.

After an interval of five years Olmstead applied to the Supreme Court of the United States for a writ of mandamus directed to Judge Peters requiring him to execute his judgment.[2] The mandamus was granted and accordingly Judge Peters issued his writ of execution. The marshal to whom it was entrusted found himself confronted by the state militia, whereupon he called a *posse comitatus* of two thousand men and set a future date for serving the writ. At this juncture the legislature placed a sum equal to that in dispute at the disposal of the governor to be used at his discretion. The marshal, however, eluding the militia, served his writ and took one of the executrices into custody in default of payment. The state officials now weakened; a state judge refused to release the woman on habeas corpus proceedings, and the governor ended the episode by paying the money to the court. The commander of the militia was prosecuted for resisting a federal officer and sentenced to fine and imprisonment. Federal authority having been completely vindicated by this time, President Madison pardoned the convicted official, on the ground that he had acted from a mistaken sense of duty.

Olmstead's application for the writ of mandamus led Chief Justice Marshall to review the issue. Referring to the decision of 1795, he declared: "By the highest judicial authority of the nation it has been long since decided, that the Court of Appeals erected by Congress had full authority to revise and correct the sentence of the courts of admiralty of the several states, in prize causes. That question, therefore, is at rest. Consequently, the decision of the Court of Appeals in this case annulled the sentence of the Court of Admiralty, and extinguished the interest of the state of Pennsylvania in the *Active* and her cargo, which was acquired by that sentence. The full right to that property was immediately vested in the claimants, who might rightfully pursue it, into whatsoever

[2] United States v. Peters, 5 Cranch 115, 138 (1809).

hands it might come. . . ." "If the legislatures of the several states may, at will, annul the judgment of the courts of the United States, and destroy the rights acquired under those judgments, the constitution itself becomes a solemn mockery, and the nation is deprived of the means of enforcing its laws by the instrumentality of its own tribunals." [3]

Meeting the contention that the federal courts were deprived of jurisdiction by the eleventh amendment, Marshall held that "in this case the suit was not instituted against the state or its treasurer, but against the executrices of David Rittenhouse." "Since, then, the state of Pennsylvania had neither possession of, nor right to, the property on which the sentence of the District Court was pronounced, and since the suit was neither commenced nor prosecuted against that state, there remains no pretext for the allegation that the case is within that amendment of the constitution."

WAR MEASURES

Measures of the federal government during the Napoleonic Wars threw New England into strenuous opposition. The rupture of the Peace of Amiens in 1803 drew the whole of Europe into the vortex of war and placed the fortunes and peace of the United States in jeopardy. Caught between the British orders in council and Napoleon's decrees her rights as a neutral were completely disregarded. Believing that "commercial coercion" would prove quite as effective as war, Jefferson hoped to compel both belligerents to do us justice by stopping the trade with them on which they depended for necessities. After certain half-way measures had been tried, he recommended an embargo forbidding the departure of all ships for foreign ports except those of other countries in port at the time of the passage of the bill; these were to be allowed to depart in ballast or with cargoes already on board. Coasting vessels were required to give bond to land their freight at domestic ports. The House of Representatives passed the bill after three days consideration, while the Senate devoted only four hours to it. It became law on December 22, 1807.

[3] On the origin and scope of the admiralty jurisdiction of the United States, see H. Putnam, "How the Federal Courts were Given Admiralty Jurisdiction."

The administration based the act on the power of Congress to regulate foreign trade, but the Federalists declared that an embargo running for an unlimited period was not a regulation, but an *annihilation* of commerce. Said Webster, it is "as perpetual as the law against murder." The power to lay an embargo even for a single day, the friends of the measure answered, means that it may be renewed from day to day, which is equivalent to laying it for an indefinite period in the first place. On substantially this ground, Judge John Davis, of the United States district court in Massachusetts, although a Federalist, upheld the act in the autumn of 1808.[4]

By midsummer of that year evasion of the law had become widespread in New England, and the Republicans found themselves compelled to choose between repeal and stern measures of enforcement. They chose the latter alternative, and an act for the purpose became law on January 9, 1809. It made the attempt to carry on commerce, even to the extent of loading a vessel, a high misdemeanor. Even a wagon might be put under bond not to cross the international boundary into Canada. Supplementing the act of 1795, which authorized the President to use the militia to compel observance of federal law, the new measure made it lawful for him, or his appointee, to employ also the land and naval forces to prevent the illegal departure of any vessel or to suppress any armed or riotous assemblage engaged in any way in opposing the embargo.

When at length war came in spite of the policy of peaceful coercion, the federal government was driven to other extreme measures. In the autumn of 1814, after the British had invaded the coast of Maine, Congress took up two extraordinary bills for raising troops. Both originated in the Senate. The first, known as the conscription bill, proposed to draft 80,000 militia to serve in their own or adjoining states. The second permitted the enlistment of minors without the consent of their parents or guardians. The House made amendments to the conscription bill which the Senate refused to accept, but the measure for the enlistment of minors was passed and became law on December 10.

[4] Adams, *History*, IV, 268–269.

STATE RECALCITRANCY

All of these measures were distasteful to New England Federalists. As early as the Louisiana Purchase a few of the ultras had contemplated secession and the formation of a northern confederation. "The people of the East," wrote Pickering, "cannot reconcile their habits, views, and interests with those of the South and West. . . . I do not believe in the practicability of a long-continued union." [5] The secession scheme made little headway at that time against the conciliatory policies of Jefferson, which rapidly won the good will of the masses in New England, as was shown by the vote in the election of 1804. Much of his support was forfeited, however, when commercial restriction was taken up. Although Massachusetts at first endorsed the embargo as "a wise and highly expedient measure," the action was due to the control of the state government by Republicans. They met defeat in the next election, however, and thereafter that state like its neighbors went into opposition.

When the Pennsylvania legislature virtually admitted defeat in the Olmstead matter by placing money at the governor's disposal for its settlement, it found a safety valve for its emotions in resolutions declaring, as Jefferson had done ten years earlier, "that no provision is made in the constitution for determining disputes between the general and state governments." [6] It urged the need of an amendment establishing an impartial tribunal for that purpose, since "it is impossible, from the imperfections of language, so to define the limits [of the powers] of each, that difficulties should not some times arise from a collision." In the absence of such a tribunal, it reiterated the doctrine of sentinelship, and asserted that as *"guardians of the State rights,* [it] can not permit an infringement of those rights, by an unconstitutional exercise of power in the United States' courts."

These resolutions were passed on April 3, 1809. No state concurred with Pennsylvania at the time, but at least eleven passed

[5] To George Cabot, Jan. 29, 1804, in Henry Adams, ed., *Documents relating to New England Federalism, 1800–1815,* 339.
[6] Ames, *State Docs.,* 47.

resolutions of disapproval. Even Virginia, repudiating for the moment the doctrines of her distinguished statesman who had just left the presidency, declared that "a tribunal is already provided by the constitution of the United States, *to wit:* the Supreme Court, more eminently qualified from their habits and duties, from the mode of their selection, and from the tenure of their offices, to decide the disputes aforesaid in an enlightened and impartial manner, than any other tribunal which could be erected." [7]

The next year Pennsylvania reaffirmed her conviction that the settlement of disputes between states and nation was "unprovided for in the constitution, and there is no common umpire"; and in spite of the fact that she won no sympathy for her position on the Olmstead issue, her position on the matter of the *lacunae* and ambiguities of the Constitution was substantially that which every state was to take when its turn came to feel aggrieved by the conduct of the federal administration. "How are the powers reserved to the States . . . to be maintained," inquired Timothy Pickering in a letter to a friend upon the passage of the bill to enforce the embargo, "but by the respective States judging for themselves and putting their negative on the usurpations of the general government?" [8] In answer the Federalists appropriated the teachings of Jefferson and Madison—they seized the enemy's guns and turned them against their owners.

The enforcement act of 1809 was greeted in New England by newspaper headlines with such readings as "Liberty is Dead"; "Resistance to Arbitrary Laws is a Duty to God." As in the revolutionary era, many towns forwarded resolutions to the state legislatures denouncing the act and threatening dissolution of the Union. Members of Congress corresponded with the malcontents at home. Harrison Gray Otis wrote to Josiah Quincy that the next session of the Massachusetts legislature would require a bridle rather than a spur, but held that the New England states should adhere to the Union as long as possible.

The session of the Massachusetts legislature which met early in 1809 found the Federalists in control in both houses. They de-

[7] *Ibid.*, 49.
[8] To Christopher Gore, Jan. 8, 1809, in Adams, *New England Federalism*, 378.

nounced the enforcement act as "unjust, oppressive and unconstitutional, and not legally binding on the citizens of this state." They advised against forcible resistance, but went so far as to pass an act against "unconstitutional" searches which was intended to prevent the operation of the enforcement act within the bounds of the state.[9] This was vetoed by the governor, a Republican, who had come to the office from the lieutenant-governorship through the death of his Federalist predecessor.

In Connecticut affairs took a somewhat different turn, under the leadership of Governor Trumbull. In accordance with the terms of the enforcement act, the secretary of war, under the President's directions, called for militia in the New England states to assist the revenue officers at each port of entry. To the request that he, "as commanding officer of the militia" in Connecticut, appoint a subordinate officer to carry out the President's plans, Governor Trumbull replied that in his opinion he had no authority under the constitution or laws of the state to make such an appointment; nor did he think that the Constitution or laws of the United States gave the President the authority to ask him to do so. Conceiving that the enforcement act was unconstitutional, he deemed it improper "to contribute his *volunteer* aid in support of" it.[10]

Following this reply the governor called the general assembly in special session and laid the matter before it. Borrowing from the Virginia Resolutions of 1791 and 1798, he said that "it would be useful for the general good, if the State Legislatures were often to cast a watchful eye towards the general government, with a view, candidly to consider, and judiciously discern, whether the powers delegated to the United States are not exceeded. . . . Whenever our national legislature is led to overleap the prescribed bounds of their constitutional powers, on the State Legislatures, in great emergencies, devolves the arduous task—it is their right— it becomes their duty, to interpose their protecting shield between the right and liberty of the people, and the assumed power of the

[9] Ames, *State Docs.*, 27.
[10] The letter of the secretary of war and Trumbull's reply are reprinted in Johnson, *Readings*, 263–266.

General Government." [11] The legislature promptly endorsed the stand taken by the governor and passed resolutions asserting the right of sentinelship. The governor of Rhode Island followed the course of Governor Trumbull and received the support of similar resolutions of the legislature.[12]

Failure to produce the desired concessions from the European powers, the rising protest of the agricultural states, and the opposition of the Federalist states led the Republicans at length to decide upon the repeal of the embargo and the acts to enforce it. The constitutionality of the measure was involved in the case of Gibbons *v.* Ogden, which came before the Supreme Court in 1824.[13] The power to make rules governing commerce, the court held, is complete and without other limitations than those mentioned in the Constitution. The wisdom and discretion of Congress and the votes of the people are the only restraints on abuse of the power.

THE MILITIA QUESTION

In the Southwest Americanization proceeded so rapidly that by 1811 the Territory of Orleans was asking for statehood. The Federalists had not forgotten the fight they had made in 1803 against a policy which seemed likely to lead to the creation of states from the territory purchased from France, and the bill for the admission of Louisiana awakened the secession sentiment which had slumbered since 1804. Speaking against the bill, Josiah Quincy of Massachusetts was "compelled to declare it as" his "deliberate opinion, that if this bill passes, the bonds of this union are, virtually, dissolved; that the states, which compose it are free from their moral obligations, and that as it will be the right of all, so it will be the duty of some to prepare, definitely for a separation; amicably, if they can, violently, if they must." [14]

Never before had Jefferson's doctrine that a state, in judging of breaches of the Constitution, might decide also upon the mode and measure of redress, been carried publicly to the point of

[11] Ames, *State Docs.*, 39–40.
[12] *Ibid.*, 40–44.
[13] 9 Wheaton I, 384 *et seq.*
[14] *Ann. of Cong.*, 11 Cong., 3 sess., 525 *et seq.*

asserting the right to secede from the Union. It had been implied, perhaps, in a resolution of Pennsylvania which called the Constitution "to all intents and purposes a treaty between sovereign states," [15] but the protests against federal measures during the years preceding the War of 1812 were generally concerned with the effort to protect what the states considered to be their reserved rights. Quincy went on to expound his view of the nature of the Constitution and the grievances and rights of the states of his section.

The bill, he said, was based on the assumption that the national government can admit "new partners to a share of the political power, in countries out of the original limits of the United States." The proposal to admit such a new partner raised the question "whether the proprietors of the good old United States shall manage their own affairs in their own way; or whether they, and their constitution, and their political rights, shall be trampled under foot by foreigners, introduced through a breach of the constitution. The proportion of the political weight of each sovereign state, constituting this union depends upon the number of the states, which have a voice under the compact. . . . This constitution never was, and never can be, strained to lap over all the wilderness of the west, without essentially affecting both the rights and convenience of its real proprietors. It was never constructed to form a covering for the inhabitants of the Missouri and the Red River country. And whenever it is attempted to be stretched over them, it will rend assunder. . . ." "Do you suppose the people of the Northern and Atlantic States will, or ought to look on with patience and see representatives and senators from the Red River and Missouri, pouring themselves upon this and the other floor, managing the concerns of a seaboard fifteen hundred miles, at least, from their residence; and having a preponderancy in councils, into which, constitutionally, they could never have been admitted?"

All of the conservative fear of the influence of the West on the interests and culture of the old sections was compressed into Quincy's utterance. Declining reelection to Congress, he entered

[15] Jan. 11, 1811, against the Bank of the United States. Ames, *State Docs.*, 8–10.

the state senate, and in 1813 was responsible for a report and resolutions adopted by the legislature denouncing the admission of
Louisiana.[16] By this time war issues were absorbing attention and
the Louisiana question fell into abeyance. When Congress declared war the Federalist members issued a protest addressed to
their constituents which appears to have been written by Quincy.
They abhorred the war; it was a party war; the United States
entered it with the people divided; the government was an experiment in the association of sovereign states, and to subject the
moral bonds which held the Union together to such severe strain
was suicidal; the war took sides with a tyrant; the Federalists disclaimed all share in the misfortunes which would follow; the
people should organize a peace party and express loud and deep
disapprobation; there should be no volunteering except for defense.[17]

Early acts of the administration revived the controversy over
the use of the state militia. During the first stages of the war it
was the plan of the government to rely largely upon them. On
June 22, 1812, calls were sent to the governors of Massachusetts,
Connecticut, and other states for quotas of militia to guard the
seacoast. Some of the troops were to be sent out of their own
states, and no high officers were asked for, as it was intended to
place the contingents under officers of the United States army.[18]

Neither Strong of Massachusetts nor Griswold of Connecticut
responded to this call. The former held that the governors of the
states were the judges of the existence of any of the exigencies
mentioned in the Constitution as warranting the calling of the
militia into the service of the United States. In his opinion none
of them did exist. The mere possibility of invasion he thought
did not warrant the call. He also questioned the right of the
President to place the men under federal officers.[19]

Upon receiving a second call from the war department in July,

---

[16] *Ibid.*, 66–67.
[17] "An Address . . . to their Constituents, on the subject of the war with Great
Britain," in *Niles Weekly Register*, July 11, 1812. On Quincy's authorship, see
Edmund Quincy, *Life of Josiah Quincy*, 260.
[18] *Ann. of Cong.*, 12 Cong., 1 sess., 2196–2221; 2 sess., 1296–1310.
[19] Ames, *State Docs.*, 54 *et seq.*

Governor Strong consulted the council, and under their advice referred the issues to the state supreme court. To the governor's inquiries the judges replied that the Constitution gave no power either to President or Congress "to determine that either of the said exigencies do in fact exist." Not being delegated to the United States nor prohibited to the states, it must belong to the person designated by the state as commander of the militia, namely, the governor. Nor could an officer of the United States army command the militia, for by the Constitution of the United States the officers of the militia are to be chosen by the states.[20]

In Connecticut the council advised the governor to call a special session of the general assembly. The assembly supported his refusal to place militia under federal officers, believing that it was not "intended that they should be liable, on demand of the president . . . to be ordered into the service of the United States, to assist in carrying on an offensive war."[21] Other New England states took similar stands. Governor Chittenden of Vermont, addressing the assembly in October, 1813, was convinced that "it never could have been contemplated by the framers of our excellent constitution, who, it appears, in the most cautious manner, guarded the sovereignty of the States, or by the States, who adopted it, that the whole body of the militia were, by any kind of magic, at once to be transformed into a regular army for the purpose of foreign conquest."[22] Receiving the endorsement of the law-makers, the governor recalled the militia which had gone beyond the state's borders in the federal service, but the troops refused to heed his order.

The administration left the states which did not comply with the request for troops largely to their own defensive devices. For a time the British refrained from attacking them, hoping thereby to encourage the spirit of disunion. In 1814 they abandoned this lenient course and invaded the coast of Maine, then a part of Massachusetts. Besides carrying her share of national taxation the state was now under the necessity of assuming a load of special

[20] Art. I, sec. 8, par. 16.
[21] Ames, *State Docs.*, 62.
[22] *Ibid.*, 65.

taxation to meet extraordinary military expenditures for the defense of her territory. At the close of the war she presented a claim for these disbursements, and after thirteen years Congress consented to an appropriation of about half of the amount asked for, on condition that the state legislature renounce its former stand on the militia question.

This controversy had raised several constitutional issues: (1) who is the judge of the existence of the exigencies which permit the calling of the militia into the service of the United States? (2) must officers be called with the men, or can the men be placed under officers of the regular army? (3) can the militia be required to serve beyond the limits of their own states? (4) can they be required to serve outside of the United States?

The Supreme Court passed on several of these questions in the case of *Martin v. Mott*, decided in 1827.[23] Justice Joseph Story delivered the opinion of the court, which may be summarized as follows: The Constitution allows Congress to *provide* for calling forth the militia for the three purposes specified. By the act of 1795 Congress did so provide, authorizing the President to issue the call in any of the three contingencies. Under this statute he is the sole judge of the existence of the exigency, and when he has made his decision it is conclusive upon all others. The executive is in better position than any one else to make the decision. The militia when called are subject to the President or any superior officer whom he may place over them.

In later cases it has been held that officers as well as men should be called, although both may be placed under superior officers designated by the President. Militia may be sent beyond the bounds of their own states, but not beyond the borders of the United States, since there can be neither invasion, insurrection, nor occasion for enforcing United States law, on foreign soil. When, during the Spanish-American War, it was desired to send state troops to Cuba, they were mustered out of the service of their respective states and into that of the United States. This experience led to the revision of the laws and the organization of the national guard, under regulations which provide that men who en-

[23] 12 Wheaton 19 *et seq.*

list in the state militia become by the same act a part of the national military organization, subject to service on terms similar to those which govern the regular army.

NEW ENGLAND AND THE WAR

In December, 1813, Congress passed a new embargo as a war measure. This added a new grievance to those under which New England was already groaning, and it was believed that the act was intended to punish that section for its obstruction of federal policies. When the legislature of Massachusetts met early in 1814 many memorials and remonstrances from town meetings were referred to a committee which made a report in February summarizing the grievances of the section. The report complains of the admission of new states, the war, and especially of the recent embargo, and points to the sovereignty reserved to the states as intended to protect their citizens "from acts of violence by the United States, as well as for purposes of domestic regulation. We spurn the idea that the free, sovereign and independent State of Massachusetts is reduced to a mere municipal corporation, without power to protect its people, and to defend them from oppression, from whatever quarter it comes. Whenever the national compact is violated, and the citizens of this state are oppressed by cruel and unauthorized laws, this legislature is bound to interpose its power, and wrest from the oppressor his victim. This is the spirit of our Union, and thus has it been explained by the very man, who now sets at defiance all the principles of his early political life. The question . . . is not a question of power or right with this legislature, but of TIME AND EXPEDIENCY." As a measure promising relief and not yet tried the committee recommended "the Wise and Good, of those States, which deem themselves oppressed, to assemble . . . and to propose, urge, and even insist upon such explicit declarations of power, or restriction, as will prevent the most hardy from any future attempts to oppress, under the color of the constitution." The calling of the convention was left to the next legislature, which would "come from the people still more fully possessed of their views and wishes." [24]

[24] Ames, *State Docs.*, 72 *et seq.*

The next session did not take up the proposal of a convention, as the embargo was repealed before it assembled. But the conscription bill and bill for the enlistment of minors raised new causes of discontent. In Congress Daniel Webster said that if these measures were enacted it would become the duty of state governments to interpose their authority to prevent their enforcement. That, he asserted, was among the purposes for which those governments existed.[25] While the conscription bill was pending the Connecticut legislature adopted resolutions denouncing it as "utterly subversive of the rights and liberties of the people of this state, and the freedom, sovereignty, and independence of the same, and inconsistent with the principles of the constitution of the United States," and requesting the governor to convoke the general assembly in special session in case the bill or one like it should be passed, "to the end that opportunity may be given to consider what measures may be adopted to secure and preserve the rights and liberties of the people of this state, and the freedom, sovereignty and independence of the same."[26]

At about the same time a special session of the Massachusetts legislature met to take up the matter of additional military forces for the defense of the state. Besides providing for a force of ten thousand men, the session adopted a committee report recommending anew a convention of delegates from the northeastern states, and sent out a call on October 17 for a meeting at Hartford. In this call the objects of the meeting were stated.[27] First mentioned was the problem of military defense, but "it seems also expedient" to consider whether efforts should be made to procure amendments to the federal Constitution, if necessary by bringing about a convention of all the states in the Union.

The legislatures of Connecticut and Rhode Island, as well as that of Massachusetts, chose delegates to meet at Hartford. Those of New Hampshire and Vermont did not act, but delegates came from some of the counties in those states. In all twenty-six dele-

[25] When the *Annals of Congress* were printed in the thirties, Webster prevented the inclusion of this speech. See Claude H. Van Tyne, ed., *Letters of Daniel Webster*, 56.
[26] Ames, *State Docs.*, 76–77.
[27] *Ibid.*, 80.

gates assembled in December and spent three weeks in deliberation.

The secrecy of the sessions of the Hartford Convention caused grave apprehension on the part of friends of the administration. President Madison stationed troops in the neighborhood ostensibly to engage in recruiting but really to watch what went on. It was generally believed that the leaders contemplated secession, and the utterances of some of the radical Federalists lent color to the surmise. One of them, writing in the Boston *Advertiser*, urged the Hartford meeting to recommend that the states declare the Constitution "suspended." The *Centinel* of the same city announced Connecticut's decision to send delegates to Hartford as the rearing of the "second pillar of a new federal edifice." Gouverneur Morris said that the deeds of Congress were "indifferent to one whose eyes are fixed on a Star in the East, which he believes to be the day spring of freedom and glory. The traitors and madmen assembled at Hartford will, I believe, if not too tame and mild, be hailed hereafter as the patriots and sages of their day and generation."

Vague as these expressions were, they indicated that undercurrents were flowing which carried more radical possibilities than the words of the formal call indicated. Now and then an individual proposed an effort to achieve definite ends. Thus "Refederator," who was quoted with apparent approval by many papers, wanted, not the secession of New England, but the expulsion of the western states from the Union. "Let the Western States go off," he urged; "then let us, who belonged to the old family, try, by the agency of such men as are to meet at Hartford . . . to revise our family compact."

The gathering seems in truth to have been quite mild in temper. The man chosen to act as president, George Cabot, was a moderate man, sixty-two years of age at the time. Although one of the founders of the Federalist party, he had said to Pickering in 1813, "Why can't you and I let the world ruin itself in its own way?" The persistent report that under cover of secrecy treasonable proposals were discussed in the convention led to the publication of its journal after a few years. It showed no evidence to support the rumors, and members declared that it recorded every motion and vote, and that no proposal was made to divide the Union, organize a separate government, or form any foreign alliance.[28]

The convention issued a report making certain recommendations to the states represented, and formulated certain demands to be made upon the federal administration.[29] These demands took the form of amendments to the Constitution: apportionment of taxes and representatives in the House on the basis of free population; a two-thirds vote of both houses for the admission of new states, the interdiction of foreign commerce, or the declaring of war; the limitation of embargoes to sixty days; the disqualification of naturalized citizens for federal office; and the limitation of the President's tenure to a single term, no two Presidents to come in succession from the same state. The first of these proposals sprang from long-standing dissatisfaction with the three-fifths compromise; the rest from jealousy of Virginia and the growth of the West. Looking backward it is doubtful if any one of the changes would have been wise.

Massachusetts and Connecticut appointed commissioners to present the demands at Washington. In spite of appearances, most of the Federalists probably wished for nothing more than a redress of their supposed grievances. It is more than doubtful whether a majority of the people in any New England state would have supported secession. On the way to Washington the commissioners learned that peace had been agreed upon, and realizing that the moment was inauspicious for completing their errand they quietly turned their faces homeward.

The most radical of the recommendations made to the states by the convention was that the legislature of each should adopt measures to protect its citizens from acts of Congress subjecting them to "drafts, conscriptions, or impressments" not authorized by the Constitution.[30] In January, 1815, the Connecticut legislature in special session passed "An Act to secure the rights of Parents, Masters and Guardians," which declared the act of Congress per-

---

[28] S. E. Morison thinks that Pickering tried in vain to steer the convention towards secession. *The Life and Letters of Harrison Gray Otis,* I, 269–270.

[29] Ames, *State Docs.,* 83–86.

[30] The constitutionality of conscription by the United States was upheld by the Supreme Court in 1918 in the Selective Draft Cases, 245 U. S. 366.

mitting the enlistment of minors without the consent of parents or guardians to be "repugnant to the spirit of the constitution of the United States, and an unauthorized interference with the laws and rights of this State." The measure required judges to release on habeas corpus all minors so enlisted, and subjected to fine or imprisonment any person concerned in such enlistment who should remove any such minor out of the State.[31] Massachusetts passed a similar law the next month,[32] and only the end of the war, in all probability, prevented conflict between the federal government and the authorities of these states. No more out and out attempt at nullification was made prior to 1832.

The amendments proposed by the Hartford Convention failed to obtain the endorsement of any states except Massachusetts and Connecticut.[33] Nine legislatures passed dissenting resolutions. These were Vermont, New York, New Jersey, Pennsylvania, Virginia, North Carolina, Ohio, Tennessee, and Louisiana. Three states gave their reasons for disapproval. The merits of the amendments were hardly dealt with fairly, however, as they were viewed as the fruits of the spirit of faction. The New Jersey report will illustrate the type of response elicited: "The . . . master principle pervading all the propositions . . . is to reduce within a narrower sphere the power and influence of the general government, and thereby weaken its arm, at a time when, above all others, it requires to be strengthened. Their obvious tendency also, is, to throw amongst the states of the union the apple of discord—to increase those jealousies and suspicions, which have been already too far excited, and to give new life, activity and nurture to those seeds of dissention [sic] and disunion which have been recently sown with an unsparing hand by insidious combinations and associations, all of them professing to promote the general good, but acting in direct opposition to their professions."

[31] Ames, State Docs., 76.
[32] Ibid.
[33] Ames, State Docs., 86–88.

XVII

BROAD CONSTRUCTION IN CONGRESS

THE UNITED STATES BANK

THE War of 1812 was one of the most futile of conflicts, judged by the contrast between its avowed purposes and its achievements. Yet it possesses significance for constitutional history because of the impetus it gave to American nationality. Never before had the spirit of nationalism attained the vigor it showed at the close of this second contest with England.

The Republicans had been undergoing a process of nationalization from the beginning of their control of the federal government. Jefferson had won the presidency as the foe of centralized authority but the logic of circumstances had proved stronger than his theories. As he and his party had swung around in practice to the pattern of strong government set by the Federalists, the latter, aggrieved by administration policies, had defended themselves as best they could by seizing the weapons dropped by their opponents. Thus the two parties had actually exchanged positions. But the factional opposition of the war period had taught the whole country the danger of weakening the government by insistence on state sovereignty in a national crisis, and a marked reaction followed the Peace of Ghent.

The new temper was partly due also to the growth of the West, to the ascendancy of a group of new leaders, and to the novelty of the questions which claimed attention upon the return of peace. These new questions concerned domestic affairs which had been overshadowed by the issues arising in the sphere of foreign relations.

For several years the tone of Congress in discussing measures of reconstruction and domestic policy was strongly nationalistic. Within these years also the Supreme Court rendered several great decisions which served as it were to focus or crystallize the prevalent sentiment. It was not long, however, before dissent began to be manifest. The Presidents of the period, Madison and Monroe, were the first responsible persons to show a tendency to revert to more conservative positions; they revived the traditional Republican theories, and vetoed bills from time to time which they regarded as transgressing the limits of federal power, even when the ends sought met their approval. Nor was it long before sectional interests began to clash over the new issues; in consequence, divisions appeared in Congress and party lines tended to re-form. First the Federalist organization disintegrated and disappeared, discredited by its opposition to the war and undermined by the growth of the West where Republicanism proved to be more congenial to the situation and mood of the people. Next, a divergence of interest between the Old South and the new states of the Mississippi Valley disrupted the Republican Party. After the presidential election of 1824 these various elements began to recombine, giving rise first to the Jacksonian Democratic and National Republican parties, and then, after further shiftings, to the Democratic and Whig parties of the 1830's, 1840's, and 1850's.

Among the most important of the domestic questions of this new era was that of banking. Even during the Confederation the lack of a provision in the Articles authorizing Congress to establish a bank had been deplored, and both Madison and Jefferson had favored adding that power. Congress actually did incorporate the Bank of North America, and was sustained in this stretch of authority by a strained interpretation of the Articles. In the Constitutional Convention Madison proposed to give Congress a general power to grant charters of incorporation, but the suggestion was rejected because some delegates disliked the idea of a great central bank, and others feared the power might be used to create commercial monopolies.[1]

Under the Constitution, Hamilton's representations, as secretary of the treasury, concerning the utility of a bank as a fiscal agent of the government, supported by his plausible exposition of the theory of implied powers, wrung the twenty-year charter of the first United States Bank from a reluctant Congress. When that charter expired in 1811, the war had not yet brought its bitter

[1] Farrand, *Records,* II, 615–616.

experiences to show the necessity of such an institution. Albert
Gallatin, the secretary of the treasury, was aware of its value, but
sought in vain the renewal of the charter. Recharter bills were introduced in both houses and failed by narrow margins; in the lower
by a vote of 64 to 65, in the Senate by the casting vote of the Vice-
President.[2] The arguments of 1791 had not yet been forgotten.
Said Henry Clay, "the power to charter companies is not specified in
the grant, and I contend is of a nature not transferable by mere
implication." Others pointed to the foreign ownership of the
majority of the shares of stock, or predicted that the great bank
would wield a dangerous influence in politics. Friends of state
banks found a reason for opposition, as they had twenty years
earlier, in their economic interests. Some of the state legislatures
adopted resolutions denying the power of Congress to charter any
corporation.[3] The charter provision giving the bank the right
to establish branches within the states without obtaining their
consent was denounced in particular as an encroachment upon
their retained sovereignty.

Nevertheless the close votes show that many Republicans had
become friendly to the central bank, and following its dissolution,
the disorganization of the currency under the strain of war converted many others. By 1815 President Madison had come to
regard the constitutional issue as settled "by repeated recognitions
. . . of the legislative, executive, and judicial branches of the
Government, accompanied by indications . . . of a concurrence
of the general will of the nation." [4] Such "evidence of the public
judgment," he thought, necessarily superseded individual opinions.[5] In his message to Congress in that year he urged that steps
be taken to restore a "general medium of exchange," and in the
temporary absence of the money metals recommended that "if
the operation of the State banks can not produce this result, the
probable operation of a national bank will merit consideration." [6]

Thus Madison and his Republican followers adopted Hamilton's

[2] *Ann. of Cong.*, 11 Cong., 3 sess.
[3] Ames, *State Docs.*, 52–54.
[4] Richardson, *Messages*, I, 555.
[5] Letter to N. P. Trist, December, 1831. *Letters and Other Writings*, IV, 211.
[6] Richardson, *Messages*, I, 565–566.

policy. John C. Calhoun, of South Carolina, one of the group of new leaders which included Henry Clay of Kentucky and Daniel Webster of Massachusetts, was chairman of the committee which reported the bill chartering the Second Bank of the United States. The measure originated with A. J. Dallas, secretary of the treasury, and was drawn upon the model of the bill which Hamilton had drafted in 1791, but on a larger scale. The capital was increased from $10,000,000 to $35,000,000, and again the central bank was given the privilege of establishing branches in the states as needed. A new feature was a clause requiring the bank to pay to the government a bonus of $1,500,000 in return for its privileges. In presenting the bill in the House of Representatives Calhoun followed Madison in maintaining that the constitutional question was at rest, and that to discuss it would be "a useless consumption of time." [7] Clay, changing front, came to the support of the measure, explaining that in 1811 he had been instructed by his state to oppose the recharter of the first bank, but that "the force of circumstances, and the light of experience" had convinced him that the bank was indispensably necessary, and that Congress did possess the "constructive power" to incorporate it. Republican papers went so far as to reprint Hamilton's argument in support of the bill of 1791, as a justification of the action which their own party was now proposing. Oddly enough, the Federalists, led by Webster, were in opposition: the vote in the House stood 80 to 69, and of the 69 members who voted Nay, 38 were Federalists. The act received the President's signature in April, 1816.

INTERNAL IMPROVEMENTS

The War of 1812, which was fought in large part along the Canadian border amid wilderness conditions, emphasized the importance of military roads, and the rapid growth of the West which followed the return of peace made it imperative to improve the means of communication and transportation between the older and newer areas of population. Internal improvements became one of the pressing problems of the years following the war.

But the question was already an old one. Madison's proposal

[7] *Ann. of Cong.*, 14 Cong., 1 sess., 1189–1195.

in the Constitutional Convention to confer on Congress the power to incorporate had canal and road companies in contemplation quite as much as banks. From the beginning even the advocates of strict construction regretted the failure to include within the powers of Congress that of providing for internal improvements. When a surplus began to accumulate during Jefferson's second term he preferred to use it for public purposes, including the construction of roads and canals, rather than to cut it off by reducing import duties. He broached the matter in his message to Congress in 1806, carefully pointing out at the same time that an amendment to the Constitution would be necessary to authorize the expenditure of money for purposes which were not enumerated in the grant of power.[8] Congress having taken no action, Jefferson raised the question again after two years: "Shall the revenue be reduced? Or shall it not rather be appropriated to the improvement of roads, canals, rivers, education and other great foundations of prosperity and union, under the powers which Congress may already possess, or such amendment of the constitution as may be approved by the states? While uncertain of the course of things, the time may be advantageously employed in obtaining the powers necessary for a system of improvement, should that be thought best." [9]

This recommendation was followed, not by an amendment of the Constitution, but by a report prepared by Secretary of the Treasury Gallatin showing what improvements might wisely be made. Beyond a few miles of the Cumberland Road, however, no works were attempted before the War of 1812, for the policy of commercial restriction adopted by the government cut down the revenues as effectually as a reduction of duties would have done. In his first annual message after the war, President Madison advocated federal activity in this sphere with enthusiasm, but not without reminding Congress of the need of an amendment: "No objects within the circle of political economy so richly repay the expense bestowed on them; there are none the utility of which is more universally ascertained and acknowledged; none that do

[8] Richardson, *Messages*, I, 405 *et seq.*
[9] *Ibid.*, I, 451 *et seq.*

more honor to the governments whose wise and enlarged patriotism duly appreciates them. Nor is there any country which presents a field where nature invites more the art of man to complete her own work for his accommodation and benefit. These considerations are strengthened, moreover, by the political effect of these facilities for intercommunication in bringing and binding more closely together the various parts of our extended confederacy." [10] The general government was urged to supplement the undertakings of the states by additional works "requiring a national jurisdiction and national means." The hint of the need of amending the Constitution, after this glowing endorsement, seemed almost incidental: "It is a happy reflection that any defect of constitutional authority which may be encountered can be supplied in a mode which the Constitution itself has providently pointed out."

Madison found it necessary to repeat his recommendation before Congress responded. In his message of 1816 he wrote: "I particularly invite again . . . attention to the expediency of exercising . . . existing powers, and, where necessary, of resorting to the prescribed mode of enlarging them, in order to effectuate a comprehensive system of roads and canals, such as will have the effect of drawing more closely together every part of our country by promoting intercourse and improvements and by increasing the share of every part in the common stock of national prosperity." [11]

Overlooking the President's mild caution, Congress passed a bill appropriating the bonus of a million and a half paid by the United States Bank for its charter to finance the beginning of a comprehensive system of improvements. In presenting the bill from committee, John C. Calhoun explained that it could not be objected to as proposing that the government should itself construct roads or canals, for it "simply appropriates money for the purpose of improving the means of communication." [12] He found the authority for spending money on public improvements in the general welfare clause. To the argument that Congress could apply money only in execution of the enumerated powers, he replied: "If the

[10] *Ibid.*, I, 567 *et seq.*
[11] *Ibid.*, 576.
[12] *Ann. of Cong.*, 14 Cong., 2 sess., 851 *et seq.*

framers had intended to limit the use of the money to the powers afterwards enumerated and defined, nothing could be more easy than to have expressed it plainly. . . . Why should we be confined in the application of money to the enumerated powers? There is nothing in the reason of the thing, that he could perceive, why it should be so restricted; and the habitual and uniform practice of the Government coincided with his opinion. Our laws are full of instances of money appropriated without any reference to the enumerated powers. We granted, by an unanimous vote, or nearly so, fifty thousand dollars to the distressed inhabitants of Caraccas, and a very large sum at two different times, to the Saint Domingo refugees. If we are restricted in the use of our money to the enumerated powers, on what principle . . . can the purchase of Louisiana be justified? To pass over many other instances, the identical power which is now the subject of discussion, has, in several instances, been exercised. To look no further back, at the last session a considerable sum was granted to complete the Cumberland Road."

This "bonus bill" Madison vetoed, evidently for the purpose of emphasizing the method of enlarging constitutional powers which he regarded as the only safe and sound one: "Seeing that such a power is not expressly given by the Constitution, and believing that it cannot be deduced from any part of it without an inadmissible latitude of construction and a reliance upon insufficient precedents; believing also that the permanent success of the Constitution depends on a definite partition of powers between the General and the State Governments, and that no adequate landmarks would be left by the constructive extension of the powers of Congress as proposed in the bill, I have no option but to withhold my signature from it, . . . cherishing the hope that its beneficial objects may be attained by a resort for the necessary powers to the same wisdom and virtue in the nation which established the Constitution in its actual form and providently marked out in the instrument itself a safe and practicable mode of improving it as experience might suggest." [13]

The contrast in Madison's stand on the questions of the bank

[13] Richardson, *Messages*, I, 584 *et seq.*

and internal improvements is significant. In the case of the bank he regarded the issue as *res judicata*, as the result of the repeated action of the several branches of government and the evident acquiescence of the people. For lack of equally conclusive precedents he held that Congress was not warranted in passing internal improvement legislation resting on a constructive interpretation of its powers. He still believed, as he did in 1791, that Congress could collect and spend money only for the purposes enumerated in the Constitution. This, of course, was the position which Jefferson had taken while President. On the occasion of the veto the latter wrote to Gallatin: "I think the passage and rejection of this bill a fortunate incident. Every State will certainly concede the power; and this will be a national confirmation of the grounds of appeal to them, and will settle forever the meaning of this phrase [general welfare] which, by a mere grammatical quibble, has countenanced the General Government in a claim of universal power. . . ." [14] "Our tenet ever was . . . that Congress had not unlimited powers to provide for the general welfare, but was restrained to those specifically enumerated; and that, as it was never meant they should provide for that welfare but by the exercise of the enumerated powers, so it could not have been meant they should raise money for purposes which the enumeration did not place under their sanction; consequently, that the specification of powers is a limitation of the purposes for which they may raise money." He did not, however, attempt to show how this principle covered the purchase of Louisiana! Calhoun's challenging question remained unanswered.

In the debate on the bonus bill Philip P. Barbour of Virginia presented the Jeffersonian viewpoint in the House of Representatives. In a speech delivered two days after that of Calhoun he said: "It was certainly true, that internal improvement, upon an extended scale, by means of artificial roads and inland navigation, was in itself a desirable object. . . . But . . . whatever might be the expediency of the measure whatever advantage it might promise, he should feel himself constrained to vote against the bill, upon

[14] June 16, 1817. Ford, *Writings of Jefferson*, X, 90–92.

the ground, that it embraced objects not within the sphere of the constitutional powers of Congress." [15]

James Monroe came to the chief magistracy in 1817, a short time after this veto, entertaining views apparently quite in harmony with those of his illustrious fellow Virginians. In his inaugural address he referred to roads and canals as among the most important subjects which could claim the attention of Congress, but went out of his way, as some thought, to warn the law-makers that he had constitutional scruples concerning federal activity in that field.[16] Following up the topic in his first message, he wrote in the same vein: "As this subject was acted on by Congress at the last session, and there may be a disposition to revive it at the present, I have brought it into view for the purpose of communicating my sentiments on a very important circumstance connected with it with that freedom and candor which a regard for the public interest and a proper regard for Congress require. A difference of opinion has existed from the first formation of our Constitution . . . respecting the right of Congress to establish such a system of improvement. . . . I have bestowed on the subject all the deliberation which its great importance and a just sense of my duty required; and the result is a settled conviction in my mind that Congress do not possess the right. It is not contained in any of the specified powers granted to Congress, nor can I consider it incidental to or a necessary means, viewed on the most liberal scale, for carrying into effect any of the powers which are specifically granted. In communicating this result I cannot resist the obligation which I feel to suggest to Congress the propriety of recommending to the States the adoption of an amendment to the Constitution which shall give to Congress the right in question." [17]

Monroe's warning was as emphatic as Madison's had been mild. Yet his reference to "the right in question" was obscure, since it did not specify whether he referred to the right to construct works or merely to appropriate money for them—powers quite distinct. As he referred to the bonus bill, however, which involved only the

[15] *Ann. of Cong.*, 14 Cong., 2 sess., 893.
[16] Richardson, *Messages*, I, 585.
[17] *Ibid.*, II, 18.

latter power, it was a fair inference that he believed funds could be appropriated only for the purposes enumerated in the Constitution.

When Monroe's message of December, 1817, reached Congress, James Barbour of Virginia introduced in the Senate a resolution designed to set in motion the machinery of amendment. "Congress shall have power," ran his proposal, "to pass laws appropriating money for constructing roads and canals, and improving the navigation of water-courses; *Provided, however,* That no road or canal, shall be conducted in any State, nor the navigation of its waters improved, without the consent of such State: *And provided also,* That whenever Congress shall appropriate money to these objects, the amount thereof shall be distributed among the several States, in the ratio of representation which each State shall have in the most numerous branch of the National Legislature. But the portion of any State, with its own consent, may be applied to the purpose aforesaid, in any other State." [18]

Barbour's resolution was read twice, referred to a select committee, reported favorably, considered, and finally postponed indefinitely by a vote of 22 to 9. Meantime the portion of the presidential message relating to internal improvements was referred in the House of Representatives to a committee of which Henry St. George Tucker, like the President and the Barbours from Virginia, but not of the strict school, was chairman. This committee made a report rejecting the President's constitutional views and recommending once more that the bank bonus be set aside as a fund for roads and canals. Supporting the report the chairman spoke in March, 1818. Referring to the President's intimation that he would not sign any bill which Congress might pass unless an amendment were previously obtained, Tucker said: "I will not upon such a suggestion yield in hopeless despair the prospect of availing ourselves of the power vested in us by the Constitution. . . . If this House is to be dissuaded from an attempt to legislate on an important subject, by a suggestion of Executive opinion, its Constitutional powers are gone. . . ." "But why . . . not amend the Constitution? The answer is easy. Those who do

[18] *Ann. of Cong.,* 15 Cong., 1 sess., 21 *et seq.*

not believe we possess the power, are right in wishing an amendment. Those who believe we have it, would be wrong in referring it to the States; and as the Committee were of this opinion, they could not recommend an amendment. For, if an amendment be recommended, and should not be obtained, we should have surrendered a power, which we are bound to maintain if we think we possess it. . . . We must decide according to our conscience, on the Constitutional question, and not refer the matter to State decision." [19]

Several of the Virginia members spoke in opposition to Tucker, but he was eloquently supported by Henry Clay. Admitting that he had imbibed his political principles from "the celebrated production of Mr. Madison, when a member of the Virginia Legislature, of the period of 1799," he declared that "the attempt then was to destroy the Constitution by a plethora; but he begged the gentleman from Virginia [James Barbour] to reflect, that that was not the only malady by which the Constitution could be afflicted; another complaint, equally dangerous to that Constitution, was an atrophy; and if . . . I do not go along with them in the water-gruel regimen they would administer to the Constitution, in construing it to a dead letter, and reducing it to an inanimate skeleton, let me not be charged with abandoning principle, but let them answer to the charge of thus attenuating the strength of that instrument. . . ." Was the Constitution with its grant of power to establish post offices and post roads and to regulate commerce between the states (in all of which he found the implied power to build roads and canals) made for the Atlantic margin of the country only? "We . . . are not legislating for this moment only, or for the present generation, or for the present populated limits of these States; but our acts must embrace a wider scope— reaching northwestwardly to the Pacific, and more southwardly to the river Del Norte. Imagine this extent of territory covered with sixty, or seventy, or an hundred millions of people. The powers which exist in this Government now will exist then; and those which will exist then exist now." [20] Clay seemed to believe

[19] *Ibid.*, 1116 *et seq.*
[20] *Ibid.*, 1165 *et seq.*

that the doctrine of implied powers was adequate to provide for every new need as the Republic grew, and that the amending process should virtually be abandoned.

Clay and his friends did not rely merely upon the general welfare clause to support their program. As intimated in this speech they found ample constitutional warrant for constructing as well as financing federal internal improvements in several of the enumerated powers, particularly the authority to establish post offices and post roads, to make war (which they thought involved that of constructing military roads and canals), and to regulate interstate commerce. The House debate culminated in a series of votes on March 14, which tested the views of members on these several points. The votes showed that a fair majority of members believed that Congress had the power to *appropriate money* for post, military, and other roads, as well as canals, and for improving water courses, but not the power to *construct* post roads, military roads, and canals, or roads and canals needed in interstate commerce.[21] These votes revealed the rift between the old line Republicans and the new western branch of the party, and proved as well that the latter possessed too slight a majority to carry any measure over the veto of the President. The liberals had to be content for awhile with surveys of possible improvements such as the one made, at the direction of the House, in 1818, by Calhoun, who had entered Monroe's cabinet in 1817 as secretary of war.

Despite the firm convictions which the President professed in his first message, however, he was gradually shifting his position. While the discussion was in progress in Congress, he engaged in correspondence with ex-President Madison with reference to the appropriations for the Cumberland Road which Calhoun had mentioned as precedents for the bonus bill. The plans for the Cumberland Road had been made at the time of the admission of the State of Ohio; an agreement had then been entered into between Congress and the new state for the expenditure of a percentage of the proceeds of the sales of public lands situated within the state in the construction of a road to connect it with the Atlantic seaboard. In reply to Monroe's inquiry Madison gave his opinion

[21] *Ibid.*, II, 1380–1389.

that the case of the Cumberland Road differed from the improvements contemplated by the bonus bill, first, in "that the road was undertaken essentially for the accommodation of a portion of the country [that is, a portion just emerging from the territorial status] with respect to which Congress have a general power not applicable to other portions"; and second, in "that the funds appropriated, and which alone have been applied, were also under a general power of Congress [that is, derived not from taxes but from the sale of public lands], not applicable to other funds." He thought that as a precedent the case of this road was "without the weight allowed to that of the national bank," and that the arguments used on behalf of the bonus bill threatened the genuine sense of the Constitution "not only by an unwarrantable latitude of construction, but by the use of precedents which cannot be supposed to have had in the view of their authors the bearing contended for." [22]

As a result of his reflections and consultations Monroe arrived at the conclusion that it was not beyond the power of Congress to appropriate money for the construction of improvements if they were of more than local importance. He was by no means converted to the views of Calhoun and Clay, and in May, 1822 vetoed a bill providing for the collection of tolls for the upkeep of the Cumberland Road, on the ground that the punishment of violators of the act would infringe upon the police power of the states.[23] Again he emphasized the desirability of a comprehensive system of improvements carried out under a new grant of power. In the case of the Cumberland Road the legislature of each state through which it passed had been asked to approve the route and provide for the condemnation of the land, the United States exercising no act of jurisdiction or sovereignty. Existing constitutional limitations hampered the federal government, which should have the "right to take up the subject on principle; to cause our Union to be examined by men of science, with a view to such improvements; to authorize commissioners to lay off the roads and canals in all proper directions; to take the land at a valuation if necessary,

[22] Dec. 27, 1817. *Letters and Other Writings*, III, 55 *et seq.*
[23] Richardson, *Messages*, II, 142 *et seq.*

and to construct the works; to pass laws with suitable penalties for their protection; and to raise a revenue from them, to keep them in repair, and make further improvement by the establishment of turnpikes and tolls, with gates to be placed at proper distances. . . . This power will operate, like many others now existing without affecting the sovereignty of the States except in the particular offices to be performed. . . . The right of Congress to protect the works by laws imposing penalties would operate on the same principles as the right to protect the mail. The act being punishable only, a jurisdiction over the place would be altogether unnecessary and even absurd." As such new powers could be vested in the United States only by means of an amendment, the President was of the "opinion that such an amendment ought to be recommended to the States for their adoption. . . . The power should be confined to great national works only."

When Monroe in his annual message in December of the same year reminded Congress of the need of the amendment, that part of the message was referred by the House to a special committee. On January 15, 1823, Robert R. Reid of Georgia reported from this committee a resolution reading "Congress shall have power to establish and construct roads and canals." Reid declared that he himself believed that Congress already possessed the power in question, but that in view of the diversity of opinion and the President's recommendation it seemed wise to obtain an amendment "in terms so explicit as to preclude all dispute." [24]

After one reading the resolution was laid on the table. Its terms were too sweeping; but a new proposal, more guardedly phrased, fared little better. This second attempt, in February, 1823, was in the form of a joint resolution providing that "Congress shall have power to adopt and execute a system of internal improvements, confined to great national purposes." After a second reading this resolution, like its predecessor, was laid on the table by the Senate.[25] One more effort was made, in January, 1824, when a resolution was introduced in the Senate by Martin Van Buren of New York, who hoped by an amendment to break

[24] *Ann. of Cong.*, 17 Cong., 2 sess.
[25] *Ibid.*, 200.

the deadlock. Assuming that it was agreed that it was desirable to have government funds spent upon internal improvements under such restrictions as would guard the sovereignty and equal interests of the states, he appealed to those who believed that Congress had the power without an amendment, to consent to one, "to place the matter on well defined ground" and end the conflict.[26] His resolutions differed from Barbour's of 1817 only in proposing that Congress should "have power to make roads and canals" instead of merely power to appropriate money to promote their construction. Van Buren's effort shared the fate of the earlier proposals.

Meantime the President had taken the initiative. In spite of his scruples Monroe was thoroughly friendly to improvements and desired to make full use of such constitutional powers as the federal government possessed. Unable to obtain the comprehensive grant by amendment which he sought, he completely abandoned the position he had taken in 1817, and informed Congress in his annual message of 1823 that in his opinion an appropriation might be made to aid the projected Chesapeake and Ohio canal, the jurisdiction remaining in the states through which it would pass. He also submitted the question "whether it may not be advisable to authorize by an adequate appropriation the employment of a suitable number of the officers of the Corps of Engineers to examine the unexplored ground during the next season and to report their opinion thereon," extending their examination to the several routes proposed for connecting the Ohio with Lake Erie.[27]

The President and the liberals in Congress had at last found common ground. A bill for a general survey was the result of the message, and all members who were in favor of any of the many mooted projects for connecting eastern and western waters united in its support. New England and the South Atlantic states supplied the chief opposition, since neither of these sections was

---

[26] *Ibid.*, 18 Cong., 1 sess., 136.

[27] Richardson, *Messages*, II, 216. There is reason to believe that Monroe's change of attitude was due at least in part to the discovery that his original view tended to make him unpopular with the people of the West.

likely to profit by any works which might result. Especially in the latter the new improvement policy was a factor in bringing about a reaction against nationalism. But Monroe had opened the flood gates, and while he insisted that federal aid should be given only to works of general, not local, value, under his successors congressional appropriations to assist projects fostered by states and private corporations became the order of the age. Subscriptions for stock in corporate undertakings were supplemented under President John Quincy Adams by land grants to states which undertook to construct canals. Jackson's famous Maysville Road veto was an attempt to recall the country to Monroe's principle that only works of general importance should receive federal aid. This effort to stem the tide was of no avail, and little by little conservative views gave way until it became possible for the Supreme Court to rule in 1888 that Congress has authority, under its power to regulate interstate commerce, to empower corporations to construct railways and other highways across states without their consent.[28] It would seem to follow that the federal government possesses the power to protect such works within the states independently of the police jurisdiction of the states—the identical power which Monroe believed required an amendment. Another growth from these beginnings was the continuous series of river and harbor appropriations, known as the "pork barrel," because of the scramble in which states engaged to get their share of federal largesse for local works. After the Civil War even representatives of the southern states joined in the mad scramble. The pork barrel cannot be overlooked as a factor in the destruction of state's rights republicanism of the early Jeffersonian type.

[28] California v. Central Pacific Ry. Co., 127 U. S. 1.

XVIII

THE SUPREME COURT AND THE CONSTITUTION

THE BANK CASES

THE discussion which has been traced shows that although the general course of development in the era of Monroe's presidency was nationalistic, there was a strong undercurrent of dissatisfaction. The constitutionality of federal internal improvements did not come before the Supreme Court in the years under consideration, but the history of the Second Bank of the United States illustrates the conflicting tendencies, and presents besides the contribution of the court to nationalistic patterns of thought. Not long after the establishment of the bank hard times broke upon the country. The jealousy which the friends of the state banks felt towards the federal corporation was now reinforced by popular discontent due to the belief that the latter was responsible for much of the distress. An investigation made by Congress revealed various abuses in its administration, and showed that defalcations had occurred in some of the branches, especially the one at Baltimore. On March 19, 1819, the legislature of Pennsylvania, the state in which the central office was located, passed resolutions recommending the adoption of an amendment to the Constitution forbidding the establishment by Congress of any bank outside of the District of Columbia. Tennessee, Ohio, Indiana, and Illinois concurred in the resolutions, and the proposal was laid before Congress early in 1820.[1] No action followed.

Meantime some of the states attempted to take matters into their own hands. Although by the Constitution the citizens of each state were entitled to the privileges and immunities of citizens in the several states, corporations were unknown to the Constitution, and it seemed to many that retained "sovereignty" warranted any state in excluding a "foreign" corporation at its discretion. It

[1] Ames, *State Docs.*, 89–92.

also seemed feasible to drive branches of the United States Bank from any state where they were unwelcome, by means of special taxation. Maryland was the pioneer in this type of experiment. A law of that state went into effect on May 1, 1818 requiring all banks or branches of banks doing business within the state, except those chartered by it, to print their notes on stamped paper sold by the state, or as an alternative to pay the sum of $15,000 annually into the state treasury. When the cashier of the Baltimore branch of the United States Bank failed to comply with this law, a suit was instituted against him and eventually the highest Maryland court gave judgment for the state. Thereupon the cashier, McCulloch, took the case on writ of error to the Supreme Court of the United States.[2]

The counsel for Maryland held that the powers of the general government are delegated by the states, and are "to be exercised in subordination to the states, who alone possess supreme dominion." Reviving Jefferson's argument of 1791, they contended that Congress did not have the constitutional right to charter the bank. Even more plausible was the argument that, granting the power to incorporate a central bank, Congress could not authorize it to establish branches in the states without their consent. Finally it was argued that the power of taxation was a sovereign power of the state from which no such institution as the bank could gain immunity by virtue of congressional incorporation. It was denied, moreover, that the branches were set up for the convenience or use of the government; it was alleged, on the contrary, that they were created solely at the will of the directors who regarded only the matter of profit for the stockholders. "The power to raise the bank is founded on no provision of the constitution that has the most distant allusion to such an institution . . . the bank is created by . . . a very subtle course of reasoning. . . ." Then "this creature of construction claims the right to enter the territory of a state without its assent; to carry on its business when it pleases, and where it pleases, against the will, and perhaps in contravention of the policy, of the sovereign owner of the soil . . . and not contented with having obtained two rights in this extraordinary way,

[2] McCulloch v. Maryland, 4 Wheaton 316.

the fortunate adventurer assails the sovereignty of the state, and would strip from it its most vital and essential power. . . ."

The Maryland case raised three main issues: the power of Congress to incorporate a bank, which included the question of the validity of the doctrine of implied powers; the power of Congress to authorize a corporation to do business within a state without the latter's consent; and the right of a state to tax such a corporation. It involved incidentally questions concerning sovereignty, the scheme of distributed powers, and the old problem as to who is the judge of the actual assignment of powers in case of dispute between the nation and a state over the assignment. In dealing with cases involving such fundamental issues the Supreme Court found itself playing the part of a pioneer. Marshall had frequent occasion to consider the basic philosophy on which the American government rests because it bore directly upon the decisions to be given, and was thus led into expositions which his critics regarded as *obiter dicta*. The body of constitutional precedents which he built up is of almost incalculable significance in our history, and he must forever rank with Hamilton and Jefferson as one of the great architects of our actual constitutional system, as contrasted with the document inscribed on paper in 1787. But it must be admitted that his expositions rested upon a philosophy which was not universally accepted, and that another statesman in his position might have given our development a very different direction.

The assumption by the Maryland counsel that the states alone possess supreme dominion led Marshall, in rendering the decision of the court, to examine the origin of the Constitution and the duality of the system of government. His language is somewhat confusing to the modern reader, because, following the fashion of his generation, he spoke in terms of divided sovereignty where today one would talk of distributed powers. "In America," he said, "the powers of sovereignty are divided between the government of the Union, and those of the States. They are each sovereign, with respect to the objects committed to it, and neither sovereign with respect to the objects committed to the other." But the source of their authority is the people. "The government proceeds directly from the people . . . the assent of the states, in their

sovereign capacity, is implied in calling a convention, and thus submitting" the Constitution "to the people" who were at liberty to
accept or reject. Their act could not be negatived by the state
governments, and "the constitution, when thus adopted, was of
complete obligation, and bound the state sovereignties." "The
nation, on those subjects on which it can act, must necessarily bind
its component parts," for the people have ordained that the Constitution and the laws of the United States shall be the supreme law of
the land. Of course even Jefferson agreed with Marshall's premise that states have a portion of sovereignty, and would not have
combatted his assertion of the supremacy of the United States
within its own sphere. But Marshall's assumption that the United
States, through the judiciary, was judge of its own powers, was
what Jefferson had denied for many years. The incompetence of
any state to interfere with any constitutional act of Congress was
self-evident; but who was to say whether an act of the national
government was or was not constitutional? This fundamental issue
Marshall treated as non existent.

Having thus asserted that federal law was supreme within its
sphere, Marshall examined the power of Congress to incorporate
the bank. The argument of Maryland's counsel that the power to
create a corporation appertains to sovereignty he did not admit as
conclusive, since both states and nation were sovereign within
their respective spheres. The question was, rather, he said, "to
what portion of sovereignty does it appertain?" The power to
establish a bank is not among the enumerated powers of Congress,
but the Constitution, unlike the Articles of Confederation, does not
exclude all powers not expressly granted, leaving the question as to
any particular power to depend on a fair construction of the whole
instrument.

While it cannot be contended, he continued, that the enumerated powers draw others of inferior character with them merely
because they are inferior, it is reasonable to believe that a government entrusted with such ample powers must also be entrusted
with ample means for their execution. The Constitution does not
profess to enumerate the means. The "necessary and proper"
clause is added to give Congress the choice of means in executing

the enumerated powers, and the word "necessary" is not used in a sense which limits the choice to such means as are indispensable. The clause is intended to enlarge rather than restrict the powers of Congress, and is placed among the powers and not among the limitations. If intended as a limitation, it would be phrased in some such terms as "in carrying into execution the foregoing powers, . . . no laws shall be passed but such as are necessary and proper," etc. "We think the sound construction of the constitution must allow to the national legislature that discretion, with respect to the means by which the powers it confers are to be carried into execution, which will enable that body to perform the high duties assigned to it, in the manner most beneficial to the people. Let the end be legitimate, let it be within the scope of the constitution, and all means which are appropriate, which are plainly adapted to that end, which are not prohibited, but consist with the letter and spirit of the constitution, are constitutional." "After the most deliberate consideration, it is the unanimous and decided opinion of this court, that the Act to incorporate the Bank of the United States is a law made in pursuance of the Constitution, and is a part of the supreme law of the land."

The power of states to exclude from their limits corporations not chartered by themselves was later to become an issue of great importance. After many years the rule became established that a corporation engaged in activities falling under federal control, such as interstate commerce, cannot be excluded by a state. Yet Marshall passed by this point in the argument of the Maryland case, to take up the question whether the state could constitutionally lay a tax upon the branch of the United States Bank. Having already determined that the bank was a legitimate creation of Congress as an agency in the performance of federal functions, it was easy to deny the state's power to tax it. The power to tax was the equivalent of the power to destroy. "If we apply the principle for which the State of Maryland contends, to the constitution generally, we shall find it capable of changing totally the character of that instrument. We shall find it capable of arresting all the measures of the government, and of prostrating it at the foot of the States. . . . This principle would transfer the supremacy, in fact, to the

State. . . ." In short, the power to tax, instead of being the sovereign power which Maryland counsel had called it, is limited by the extent of the sovereignty which the people of a single state possess. Under this principle the state cannot interfere with powers conferred by the people of the United States upon the government of the Union, or with the means employed by that government in carrying those powers into execution. The principle avoids the danger of a clash of sovereignties, but it "does not deprive the states of any resources which they originally possessed. It does not extend to a tax paid by the real property of the bank, in common with the other real property within the state, nor to a tax imposed on the interest which the citizens of Maryland may hold in this institution, in common with other property of the same description throughout the state." But the tax involved in the suit "is a tax on the operations of the bank, and is, consequently, a tax on the operation of an instrument employed by the government of the Union to carry its powers into execution. Such a tax must be unconstitutional."

Kentucky and Ohio vied with Maryland in efforts to drive the branches of the United States Bank from their borders by taxation. The *Kentucky Herald* greeted the Maryland decision with the comment: "This monster of iniquity is to be saddled upon us. We are to be taxed by a corporation unknown to the Constitution, and known to us only by its oppressive and vindictive acts. . . . If the bank may tax us without our consent, and if these branches are to be free from State taxation, we had better give up our Constitution and return to the condition of a territory." [3] Since, of course, the branches in the state refused to pay the state tax, the governor urged the legislature "to inquire how far it was compatible with the supreme power of the State to be manacled, . . . for, if one department of the national Government could usurp the sovereignty of the States and another department consecrate the usurpation by calling it constitutional, State sovereignty was a fit subject of derision." The assembly responded by passing several acts intended to place the Bank of the United States at a disadvantage by discriminations against its notes.

[3] Quoted by McMaster, *History*, IV, 505.

In Ohio a branch was established at Cincinnati in the spring of 1817, and another at Chillicothe, a year later.[4] In February, 1819, the legislature levied a tax of $50,000 per annum on each branch. This tax remaining unpaid, an act was passed six months after the McCulloch decision, requiring the state auditor to levy upon the chattels of the branches. Disregarding a restraining order issued by the United States circuit court at Chillicothe, Osborn, the state auditor, sent one Harper armed with his warrant, who seized funds to the amount of the tax in the vaults of the Chillicothe branch and carried them to the capital. The bank brought both criminal and civil suits against the auditor and his agent. The criminal suit was soon dismissed, but the action for recovery of the seized funds was pending in the United States court when the state legislature met in December, 1820. One of its first acts was to appoint a committee to canvass the bank question.

The report of the committee reviewed the relations of the state with the United States Bank and declared that the action against the state officials was in effect a suit against the state, forbidden by the eleventh amendment.[5] Citing the Virginia and Kentucky Resolutions of 1798, which the committee declared had been approved by the people in the election of 1800, the report denied the right of the federal courts to act as the final interpreters of the Constitution where the sovereign rights of the states are in question, maintaining, on the contrary, that the states have an equal right to interpret the Constitution for themselves. The committee recommended that an attempt be made to compromise, the state agreeing to refund the sum seized on condition that the bank discontinue its suit and withdraw its branches from the state. In conclusion, to vindicate the authority of the state, the report recommended that the legislature outlaw the bank "forbidding the keepers of our jails from receiving into their custody any person committed at the suit of the Bank of the United States, or for any injury done to them; prohibiting our judicial officers from taking acknowledgments of conveyances where the Bank is a party, or when made for their use, and our recorders from receiving or re-

[4] *Ibid.*, 497–504.
[5] Ames, *State Docs.*, 93–101.

cording such conveyances; forbidding our courts, justices of the peace, judges and grand juries from taking any cognizance of any wrong alleged to have been committed upon any species of property owned by the Bank, or upon any of its corporate rights or privileges, and prohibiting our notaries public from protesting any notes or bills held by the Bank or their agents or made payable to them."

In the case against Osborn the bank won in the circuit court, and when the defendant appealed to the Supreme Court a judgment rendered on March 19, 1824, affirmed that of the lower court.[6] Following the Maryland precedent, Ohio's tax law was pronounced unconstitutional, and the state officials were directed to return the tax money to the branch bank at Chillicothe.

The contention that the State of Ohio was a party to the suit, and that consequently the action was barred by the eleventh amendment, was held to be untenable. A Kentucky newspaper said that this part of the decision repealed the amendment. In truth, although not the first, it was one of a series of decisions the net effect of which was to circumscribe the amendment rather narrowly. Marshall made perhaps too much of the fact that the state was not a party of record. More important was the transfer to constitutional law of the old English principle that an agent who inflicts a wrong cannot shift the responsibility for his deed. Consequently the agent of a state, acting under authority of a statute which the state is without power to pass, is individually liable for wrongs inflicted. In the words of a later decision of the Supreme Court, "If . . . an individual, acting under the assumed authority of a State, as one of its officers, and under color of its laws, comes into contact with the superior authority of a valid law of the United States, he is stripped of his representative character, and subjected in his person to the consequences of his individual conduct." [7]

Carrying out the recommendation of its committee the Ohio legislature had passed a bill on January 29, 1821, entitled "An Act to

[6] Osborn *et al. v.* the Bank of the United States, 9 Wheaton 738.
[7] *In re* Ayers, 123 U. S. 443 (1887). See Daniel H. Chamberlain, "Osborn *v.* The Bank," and W. C. Coleman, "The State as a Defendant under the Federal Constitution."

withdraw from the Bank of the United States the protection of the laws of this State in Certain Cases,"[8] with the intent to "leave the Bank exclusively to the protection of the federal government" and to test the constitutional power of the latter "to preserve it in the sense maintained by the Supreme Court" in the McCulloch decision. The Osborn decision did not touch this act directly, although Marshall did say that "if the courts of the United States cannot rightfully protect the agents who execute every law authorized by the constitution, from the direct action of state agents in the collection of penalties, they cannot rightfully protect those who execute any law." This statement, of course, did not cover a case of passive resistance such as the Ohio act contemplated, and in view of the solicitude for the jurisdiction of the states which Monroe showed in vetoing the Cumberland Road Bill of 1822, it is doubtful whether the federal government would have attempted to force the bank upon Ohio in the face of the outlaw act. After the Civil War, however, the fourteenth amendment forbade a state to "deny to any person within its jurisdiction the equal protection of the laws"; and since the word "person," included corporations ("artificial persons"), such a measure as Ohio's outlaw act would have been illegal thereafter. Moreover, the right of a state to exclude a corporation chartered by another state has been established, but an exception is made in the case of those serving as agencies of the federal government in the performance of its functions.

The operations of the United States Bank in these years created an interesting situation in the State of Georgia.[9] The bank had no branch in the state, but its habit of presenting notes of state institutions for redemption in specie led to legislation permitting the local banks to refuse specie payment if it appeared that the great corporation was the beneficiary. Out of such a refusal arose a suit of the latter against the Planters Bank, a state corporation. In its defense the state bank challenged the provision in the charter giving the United States Bank the right to sue in the federal courts. This case also reached the Supreme Court and was argued in connection with the Ohio case. The charter provision was up-

[8] *Acts of Ohio*, XIX, 108–110.
[9] Warren, *Sup. Court*, I, 628–631.

held, but issues came into view in this way which foreshadowed important developments of the 1840's.

These several cases touching the United States Bank marked significant advances in constitutional law. The Supreme Court gave its endorsement to the doctrine of implied powers, upheld the supremacy of federal law, and maintained its own right to draw the line between the powers of the states and those of the federal government. The right of states to tax agencies of the latter was denied, questions of sovereignty were clarified, the scope of the eleventh amendment was partially defined, and portentous problems concerning the rights of corporations were brought above the horizon. In the same years the court met successfully an attack upon its right to hear appeals from the highest state tribunals in causes involving federal law.

THE QUESTION OF APPELLATE JURISDICTION

Lord Fairfax, proprietor of rich lands in northern Virginia, had devised these lands to a nephew, Denny Martin, an Englishman.[10] In 1777, however, four years before Fairfax's death, the state confiscated the property of loyalists, and decisions of state courts from time to time held that aliens could not inherit Virginia lands. The treaty of 1783 with England promised that Congress would "earnestly recommend it to the legislatures of the respective States, to provide for the restitution of all estates . . . which have been confiscated," and by the Constitution treaties became a part of the supreme law of the land. In spite of the treaty and the recommendation of Congress, Virginia granted a portion of Martin's land to David Hunter, who brought suit to eject Martin. Prolonged litigation ensued. In 1810 the Virginia Court of Appeals upheld Hunter's claim, but on writ of error the case went to the Supreme Court of the United States under the title Fairfax's Devisee v. Hunter's Lessee.[11] Chief Justice Marshall, having in an early stage of the litigation represented Martin before the Virginia courts, absented himself from the bench during the hearing, and the decision was rendered by Justice Joseph Story, supported by

[10] *Ibid.*, I, 433–450.
[11] 7 Cranch 602.

the concurring opinions of two other justices. The three men who joined in the decision composed a majority of those sitting but not of a full bench. This abbreviated court issued a mandate to the Virginia court reversing the latter's decision on the ground that the act under which the Fairfax estate was confiscated was in conflict with the treaty. The rulings of state courts against inheritance of lands by aliens were disregarded.

Among the judges of the Virginia court of appeals was Spencer Roane, famous as a jurist of the Jeffersonian school, and no less as a critic of the United States courts in this period. The state judges, confronted by the mandate of the Supreme Court, decided that the twenty-fifth section of the Judiciary Act of 1789 was unconstitutional. "The court is unanimously of the opinion," they declared, "that the appellate power of the Supreme Court of the United States does not extend to this court under a sound construction of the constitution of the United States; that so much of the twenty-fifth section of the act of Congress to establish the judicial courts of the United States as extends the appellate jurisdiction of the Supreme Court to this court, is not in pursuance of the constitution of the United States; that the writ of error, in this cause, was improvidently allowed under the authority of that act; that the proceedings thereon in the Supreme Court were, *coram non judice*, in relation to this court, and that obedience to this mandate be declined by the court." [12]

Another writ of error brought the issue again to the Supreme Court under the title Martin *v.* Hunter's Lessee.[13] St. George Tucker, whom we have met as a liberal Virginian in the discussion of internal improvements, was associated with Samuel Dexter of Massachusetts as counsel for the state. Tucker said that Congress might provide for trial in federal courts of suits in which parties based their claims on federal law, but had no constitutional warrant for calling such cases on appeal from the state courts after trial there. The decision of the Supreme Court rejecting this argument was presented by Justice Story.

[12] On this case, and on the attitude in general of Virginia on the judiciary issues, see Henry H. Simms, *Life of John Taylor*, Chap. XI.
[13] 1 Wheaton 304.

Joseph Story was easily the greatest of Marshall's associates.[14] Reared in a Republican home in Massachusetts, he had risen within ten years after graduation from Harvard to a position of leadership at the New England bar. He had always held himself above party, or faction as he called it, and while generally respected and even admired by the Republicans, he was distrusted by the extremists, and was appointed to the bench by Madison in 1811 against Jefferson's advice. His first appearance before the Supreme Court was as an attorney in the case of Fletcher v. Peck, which will be discussed presently. Always a scholar in his tastes, he became a man of profound learning, versed in the Roman law and the English common law, and author of numerous legal treatises. In all the great cases decided while Marshall and he were colleagues his conclusions were in essential harmony with his chief's.

Writing the opinion of the court in the case of Martin v. Hunter's Lessee, Story explained the relations between federal and state jurisdiction. In passing the judiciary act Congress, he said, had proceeded on the "supposition that in all the cases to which the jurisdiction of the United States extends," it might rightfully have been vested in federal courts. Congress had preferred to allow some cases to be tried in state courts, but by so doing had not divested the federal tribunals of jurisdiction, including the right of appeal to the highest federal tribunal. Then in a brilliant epigram which illuminated the problem in hand, he declared: "It is the case, and not the court, that gives the jurisdiction."

The framers of the Constitution foresaw, he continued, that state courts would necessarily hear cases falling within the cognizance of the federal courts and would necessarily interpret the supreme law in the exercise of their ordinary jurisdiction; hence they included the provision that the Constitution, laws, and treaties of the United States should be the "supreme law of the land." As local courts would undoubtedly vary in their construction of this supreme law, uniformity of federal law throughout the country required that there be a central court of appeals or revision.

Five years later (1821) the Supreme Court decided the case of

[14] William W. Story, *Life and Letters of Joseph Story.*

Cohens *v.* Virginia, which arose from the fact that Cohens undertook to operate a lottery in the state under an act of Congress, in disregard of laws of that commonwealth forbidding lotteries.[15] When he was prosecuted and convicted in the state courts, he appealed to the Supreme Court on the ground that the case came under federal jurisdiction because his action was based on the law of Congress. In the sequel the court ruled that the act of Congress was not intended to override the police regulations of any state, and Cohens's claims were not upheld. But the immediate question raised by his appeal was the same question of jurisdiction as that involved in Martin *v.* Hunter's Lessee.

As in the previous case, counsel for Virginia argued that the appellate jurisdiction of the United States Supreme Court extended only to inferior courts of the same jurisdiction, that is, federal courts, and not to state courts which pertained to a different "sovereignty." Thus again the plea of the state disregarded the fact that the concurrent jurisdiction clauses of the Judiciary Act of 1789 had adopted the state courts into the federal system. State counsel contended also that since the state was a party to the suit, it could not be summoned to the bar of the Supreme Court on the appeal of Cohens, because of the prohibition imposed by the eleventh amendment.

As to jurisdiction the court ruled that the judicial department "is authorized to decide all cases, of every description, arising under the constitution or laws of the United States. From this general grant of jurisdiction, no exception is made of those in which a state may be a party," beyond the strict letter of the eleventh amendment, which forbids suits commenced against a state by a citizen of another state or country. In the case before it, the suit was not commenced by Cohens but by the state. "By a suit commenced by an individual against a State, we should understand the process sued out by that individual against the State, for the purpose of establishing some claim against it by the judgment of a court; and the prosecution of that suit is its continuance. Whatever may be the stages of its progress, the actor is still the same. . . . If a suit brought in one court, and carried by a legal process to a supervising

[15] 6 Wheaton 264.

court, be a continuation of the same suit, then this suit is not commenced or prosecuted against a State. It is clearly in its commencement the suit of a State against an individual, which suit is transferred to this court, not for the purpose of asserting any claim against the State, but for the purpose of asserting a constitutional defense against a claim made by a State." Being a continuation of the case originally begun against Cohens by the State, the eleventh amendment did not prohibit the present action.

THE OBLIGATION OF CONTRACTS

In a case decided before the War of 1812, that of Fletcher v. Peck,[16] the Supreme Court had made an interpretation of the provision of the Constitution which forbids the passage by any state of an act impairing the obligation of contracts. In this case the State of Georgia was involved. The legislature had made a grant of lands as the result, it later appeared, of bribery on the part of the grantees. A subsequent legislature had consequently annulled the grant. Meantime some of the lands had come into the possession of innocent third parties and the suit of Fletcher v. Peck involved the validity of the title of such innocent purchasers. The court held that the act making the grant was, so far as the rights of such purchasers were concerned, a contract which the legislature could not repudiate. Nor did the eleventh amendment deprive the court of jurisdiction.

Much more important in its influence was the case of Dartmouth College v. Woodward,[17] which involved the same provision of the Constitution. The legislature of the State of New Hampshire had, contrary to the wishes of the trustees of Dartmouth College, modified the charter granted to the institution in colonial days. The court held that such a charter was a contract which could be modified only by the mutual consent of the parties. Thus it appeared that the police power of a state, when once restricted by the terms of a charter granted to a corporation, was permanently sacrificed. As in the years which followed corporations became a favorite form of business organization, the principle of the Dartmouth

[16] 6 Cranch 87 (1810).
[17] 4 Wheaton 518 (1819).

College decision threatened to tie the hands of the states in regulating them, and the decision brought the court under suspicion
of unduly favoring "big business." Under the pressure of public
opinion the doctrine of the Dartmouth College decision was therefore later gradually modified.[18]

In this same year the court interpreted the relation of the bankruptcy clause of the Constitution to this provision against impairing the obligation of contracts. Holding that the power of Congress to pass a uniform rule of bankruptcy did not prevent the
states from dealing with the question so long as Congress did not
legislate, state bankruptcy laws were nevertheless held to be subject to the constitutional provision concerning the impairing of
the obligation of contracts. In the case of Sturges v. Crowninshield,[19] the court held invalid an act which discharged a debtor
from a contract made previous to its passage. In 1827, in the case
of Ogden v. Saunders,[20] however, the court upheld a state law
which discharged debtors from liability for debts incurred after the
passage of the act. This discharge was not to be regarded as valid
in case of a debt owed outside of the state since its police power
could not have operation beyond its limits. In both of these decisions the law existing at the time the contract was made was
virtually read into it and made a part of it.

THE REGULATION OF COMMERCE

Gibbons v. Ogden [21] was the first great case involving the interpretation of the constitutional provision which gives Congress
power "to regulate Commerce with foreign Nations, and among
the several States, and with the Indian Tribes." It appears that the
framers of the Constitution in adopting this clause had in mind
especially the confused condition of foreign commerce caused by
the conflicting systems of the states. Nothing seemed more vital
to them than a uniform system in commercial relations with other

---

[18] Between 1809 and 1824 eleven acts of eleven states were set aside wholly or
in part by the federal courts. For list of these cases see McMaster, *History*, V, 412,
note. *Cf.* Moore, "Federal Statutes Nullified by the Supreme Court," 151.
[19] 4 Wheaton 122 (1819).
[20] 12 Wheaton 213.
[21] 9 Wheaton 1 (1824).

countries. Utilizing this power, Congress at an early date passed registration and tonnage laws designed to protect American ships in their competition with foreign vessels trading with the United States. No question relating to interstate commerce came into prominence for more than a generation after the adoption of the Constitution. Then in 1824 the whole problem of the respective powers of states and federal government over commerce was brought forward by a suit arising from an act of the State of New York granting a monopoly of the use of steamboats in the navigation of the waters of the state. The grantees were Robert Fulton, the inventor of the steamboat, and his associate Robert R. Livingston, who had assigned their rights to Aaron Ogden, the operator of a steam ferry between New York City and Elizabethtown, New Jersey. Thomas Gibbons, a competitor who held no such license, was enjoined by the state courts, on Ogden's application, from operating his boats. Relying upon the fact that his vessels were duly registered and licensed under the laws of the United States governing the coasting trade, Gibbons carried the case to the Supreme Court. He alleged that the New York act violated the right of Congress to control commerce with foreign countries and among the states.

Ogden's counsel argued that this power of regulation was a concurrent power which the states might exercise in the absence of legislation by Congress; moreover, that the New York law regulated navigation only within the waters of the state, thus affecting interstate commerce only indirectly, as do quarantine laws, inspection laws, and other regulations the validity of which was not questioned. In other words, Ogden's counsel urged that the navigation of the waters of the state was controlled by the state under its police power.

The reasoning of counsel in Gibbons v. Ogden was epochal in character, due in part to the novelty of the questions discussed but also in large measure to the fact that several of the ablest lawyers in the country were engaged in the case.

On Ogden's side was Thomas J. Oakley, one of the luminaries of the New York bar, while opposed to him was Daniel Webster, then near the height of his career as an advocate. It is well to realize that to the arguments of such eminent attorneys, who were accustomed to bring to bear upon their cases vast knowledge of both American and English law, gained through habitual research as well as by preparation for pleading particular causes, the justices of the supreme bench in every period of our history are greatly indebted. The arguments of learned counsel have often been so comprehensive as to supply the bench with information essential to the right determination of causes, information which the most learned judge could not be expected to acquire through his individual studies. So it was in this first great commerce case. The justices were profoundly impressed by Webster's argument, and in rendering judgment Marshall in large part accepted his views. On the other hand, although Oakley lost his cause, his reasoning was hardly less influential on later decisions.

Oakley's plea was a masterly exposition of the doctrine that the power to regulate interstate and foreign commerce was not committed exclusively to Congress. The states had possessed the power, he reasoned, before the Constitution was adopted, and by that instrument it was neither expressly forbidden to them nor granted in exclusive terms to the Union. Nor was it by nature so incapable of concurrent exercise that the grant to Congress necessarily precluded any further employment by the states. The retention of the concurrent power was implied, he thought, in the restrictions which forbade states to enter into compacts or treaties with other states or nations, or to levy duties. Since these acts were prohibited, those not prohibited must be tacitly recognized.

Webster's argument, without quite rejecting outright the concept of concurrent power, tended distinctly towards the conclusion that the power to regulate commerce was by nature indivisible. "All useful regulation does not consist in restraint; and that which Congress sees fit to leave free, is a part of its regulation, as much as the rest." He evidently believed that the admission of the states' power to deal with a commercial matter on the ground that Congress had not yet done so would defeat the purpose of the constitutional provision, which he held was to empower Congress gradually, as need arose, to develop a *system*. State legislation, by regulating that which Congress intentionally left unregulated, would clash with the congressional plan. It was consequently incompatible with the congressional power of regulation.

The decision of the case did not require the court to determine which of these views was the correct one. Only one point was actually decided. This was that under a federal law, duly passed in pursuance of the power to regulate interstate and foreign commerce, Gibbons possessed a right to navigate the waters of the State of New York of which the attempted grant of a monopoly by the state could not deprive him. Marshall did, nevertheless, remark, relative to Oakley's arguments, "we think they do not establish the proposition they were intended to prove"; while referring to Webster's contention he said, "the court is not satisfied that it has been refuted." The public was justified in thinking that the chief justice had revealed his belief in the exclusiveness of the power of Congress, but his words were, strictly speaking, extrajudicial at this point.

Marshall, in giving the opinion of the court, first defined the word commerce broadly, as including navigation. "The completely internal commerce of a state may be considered as reserved for regulation by the state itself, but in regulating commerce with foreign countries and among the states the power of Congress does not stop at the jurisdictional lines of the several states." "If Congress has the power to regulate it, that power must be exercised wherever the subject exists. If it exists within the states, if a foreign voyage may commence or terminate at a port within a state, then the power of Congress may be exercised within a state. This principle is, if possible, still more clear when applied to commerce 'among the several States.' . . . The power of Congress . . . comprehends navigation within the limits of every State in the Union, so far as that navigation may be, in any manner, connected with 'commerce with foreign nations, or among the several States, or with the Indian tribes.' It may, of consequence, pass the jurisdictional line of New York, and act upon the very waters to which the prohibition now under consideration applies. . . ."

In the course of Webster's argument he had briefly examined the bearing of the state's police power upon the issue. The monopoly act of New York, he decided, was "not an inspection law, nor a health law," thus implying that if it were it might be regarded as a valid exercise of the police power, even though it could not be upheld on the basis of a concurrent power over commerce. Marshall's opinion went further into this phase of the discussion. "If a state . . . shall adopt a [valid] measure of the same character with one which Congress may adopt, it does not derive its authority from the particular power which has been granted [to Congress], but from some other which remains with the state, and may be executed by the same means. . . . Measures scarcely distinguishable from each other, may flow from distinct powers." Thus a state police measure may affect commerce and yet come within the legislative competence of the state, but it could not rest upon any claim to a share in the power over commerce. Moreover, in case of conflict between a state police measure and a federal regulation of commerce the latter would be paramount. Marshall's most significant words in exposition of the police power and its relations to commerce were the following:

"That inspection laws may have a remote and considerable influence on commerce will not be denied; but that a power to regulate commerce is the source from which the right to pass them is derived, cannot be admitted. . . . They form a portion of that immense mass of legislation, which embraces everything within the territory of a state, not surrendered to a general government; all which can be most advantageously exercised by the states themselves. Inspection laws, quarantine laws, health laws of every description, as well as laws regulating the internal commerce of a state, and those which respect turnpike roads, ferries, etc., are component parts of this mass." [22]

It is to be repeated that the decision in this case did not rest upon the ground that Congress has exclusive control over commerce.

[22] This police power "is the unclassified residuary power of government vested by the constitution of the United States in the respective States." W. W. Cook, "What is Police Power?" Marshall made use of the term in Brown v. Maryland. See Collins Denny, "Growth and Development of Police Powers." The term "internal police" was in use in colonial times to designate those matters of domestic concern over which it was believed each colony should have autonomous control. These matters were substantially identical with those reserved to the states by the tenth amendment.

Marshall's utterance left that point undetermined, and many persons continued to believe that the states and nation had concurrent power to regulate commerce, state regulations being valid as in bankruptcy until Congress exercised its superior authority. In the present case, the New York law was held to be invalid because it was in contravention of an act which Congress had already passed.

No dissent from Marshall's views in this case was expressed by any of the associate justices, but Justice Johnson presented a concurring opinion, in which he adopted without reservation the doctrine of the exclusiveness of the commercial power of Congress. "Since the power to prescribe the limits of its freedom necessarily implies the power to determine what shall remain unrestrained, it follows that the power must be exclusive; it can reside but in one potentate; and hence, the granting of this power carries with it the whole subject, leaving nothing for the State to act upon." Johnson went beyond both Webster and Marshall, although his view may very well have been suggested to him by Webster's argument. He also predicted, correctly, that "in the advancement of society, labor, transportation, intelligence, care, and various mediums of exchange" would "become the objects of commercial regulation."

Three years later (1827) in Brown v. Maryland [23] Marshall ruled that a state could not require an importing merchant to take out a license as a condition precedent to disposing of imported merchandise. By this judgment he rejected the argument of the future Chief Justice Taney, who appeared as counsel for Maryland, to the effect that the state's power of taxation was paramount to the federal government's power to regulate commerce. The state's power to tax, said Marshall, could not "be used to obstruct or defeat the power to regulate commerce." Under this power "Congress has a right, not only to authorize importation, but to authorize the importer to sell." With this process, including sale as the final step, the state could not interfere. Thus Marshall gave force to the view expressed in Gibbons v. Ogden, that in case of conflict between the police power of a state and the

[23] 12 Wheaton 434.

powers of the Union, when operating upon the same subject, the latter are paramount.[24]

The two decisions which have been analyzed were followed, in 1829, by the case of Willson v. Blackbird Creek Marsh Company.[25] The defendant company had been incorporated by the State of Delaware with permission to construct a dam across Blackbird Creek for the purpose of redeeming lowlands subject to tidal inundation, and owned by the company. Willson, owner of a brig licensed for the coasting trade, finding his vessel excluded by the dam from its customary navigation of the river, broke through the obstruction and was sued for trespass. His counsel contended that the Delaware act incorporating the company conflicted with the congressional power to regulate commerce and navigation. Counsel for the company maintained that Delaware was dealing with property rights within her own bounds, and was therefore acting within her police powers; and that the congressional power over commerce did not interfere with her freedom in such matters unless exercised. Each side cited Gibbons v. Ogden and sought to find in the judgment in that case precedents for its contentions.

In rendering the court's opinion in this case Marshall said: "If Congress had passed any act which bore upon the case; any act in execution of the power to regulate Commerce the object of which was to control State legislation over those small creeks . . . then a State law coming in conflict with such an act would be void. But Congress has passed no such law. . . . We do not think, that the Act empowering the Blackbird Creek Marsh Company to place a dam across the Creek can under the circumstances be considered as repugnant to the power to regulate Commerce in the Dormant state, or as being in conflict with any law passed on the subject."

This decision was generally misunderstood for two or three

[24] Marshall's decision in this case became the basis for the "original package" doctrine, that an imported article is not subject to state control until the original package has been broken and the contents thereof have become intermingled with the general property mass of the state. To Justice Thompson, Marshall's position seemed extreme, and he wrote one of the few dissenting opinions rendered during Marshall's life. To him it seemed that external commerce ended when goods brought into the country had complied with the provisions of the revenue laws.

[25] 2 Peters 245.

decades, and was even cited as an admission of the doctrine of concurrent commercial powers.   A recent historian of the Supreme
Court says: "To reconcile this expression as to the 'dormant state'
of congressional power, with the broad lines of the decision in
Gibbons *v*. Ogden, . . . became a difficult task in later years; and
for a long time produced great uncertainty in the whole law of
interstate commerce." [26]   The words in question were taken to
mean that so long as Congress allowed its power to lie dormant, a
state might pass commercial legislation, and the decision was regarded as pointing in a direction opposite to that in Gibbons *v*. Ogden.   But Marshall was not guilty of this inconsistency.   He remarked that by excluding the water from the marsh the value of
the lands was doubtless enhanced, and the health of the inhabitants
improved.   He therefore took the position that the Delaware law
was a health measure, and such measures he asserted were valid so
long as there was no regulation of Congress, under its commercial
power, colliding with them, which was the case in this instance.
The decision rested, not on any admission of concurrent power
over commerce, but upon the power of the state to pass health laws
as a matter of internal police.

Even some recent students have said that Marshall left no satisfactory precedent for the interpretation of the commerce clause.[27]
This is true in the sense that his decisions were not clearly grasped,
or at least were not followed by the court under his successor.
The departure did not result from any lack of clarity in his own
thinking.   Other jurists either failed to grasp the subtle distinctions which he perceived, or were unwilling to accept his nationalistic interpretations.   Careful study of his opinions reveals that the
doctrine of this great expounder of the Constitution, with regard
to the commercial power, may be summed up as follows:

The states have the power to regulate all their internal affairs and
in some instances while doing so may incidentally affect matters
lying within the field of federal regulation.   Such state regulations
do not rest upon a concurrent power to regulate commerce, for a

[26] Warren, *Sup. Court*, I, 709.
[27] *Cf.* D. W. Brown, "The Exclusive Power of Congress to Regulate Interstate
and Foreign Commerce," 491.

state has no such power. The federal government has the entire power of regulating commerce "with foreign nations, and among the several States, and with the Indian tribes." If a state police regulation collides with a federal regulation of commerce, the "supreme law" clause gives paramountcy to the act of Congress. Even though the state bases its measure on such a prerogative as the taxing power, the state act falls before the federal. Under Marshall's successors, however, concurrent powers received limited recognition.[28]

These decisions of the Supreme Court helped to clarify the scheme of distribution of power between states and federal government by actually tracing the boundary in concrete instances. Some of them set limits upon the authority of the states while others asserted the prerogatives of the national government. Marshall clearly grasped the dual nature of the governmental system and in connection with the Gibbons case explained it in the following words:

"The genius and character of the whole government seem to be, that its action is to be applied to all the external concerns of the nation, and to those internal concerns which affect the states generally; but not to those which are completely within a particular state, which do not affect other states, and with which it is not necessary to interfere, for the purpose of executing some of the general powers of the government."

Nevertheless the court under Marshall showed a distinct nationalistic bias, apparently emphasizing the power of the federal government upon every possible occasion and limiting the state powers narrowly. The nationalistic trend of constitutional interpretation during these years indicated the permanent direction which the developing constitutional system was to take. An immediate result, however, was a well-marked reaction towards greater em-

[28] Clyde E. Feuchter, *The Relation of the Police Power of the States to the Commercial Power of Congress.* See the recent discussion by Felix Frankfurter, *The Commerce Clause under Marshall, Taney and Waite.* In regard to concurrent powers, Marshall laid down the following rule: "Whenever the terms in which a power is granted to Congress, or the nature of the power requires that it should be exercised exclusively by Congress, the subject is as completely taken from the state legislatures as if they had been expressly forbidden to act on it."—Sturges *v.* Crowninshield, 4 Wheaton 122.

phasis on state powers; indeed, this stream of thought accompanied the stronger current with force sufficient to produce more than one crisis and even to threaten the disruption of the Union. The story of this conflict of contrary opinions is the theme of the volume dealing with the second half-century of the history of the United States as an independent nation.

LIST OF REFERENCES

Abbot, Wilbur C., *Adventures in Reputation*. Cambridge, Mass., 1935.

——, "David Hume: Philosopher—Historian," in *Adventures in Reputation*, 118–146.

Abernethy, Thomas P., *Western Lands and the American Revolution*. New York, 1937.

Acts . . . [Passed by the] General Assembly [of Ohio] (1803–1838). 37 v. Columbus, 1803–1839.

Adams, Charles Francis, ed., *Memoirs of John Quincy Adams*. 12 v. Philadelphia, 1874–1877.

——, "The Life of John Adams," in *Works of John Adams*, edited by C. F. Adams, I.

——, ed., *The Works of John Adams*. 10 v. Boston, 1856.

Adams, George Burton, *The Council and Courts of Anglo-Norman England*. New Haven, 1926.

Adams, Henry, *History of the United States during the Administrations of Jefferson and Madison*. 9 v. New York, 1889–1891.

——, ed., *Documents Relating to New England Federalism, 1800–1815*. Boston, 1877.

——, ed., *The Writings of Albert Gallatin*. 3 v. Philadelphia, 1879.

Adams, Herbert Baxter, *Maryland's Influence upon Land Cessions to the United States*. Johns Hopkins University *Studies in Historical and Political Science*, 3d series, No. 1. Baltimore, 1885.

Adams, John, *Works of*. See Adams, Charles Francis, editor.

——, "Autobiography," in *Works of John Adams*, edited by C. F. Adams, II.

Adams, John Quincy, *Memoirs*. See Adams, Charles Francis, editor.

Adams, Randolph G., *Political Ideas of the American Revolution*. Durham, N. C., 1922.

Adams, Samuel, *Writings of*. See Cushing, Harry A., editor.

Alden, G. H., *New Governments West of the Alleghanies before 1780*. University of Wisconsin *Bulletin*, Historical Series, II, No. 1. Madison, 1897.

Alvord, Clarence W., *The Mississippi Valley in British Politics*. . . . 2 v. Cleveland, 1917.

American Archives. See Force, Peter, editor.

American History Leaflets. See Hart, Albert Bushnell, editor.

American Nation. See Hart, Albert Bushnell, editor.

American State Papers: Documents, Legislative and Executive. 38 v. Washington, 1832–1861.

Ames, Herman V., *Proposed Amendments to the Constitution*. American Historical Association *Report* for 1896, II.

——, *State Documents on Federal Relations, 1789–1861*. New York, 1907.

Ames, Fisher, *Works of*. See Ames, Seth, editor.

Ames, Seth, ed., *The Works of Fisher Ames, with a Selection from his Speeches and Correspondence*. 2 v. Boston, 1854.

Anderson, Dice R., "Jefferson and the Virginia Constitution." *American Historical Review*, XXI, 750–754 (July, 1916).

Anderson, Frank M., "Contemporary Opinion of the Virginia and Kentucky Resolutions." *American Historical Review*, V, 45–63, 225–252 (Oct., 1899, Jan., 1900).

——, "Enforcement of the Alien and Sedition Acts." American Historical Association *Report* for 1912, 113–126.

Andrews, Charles M., *Our Earliest Colonial Settlements*. New York, 1933.

——, "The Royal Disallowance." American Antiquarian Society *Proceedings*, n. s., XXIV, 342–362 (Oct., 1914).

Annals of the Congress of the United States. 42 v. Washington, 1834–1856.

Aronson, Julian, "The 'Forgotten Man' of Yesterday." *Scholastic*, XXIV, 15–16 (Feb. 3, 1934).

Bacon, Matthew, *et al.*, *A New Abridgment of the Law*. 5 v. [London], 1736–1766.
   An American edition in ten volumes, edited by Bird Wilson, was published at Philadelphia in 1876.

Baldwin, Alice M., *The New England Clergy in the American Revolution*. Durham, N. C., 1928.

Baldwin, E. H., *Joseph Galloway, the Loyalist Politician*. Philadelphia, 1902.

Baldwin, J. F., *The King's Council in England during the Middle Ages*. Oxford, 1913.

Ballagh, James C., ed., *The Letters of Richard Henry Lee*. 2 v. New York, 1911–1914.

Bancroft, George, *The History of the Formation of the Constitution of the United States of America*. 2 v. New York, 1882.

Barrett, J. A., *Evolution of the Ordinance of 1787*. New York, 1891.

Beard, Charles A., *An Economic Interpretation of the Constitution*. New York, 1913. Revised edition, 1935.

——, *The Supreme Court and the Constitution*. New York, 1922.

Becker, Carl L., *Beginnings of the American People*. Boston, 1915.

——, *The Declaration of Independence, a Study in the History of Political Ideas.* New York, 1922.

——, *The History of Political Parties in the Province of New York, 1760–1776.* University of Wisconsin *Bulletin,* History Series, II, No. 1. Madison, 1909.

Beer, George Louis, *British Commercial Policy, 1754–1765.* New York, 1907.

——, *The Old Colonial System, 1660–1754.* New York, 1912.

——, *The Origins of the British Colonial System.* New York, 1908.

Bernard, Francis, *Select Letters. . . .* London, 1774.

Beveridge, Albert J., *Life of John Marshall.* 4 v. Boston, [c1916–1919].

Bigelow, John, ed., *The Complete Works of Benjamin Franklin.* 10 v. New York, 1905–1907.

Birkenhead, Lord F. E. S., *Fourteen English Judges.* London, 1926.

Blackstone, William, *Commentaries on the Laws of England.* See Cooley, Thomas M., editor.

Borgeaud, Charles, *The Rise of Modern Democracy in Old and New England.* New York, 1894.

Boudin, Louis B., *Government by Judiciary.* 2 v. New York, 1932.

Bowers, Claude G., *Jefferson and Hamilton.* Boston, [c1925].

Brown, David Walter, "The Exclusive Power of Congress to Regulate Interstate and Foreign Commerce." *Columbia Law Review,* IV, 490 *et seq.* (1904).

Brown, Everett S., *The Constitutional History of the Louisiana Purchase, 1803–1812.* University of California *Publications in History,* X. Berkeley, 1920.

Brown, William Garrott, *The Life of Oliver Ellsworth.* New York, 1905.

Burke, Edmund, *The Works of. . . .* 6 v. London, 1890–1894.

——, "Resolutions for Conciliation with America." *American Archives,* 4th series, I.

Burnett, Edmund C., ed., *Letters of Members of the Continental Congress.* 4 v. Washington, 1921–1928.

Cabot, George, *Life and Letters of.* See Lodge, Henry Cabot, editor.

Caldwell, Robert Granville, "The Settlement of Interstate Disputes." *American Journal of International Law,* XIV, 38–69 (1920).

Carpenter, William Seal, *The Development of American Political Thought.* Princeton, 1930.

——, "The Repeal of the Judiciary Act of 1801." *American Political Science Review,* IX, 519–528 (Aug., 1915).

——, "The Separation of Powers in the Eighteenth Century." *American Political Science Review*, XXII, 32–44 (Feb., 1928).

Carson, Hampton L., "Pennsylvania's Defiance of the United States." *Harper's Magazine*, CXVII, 670–678 (Oct., 1908).

Carter, Clarence E., *Great Britain and the Illinois Country, 1763–1774*. Washington, 1910.

Cawston, George, and Keane, Augustus H., *The Early Chartered Companies*. London, 1896.

Chamberlain, Daniel H., "Osborn *v.* The Bank." *Harvard Law Review*, I, 223 *et seq.* (1887).

Chandler, Peleg W., *American Criminal Trials*. 2 v. Boston, 1841–1844.

Channing, Edward, and Coolidge, Archibald Cary, eds., *The Barrington-Bernard Correspondence, 1760–1770. Harvard Historical Studies*, XVII. Cambridge, 1912.

Chronicles of America. See Johnson, Allen, editor.

Clune, Mary Catherine, "Joseph Hawley's Criticism of the Constitution." Smith College *Studies in History*, III, No. 1, 5–55 (Oct., 1917).

Cobbett, William, *The Parliamentary History of England*. 36 v. London, 1806–1820.

Coke, Sir Edward, biographies of. See Birkenhead, *Encyclopedia Britannica*, Johnson, and Lyon and Block.

——, *The First Part of the Institutes of the Laws of England. Or, A Commentary upon Littleton*. Fourteenth edition, revised and corrected. . . . Dublin, 1791. *The Second Part*. . . . London, 1797. *The Third Part*. . . . London, 1797. *The Fourth Part*. . . . London, 1797.

    Many reprints have been issued.

Coker, Francis W., *Readings in Political Philosophy*. New York, 1914.

Coleman, William C., "The State as Defendant under the Federal Constitution; the Virginia-West Virginia Debt Controversy." *Harvard Law Review*, XXXI, 210 *et seq.* (1917).

Comyns, Sir John, *A Digest of the Laws of England*. First American edition, from fifth London edition. 8 v. Philadelphia, 1824–1826 (place of publication varies with the successive volumes).

    The original work was written before 1740 (in which year the author died), and published 1762 to 1767.

Connecticut, *Public Records of the Colony of*, compiled by J. H. Trumbull and C. J. Hoadly. 15 v. Hartford, 1850–1890.

Cook, Walter Wheeler, "What is the Police Power?" *Columbia Law Review*, VII, 322 *et seq.* (May, 1907).

Cooley, Thomas M., "The Acquisition of Louisiana." Indiana Historical Society *Publications*, II, No. 3. Indianapolis, 1887.

——, ed., *Blackstone's Commentaries on the Laws of England*. Third edition. 2 v. Chicago, 1884.

Corwin, Edward S., *The Doctrine of Judicial Review*. Princeton, 1914.

——, "The Higher Law Background of American Constitutional Law." *Harvard Law Review*, XLII, 148–185, 365–409 (1928–1929).

——, "Marbury *v.* Madison and the Doctrine of Judicial Review," in Corwin, *The Doctrine of Judicial Review*, 1–78.

——, *National Supremacy*. New York, 1913.

——, "The Progress of Constitutional Theory between the Declaration of Independence and the Meeting of the Philadelphia Convention." *American Historical Review*, XXX, 511–536 (April, 1925).

Coxe, Brinton, *Essay on Judicial Power and Unconstitutional Legislation*. Philadelphia, 1893.

Crandall, Samuel B., *Treaties, their Making and Enforcement*. Columbia University *Studies in History, Economics and Public Law*, XXI, No. 1. New York, 1904.

Currey, C. H., *British Colonial Policy, 1783–1915*. Oxford, 1916.

Curtis, George Ticknor, *History of the Origin, Formation, and Adoption of the Constitution of the United States*. 2 v. New York, 1854. Revised and enlarged edition, 2 v., New York, 1889–1896.

Cushing, Harry Alonzo, *History of the Transition from Provincial to Commonwealth Government in Massachusetts*. Columbia University *Studies in History*, etc., VII, No. 1. New York, 1896.

——, ed., *The Writings of Samuel Adams*. 4 v. New York, 1904–1908.

Davis, J. C. B., "Federal Courts Prior to the Adoption of the Constitution," in 131 U. S., Appendix, XIX.

Davis, John P., *Corporations: A Study of the Origin and Development of Great Business Combinations and their Relation to the Authority of the State*. 2 v. New York, 1905.

Denny, Collins, "Growth and Development of Police Powers." *Michigan Law Review*, XX, 173–214 (Dec., 1921).

Dickinson, John, *Writings of*. See Ford, P. L., editor.

——, *Life and Times of*. See Stillé, Charles J.

Dickerson, Oliver Morton, *American Colonial Government, 1696–1765: A Study of the Board of Trade in its Relation to the American Colonies*. Cleveland, 1912.

Dodd, W. F., "Constitutional Convention," in *Cyclopedia of American Government*, I, 425.

——, "The First State Constitutional Conventions, 1776–1783." *American Political Science Review*, II, 545–561 (Nov., 1908).

Egerton, Hugh E., *The Causes and Character of the American Revolution.* Oxford and New York, 1923.

Elliot, Jonathan, ed., *Debates in the Several State Conventions, on the Adoption of the Federal Constitution . . . together with the Journal of the Federal Convention.*
    Various editions. Second edition, 4 v., Washington, 1836. Edition of 1845 includes a fifth volume containing Madison's notes.

Eno, Joel N., "First Court Trials in America." *Journal of American History*, II, 479 *et seq.* (July–Sept., 1908).

Farrand, Max, *The Fathers of the Constitution. Chronicles of America*, XIII.

——, "The First Hayburn Case, 1792." *American Historical Review*, XIII, 281–285 (Jan., 1908).

——, *The Framing of the Constitution.* New Haven, 1913.

——, *The Records of the Federal Convention of 1787.* 3 v. New Haven, 1911.

Feuchter, Clyde E., *The Relation of the Police Power of the States to the Commercial Power of Congress as Reviewed by the Supreme Court, 1824–1852.*
    Manuscript thesis submitted for the degree of Master of Arts at The Ohio State University, 1929.

Fisher, Sydney G., *The Evolution of the Constitution.* Philadelphia, 1900.

Force, Peter, ed., *American Archives. . . .* 9 v. Washington, 1837–1853.

Ford, Paul Leicester, ed., *Essays on the Constitution . . . 1787–1788.* Brooklyn, 1892.

——, ed., *The Federalist.* New York, 1898.

——, ed., *Pamphlets on the Constitution . . . 1787–1788.* Brooklyn, 1888.

——, ed., *The Writings of John Dickinson.* Pennsylvania Historical Society *Memoirs*, XIV. Philadelphia, 1895.

——, ed., *The Writings of Thomas Jefferson.* 10 v. New York, 1892–1899.

Ford, Worthington C., "Jefferson's Constitution for Virginia." *The Nation*, LI, 107–109 (Aug. 7, 1890).

——, ed., *The Writings of George Washington.* 14 v. New York, 1889.

——, and Hunt, Gaillard, eds., *Journals of the Continental Congress, 1774–1789.* . . . 33 v. Washington, 1904–1936.

Frankfurter, Felix, *The Commerce Clause under Marshall, Taney and Waite.* Chapel Hill, N. C., 1937.

Franklin, Benjamin, *Works of.* See Bigelow, John, editor.

——, *Writings of.* See Smyth, A. H., editor.

Friedenwald, Herbert, *The Declaration of Independence, an Interpretation and Analysis.* New York, 1904.

Frothingham, Richard, *The Rise of the Republic.* . . . Boston, 1872. Tenth edition. Boston, 1910.

Furniss, E. S., *The Position of the Laborer in a System of Nationalism: A Study in the Labor Theories of the Later English Mercantilists.* Boston, 1920.

Gallatin, Albert, *Writings of.* See Adams, Henry, editor.

Garver, Frank H., "The Transition from the Continental Congress to the Congress of the Confederation." *Pacific Historical Review*, I, 221–234 (June, 1932).

Gibbs, George, *Memoirs of the Administrations of Washington and Adams.* New York, 1820.

Giesecke, A. A., *American Commercial Legislation before 1789.* University of Pennsylvania *Publications*, Series in Political Economy and Public Law, No. 23. New York, 1910.

Goodwin, John A., *The Pilgrim Republic: An Historical Review of the Colony of New Plymouth.* Boston, 1895. Tercentenary edition, Boston, 1920.

Gray, Horace, ed., *Quincy Reports on Constitutional Law, with Notes, 1761–1772.* 2 v. Cambridge, 1894–1895.

Greene, Evarts Boutell, *The Provincial Governor in the English Colonies of North America.* *Harvard Historical Studies*, VII. New York, 1898.

Grigsby, H. B., *The Virginia Convention of 1776.* Virginia Historical Society *Collections*, n. s., IX, X. Richmond, 1890–1891.

Gross, Charles, *The Gild Merchant, A Contribution to British Municipal History.* 2 v. Oxford, 1890.

Guggenheimer, J. Caesar, "The Development of the Executive Departments, 1775–1789," in Jameson, ed., *Essays in the Constitutional History of the United States*, 116–185.

Guthrie, William D., "The Eleventh Article of Amendment to the Constitution of the United States." *Columbia Law Review*, VIII, 183 *et seq.* (March, 1908).

Haines, Charles Grove, *The American Doctrine of Judicial Supremacy.* Second edition, revised and enlarged. Berkeley, Cal., 1932.

Hamilton, Alexander, *Works of.* See Lodge, Henry Cabot, editor, and Hamilton, John C., editor.

Hamilton, John C., ed., *The Works of Alexander Hamilton, Comprising his Correspondence.* 7 v. New York, 1850–1851.

Harding, Samuel Bannister, *The Contest over the Ratification of the Federal Constitution in the State of Massachusetts. Harvard Historical Studies,* II. New York, 1896.

——, "Party Struggles over the First Pennsylvania Constitution." American Historical Association *Report* for 1894, 371–402.

Harmon, George D., "The Proposed Amendments to the Articles of Confederation." *South Atlantic Quarterly,* XXIV, Nos. 3 and 4 (July and Oct., 1925).

Hart, Albert Bushnell, ed., *American History told by Contemporaries.* 5 v. New York, 1897–1929.

——, ed., *The American Nation; A History from Original Sources.* 28 v. New York, 1904–1918.

——, and Channing, Edward, eds., *American History Leaflets.* New York, 1892–1896.

Hart, James, *The Ordinance Making Powers of the President.* Baltimore, 1925.

Hazeltine, Harold D., "Appeals from the Colonial Courts to the King in Council, with Especial Reference to Rhode Island." American Historical Association *Report* for 1894, 299–350.

Hening, William W., ed., *The Statutes-at-Large, Being a Collection of all the Laws of Virginia (1619–1792).* 13 v. Philadelphia and New York, 1823.

Henry, W. W., "The First Legislative Assembly in America." *Virginia Magazine of History,* II, 55–67 (July, 1894).

Higginson, Stephen, "Letters of Stephen Higginson." American Historical Association *Report* for 1896, I, 704–841.

Hildreth, Richard, *History of the United States.* 6 v. New York, 1849–1852.

Hilkey, Charles J., *Legal Development in Colonial Massachusetts, 1630–1686.* Columbia University *Studies in History,* etc., XXXVII. New York, 1910.

Hinsdale, Mary L., *A History of the President's Cabinet.* University of Michigan *Historical Studies.* Ann Arbor, 1911.

Hoar, R. S., "When Concord Invented the Constitutional Convention." *Boston Transcript,* July 3, 1917.

Hockett, Homer C., "Little Essays on the Police Power." *Mississippi Valley Historical Review,* XVII, 3–23 (June, 1930).

——, *Western Influences on Political Parties to 1825.* Ohio State

University *Contributions in History and Political Science*, No. 4. Columbus, 1917.

Holdsworth, William S., *History of English Law*. 9 v. London, 1922–1926.

Holmes, Oliver Wendell, Jr., *The Common Law*. Boston, 1881.

Holst, Hermann E. von, *The Constitutional and Political History of the United States*. Translated from the German by Lalor and Mason. 7 v. and index vol. Chicago, 1876–1892. New edition, 1899.

Horwill, Herbert W., *The Usages of the American Constitution*. New York, 1925.

Hosmer, James K., *Life of Thomas Hutchinson*. Boston, 1896.

——, *Samuel Adams*. Boston, 1898.

House, Lolabel, *The Twelfth Amendment*. Philadelphia, 1901.

Hunt, Gaillard, "Virginia Declaration of Rights and Cardinal Bellarmine." *Catholic Historical Review*, III, 276–289 (Oct., 1917).

——, ed., *Writings of James Madison*. 9 v. New York, 1900–1910.

Hutchinson, Thomas, *History of the Colony . . . of Massachusetts Bay*. 3 v. London, 1765, 1768, 1828.

Jameson, John Franklin, ed., *Essays in the Constitutional History of the United States*. Boston, 1889.

——, "The Predecessor of the Supreme Court," in Jameson, ed., *Essays in the Constitutional History of the United States*, 1–45.

Jay, John, *Correspondence and Public Papers of*. See Johnston, H. P., editor.

Jay, William, *Life of John Jay*. 2 v. New York, 1833.

Jefferson, Thomas, *Writings of*. See Ford, P. L., editor, and Washington, H. A., editor.

Jennings, W. Ivor, *Cabinet Government*. New York, 1936.

Johnson, Allen, *Readings in American Constitutional History, 1776–1876*. Boston, 1912.

——, *et al.*, eds., *The Chronicles of America*. 50 v. New Haven, 1918–1920.

Johnson, Cuthbert W., *Life of Sir Edward Coke*. Second edition. 2 v. London, 1845.

Johnson, Samuel, *Taxation No Tyranny*. London, 1774.

Johnston, H. P., ed., *Correspondence and Public Papers of John Jay*. 4 v. New York, 1890–1893.

Journals of the American Congress. 4 v. Washington, 1823.

Journals of the Continental Congress. See Ford, W. C., and Hunt, G., editors.

Kelsey, Rayner, "The Originator of the Federal Idea." *The Nation*, XCIV, 562–563 (June 6, 1912).

King, Charles R., ed., *Life and Correspondence of Rufus King*. 6 v. New York, 1894–1900.

King, Rufus, *Life and Correspondence of*. See King, Charles R., editor.

Kittredge, **G. L.**, "Dr. Robert Child, the Remonstrant." Colonial Society of Massachusetts *Publications*, XXI, 1–146 (1920).

Klingelsmith, Margaret C., "Two Theories in regard to the Implied Powers of the Constitution." *American Law Register*, LIV, 214 *et seq*. (April, 1906).

Kraus, Michael, *History of American History*. New York, 1937.

Lambert, Rev. J. Malet, *Two Thousand Years of Guild Life*. Hull, 1891.

Lapsley, G. T., *The County Palatine of Durham. Harvard Historical Studies*, VIII. New York, 1900.

Laski, Harold J., *The Rise of Liberalism: the Philosophy of a Business Civilization*. New York, 1936.

Leake, James Miller, *The Virginia Committee System and the American Revolution*. Johns Hopkins University *Studies in Historical and Political Science*, XXXV, No. 1. Baltimore, 1917.

Learned, H. B., *The President's Cabinet*. New Haven, 1912.

Lee, Richard Henry, *Letters of*. See Ballagh, James C., editor.

Libby, Orin G., *The Geographical Distribution of the Vote of the Thirteen States on the Ratification of the Federal Constitution, 1787–1788*. University of Wisconsin *Bulletin*, History Series, I, No. 1. Madison, 1894.

Lincoln, Charles Henry, *The Revolutionary Movement in Pennsylvania, 1760–1776*. University of Pennsylvania *Publications*, Series in History, No. 1. Philadelphia, 1901.

Lingelbach, William E., *The Merchant Adventurers of England, their Laws and Ordinances, with Other Documents*. Philadelphia, 1902.

Lingley, Charles R., *The Transition in Virginia from Colony to Commonwealth*. Columbia University *Studies in History*, etc., XXXVI, No. 2. New York, 1910.

Locke, John, *Two Treatises on Civil Government*. See Morley, Henry, editor.

Lodge, Henry Cabot, ed., *Life and Letters of George Cabot*. Boston, 1878.

——, *Works of Alexander Hamilton*. 9 v. New York, 1885–1886.

Lord, Arthur, "Some Objections Made to the Massachusetts State

Constitution, 1780." Massachusetts Historical Society *Proceedings*, L, 54–60 (Oct., 1916).

Lucas, Sir Charles P., *The Beginnings of English Overseas Enterprise*. Oxford, 1917.

Lyon, H., and Block, H., *Edward Coke, Oracle of the Law*. Boston, 1929.

Macaulay, Thomas Babington, *The Life and Works of Lord Macaulay Complete*. New impression. 10 v. London, 1903–1912.
 The *History of England* fills volumes I to IV.

MacDonald, William, *Select Charters*. New York, 1899.

——, *Select Documents*. New York, 1903.

McIlwain, Charles H., *The American Revolution: A Constitutional Interpretation*. New Haven, 1923.

——, *The High Court of Parliament and Its Supremacy*. New Haven, 1910.

McIlwaine, Henry R., ed., *Journals of the House of Burgesses*. 9 v. Richmond, 1908–1915.

McKinley, Albert E., *The Suffrage Franchise in the Thirteen English Colonies in America*. University of Pennsylvania *Publications*, Series in History, No. 2. Philadelphia, 1905.

McLaughlin, Andrew C., *America and Britain*. New York, 1919.

——, "American History and American Democracy." *American Historical Review*, XX, 255–276 (Jan., 1915).

——, "The Background of American Federalism," in McLaughlin, *America and Britain*, 177–221.

——, *The Confederation and the Constitution*. *The American Nation*, X.

——, *Constitutional History of the United States*. New York, 1935.

——, *The Courts, the Constitution, and Parties*. Chicago, [1912].

——, *Foundations of American Constitutionalism*. New York, 1932.

——, "Power of a Court to Declare a Law Unconstitutional," in McLaughlin, *The Courts, the Constitution, and Parties*, 63–69.

McMaster, John Bach, *Benjamin Franklin as a Man of Letters*. Boston, 1887.

——, *The History of the People of the United States*. 8 v. New York, 1883–1913.

——, and Stone, F. D., eds., *Pennsylvania and the Federal Constitution, 1787–1788*. Philadelphia, 1888.

Maclay, Edgar S., ed., *Journal of William Maclay*. New York, 1890.

Madison, James, *Writings of*. See Hunt, Gaillard, editor.

——, *Letters and Other Writings* (Congress edition). 4 v. Philadelphia, 1865.

——, *Life and Times.* See Rives, W. C.

Marshall, John, *Life of.* See Beveridge, A. J.

Mason, Edward C., "Congressional Demands upon the Executive for Information." American Historical Association *Papers,* V, 365–375.

Mathews, John M., *The Conduct of American Foreign Relations.* Revised edition. New York, 1938.

Mathews, Lois K., "Benjamin Franklin's Plan for a Colonial Union, 1750–1775." *American Political Science Review,* VIII, 393–412 (Aug., 1914).

——, "The Mayflower Compact and Its Descendants." Mississippi Valley Historical Association *Proceedings,* VI, 79–106.

Miller, Elmer I., *The Legislature of the Province of Virginia.* Columbia University *Studies in History,* etc., XXVIII. New York, 1907.

Minot, George R., *Continuation of the History of the Province of Massachusetts Bay.* 2 v. Boston, 1798–1803.

——, *History of the Insurrections in Massachusetts, in the Year 1786, and the Rebellion Consequent Thereon.* Worcester, 1788. Second edition, Boston, 1810.

Moore, Blaine Free, *The Supreme Court and Unconstitutional Legislation.* Columbia University *Studies in History,* etc., LIV, No. 2. New York, 1913.

Morey, W. C., "Genesis of a Written Constitution." *Annals of the American Academy of Political and Social Science,* I, 529–557 (April, 1891).

Morison, Samuel E., ed., *The Life and Letters of Harrison Gray Otis.* 2 v. Boston, 1913.

——, "The Struggle over the Adoption of the Constitution of Massachusetts, 1780." Massachusetts Historical Society *Proceedings,* L, 353–412 (Oct., 1916–June, 1917).

——, "The Vote of Massachusetts on Summoning a Constitutional Convention." Massachusetts Historical Society *Proceedings,* L, 241–249 (Oct., 1916–June, 1917).

Morley, Henry, ed., *John Locke's Two Treatises on Civil Government.* London, 1884.

Morris, R. B., "Massachusetts and the Common Law: the Declaration of 1646." *American Historical Review,* XXXI, 443–453 (April, 1926).

Mullet, Charles F., ed., "Some Political Writings of James Otis." University of Missouri *Studies,* IV, Nos. 3 and 4 (July and Oct., 1929).

Nevins, Allan, *The American States during and after the Revolution, 1775–1789.* New York, 1927.

——, ed., *The Diary of John Quincy Adams, 1794–1845*. New York, 1928.

Osgood, Herbert L., *The American Colonies in the Eighteenth Century*. 4 v. New York, 1924–1925.
——, *The American Colonies in the Seventeenth Century*. 3 v. New York, 1904–1907.
Otis, James, *Writings of*. See Mullet, Charles F., editor.
Otis, Harrison Gray, *Life and Letters of*. See Morison, S. E., editor.

Palm, Franklin Charles, *The Middle Classes, Then and Now*. New York, 1936.
Pargellis, S. M., "The Procedure in the Virginia House of Burgesses," second installment. *William and Mary College Quarterly*, second series, VII, No. 3.
Parkman, Francis, *Pioneers of New France*. Volume I in Centenary edition of *The Works of Francis Parkman*. 13 v. Boston, 1925–1929.
Parrington, Vernon L., *Main Currents in American Thought*. 3 v. New York, 1927–1930.
Pasquet, D., *Origin of the House of Commons*. Translated from the French by R. G. D. Laffan. Cambridge, 1925.
Phillips, Ulrich B., *Georgia and State Rights*. American Historical Association *Report* for 1901, II.
Plucknett, F. T., "Bonham's Case and Judicial Review." *Harvard Law Review*, XL, 30–70 (Nov., 1926).
Pollard, Albert F., *Evolution of Parliament*. New York, 1920.
Porritt, Edward, *The Unreformed House of Commons: Parliamentary Representation before 1832*. 2 v. Cambridge, 1909.
Pound, Roscoe, *The Spirit of the Common Law*. Boston, [c1921].
——, and Plucknett, Theodore F. T., comps., *Readings on the History and System of the Common Law*. Third edition, revised. Rochester, 1927.
Pownall, Thomas, *Administration of the Colonies, Wherein their Rights and Constitutions are Discussed and Stated*. London, 1768.
Putnam, Harrington, "How the Federal Courts were Given Admiralty Jurisdiction." *Cornell Law Quarterly*, X, 460–470 (June, 1925).

Quincy, Edmund, *Life of Josiah Quincy*. Boston, 1867.

Read, Conyers, ed., *The Constitution Reconsidered*. New York, 1938.
——, "Mercantilism: the Old English Pattern of a Controlled Economy," in Read, ed., *The Constitution Reconsidered*.

Reinsch, Paul Samuel, "English Common Law in the Early American Colonies." University of Wisconsin *Bulletin*, Economics, Political Science, and History Series, II, No. 4. Madison, 1899.

Reprinted in *Select Essays in Anglo-American Legal History*, I, 367–415. 3 v. Boston, 1907–1909.

Richardson, James D., comp., *A Compilation of the Messages of the Presidents*. 10 v. Washington, 1896–1899.

Rives, W. C., *Life and Times of James Madison*. 3 v. Boston, 1859–1868.

Roosevelt, Theodore, *The Winning of the West*. 4 v. New York, 1903.

Rowland, Kate M., *Life of George Mason, 1725–1792*. 2 v. New York, 1892.

Russell, Elmer Beecher, *The Review of American Colonial Legislation by the King in Council*. Columbia University *Studies in History*, etc., LXIV, No. 2. New York, 1915.

Schaper, William A., "Sectionalism and Representation in South Carolina." American Historical Association *Report* for 1900, I, 237–463.

Schechter, Frank I., "The Early History of the Tradition of the Constitution." *American Political Science Review*, IX, 707–734 (Nov., 1915).

Schlesinger, Arthur M., "Colonial Appeals to the Privy Council." *Political Science Quarterly*, XXVIII, 279–297, 433–450 (1913).

——, *Colonial Merchants and the American Revolution*. Columbia University *Studies in History*, etc., LXXVIII. New York, 1918.

Schuyler, Robert L., "Agreement in the Federal Convention." *Political Science Quarterly*, XXXI, 289–299 (June, 1916).

——, *The Constitution of the United States*. New York, 1923.

——, *Parliament and the British Empire*. New York, 1929.

——, "A Retrospect and a Theory," in Schuyler, *Parliament and the British Empire*, 1–39.

Scott, Austin, "Holmes v. Walton, the New Jersey Precedent." *American Historical Review*, IV, 456–469 (April, 1899).

Simms, Henry H., *Life of John Taylor*. Richmond, 1932.

Simpson, Alexander, Jr., *A Treatise on Federal Impeachments*. Philadelphia, 1916.

Smith, Edward P., "The Movement towards a Second Constitutional Convention in 1788," in Jameson, ed., *Essays in Constitutional History*, 114 *et seq.*

Smith, Joshua Toulmin, *English Gilds*. London, 1870. Reprinted, 1892.

Smyth, A. H., ed., *Writings of Benjamin Franklin*. 10 v. New York, 1905–1907.

Snow, A. H., *The Development of the American Doctrine of Jurisdiction of Courts over States*. *Publications* of the American Society for Judicial Settlement of International Disputes, No. 4 (May, 1911).

Sparks, Jared, *Life of Gouverneur Morris*. 3 v. Boston, 1832.

——, ed., *The Writings of George Washington*. 12 v. Boston, 1837.

Stillé, Charles J., *The Life and Times of John Dickinson, 1732–1808*. Pennsylvania Historical Society *Memoirs*, XIII. Philadelphia, 1891.

Story, Joseph, *Life and Letters of*. See Story, William W., editor.

Story, William W., ed., *Life and Letters of Joseph Story*. 2 v. Boston, 1851.

Stubbs, Bishop William, *The Constitutional History of England*. Second edition. 2 v. Oxford, 1877.

Taft, William Howard, "The Selection and Tenure of Judges." American Bar Association *Report*, XXXVIII, 418–435 (1913).

Tawney, Richard Henry, *Religion and the Rise of Capitalism*. New York, [c1926].

Taylor, Hannis, *The Origin and Growth of the American Constitution*. Boston, 1911.

Thorne, S. E., "The Constitution and the Courts: A Reexamination of the Famous Case of Dr. Bonham," in Read, ed., *The Constitution Reconsidered*.

Thorpe, Francis N., *Constitutional History of the United States, 1765–1895*. 3 v. Chicago, 1901.

——, comp., *Federal and State Constitutions*. 7 v. Washington, 1909.

Tocqueville, Alexis de, *Democracy in America*. 2 v. Boston, 1873.

Treat, Payson J., *The National Land System*. New York, 1910.

Tucker, Henry St. George, *Limitations on the Treaty-Making Power under the Constitution of the United States*. Boston, 1915.

Tudor, William, *Life of James Otis*. Boston, 1823.

Turner, Frederick J., *The Significance of Sections in American History*. New York, 1932.

——, "Social Forces in American History." *American Historical Review*, XVI, 217–233 (Jan., 1911).

——, "Western State-making in the Revolutionary Era," in Turner, *The Significance of Sections in American History*, 86–138.

Tyler, Moses Coit, *Literary History of the American Revolution*. 2 v. New York, 1897.

——, *Patrick Henry*. Boston, 1898.

United States Statutes at Large. Boston, 1845–1873. Washington, 1875–.

Van Tyne, Claude H., *The American Revolution. The American Nation*, IX.

——, *The Causes of the War of Independence*. Boston, 1922.

——, ed., *The Letters of Daniel Webster*. New York, 1902.

Viner, Charles, *A General Abridgment of Law and Equity*. 23 v. 1741–1751.

Von Holst. See Holst.

Walker, Joseph B., *A History of the New Hampshire Convention . . . 1788*. Massachusetts Historical Society *Collections*, 5th ser., II, III; 6th ser., IV.

Warfield, E. D., *The Kentucky Resolutions of 1798*. New York, 1887.

Warren, Charles, *The Making of the Constitution*. Boston, 1928.

——, "The Mississippi River and the Treaty Clause of the Constitution." *George Washington Law Review*, II, 271–302 (March, 1934).

——, "New Light on the History of the Federal Judiciary Act of 1789." *Harvard Law Review*, XXXVII, 49–132 (Nov., 1923).

——, *The Supreme Court in United States History*. Revised edition. 2 v. Boston, 1926.

Washington, H. A., ed., *The Writings of Thomas Jefferson, Being his Autobiography, Correspondence, . . . and Other Writings*. 9 v. Washington, 1853–1854.
Often called "Congress edition."

Washington, George, *Writings of*. See Ford, W. C., editor, and Sparks, Jared, editor.

Weber, Max, *The Protestant Ethic and the Spirit of Capitalism*. Translated by Talcott Parsons . . . with a Foreword by R. H. Tawney. London, [1930].

Webster, Daniel, *Letters of*. See Van Tyne, C. H., editor.

Webster, Noah, *Sketches of American Policy*. See *American History Leaflet*, No. 28.

Webster, Pelatiah, *A Dissertation on the Political Union and Constitution of the Thirteen United States*. See *American History Leaflet*, No. 28.

Wharton, Francis, ed., *The Revolutionary Diplomatic Correspondence of the United States*. 6 v. Washington, 1889.

Wigmore, John H., *Panorama of the World's Legal Systems*. 3 v. St. Paul, 1928.

Wild, Robert, "Belknap Impeachment Trial." *Wisconsin Magazine of History*, December, 1926.

Winsor, Justin, ed., *Narrative and Critical History of America*. 8 v. Boston, 1884–1889.

——, *The Westward Movement.* Boston, 1899.

Wright, B. F., Jr., "American Interpretations of Natural Law." *American Political Science Review,* XX, 524–547 (Aug., 1926).

Wright, Philip Quincy, *The Control of the Foreign Relations of the United States.* New York, 1922.

Zwierlein, Frederick J., "Jefferson, Jesuits, and the Declaration." *America,* July 8, 1933.

INDEX

Adams, John,
and Governor Hutchinson, 94;
electoral vote for, 298;
in First Cont. Cong., 99;
in Second Cont. Cong., 109 and *n.*;
mentioned, 126;
minister in England, 164;
on apportionment, 141;
on dissolution of Confederation,
201 *n.*, 203;
on Stamp Act, 84 *f.*;
rejects Parliament, 97;
Vice-President, 234, 242.
Adams, John Quincy,
disgust at mob, 258;
internal improvement policy, 356;
reports Republican plans for impeachments, 314;
resolution on taxation of Louisiana,
322.
Adams, Samuel,
drafts reply to governor, 83;
leads colonial argument, 93 *f.*;
mentioned, 126;
on checks and balances, 92 *n.*
Addison, Alexander, on Virginia Resolutions, 294.
Admiralty courts,
descent of jurisdiction, 155 *f.*;
forerunner of federal courts, 59;
in colonies, 48, 49.
Agent, colonial, 56, 58, 59.
Albany Congress, 132 *f.*
Albany Plan, 50, 132 *f.*, 158.
Alien and Sedition Acts, 288;
endorsed by states, 292;
Republican criticism, 288 *f.*
Alliance, French, 250.
Almon, John, 90.
Amendment,
a. *vs.* interpretation, 272 *f.*;
difficulty of a. process, 301;
effect of adoption, 259;
Eleventh, 235, 287; in Olmstead case,
326; in Osborn case, 364; in Cohens
case, 369;
first ten a., 225 *f.*;
Fourteenth a. and corporations, 365;
influence of Louisiana purchase, 323;

Amendment—*Continued*
needed for internal improvements,
345 *f.*;
obstacles to a., 181 *f.*;
proposals, 350 *f.*;
proposals of Hartford Convention,
339 *f.*;
proposed abolition of three-fifths
clause, 322;
proposed a., to Articles, 184 *f.*;
proposed for branches of Bank, 357;
provision for a. in Constitution, 217;
provision of Articles of Confed., 177;
significance of provision, 217 *f.*;
Twelfth, 234, 297 *f.*; adoption, 299 *f.*;
significance, 301; text of, 301 *n.*;
Washington on a., 222.
American constitutionalism. See Constitutionalism.
American Insurance Company *v.* Canter, 323.
Ames, Fisher,
fears federal courts, 279;
on Jay's treaty, 254.
Amor Patriae. See Crowley, Thomas.
Anglican Church, 9;
supported by landed class, 13 *n.*
Annapolis Convention,
hopes concerning, 197;
New England opinion of, 202;
proposed, 196 *f.*;
report, 198;
scheme of leaders, 198.
Antifederalists,
criticisms of Constitution, 223 *f.*;
debt due them, 226;
demand bill of rights, 224;
on suits against states, 284;
pose as friends of Constitution, 259;
program, 223.
Appeals,
from colonial courts, 53 *f.*;
to Supreme Court anticipated, 59.
See Privy Council.
Appointments,
provisions of Constitution, 235;
Washington's a., 235, 239.
See Removals.
Articles of Confederation,
adoption by Congress, 144;

399